D1553653

POLICIES FOR COMPETITIVENESS

FUJI CONFERENCE SERIES 3

POLICIES FOR COMPETITIVENESS

Comparing Business–Government Relationships in the 'Golden Age of Capitalism'

Edited by

HIDEAKI MIYAJIMA, TAKEO KIKKAWA,

and

TAKASHI HIKINO

OXFORD

UNIVERSITY PRESS

OXFORD

Great Clarendon Street, Oxford OX2 6DP

Oxford University Press is a department of the University of Oxford.
It furthers the University's objective of excellence in research, scholarship,
and education by publishing worldwide in

Oxford New York

Athens Auckland Bangkok Bogotá Buenos Aires Calcutta
Cape Town Chennai Dar es Salaam Delhi Florence Hong Kong Istanbul
Karachi Kuala Lumpur Madrid Melbourne Mexico City Mumbai
Nairobi Paris São Paulo Singapore Taipei Tokyo Toronto Warsaw

and associated companies in Berlin Ibadan

Oxford is a registered trade mark of Oxford University Press
in the UK and in certain other countries

Published in the United States
by Oxford University Press Inc., New York

© The Business History Society of Japan 1999

The moral rights of the author have been asserted

Database right Oxford University Press (maker)

First published 1999

British Library Cataloguing in Publication Data

Data available

Library of Congress Cataloging in Publication Data

Policies for competitiveness: comparing business-government
relationships in the 'golden age of capitalism' / edited by
Hideaki Miyajima, Takeo Kikkawa, and Takashi Hikino.
p.   cm.—(Fuji conference series; 3)
"Compendium of papers presented at the 23rd International
Conference on Business History, 5–8 January 1996 at the foot of Mt.
Fuji"—Acknowledgments
Includes bibliographical references and index.
1. Industrial policy—Congresses.   2. Competition, International—
Congresses.   I. Miyajima, Hideaki.   II. Kikkawa, Takeo, 1951–   .
III. Hikino, Takashi.   IV. International Conference on Business
History (23rd : 1996)   V. Series.
HD3611.P636   1999   338.9—dc21   99–21238

ISBN 0–19–829323–2

1 3 5 7 9 10 8 6 4 2

Typeset by Hope Services (Abingdon) Ltd.
Printed in Great Britain
on acid-free paper by
Biddles Ltd.,
Guildford & King's Lynn

ACKNOWLEDGEMENTS

The role of government in economic development—especially when it comes to international competitiveness—has been one of the most contentious issues for many countries. It is true that public-policy activism is now attacked and that deregulation seems to be the most popular worldwide policy orientation. Because less state intervention has become the guiding principle, it is important to review the dynamic interaction between industrial development and government policies from the historical and cross-national perspectives. This book examines this critical question. It is a compendium of papers presented at the 23rd International Conference on Business History, which took place 5–8 January 1996 at the foot of Mount Fuji.

Gaining worldwide recognition as the Fuji Conference, the International Conference on Business History has been held in Japan in January of every year since 1974. These conferences have been made possible by the gracious co-operation of business historians and other related experts from all parts of the world. The continued generous support of the Taniguchi Foundation made it possible to inaugurate a fifth series of these conferences, which ran from January 1994 to January 1998. The Organizing Committee of this fifth series of the International Conference, chaired by Professor Akira Kudo, decided to turn the spotlight towards enterprise growth after the Second World War in all industrial countries (though focusing particularly on Japan) within a long-term perspective. Already the series has generated two books, *Fordism Transformed* and *Beyond Firms*, both of which were published by Oxford University Press, in 1996 and 1997 respectively.

Takeo Kikkawa, Takashi Hikino, and myself were entrusted with the task of organizing the third conference in the fifth series around a general topic relating to industrial policy. In line with the wishes of the Organizing Committee, we entitled it 'Policies for Competitiveness: Comparing Business–Government Relationships in the Golden Age of Capitalism'. It was our intention to characterize the business–government relationship in the many ways in which it has diversified across nations, and to review the role of government in economic development from the business historians' perspective.

The organizers of the conference were extremely fortunate in being able to arrange for the participation of several distinguished contributors from a variety of countries. The conference was exciting and successful, and the papers in this book were revised in accordance with discussions and suggestions raised at the conference.

The Taniguchi Foundation's financial support has also made it possible to publish these papers. The editors, as well as the Organizing Committee, would like to express their deepest gratitude to the Taniguchi Foundation for its continuing sponsorship of the conference. Professor Mark Mason was kind enough to act as adviser for the publication of the papers in this fifth series of the International Conference on Business History, and his steadfast support and expert advice greatly facilitated this book's publication.

This book is, in a sense, the joint product of both the authors and the conference attendees. Besides the papers' authors, the following attended the conference: Etsuo Abe, Akihiko Amemiya, Takashi Hotta, Joung-Hae Seo, Akira Kudo, Hidemasa Morikawa, Masachika Shinomiya, Akifumi Nakase, Tamotsu Nishizawa, Jun Sakudo, Minoru Sawai, Akitake Taniguchi, Junko Watanabe, and Kazuomi Tamaguchi. They all took part in the discussion, and raised many questions and suggestions. Shigeru Matsushima, from the Ministry of Trade and Industry, also participated in this conference and gave useful comments from the policy-maker's perspective. The editors would like to thank everyone for their participation and much valued contributions.

Much secretarial and administrative support is required when putting together a conference such as this. That support was ably provided by the following staff: Yuichi Ikemoto, Simon Partner, and Osamu Uda. Two interpreters, R. Hanna Brendon and Kyoko Sakuma, helped ensure smooth communication among participants. Eilene Zimmermen, from the Harvard Business School, checked and polished the English of all the papers in the book; without her efforts, readers might have had to cope with numerous eccentric expressions, especially in the non-English speakers' papers. Last but not least, the editors would like to express their gratitude to the numerous business historians—not mentioned above—who helped us in many ways.

H.M.

CONTENTS

LIST OF CONTRIBUTORS

Alice H. Amsden
  Ellen Swallow Richards Professor of Industrial Development, Department of Urban Studies and Planning, Massachusetts Institute of Technology
William H. Becker
  Professor of History and Strategic Management and Public Policy, The George Washington University
Giovanni Federico
  Life Fellow, Dipartmento di Storia Moderna e Contemporanea, University of Pisa
Takashi Hikino
  Professor of Industrial and Business Organization, Graduate School of Economics, Kyoto University
Takeo Kikkawa
  Professor of Business Management, Institute of Social Science, University of Tokyo
Philippe Mioche
  Professor of Contemporary History, Jean Monnet Chair of European Integration History, University of Provence
Hideaki Miyajima
  Professor of Japanese Economy and Economic History, School of Commerce, Waseda University
Kiyoshi Nakamura
  Professor of Business History, School of Business, Chiba Keizai University
Werner Plumpe
  University Lecturer, Historishes Seminar, Johann Wolfgang Goethe-Universität, Frankfurt-on-Main
Tsuneo Suzuki
  Professor of Industrial Evolution, Faculty of Economics, Gakushuin University
Jim Tomlinson
  Professor of Economic History, Department of Government, Brunel University
Richard H. K. Vietor
  Senator John Heinz Professor of Environmental Management, Graduate School of Business Administration, Harvard University

LIST OF FIGURES

LIST OF TABLES

Introduction

HIDEAKI MIYAJIMA, TAKEO KIKKAWA, AND TAKASHI HIKINO

All over the world public-policy activism is now under siege. Economists and policy-makers claim that the era of Big Government is over. The historic controversy over government's role in industrial competitiveness and economic welfare, they insist, has finally been settled. Government initiative, it is argued, tends to discourage private-sector viability. Government actions tend to be distorted by narrow-interest groups. Government involvement tends to result in the so-called crony capitalism. Government planning tends to be rigid and inflexible. Government controls tend to distort resource allocation. Goodbye state intervention, hello free market forces. So long Keynes and Japan's 'Notorious MITI,' welcome back Adam Smith.

Despite all the negative publicity concerning government's economic actions, nobody yet categorically denies that government historically played a critical role in modern economic development. Everybody accepts the importance of public institutions that ensure property rights and effective markets. There is little question concerning the positive effects of public spending on infrastructure such as basic education and transportation. Public investment in technology has been universally encouraged. Above all, sound macroeconomic policies, accountable public finance, and monetary stability are accepted as necessary conditions for continuous economic growth.[1] The contentious question, then, is not if government is necessary, but what appropriate roles government could and should play. Which government actions are useful public policy and which represent unnecessary intrusion and harmful interference?[2]

Competing Policies for Competitiveness

For the past generation, economic thinking on the appropriate role of the government has shifted drastically. Up to the early 1970s a main focus of economic policy, at least in advanced industrial economies, was demand-side, macroeconomic management in the Keynesian tradition, which aimed to increase demand, often with extensive government spending, to boost economic expansion.[3] Within this macroeconomic framework, however, microeconomic interventions to tamper with the price mechanism remained an important undercurrent. Across nations, economic concerns and political realities propelled individual governments to adopt different mixes of microeconomic policies such as industrial policies, antitrust measures, and price-regulatory regimes in order to ensure the maximum economic output of individual industries and enterprises.

As conventional Keynesian demand management became problematic in many industrialized nations in the second half of the 1970s, due mainly to hyper-inflation, unemployment, and overall poor economic performance, the focal point of economic policies shifted towards the supply-side, emphasizing production and efficiency.[4] Supply-oriented policies actually went in two conflicting directions: first, microeconomic, particularly industrial policies, which aimed to increase output and productivity through government guidance of individual industries; and, macroeconomic, particularly financial policies, which attempted to maximize economic welfare by encouraging saving and investment.

In the 1980s policy-makers in many industrial as well as industrializing nations became acutely interested in supply-side microeconomic policies, particularly sector-specific industrial development policies, thanks mostly to the powerful impression of rapid economic growth achieved in Japan and, later, in other East Asian countries. Chalmers Johnson's *MITI and the Japanese Miracle* appeared in 1982 and soon became the most influential volume on industrial policy among policy-makers as well as academics. The European Union actively sought to establish a systematic 'European Industrial Policy' following its formation in 1992, based on elements of the industrial policies of different members from the end of the Second World War, or earlier. In 1993 even the World Bank endorsed the 'market-friendly' approach to economic policy management which recognized de facto the positive effects of industrial policy in East Asia (World Bank, 1993).

By the 1990s, however, the tide of public policy worldwide had again shifted, as market forces revived themselves as the major administrative mechanism for economic growth and efficiency. Behind this change were the historic collapse of socialist economies and the revitalization of the US economy, widely attributed to deregulation and liberalization. This trend accelerated as many of the Asian economies started experiencing economic troubles in the mid-1990s. Now the popular direction is towards supply-side macroeconomic policies. These policies encourage private saving and investment in order to increase the capacity and capability of the economy to produce more goods at a lower cost. This goal is supposed to be achieved by reducing macroeconomic instability through the correction of imbalances in government budgets, money supply, exchange rates, and foreign payments. Such a policy assumes that all goods produced can find a market so that demand-side management is not required. One necessary condition is that all goods are free to move across international borders, and this demands an absence of trade barriers among nations. The original form of this economic thinking can be found in nineteenth-century France when it was known as 'Say's Law', the belief that supply creates its own demand. This law was the main target of Keynes's criticism of unemployment. The times seem to have finally come back to the pre-Keynesian era (Uchitelle, 1996, 1998).

Public Policy and Business Decisions Since the Second World War

As enthusiasm for having an industrial policy fades, this is an appropriate time to review the dynamic interactions between government policies and industrial developments from a broad historical perspective.[5] Business historians can contribute to this controversial subject in two ways. First, they can provide empirical research centred around sector-specific microeconomic policies which directly alter the industry structure and the product characteristics of individual firms. More importantly, they can evaluate the actual outcome of policies in terms of the performance of firms and the competitiveness of targeted industries.

Individual chapters of this book share some of the common approaches and goals to be seen in historical contributions. All the chapters try to clarify the national characteristics of economic policy-making and business–government relations. All the authors are interested in pinning down the determinants that historically moulded each nation's particular pattern of business–government relations, and each aims to achieve this goal by presenting stylized facts concerning the dynamic process of business–government interactions in individual countries.

Many chapters attempt to assess how a nation's particular policies and business–government relations have affected its international competitiveness in specific industries. The guiding questions are: How important are industrial policies for export-oriented manufacturing industries in Japan? What is the hidden cost of these policies? Are the famed cooperative relations between government and business in East Asia instrumental in the international success of many industries? *Per contra*, have apparently adversarial business–government relationships harmed American firms? Some chapters try to find an answer to the question of why similar government interventions gave birth to different results in different nations. Tariff protection or direct subsidies, for instance, seem to have resulted in enhancing the industrial competitiveness in some countries but not in others. What accounts for these differences in policy outcomes? Why have individual firms in different nations responded in different ways to similar policy incentives? Why was the targeting of one industry effective in one nation but inconsequential in another?

In trying to find fact-based answers to these complicated questions, the book's chapters are concerned with three major policy instruments related to industrial development: industrial policy; antitrust and competition policy; and price regulations. First, many chapters examine the backgrounds, contents, and effects of industrial policy, broadly defining industrial policy as government policies that directly affect resource allocation and cost position through various means such as straight subsidies, low-interest credit, tariff protection, and import restrictions.[6] As long as industrial policy assumes the priority of certain targeted industries among many possible choices, government-owned enterprises can be a part of industrial policy. Second, some chapters examine antitrust policy. Those actions which affect ownership structure and the scale and scope of enterprises have a potentially serious impact on the competitive nature of industries. Confined mostly to the United States until the Second World War, antitrust measures then spread to other industrial nations through the 'Americanization of institutions'. For instance, Japan and West Germany introduced antitrust measures as a part of US occupation policy. Other nations followed through the GATT regime. Third, a few chapters analyse price regulations. One of the major sectors that price regulation targeted was that of financial services, because the regulatory framework for that industry inevitably affected the corporate finance of industrial enterprises.

The history of individual countries is complicated by the uniqueness of their background, choices, implementation, effectiveness, and the outcome of their policy instruments. Japan utilized industrial policies extensively in many industries. The United States emphasized antitrust policies and price regulation. Many European nations tried to create government-owned 'national champions' in several strategic industries. This does not mean that a country exclusively adopted one single model. But each nation has its own specific mix of policy tools. These policy mixes, however, have changed historically even within a single country. In the case of Japan, it has, since the early 1980s, followed the North Atlantic fashion of deregulation, while industrial policy has become dysfunctional in many industries.

Three historical factors should be singled out as the major determinants of overall policy choices for individual countries. First, the basic experience of economic management during the Second World War left a profound impact on government policy. Japan's industrial policy in its mature version, popularized in the 1950s and 1960s, originated in public mechanisms devised under wartime government control. Second, the role of ideology should not be ignored. Scepticism about government-owned enterprises in Japan partially resulted from the absence of socialist government after the Second World War. An intense distrust of the government in the United States went at least as far back as Thomas Jefferson. Third, industrial organization and firm capabilities affect policy choices. Industrial policy in Japan (and South Korea) was introduced as a co-ordination mechanism to supplement the competencies of individual companies and to create oligopolistic structures in affected industries.

A key issue then is how these various means of government actions influence the strategic behaviour of individual firms and the growth patterns of specific industries. Here a consensus among scholars barely exists, as has been illustrated in the conflicting interpretations of Japan's industrial policy. Some authors credit industrial policy for Japan's rapid economic growth in the 1950s and 1960s, while others discredit it as irrelevant or even harmful. In basically empirical research, such as that in this book, the challenge for each author is to identify the exact mechanism through which incentives induced by public policy affect a firm's strategic decision-making and resulting economic performance. There are many paths and routes through which government actions influence firm behaviour. Here each author attempts to clarify the complex causal chain of policy implementation, corporate response, and industry competitiveness.

Diversity of National Economies, Public Policies, and Business Enterprises

This book attempts to utilize the Japanese case as an analytical tool against which the experiences of other economies may be examined. A volume that resulted from a conference in Japan should extract some lessons from Japanese experience. The heavy emphasis on industrial policy in many of the chapters reflects this perspective, but from a historian's stance. The framework is not that of an orthodox economist whose theory discusses a price-tampering economic policy as a deviation from optimal market forces. Rather, individual chapters of the book try to find empirical regularities concerning the background, process, and outcome of individual policy decisions in their particular historical settings.[7] The results are neither always positive nor negative.

In examining the dynamic relationships between government policies and efficiency and competitiveness, this book mostly focuses on the so-called 'Golden Age of Capitalism'—-the period from the end of the Second World War to the early 1970s.[8] Those decades were an intriguing era for two reasons. First, most economies under consideration in this volume experienced quick economic recovery after the Second World War and subsequently enjoyed rapid economic growth. At the same time, the dynamics of international economic rivalry changed drastically as the West European nations, and then Japan and the greater East Asian region, steadily caught up in terms of industrial competitiveness with the United States. Second, as pointed out earlier, this was an era when many nations experimented with their own mix of industrial policy, antitrust actions, and price regulations, while macroeconomic policy was uniformly Keynesian in spirit. The World Bank and IMF did not necessarily discourage these experiments, although they started doing so in the 1980s.

For analytical convenience the nations which are examined in this book are classified into three groups based roughly on income level following the Second World War, as is illustrated in Table 1.1. At one pole are the prime movers, which include the United States and Great Britain, whose income levels were higher historically than those of the other two groups. The United States and Great Britain were instrumental in establishing

Table 1.1   *Growth of GDP per capita in 1990 International Dollars, 1900–1992*

	GDP per capita					Growth coefficient 1973/1950
	1900	1913	1950	1973	1992	
Prime movers						
United States	4,096	5,307	9,573	16,607	21,558	1.7
Great Britain	4,593	5,032	6,847	11,992	15,738	1.8
Followers						
France	2,849	3,452	5,221	12,940	17,959	2.5
Germany	3,134	3,833	4,281	13,152	19,351	3.1
Italy	1,746	2,507	3,425	10,409	16,229	3.0
Latecomers						
Mexico	1,157	1,467	2,085	4,189	5,112	2.0
Japan	1,135	1,334	1,873	11,017	19,425	5.9
Brazil	704	839	1,643	3,913	4,637	2.4
Taiwan	759	794	922	3,669	11,590	4.0
South Korea	850	948	876	2,840	10,010	3.2
India	625	663	597	853	1,348	1.4

Note: Nations are listed in the order of income levels of 1950.

Source: Compiled from Angus Maddison, *Monitoring the World Economy, 1820–1992* (Paris: OECD, 1995).

various economic regimes in the post-Second World War economy, which set a generally liberal tone for trade and economic policies. The second group, Germany, France, and Italy, is comprised of European followers, whose income levels were historically lower than those of the prime movers. Emerging from massive destruction during the Second World War, these three countries experienced an 'economic miracle' through which they gradually caught up in income with the prime movers. The third group contains latecomers, including Japan, South Korea, and other Asian emerging economies. The income levels of these countries immediately after the Second World War were much lower than those of the other two groups. All latecomers exhibited high degrees of government economic intervention.

The book has been divided into four parts in order to illustrate the similarities and differences among each of the three groups of nations. The first two parts are concerned with the experiences of latecomers, particularly Japan. The third part focuses on the world's prime movers, especially the United States. The fourth and last part discusses followers on the European continent.

Japanese Policies as a Referent

Japan used industrial policy deliberately and extensively during its high growth era, from the 1950s to the First Oil Shock of 1973. The actual effects of government policy have understandably been controversial. The first part of this book, 'Japan's Experience in Industrial Policy: A General Overview', consists of two chapters on Japan which survey the interactions between government policy and corporate strategy during post-Second World War decades. Chapter 1, 'Industrial Policy and Japan's International Competitiveness: Historical Overview and Assessment' by Takeo Kikkawa and Takashi Hikino, deals with the theory and practice of industrial policy. The chapter first summarizes the latest policy debate in the United States in which sceptical mainstream economists criticize political scientists and political economists for their excitement about the effectiveness of industrial policy in Japan. The outcome of the controversy was mostly fruitless because the two groups of scholars employed different sets of approaches and criteria to evaluate policy outcomes.

The authors then attempt to find some common, intermediate grounds for constructive discourse. They introduce an international, comparative perspective on industrial policy, particularly that related to the recent US debate on so-called corporate welfare. A hidden policy of corporate welfare was conceivably a US equivalent of industrial policy, although it has been conveniently ignored by business and public-policy historians. Based on these theoretical and comparative examinations, the chapter presents stylized facts concerning the postwar experiences of Japan's industrial policy. In order to pin down the likely ingredients affecting the effectiveness of its application, the authors single out the 'firm-conforming' nature as the key variable of Japan's industrial policy.

The next chapter, 'Regulatory Framework, Government Intervention and Investment in Postwar Japan: The Structural Dynamics of J-Type Firm–Government Relationships' by Hideaki Miyajima, further examines the relationships between government policy and corporate investment decision-making, but from a regulatory rather than industrial policy framework. Miyajima points out that postwar reform, such as the *zaibatsu* dissolution, the democratization of shareholding, and the introduction of antitrust laws, were part of the Americanization of institutions that broadly affected corporate and industrial organization. They initially created a competitive industry structure. In the early 1950s, however, the Japanese government gradually revised the original regulatory framework and introduced several acts to encourage capital accumulation. These efforts are understood as a Japanization of the transplanted American system. The Japanese government further encouraged competitive investment among several large companies, which resulted in an oligopolistic competitive structure in many affected industries. Incentives such as subsidies, low interest loans, protective tariffs, and import restrictions, together with a discretionary application of antitrust laws, promoted competition for massive investments in the Japanese industries.

The author then explores the corporate governance structure in postwar Japan which was conducive to such investment competition. Miyajima stresses that, along with the co-operative mechanism between non-owner management and labour created within large Japanese enterprises, two major factors, cross-shareholding between group enterprises supported by an appropriate regulatory framework, and the so-called main bank system resulting from governmental regulation, contributed to competitive investment behaviour. Lastly, the author tries to clarify the relationships between governance structure and corporate behaviour using simple statistical tests.

Latecomers: Influential Industrial Policy and Competitiveness

Latecomer countries are characterized by low income levels after the Second World War. They consequently employed a wide range of industrial policy measures into the 1970s and beyond. The key question then is through what mechanism these government actions encourage industrial development? Three chapters in Part II deal with the government's role in the catch-up process of industries and nations. Chapter 3, 'Industrial Policy and the Development of the Synthetic Fibre Industry: Industrial Policy as a Means for Promoting Economic Growth', by Tsuneo Suzuki, takes the synthetic fibre industry as an example of the functions and limitations of the industrial policy of the Ministry of International Trade and Industry (MITI). Suzuki first clarifies that MITI never intended to establish a textbook perfect market condition. The ministry aimed to have 'orderly' competitive markets. It thus came up with a policy-mix to achieve a dual industrial structure by encouraging large firms to invest in the latest, most efficient plant technologies while at the same time preserving small producers for domestic political reasons. In addition to tariff protection, therefore, MITI carefully divided the entire industry into three segments, each dominated by an oligopolist. To encourage the rapid growth of the industry, the ultimate target of the ministry, a resulting monopoly-price umbrella actually worked as an incentive for the subsequent entry of firms seeking high profits.

According to Suzuki this growth mechanism functioned well as long as the Japanese economy grew rapidly and international competition was limited. In the 1970s, as the fundamental economic environment soured and the South-east Asian nations developed their own efficient synthetic fibre industries, this mechanism became less effective. The poor performance and struggle of many enterprises forced the government to alter its policies and this resulted in a lengthy restructuring of the industry.

Kiyoshi Nakamura's chapter on the Japanese computer industry, 'Government and Business in Japan's General-Purpose Computer Industry', further clarifies the public-policy mechanism that enhanced the growth of technology-intensive industries in postwar Japan. Even compared to the synthetic fibre industry, the computer manufacturing industry posed an enormous challenge to Japan's ability to catch up. The Japanese government's commitments became more direct and extensive, although Nakamura carefully points out that the government did not necessarily have a grand vision or programme for the industry's development. Through trial and error, however, the Japanese government came up with various measures to regulate imports, to control foreign capital investments, to expand domestic rental markets, and to enhance technological capabilities. The author contends that these policies helped domestic manufacturers to secure and expand their markets, to keep profitable operations, and to invest in their technical skills.

In the growth process of the Japanese computer industry, according to Nakamura, both government bureaucrats and corporate executives and engineers deliberately benchmarked IBM as the technological and commercial front runner in global markets. He discusses the government's

perception of the prospects of domestic markets, the strategies of international players, and the competencies of domestic manufacturers. By
company and by time period, concrete plans for catching up naturally varied. The author gives detailed descriptions of the interactions between
these strategies and shifting government policies. Ultimately, over time
the Japanese government came up with a coherent programme to develop
the computer industry.

   Chapter 5 by Alice Amsden, 'Early Postwar Industrial Policy in
Emerging Economies: Creating Competitive Assets or Correcting Market
Failures?', analyses how South Korea and other emerging Asian
economies caught up. She begins by criticizing the conventional wisdom
in mainstream economics, that latecomer countries can and should catch
up by 'getting the prices right' for inputs and products, as determined by
open international markets. She claims that enterprises from nations outside the North Atlantic economies and Japan actually can not compete
with international prices, not even in labour-intensive cotton spinning and
weaving, because of the enormous productivity gap between producers of
advanced and backward economies. Such theoretically assumed international competition is unrealistic. Amsden thus suggests that governments distort prices deliberately to make domestic products competitive.
This is the purpose of industrial policy, where economic development is a
process of creating competitive assets rather than perfect markets.

   Amsden, however, does not simply advocate traditional protective
measures. Government should not give anything away to business for
free. Instead subsidies should be made conditional on monitorable
performance standards related to exports, labour training, and R. & D.

                Prime Movers: Influential Antitrust Measures With Limited
                                Industrial Policy

Immediately after the Second World War, the United States and Great
Britain, at that time the two leading economies in the international economy, took the initiative in establishing a global economic order and so
became the model of learning for followers and latecomers. The general
use of antitrust policy and the limited use of industrial policy characterized these Anglo-American cases, whose international competitiveness
was profoundly affected by this policy-mix. Part III thus deals with the
American and British models. Chapter 6, 'Postwar US Antitrust Policy,
Corporate Strategy, and International Competitiveness' by William
Becker, discusses the impact of changing antitrust policies on corporate
strategy and the competitiveness of American industry. The author

focuses on the Celler–Kefauver Anti-Merger Act of 1950, which revised antitrust policy to make horizontal expansion and vertical integration extremely difficult as growth strategies of oligopolistic firms.

Becker points out that the strategic response of large enterprises to the Celler–Kefauver Act depended on the 'robustness' of their technology. In industries in which technology was relatively stable, firms were forced to grow by expanding into unrelated product markets. This conglomerate movement had a negative effect on their international competitiveness. In the high tech industries, however, the effect tended to be the reverse. By making mergers prohibitive, the author argues, the law prompted enterprises with advanced technological capabilities to concentrate their investments in research and development in such core product areas. This growth strategy actually enhanced the competitiveness of those enterprises and industries.

Chapter 7, 'Competition and Industrial Policy in Britain, 1945–1973' by Jim Tomlinson, illustrates that British economic thinking about industrial efficiency was different from that of the United States. The British policy tradition carried over from pre-Second World War years did not boost the idea that maintaining competitive market structure is critical to the efficiency of an industry. Industrialists, as well as both the Labour and Conservative governments, were basically sceptical about the economic rationale of competition. They believed rather in the benefits of the concentration and co-operation of enterprises to achieve scale economies and good export performance. A means to accomplish industrial efficiency was thus the wholesale nationalization of several key industries.

Industrial promotion policies in Britain, on the other hand, took a form that was somewhat closer to that of the United States. Policies in the 1950s targeted defence-related high technology sectors, with government purchasing and subsidies to promote high-tech industries for civilian use. But in other industries, policies were not co-ordinated the way they were in Japan (or Korea). Tariffs, for instance, were utilized for balance-of-payments purposes, rather than as an instrument to protect strategic industries. Furthermore, financial credit allocation by the government, which played a huge role in several latecomer economies, was not employed because the overall role of the government in capital markets remained very limited.

Chapter 8, 'Regulation American Style, 1933–1989' by Richard Vietor, articulates the US style of government industrial management in contrast with that experienced in Japan and Europe. The author emphasizes that the unique position of the US economy after the Second World War fostered a policy of economic regulation oriented towards domestic rather than international markets. The United States economy after the Second World War inherited extensive New Deal-inspired regulatory regimes to control the entry, price, and structure of many industries.

Vietor emphasizes the experiences of such infrastructure-related industries as financial services, transportation, telecommunications, and energy, and articulates the expansion, elaboration, and sophistication of their regulatory regimes for three decades up to the late 1960s.

The relatively non-competitive environment of regulated industries became dysfunctional in the face of intensifying international competition in various industries. Their economic performance declined compared to that of other industrial nations. Consequently, the late 1970s, during the Carter administration, saw a sudden outburst of deregulatory measures. Government-managed competition and market-oriented controls emerged as a new, *re*-regulatory regime under which US companies and industries contended for renewed competitiveness in international markets.

Followers: Insignificant Antitrust Policy and the Limited Effect of Industrial Policy

Continental European countries universally experienced drastic changes in regulatory framework and policy orientation after the Second World War, although each nation had its own unique historical and political characteristics. Part IV consists of three chapters that discuss these changes. Chapter 9, 'The State and Enterprise in the German Economy after the Second World War' by Werner Plumpe, deals with the era of economic liberalism up to the late 1960s during which non-interventionist policy was credited with the rapid recovery and reconstruction of the West German economy. The author argues that the neo-liberal policy orientation was certainly a radical departure from prior traditional measures, particularly National Socialist planning practices, that valued government control of prices and wages and the cartelization and co-operative behaviour of markets. West German enterprises welcomed the drastic change through which they could utilize and develop their accumulated competitive strength in international markets, while the federal government limited its economic role to guaranteeing the general institutional and macroeconomic setting for free enterprise.

The fundamental aspects of the West German liberal policy regime were articulated as a 'social market economy' by A. Muller-Armack in 1947. The West German federal government followed the prescriptions of the 'social market economy' in micro- and macroeconomic initiatives. The government abolished price-fixing and liberalized resource allocation. Markets were opened and private investments were promoted. The government pursued currency reform and revised the tax structure in accordance with the investment strategies of enterprises. The only visible measure of an industrial promotion policy remained massive tax concessions to companies with qualified performance, although the government directly committed substantial resources to internationally uncompetitive sectors such as agriculture and, later, the coal and shipbuilding industries. Enterprises accepted government policy, with the possible exception of control over monopolistic market structures. Actually, however, the only market in West Germany that became non-competitive was the labour market which was entirely cartelized. This liberal, non-interventionist regime did not change until the mid-1970s, when the federal government started reacting to tougher international competition.

Chapter 10, 'Coherence and Limitations of French Industrial Policy during the Boom Period: It Was Not So Bad After All' by Philippe Mioche, reviews the critical case of industrial policy in the steel industry. Until the mid-1970s steel policies were regarded as the prototype of industrial policy in France. The prime status of the steel industry subsequently resulted in bitter criticism of the inefficiency of the industry and of the flawed outcome of particular government policies. The semi-liberal Monnet Plan of 1946 was in the first phase of postwar industrial policy that introduced price control and industrial planning. One of the six key sectors covered by the plan, the steel industry received one-third of the industrial subsidies that derived mostly from United States aid, particularly under the Marshall Plan. Although price control in domestic markets depressed the profitability of steel firms, rising export markets sustained the expansion of these enterprises. Industrial subsidies and domestic price control continued, but in the early and mid-1950s industrial policy on steel became unclear and often conflicting. This happened when the international regulatory organization, the European Coal and Steel Community, eventually replaced the national government in formulating some public policies. Actual policies introduced were a mixed bag of government management and free markets. The community's executive body could control investment guidelines for modernization, but cartels and collusive conduct were theoretically prohibited and prices were unregulated.

As French industry faced intensifying international competition from the late 1950s on, the French government developed a strategy of 'national champions', in which major industries became concentrated into one or two giant enterprises. Using the incentive of extensive investment financing, the French government achieved its goal of consolidating the commodity steel segments into two companies, while leaving speciality steel in just one enterprise. The government also invested heavily in new manufacturing facilities. In the end, however, as this concentration policy did not bring visible economic improvements for steel companies, in 1978 the government was forced to convert public loans to equity stake, which led to an eventual government takeover of the entire industry in 1982.

Chapter 11, 'Harmful or Irrelevant? Italian Industrial Policy, 1945–1973' by Giovanni Federico, takes industrial policy as a representative case of the general ineffectiveness of economic policy implementation in Italy. The author actually writes positively of the effectiveness of the policy in the 1950s, when government ownership of large enterprises in strategic industries facilitated the recovery and rapid growth of various industries. The steel industry was typical in that the growing demand of the auto-mobile sector induced capacity-increasing investments in new plants and equipment. One possible reason for the success of industrial policy in this decade, according to Federico, was that enterprise management could exercise its strategic discretion without the intervention of government bureaucrats and political influence.

The optimistic trend of industrial policy changed in the 1960s and 1970s, however. When government started assigning too ambitious and often conflicting goals to industrial and related policies, their outcome inev-itably became ineffectual. The government aimed to achieve the rapid growth of key industries, the regional relocation of industries towards the southern part of the nation, and the redistribution of income, all at once. Consensus-building among private firms, labour unions, and government bureaucracies turned out not to be feasible. As a result, industrial policy in targeted industries became lavish subsidies to many enterprises that loosely fitted the broad criteria or, supposedly, had political support. The chemical industry was an exemplary case in which enterprises continued to increase the production capacity of bulk petrochemicals at a time when the Oil Shock of 1973 drove the chemical firms of other economies to cur-tail basic chemical production and to switch to high value-added fine and speciality chemicals.

NOTES

1. For consensus views in major policy areas among mainstream economists, see Fischer and Thomas (1990); Roemer and Radelet (1991).
2. The latest readable summary of the philosophical changes of the historical role of public policies is Yergin and Stanislaw (1997).
3. On the development of macroeconomic policies, particularly Keynesian doc-trine, in various nations, see Marglin and Schor (1990); Hall (1989); Hamond and Smithin (1988); Wattel (1985); Worswick and Trevithick (1984); Coats (1981).
4. 'Supply-side' policies were widely popularized by an American economist, Arthur Laffer, whose ideas particularly on tax incentives were highlighted by

the Reagan Administration in the early 1980s. While Laffer's influence did not last long, a general policy orientation towards the supply-side would last until the present date.

5. Recent books which share the interest and concern of this book are: Audretsch (1989); Chick (1990); McCraw (1986); Shoven (1988); Wilks and Wright (1987). For developing economies, see Evans (1995); Gereffi and Wyman (1990); MacIntyre (1994); Maxfield and Schneider (1997). The Fuji Conference published an earlier volume on business–government relations in Nakagawa (1980).

6. Industrial policies can be defined in various ways, as will be discussed in Chapter 1. In particular European authors tend to have a broad definition. See, for instance, Ferguson and Ferguson (1996), in which industrial policy includes competition policy and regional policy.

7. This book does not intend to engage directly in controversial debates among economists on the proper role of public policy or offer systematic implications for policy-makers. Those examinations should include a few additional important policy issues that have not been discussed here, such as labour policies which affect the internal organizational behaviour of enterprises and thereby influence the productivity level of those firms and concerned industries.

8. The general background of international economy during the Golden Age of Capitalism can be obtained in Van Der Wee (1986).

REFERENCES

Audretsch, D. B. (1989), *The Market and the State: Government Policy Towards Business in Europe, Japan and the United States* (New York and London: Harvester Wheatsheaf).

Chick, M. (1990) (ed.), *Government, Industries, and Markets: Aspects of Government–Industry Relations in the UK, Japan, West Germany, and the USA Since 1945* (Aldershot: Edward Elgar).

Coats, A. W. (1981) (ed.), *Economists in Government: An International Comparative Study* (Durham, NC: Duke University Press).

Evans, P. (1995), *Embedded Autonomy: State and Industrial Transformation* (Princeton: Princeton University Press).

Ferguson, P. R., and Ferguson, G. J. (1996), *Industrial Economics: Issues and Perception*, 2nd edn. (New York: New York University Press).

Fischer, S., and Vinod, T. (1990), 'Policies for Economic Development', *American Journal of Agricultural Economics* (Aug.), 809–13.

Gereffi, G., and Wyman, D. L. (1990) (eds.), *Manufacturing Miracle: Paths of Industrialization in Latin America and East Asia* (Princeton: Princeton University Press).

Hall, P. A. (1989), *The Political Power of Economic Ideas: Keynsianism across Nations* (Princeton: Princeton University Press).

Hamond, O. F., and Smithin, J. N. (1988) (eds.), *Keynes and Public Policy After Fifty Years* (London: Edward Elgar).

Johnson, C. (1982), *MITI and the Japanese Miracle* (Stanford, Calif.: Stanford University Press).

McCraw, T. K. (1986) (ed.), *America versus Japan* (Boston: Harvard Business School Press).

MacIntyre, A. (1994) (ed.), *Business and Government in Industrial Asia* (Ithaca, NY: Cornell University Press).

Marglin, S., and Schor, J. (1990) (eds.), *The Golden Age of Capitalism: Reinterpreting the Postwar Experience* (Oxford: Clarendon Press).

Maxfield, S., and Schneider, B. R. (1997) (eds.), *Business and the State in Developing Countries* (Ithaca, NY: Cornell University Press).

Nakagawa, K. (1980) (ed.), *Government and Business: Proceedings of the Fifth Fuji Conference* (Tokyo: Tokyo University Press).

Roemer, M., and Radelet, S. C. (1991), 'Macroeconomic Reform in Developing Countries', in Dwight Perkins and Michael Roemer (eds.), *Reforming Economic Systems in Developing Countries* (Cambridge, Mass.: HIID).

Shoven, J. B. (1988), *Government Policy Toward Industry in the United States and Japan* (Cambridge: Cambridge University Press).

Uchitelle, L. (1996), 'How Both Sides Joined the Supply Side', *New York Times*, 25 August, E1, 4.

—— (1998), 'The Accidental Inventor of Today's Capitalism: Jean-Batiste Say, No Longer a Villain, Stands Guard Over Free Market', *New York Times*, 21 February, A13, 15.

Van Der Wee, H. (1986), *Prosperity and Upheaval: The World Economy, 1945-1980* (New York: Viking).

Verdier, D. (1994), *Democracy and International Trade* (Princeton: Princeton University Press).

Wattel, H. (1985) (ed.), *The Policy Consequences of John Maynard Keynes* (New York: M. E. Sharpe).

Wilks, S., and Wright, M. (1987) (eds.), *Comparative Government–Industry Relations: Western Europe, the United States, and Japan* (Oxford: Oxford University Press).

World Bank (1993), *The East Asian Miracle: Economic Growth and Public Policy* (Oxford: Oxford University Press).

Worswick, D. N., and Trevithick, J. (1984) (eds.), *Keynes and the Modern World* (Cambridge: Cambridge University Press).

Yergin, D., and Stanislaw, J. (1997), *The Commanding Heights: The Battle Between Government and the Marketplace That Is Remaking the Modern World* (New York: Simon & Schuster).

PART I

JAPAN'S EXPERIENCE IN INDUSTRIAL POLICY

A GENERAL OVERVIEW

1

Industrial Policy and Japan's International Competitiveness
Historical Overview and Assessment

TAKEO KIKKAWA AND TAKASHI HIKINO

1.1. Introduction

In 1992, at the height of world interest in Japan's industrial policy, Karl Zinsmeister, a journalist at the conservative American Enterprise Institute, wrote a short essay called 'MITI Mouse: Japan's Industrial Policy Doesn't Work'. Even before the essay was formally published, the *Wall Street Journal* jumped at the chance to carry a summary of a piece that bluntly claimed that having an industrial policy was not effective even in Japan and, therefore, that the United States should not experiment with a policy that contained a strong socialist element of 'centralized management' (Zinsmeister, 1993).

The newspaper column outraged Chalmers Johnson, the doyen of political scientists studying Japan's economic policy-making, and James Fallows, a noted Washington journalist, who, with the signature of more than twenty notable Japanologists, jointly wrote a letter to the *Wall Street Journal* criticizing the contents of the piece and also protesting against the general 'biased' coverage of the newspaper of the Japanese economy. The *Journal* initially refused to publish the letter, and a bitter controversy resulted over the original essay as well as the alleged xenophobic tone of the American media. (Fallows (1993) later wrote an amusing piece covering the entire episode in the liberal *American Prospect*.)

In the course of the debate there were, amazingly, no serious analyses of the conceptual and practical usefulness of industrial policy, or even the facts of the case. The Japanese economy stumbled and the US economy soared, and interest in industrial policy in the 1990s evaporated. Still, postwar economic development and industrial policy were closely intertwined in many parts of the world, and their relationship is a major question in economic analysis. In spite of the heated exchange of views, however, the controversy over industrial policy achieved little in advancing our understanding of this politicized subject.[1]

1.2. Why has Industrial Policy been Controversial?

In the standard economics framework, it is theoretically recognized that government can play a positive role in the optimization of collective economic welfare (or the achievement of 'a Pareto-efficient' allocation of resources) when government corrects a 'market failure', in which the free competitive forces of a market economy fail to prevent outcomes that are not optimal for the economy in general.[2] One of the few systematic orthodox economic approaches to Japan's industrial policy, by Itoh, Kiyono, Okuno-Fujiwara, and Suzumura understands the Japanese government's involvement along these theoretical lines. They thus define industrial policy as 'the policies implemented for raising the welfare level of a given economy when the defects of a competitive market system—market failures—create problems for resource allocation and income distribution' (Itoh, Kiyono, Okuno-Fujiwara, and Suzumura, 1991: 8).[3]

The weakness of the market-failure approach is twofold: first, in reality, Japan's industrial policy (or that of any nation), contained many policy objectives and measures that did not fit neatly into the neoclassical framework. One sceptical Japanese economist thus prescribes industrial policy as 'any policy that has ever been experimented by MITI'.[4] Second, the market-failure approach does not necessarily provide *ex ante* instrumental guidelines for concrete policy-making. At best, it provides *ex post* standards to evaluate policies by giving theoretical and philosophical support to a certain type of government action in general.[5]

The absence of a coherent economics framework to analyse policy issues brought two characteristics to the industrial policy controversy. First, debates surrounding industrial policy have been centred around less theoretical and more practical and political issues. Second, a neutral evaluation of policy effects is practically impossible to achieve. It is in a sense easy to pick out either all the failures or all the successes, depending on one's point of view. The stereotypical image of 'Japan, Inc.' contains a misleading impression of Japanese economic growth dominated and controlled by the government's decision-making. On the other hand, it is also naive to put a critical emphasis on market forces and private investment alone, while dismissing the government's efforts altogether.

In the United States in particular, virtually all debates on Japan's industrial policy have been characterized by an ideological politicization that resulted from different philosophies concerning *American* policy.[6] In other words, the understanding of Japan's industrial policy history became a convenient tool to promote different agendas for the present and future economic course of the United States. Analysing Japan's industrial policy experiences became a secondary issue. There is actually a substantial amount of serious research on Japanese industrial policy done by political scientists and historians who, based on historical inquiry, tend to be more sensitive, and often sympathetic, to the policy outcome.[7] Most influential among them are Chalmers Johnson (1982), and Edward Lincoln (1984), Ira Magaziner and Thomas Hout (1980). The most detailed studies at the industry level include Marie Anchordoguy (1989) on the computer industry, Martin Fransman (1990) on information technology, David Friedman (1988) on the machine-tool industry, Daniel Okimoto (1989) on high-technology industries, and Richard Samuels (1987) on the energy industry. At a more general level, important works have been done from various perspectives: Kent Caldor (1993), James Fallows (1994), Bai Gao (1997); Jeffrey Hart (1992), Thomas Huber (1994), Eugene Kaplan (1972), Mark Mason (1992), William Nester (1991), Hiroyuki Odagiri and Akira Goto (1996), and James Vestal (1993).[8]

In spite of the vast contribution these studies have made and their rich and detailed analyses of policy formation and outcomes, with the exception of the work of Chalmers Johnson, they have had amazingly little impact on the controversy concerning the economic theory of industrial policy. The most significant reason for the relative neglect of this body of research lies, therefore, in its absence of a coherent synthesis regarding the effectiveness of industrial policy. Ironically, the most important analytical concept, 'market conformity', appeared early in Chalmers Johnson's work in 1982, but subsequent studies did little to systematize their own work around the market conformity idea or any other logical concept. This analytical weakness has turned out to be deadly when historical and political science approaches to industrial policy faced the economics critiques.

It was thus a group of political economists, relying on the work of historians and political scientists, who deliberately or unintentionally forwarded the image of Japan's postwar growth as being government led. Particularly influential among them were Ira Magaziner, Robert Reich, and Lester Thurow, all of whom were instrumental in advocating a New Industrial Policy for revitalizing the American economy which, they suggested, had been overtaken by a new form of capitalism symbolized by 'Japan, Inc.'. Thurow maintained that 'Japan Inc.' needs to be matched with 'USA Inc.' (Thurow, 1980: 216).

Advocacy of 'USA Inc.' had a sharp and negative response from conventional economists and their followers in media and policy circles who were philosophically dubious about industrial policy (or any microeconomic government intervention, for that matter). On general theoretical grounds economists cited the dead-weight costs of industrial policy (that is, the costs related to devising, monitoring and enforcing it) and the welfare loss from market distortions and possible rent-seeking.[9]

At a more concrete level, the most pointed criticism came from two economists at the Brookings Institution. Charles Schultze, chairperson of the Council of Economic Advisors under Jimmy Carter, argued that:

The first problem for the government in carrying out an industrial policy is that we actually know precious little about identifying, before the fact, a 'winning' industrial structure. There does not exist a set of economic criteria that determines what gives different countries preeminence in particular lines of business . . . The winners emerge from a very individualistic search process, only loosely governed by broad national advantages in relative labor, capital, or natural resources. (Schultze, 1983: 7–8)

Philip Trezise, on the other hand, contended that, given the huge size of the Japanese economy, it was not feasible for national plans or goals to mobilize the resources of individual firms in the way bureaucrats envision. Citing a famous case of MITI's failure to reorganize the automobile industry in the 1950s and 1960s and the prominent example of consumer electronics, that became internationally successful without visible government intervention, Trezise concluded:

the impressive economic growth and social stability of postwar Japan are not owing in any decisive degree to the microeconomic decision making [on the part of the government] that is often held up as a source of Japanese accomplishments, even though there has been a pervasive pattern of interventionism in economic life by the permanent civil service and its political masters. (Trezise, 1983: 13)

Subsequent criticism of industrial policy was usually a variation of these two themes. Scepticism became particularly evident as Japan's economy faltered in the 1990s.[10]

Given the two fundamentally different approaches and opposing assessments—of the political scientists and historians and of mainstream economists—what is needed is a reasonably operational and systematic economic framework to analyse the background and effectiveness of the various applications of industrial policy. Towards this end, as economic historians we examine Japan's past experiences with industrial policy within a loose industrial organization framework. In the course of searching for empirical regularities within many historical cases of industrial policy, this chapter tries to articulate the specific economic conditions under which industrial policy did actually contribute to the efficiency and effectiveness of individual Japanese industries, in terms of their international competitiveness. 'Industrial policy' is defined as the supply-side microeconomic policy directly related to the competitiveness of targeted industries.

1.3. Historical Review of Japan's Industrial Policy

Looking at Japan's industrial policy since the Second World War is a puzzling and frustrating experience if one removes ideological eyeglasses and looks at the facts with bare eyes. Japan's experiences pose difficult questions, particularly if one has an image of Japanese industrial policy being well organized and systematic. Why did the extent of government intervention differ among industries that apparently share similar developmental phases and characteristics? Why did internal co-ordination within the government, which had been relatively well functioning, become problematic towards the end of the 1960s? Among policy instruments utilized by MITI, why were their effects so strikingly different by industry and time period? Why did similar policies introduced by MITI at the same time result in different outcomes? And why did enterprises in the same industry targeted by MITI react to policies in different ways?

Japan's postwar experience of an industrial policy can be evaluated from five different perspectives: the evolutionary nature of industrial policy; co-ordination among bureaucratic organizations and divisions; the industrial organization and policy apparatus; the economic characteristics of industrial policy; and the leadership of business and government. The first two issues are related to the historical and institutional credentials of industrial policy. The third concerns structural variables that influence economic performance. The last two involve the behavioural and internal issues of the policies themselves.

1.3.1. The Evolutionary Nature of Industrial Policy

The basic ideas and concrete instruments of industrial policies have been the cumulative outcome of learning by doing within the dynamic workings of both the Japanese government and individual businesses. Japan did not follow or even envision any clear guidelines on microeconomic policies, but at the same time the country could and actually did emulate many foreign formulas of macroeconomic policy-making (Yamamura, 1967). The absence of a model for microeconomic policy was sharply different from the experience of economies industrializing after Japan, such as South Korea, Taiwan, and China, which had the Japanese model immediately in front of them (Amsden, 1989).

This was partly because of the timing of Japan's industrial drive: Japan's embryonic microeconomic policy-making came *before* the maturity of the neoclassical economics paradigm and the IMF-World Bank-OECD conditionality supposedly based on economic theory. The prototype of Japan's industrial policies, which exerted influence upon rapid growth from the mid-1950s, was mostly and directly derived from the experiences of economic controls set in place during the Second World War and the subsequent Occupation period (Kikkawa, 1994; Nakamura, 1981: 18). It was not until the late 1960s that the neoclassical paradigm actually started to influence concrete microeconomic policy-making in Japan and elsewhere as well as international organizations.

Japan's industrial policy thus began as an eclectic learning process rather than as a deductive application of an integrated theory, economic or political, and it has remained that way. Actually the term 'industrial policy' was not widely employed even within MITI until around 1970 (Komiya, 1990: 288). Ironically, therefore, MITI itself did not make much use of the industrial policy concept even at the height of industrial policy applications in the 1950s and 1960s, because bureaucrats in various divisions were apparently working to pursue their own narrow policy goals for specific industries. This lack of a well-organized system has understandably caused confusion on the part of scholars who have sought to find a grand vision or principle to guide bureaucratic decision-making.

The inductive, evolutionary nature of Japan's industrial policy can be illustrated by studying the differing degrees and characteristics of the government's involvement in industries at a similar developmental phase. The most telling comparisons can be made by contrasting the policies of the electrical power and petroleum-refining industries, which were managed through the Electric Power Industry Law of 1964 and the Petroleum Industry Law of 1962 respectively.[11] In terms of the execution of these laws in these two industries, both of which contain strong public utility elements, MITI's role was critically different. In the electrical power utility industry large enterprises collectively took the initiative in strategic investment decisions, while MITI *ex facto* followed and legitimized the industry structure established by these firms.[12] On the other hand, enterprises in the petroleum-refining industry fell into competitive chaos, which led MITI to involve itself actively in its structure and operation.

One important factor in determining the role of government is, in general, the ability of individual industries to maintain 'orderly competition' and to co-ordinate their own investment decisions. If enterprises collectively possess these capabilities, the role and function of government in the industry stays limited. Otherwise, the government actively involves itself in order to maintain competitive order. This criterion can be seen to differentiate government's role in different industries.

A generalization about MITI's policy effectiveness by Daniel Okimoto, an influential scholar of industrial policy, is intriguing, but ultimately does not explain the whole story. In his explanation of why ministries exhibited different degrees of effectiveness in their policy implementation, Okimoto suggests that MITI's policies were more effective in raising the competitiveness of industries compared to those of other ministries. He claims that this was because of MITI's neutrality in terms of political intervention and distortion, which, he assumes, differed from the non-neutrality of other ministries. Okimoto further believes that the industry 'life cycle' played a significant role in the effectiveness of industrial policy even among industries with similar technological and market characteristics (Okimoto, 1989: 3, 50–1, 229, 231). Although Okimoto's generalizations are intriguing, they are contradicted by the electrical-utility industry and the petroleum-refining industry which had different experiences with industrial policy but similar life cycles.

1.3.2. *Coordination among Bureaucratic Organizations and Divisions*

Internal co-ordination among various decision-making organizations within the Japanese government was usually smooth in the early years of industrial policy implementation but problematic later. From the Second World War until at least the mid-1960s, MITI (and its predecessors) made serious efforts to co-ordinate policies with the Ministry of Finance (MOF), which was responsible for macroeconomic policy-making, including control of the allocation of financial resources directly and indirectly related to industrial policy. In spite of nagging problems of balance of payments and shortages of foreign exchange, MOF did not oppose the import of the latest expensive technology. Purely macroeconomic management might have caused the ministry to encourage inward direct foreign investments rather than technical licensing and joint ventures. Instead, MOF and MITI (and other parts of the Japanese government) formed a consensus to nurture the competitive competence of Japanese firms. At the same time, macroeconomic constraints forced MOF as well as MITI to introduce vigorous monitoring to ensure the effectiveness of individual policies (Caldor, 1993).

Japan suffered from trade and current account deficits up until the mid-1960s. It experienced business cycles of three to four years duration, hitting the so-called 'ceiling of international balance of payment'. Although the Japanese economy grew rapidly in the long run, boom years brought a sudden rise of imports, which immediately resulted in trouble for the balance of payments. MOF in response had to introduce policies of financial contraction. Under these circumstances, MITI and MOF carefully co-ordinated their policies in order to regulate imports and to expand exports. While MITI chose, protected, and nurtured strategic industries which were targeted as instrumental in achieving these goals, MOF exercised its influence in steering the government-controlled Japan Development Bank to direct industrial finance towards targeted industries.[13] MOF also co-operated in allocating precious foreign exchange for the purpose of technology imports to firms which passed the MITI-set guideline for international competitiveness (Kikkawa, 1995: 106).

One hidden factor behind the well-functioning policy co-ordination within the Japanese government was a national consensus about achieving rapid economic growth under government guidance. Struggling to digest the painful experiences of the Second World War, people uniformly supported the economic idea behind the slogan, 'Catch-up and go-ahead', up to the mid-1960s. Politicians as well as government bureaucrats deliberately or unconsciously shared this national fever, which minimized differences of opinion among ministries and bureaucrats.

Co-ordination between MITI and MOF became more problematic after the mid-1960s, when the 'ceiling of international trade balance' gradually disappeared. As the major industries of Japan became internationally competitive, the Japanese economy enjoyed a long-lasting boom of fifty-seven months starting in 1965. The trade balance was no longer a problem to MITI or MOF, but since they had lost a common macroeconomic target their policy co-ordination became difficult. Potential inter-ministerial conflicts made the formation and execution of industrial policy more difficult from the beginning of the 1970s.

As the Japanese economy achieved the prestigious status of Number Two behind the United States among market economies in Gross National Product towards the end of the 1960s, people's enthusiasm for economic growth suddenly and drastically waned. They began to notice the alleged 'Distortions from Growth' such as environmental problems, uncontrollable inflation, and widening regional disparities between urban and rural areas. Some people even started believing the new expression, 'Hell to GNP'. Administrative rivalry between competing ministries became serious and harmful to flexible and coherent policy-making, a situation which lasts until today. The era of simple fine-tuning between ministries was gone.

1.3.3. Industrial Organization and Policy Apparatus

The nature of industry structure critically influences the outcome of industrial policy. Holding other factors equal, industrial policy may be expected to have more positive effects in industries dominated by oligopolistic enterprises. Although not all policies concerning oligopolistic industries result in success, the clear target of a few large enterprises is almost a necessary condition for effective policy. By contrast, in industries characterized by small competitive firms, industrial policy usually does not achieve its goals. The extensive efforts and financial resources governments invest in small and mid-sized enterprises have not visibly exhibited any substantial contribution to their economic strength. For instance, medium and small retailing enterprises in Japan have not become an integral part of a modern distribution network, despite the protection and support they received through the Large-Scale Retail Store Act and the Act for the Development of Medium and Small Retailing both enacted in 1973. An extreme is agriculture (although not strictly a target of *industrial* policy) which, in spite of long-term efficiency-aiming rationalization measures, fares badly in its competitiveness.

A possible reason behind this firm–size dichotomy may be the difficulty of preventing rent-seeking and enforcing the performance of individual economic players given many firms but limited monitoring resources. Successful examples of industrial policy in industries dominated by small and medium-sized firms are the machine-tool industry and the automobile-parts industry. In both cases MITI was assisted by powerful private organizations in the industries. In the case of machine tools the trade association, the Japan Machine Tool Industry Association, monitored and enforced MITI's policy devices while automobile manufacturers, as dominant customers, played a critical role in monitoring the automobile-parts industry.

While oligopolistic industry organization can be an important necessary condition for the effectiveness of industrial policies, such policies in return must encourage a *competitive* oligopolistic structure. This is because of 'the principle of equal opportunity for worthy competitors', which, according to Juro Hashimoto, is one common element in Japan's successful industrial policy (Hashimoto, 1991: 284). This principle meant that the Japanese government *equally* helped and subsidized all worthy enterprises in a targeted industry which passed the criteria of rationalization and international competitiveness. Beginning with the First Rationalization Plan of the iron and steel industry in the early 1950s, the principle became a widely employed guideline for Japan's industrial policy in general. In regard to the iron and steel industry, for instance, the Japan Development Bank continued to finance the identical six large firms which consecutively proved to be worthy competitors.

1.3.4. The Economic Characteristics of Industrial Policy

One of the intriguing mysteries of Japanese industrial policy is why its effectiveness differed markedly by policy objective, even when applied almost simultaneously to similar industries. Given the oligopolistic characteristics of targeted industries, the nature of economic objectives plays a decisive role. As long as the competitive nature of a particular policy is market and growth restrictive to individual firms, it has much less chance of success than a policy to ensure market and firm expansion. The best illustration is the oft-cited case of MITI's failure in the 1950s and 1960s to make a forced merger of Japanese automobile manufacturers to create a few 'national champions' in the European fashion. Actually, MITI's restrictive policy backfired and, ironically, resulted in an *increase* in the number of automobile manufacturers. MITI's original intention behind the People's Car Vision in 1955 was to concentrate the production of popular cars in a single manufacturer. Subsequently, in 1961, the ministry came up with the Group-Orientation Vision in which two or three enterprises were supposed to operate in each segment of the automobile market. Panic ensued among motor-cycle and small automobile manufacturers, who were afraid of limited opportunities to expand, and this resulted in an entry frenzy into the mid-size automobile market by motor-cycle and sub-compact automobile makers. Between 1962 and 1966 six such companies (Mazda, Mitsubishi, Daihatsu, Honda, Subaru, and Suzuki) started manufacturing mid-size automobiles (Ito, 1988: 188–9). Enterprises who were economically and politically strong enough did not need to follow MITI's guidelines

Similar incidents can be observed in the petrochemical, machine-tool, and computer industries. In the case of petrochemicals, MITI expected that the investment criteria of the Second Plan of 1959 and the minimum annual capacity criteria of 300,000 tons of 1967 would help reduce the industry's number of firms and thus calm excessive competition. In reality, however, these criteria brought about exactly what MITI had hoped to avoid—an industry crowded with a large number of players vying with each other ever more harshly. When MITI set the 300,000 tons guideline for new ethylene facilities, which was supposed to be high enough to deter entry and expansion, it assumed that the number of firms filing applications for expansion would be very limited. In reality, MITI had to approve nine plans during the short period between late 1967 and the end of 1969, with all the facilities built under these plans going into operation by April 1972.[14]

The MITI-co-ordinated merger to form Shin Nippon Steel in 1970 may be the only notable exception to this rule that policies to restrict the growth opportunities of individual firms particularly in dynamic industries have almost unanimously backfired. It is noteworthy, however, that the organization of Shin Nippon Steel did not preclude competitive pressure from other members of the iron and steel oligopoly, such as NKK, Kawasaki Steel, Sumitomo Steel, and Kobe Steel.

On the other hand, when the Japanese government introduced market- and capability-augmenting or complementary policies, results were much better. Good examples are synthetic fibres and computers (which will be examined in detail in Chapters 3 and 4). Another instance is the case of the petrochemical industry during the high-growth period, when the industry emerged in the 1950s to become the second largest global producer of petrochemicals by the end of the 1960s. The government performed various functions to put the petrochemical industry on its developmental trajectory, but by far the most important was setting short-term investment goals for the industry in various phases of development—goals that were deemed necessary for the industry to meet in order to become or remain internationally competitive. These goals were specified in the form of concrete criteria which prospective plant expansion plans were required to satisfy in order to win MITI's approval. The First Plan of 1955 required individual firms in the industry to be an efficient and internationally competitive player from the very outset of import-substituting production; the Second Plan of 1967 emphasized the building of integrated petrochemical complexes; the minimum capacity for new plants was set at an annual production level of 300,000 tons, which was meant to enable the industry to enjoy greater economies of scale, cut production costs, and prepare for the liberalization of capital investment from abroad. Especially during the period before the total lifting of restrictions on the transfer of petrochemical technologies from abroad in 1973, these criteria carried formidable bidding power. They had the effect of causing individual enterprises to scramble to invest actively in order to meet the criteria and to remain viable, which in turn had the effect of boosting the industry's competitiveness in a short span of time (Chandler, Hikino, and Mowery, 1998; Hikino *et al.*, 1998).

Thus Japan's industrial policy after the Second World War was effective in encouraging scale-oriented investments or efficiency-encouraging commitments of individual large enterprises, which consequently resulted in nurturing the international competitiveness of concerned industries. The policy remained dysfunctional, however, when the policy goal was restrictive of the competitive rivalry of other firms. The government-induced rationalization of industries through mergers and consolidation did not succeed very well. The case of the petrochemical industry cited above illustrates both sides of the effectiveness of industrial policy implementation. Japanese firms after the Second World War had a strong drive to grow, and industrial policy succeeded so long as government incentives were growth oriented.

1.3.5. *Leadership of Business and Government*

Japan's industrial policies worked best when leading firms, rather than government itself, set the standard. In manipulating common investment behaviour among oligopolistic firms, the Japanese government set an achievable target of international scale, efficiency, and competitiveness that was originally conceived by a leading pace-setting private firm. Policy was then structured as an incentive mechanism for other players to emulate.

In the case of the petrochemical industry, not all the criteria set by MITI were of its own making; rather, they were often announced as adaptations of business plans envisioned by ambitious forerunners in the industry. Take, for instance, MITI's policy document of 1951, 'On the Petroleum-based Organic, Synthetic Chemical Industry', with which the ministry took its first step towards nurturing the industry. This document was based on a business plan prepared by Nippon Soda. Similarly, when MITI worked out criteria for the First and Second Plans for domestic production, it waited until private companies demonstrated their willingness to proceed with their own investment plans. Subsequently, MITI adopted a standard for ethylene facilities of an annual capacity of 300,000 tons, as two Mitsubishi chemical enterprises (Mitsubishi Yuka and Mitsubishi Kasei) submitted their plans to build plants of that size. It seems safe to conclude, therefore, that the developmental process of the petrochemical industry in Japan unfolded in three steps: first, a few industry leaders conceived ambitious expansion plans for building plants of a size far in excess of the existing industry standard; then MITI stepped in to authorize these plans by designating the proposed plant size as its new official investment goal for application to the whole industry; and finally the remaining oligopolistic members of the industry followed suit simultaneously, emulating the expansion plans of the forerunners and striving to meet the newly set goal.

From a comparative perspective, the difference between Japan and other Asian nations in terms of leadership between business and government partially resulted from the accumulated capabilities of the government bureaucracy and the private sector. While Japanese firms, particularly oligopolies, had achieved adequate technical and managerial competencies in terms of their information processing and target setting on an international scale, a similar capacity in other East Asian countries resided less with private enterprises and more with the bureaucracy, which had often been enhanced in the ironical context of Japan's colonial rule (Myers and Peattie, 1984).

1.3.6. *Industrial Policy, American Style?*

One intriguing way to understand the basic character of Japan's industrial policy is to compare it with that of the United States, which scholars often take as a representative case without industrial policy. As Chapters 6 and 8 of this volume persuasively argue, the United States emphasized antitrust policy and regulatory measures as the major microeconomic instruments of government to shape industry structure, corporate behaviour, and international competitiveness. In this sense the United States contrasts sharply with all other nations whose experiences are examined in this volume.

The uniqueness of the United States in terms of its competitiveness policy does not necessarily mean, however, the absence of industrial policy. At least from the time of Alexander Hamilton's *Report on Manufactures* in 1791 the United States envisioned extensive government action to promote the country's industrial and trade interests. A few recent studies list many actual examples of the US government actually introducing sector-specific programmes to support industrial development (Nester, 1997; Bingham, 1997; Graham, 1992; Limerick, 1987). Historical cases often cited are the Morrill Act, the Erie Canal, land subsidies to western railroads, land-grant colleges, direct loans to farmers, agricultural experimental stations, the Federal Reserve System, price support for agricultural products, the Tennessee Valley Authority, the Reconstruction Finance Corporation, and price controls in the milk and coal industries. Contemporary cases are the Chrysler bail-out, unilateral trade initiatives, military procurements, defence-related R. & D., tariffs on Asian textiles, anti-dumping measures against foreign steel producers, import quotas for Japanese automobiles, airline and banking deregulation, and financial support to the internet and high-definition television. As impressive as this list looks, it would be much more extensive if local development programmes were included.

These examples certainly illustrate a long and often successful history of government activism in the United States, but they do not necessarily represent 'industrial policy'. A few of the programmes listed are more or less macroeconomic policies, such as the Federal Reserve System. Some can be classified as regulatory (or deregulatory) measures, such as price controls and industry deregulation. When a systematic examination is made among remaining examples of broadly construed industrial policy, six characteristics of such policy in the United States can be articulated.

First, in the nineteenth century the federal government actively promoted public infrastructures such as canals, railroads, and colleges. These investments in public goods should have had a long-term positive spillover effect on the economy, even if special interests originally captured the private gains. Second, since the late nineteenth century, agriculture has been one of the central targets of 'industrial' policy. Ideas behind agricultural experimental stations, direct loans, and price support come very close to an important core theme of industrial policy in other nations, too. Third, there is a strong American government involvement in restructuring troubled firms or industries, as was the case with the Reconstruction Finance Corporation, the Chrysler bail-out, and various anti-import measures to help firms in specific industries. This interventionism on behalf of a particular firm resembles practice in Italy, as is illustrated in Chapter 11 of this volume. Fourth, trade policies have been historically an important part of American industrial policy. This includes both the protection of domestic markets and producers and aggressive market opening in foreign countries. Fifth, military-related programmes occupy a significant position in American policy. Military purchase of industrial products ensures a huge market, while the military's involvement in civilian R. & D. has had a critical impact on American technology, including such epoch-making developments as the transistor and computer.

Related to military R. & D., the sixth and probably most critical policy instruments for industrial development were the government's subsidies for high technology. Public financing of private R. & D. is theoretically justified in terms of 'public goods' which can be shared by many constituencies in the long run. Most industrial nations, including Japan, possess extensive programmes to subsidize R. & D., and international monitoring organizations such as GATT and WTO usually accept such programmes as positive and a fair means to enhance the international competitiveness of individual industries.

When these characteristics of American industrial policy are compared to their Japanese counterparts, one notable American feature is the absence of bureaucratic administrative guidance in manufacturing industries, as has been critically important in Japan. For the development of the dynamic core of its industrial economy, the United States government has mostly utilized various programmes of technology investment and foreign market access for American companies.

If there is a facet of American policy that superficially resembles Japanese industrial policy, it is the so-called 'corporate welfare' system. Corporate welfare includes direct subsidies and tax breaks which are given to US corporations, particularly large ones, for the purpose of technical assistance, price support, or market promotion.[15] Depending on individual studies, the extent of American corporate welfare can be vastly different. One estimate claims that the total annual amount of corporate subsidies and tax breaks came to $150 billion around the mid-1990s, which was more than the cost of the core programmes for social welfare.[16]

The issue of corporate welfare has never been raised in the context of industrial policy. Yet corporate welfare in the United States shares some of the same faults that the country is so vehemently critical of in industrial policy, especially crony capitalism. Actually, the main reason why corporate welfare in the United States became contentious was not related to the industrial policy controversy. Rather it was the political and policy issue of so-called 'donor access', through which big donors buy access to policy-making circles with huge contributions to influential politicians and parties. According to a Washington observer, Elizabeth Drew, 'access can lead to influence, which can lead to a policy result . . . Virtually all of this, the public doesn't see and it's hard to prove . . . People will say, of course, that they made the decision on the merits' (quoted in Abramson, 1997).

1.4. Conclusion

Japanese industrial policies have usually complemented the strategic and functional capabilities of individual firms. The basic nature of industrial policy has not necessarily been market conforming but, rather, firm conforming. The government has been called upon to perform its intermediary functions on behalf of a given industry when that industry failed to maintain growth-oriented yet orderly competition or to make necessary co-ordination efforts for and by the firms involved. In general, government industrial policies have succeeded only when they have been consistent with the investment behaviour of private firms. The government closely watched investment patterns of individual firms and eagerly identified a certain behaviour pattern among prime-moving firms in an industry that could be of potential significance in boosting the industry's overall international competitiveness. The government then set a target which was promptly emulated by other competent firms in the same industry.

Thus the industrial policies of the Japanese government have proved instrumental in steering the economy along its growth trajectory, and in helping individual companies in targeted industries to sharpen their competitive capabilities. If the industrial policies conformed well with firms' capabilities, they functioned as an effective supplement of (or even substitute to) competition and antitrust policies. MITI did not necessarily intend to promote this policy. In applying the principle of equal opportunity for worthy competitors the ministry prevented efficiency-detracting rent-seeking behaviour in individual firms and promoted strategic and functional competition among them. As long as the industrial policy contained a strong element of competition-enhancing and efficiency-gaining on the part of individual enterprises, it is probably not a mystery that the Japanese economy has significantly developed its international competitiveness in spite of the apparently half-hearted enforcement of antitrust provisions.

If rapid economic growth is the product of a well-organized and articulate industrial policy, led by a competent bureaucracy, that is the experience of South Korea and Taiwan (and possibly China), not Japan.[17] This critical difference is the result of two historical conditions. Japan was the first country to experiment with industrial policies and the bureaucracies in the rest of East Asia learned from and systematized Japan's experiences. As the pioneer, Japanese industrial policy was not always coherently exercised by experienced bureaucrats. Second, the overall capabilities regarding investment decision-making and the general balance of power lay with private business in Japan while in Korea and Taiwan government exerted relatively more weight.

These three nations, however, share one critical element for the effectiveness of industrial policy: they are latecomers and followers striving to catch up. If in the United States pinning down the 'winning' industries or industry structure in the 1980s was really impossible, as Charles Schultze (1983) suggested, this was mostly because the United States was at the world's technological and economic edge. Uncertainty regarding the future course of strategic industries is greatest at the global frontier. Japan in the 1950s and 1960s and Korea and Taiwan in the 1970s and 1980s, by contrast, faced an easier condition in targeting industries and structures, mainly because as latecomers they could identify growing industries and existing structures in the United States and other advanced economies as models to emulate (Hikino and Amsden, 1994). As Japan quickly approaches the world frontier, its industrial policy should encounter more challenging times.

NOTES

1. For interpretations of national experiences of industrial policy in advanced economies other than Japan and the United States, see Chapters 8–11 of this volume. Also refer to Audretsch (1989); Barfield and Schambra (1986); Chick (1990); Duchene and Shephaerd (1987); Grant (1989); Hart (1992); Sletmo and Boyd (1994); Verdier (1994); Wilks and Wright (1987).
2. A classic statement of this issue can be found in Baumol (1952). The latest summary of market failure arguments is Stiglitz (1990). Stiglitz's emphasis on imperfect and incomplete markets in terms of information is sometimes called 'new market failure'.
3. The most inclusive definition of industrial policy, on the other hand, can be: 'All measures that will increase the economy's supply potential . . . [or]

anything that will improve growth, productivity, and competitiveness' (Adams and Klein, 1983: 3). If this definition is accepted, it will eventually include all the economic policies. See also Komiya, Okuno, and Suzumura (1988) for the application of their analytical framework to individual industry cases.

4. Accordingly, Itoh *et al.* (1991) add the following element of industrial policy in their definition: 'Moreover, it [industrial policy] includes the totality of policies that are designed to attain this objective through intervention in the allocation of resources between industries or sectors, or in the industrial organization of individual industries' (8). Although the inclusion of these policies makes their definition broad enough to capture most of Japan's industrial policy means, the resulting denotation compromises the coherence of their original market failure approach.

5. Given the weakness of the market-failure approach in economics, a few scholars have tried to develop a different framework in analysing industrial policy. See Alice Amsden's Chapter 5 in this volume. Also refer to Chang (1994) for a transaction costs approach to industrial policy. Evans (1995) is an influential approach by a non-economist.

6. The most comprehensive historical summary of the industrial policy debate in the American context is Graham (1992). See also Adams and Klein (1983); Barfield and Schambra (1986); Johnson (1985); Johnson, Tyson, and Zysman (1989); McCraw (1986); Wachter and Wachter (1981) for a more policy-oriented discussion.

7. Books and articles on Japan's industrial policy in the English language are too numerous to discuss individually. For a comprehensive list of them, see Boger (1988).

8. Representative articles are reprinted in Audretsch (1998); Grant (1995); Ravenhill (1995).

9. For an influential argument of the negative impact of government intervention, see Peltzman (1988) and Becker (1988).

10. For the mixed effects of industrial policy on the restructuring of the Japanese economy since the 1970s, see Callon (1995); Dore (1986); Hollerman (1988); Wood (1994).

11. For further details on the comparison between the Electric Power Industry Law and the Petroleum Industry Law, see Kikkawa (1991).

12. For further details of the Japanese electrical power industry, see Kikkawa (1995a).

13. Japan Development Bank, from its establishment in 1951, heavily financed the coal, electric power, ocean shipping, shipbuilding, and iron and steel industries, which MITI regarded as strategic sectors.

14. Kikkawa (1994: 107). For machine tools, see Friedman (1988); Sawai (1990). For the computer industry, refer to Anchordoguy (1989); Fransman (1990); and Nakamura (1992).

15. See Bingham (1997) and Nester (1997) for more detailed historical and contemporary cases.

16. The controversy surrounding corporate welfare in the United States started when social welfare for individuals became a target of reform. While social welfare was being severely cut, government subsidies and tax breaks for corporations increased.

17. For this reason it is probably misleading to treat the business–government relations of these three countries as if they are fundamentally similar, as is the case of the World Bank's *The East Asian Miracle*. For a criticism of the World Bank report, see Amsden (1994).

REFERENCES

Abramson, J. (1997), 'Money Buys a Lot More Than Access', *New York Times*, 9 Nov., wk 5.

Adams, F. G., and Klein, L. R. (1983), *Industrial Policies for Growth and Competitiveness: An Economic Perspective* (Lexington, Ky.: Lexington Books).

Amsden, A. H. (1989), *Asia's Next Giant: South Korea and Late Industrialization* (Oxford and New York: Oxford University Press).

—— (1994), 'The World Bank's *The East Asian Miracle: Economic Growth and Public Policy*', *World Development*, 22: 4.

Anchordoguy, M. (1989), *Computer, Inc.: Japan's Challenge to IBM* (Cambridge, Mass.: Harvard University Press).

Audretsch, D. B. (1989), *The Market and the States: Government Policy Towards Business in Europe, Japan, and the United States* (New York and London: Harvester Wheatsheaf).

—— (1998) (ed.), *Industrial Policy and Competitive Advantage* (Northampton, Mass.: Edward Elgar), 3 vols.

Barfield, C. E., and Schambra, W. A. (1986) (eds.), *The Politics of Industrial Policy* (Washington: American Enterprise Institute).

Baumol, W. J. (1952), *Welfare Economics and the Theory of the State* (Cambridge, Mass.: Harvard University Press).

Becker, G. S. (1988), 'Public Policies, Pressure Groups, and Dead Weight Costs', in George Stigler (ed.), *Chicago Studies in Political Economy* (Chicago: Chicago University Press).

Bingham, R. D. (1997), *Industrial Policy American Style: From Hamilton to HDTV* (Armonk, New York, and London: M. E. Sharpe).

Boger, K. (1988), *Postwar Industrial Policy in Japan: An Annotated Bibliography* (Metuchen, NJ: Scarecrow Press).

Caldor, K. E. (1993), *Strategic Capitalism: Private Business and Public Purpose in Japanese Industrial Finance* (Princeton: Princeton University Press).

Callon, S. (1995), *Divided Sun: MITI and the Breakdown of Japanese High-Tech Industrial Policy, 1975–1993* (Stanford, Calif.: Stanford University Press).

Chandler, A. D., Jr., Hikino, T., and Mowery, D. (1998), 'The Evolution of Corporate Capability and Corporate Strategy and Structure Within the World's Largest Chemical Firms: The Twentieth Century in Perspective', in Ashish Arora, Ralph Landau, and Nathan Rosenberg (eds.), *Chemicals and Long-Term Economic Growth: Insights from the Chemical Industry* (New York: John Wiley).

Chang, H.-J. (1994), *The Political Economy of Industrial Policy* (New York: St Martin's Press).

Chick, M., (1990) (ed.), *Governments, Industries, and Markets: Aspects of Government–Industry Relations in the UK, Japan, West Germany, and the USA Since 1945* (Aldershot: Edward Elgar).

Dore, R. (1986), *Flexible Rigidities: Industrial Policy and Structural Adjustment in the Japanese Economy, 1970–80* (London: Athlone Press).

Duchene, F., and Shephaerd, G. (1987) (eds.), *Managing Industrial Change in Western Europe* (London: Frances Pinter).

Evans, P. (1995), *Embedded Autonomy: States and Industrial Transformation* (Princeton: Princeton University Press).

Fallows, J. (1993), 'Up Against the Wall Street Journal', *American Prospect*, 14 (Summer).

—— (1994), *Looking at the Sun: The Rise of the New East Asian Economic and Political System* (New York: Pantheon).

Fransman, M. (1990), *The Market and Beyond: Information Technology in Japan* (Cambridge: Cambridge University Press).

Friedman, D. (1988), *The Misunderstood Miracle: Industrial Development and Political Change in Japan* (Ithaca, NY: Cornell University Press).

Gao, B. (1997), *Economic Ideology and Japanese Industrial Policy: Developmentalism from 1931 to 1965* (New York: Cambridge University Press).

Graham, O. L., Jr. (1992), *Losing Time: The Industrial Policy Debate* (Cambridge, Mass.: Harvard University Press).

Grant, W. (1989), *Government and Industry: A Comparative Analysis of the United States, Canada, and the UK* (Aldershot: Edward Elgar).

—— (1995) (ed.), *Industrial Policy* (Aldershot: Edward Elgar).

Hart, J. A. (1992), *Rival Capitalists: International Competitiveness in the United States, Japan, and Western Europe* (Ithaca, NY: Cornell University Press).

Hashimoto, J. (1991), *Nippon Keizairon* (A treatise on the Japanese economy) (Kyoto: Minerva Shobo).

Hikino, T., and Amsden, A. H. (1994), 'Staying Behind, Stumbling Back, Sneaking Up, Soaring Ahead: Late Industrialization in Historical Perspective', in William J. Baumol, Richard R. Nelson, and Edward N. Wolff (eds.), *Convergence of Productivity: Cross-National Studies and Historical Evidence* (New York: Oxford University Press).

—— et al. (1998), 'The Japanese Puzzle', in Ashish Arora, Ralph Landau, and Nathan Rosenberg (eds.), *Chemicals and Long-Term Economic Growth: Insights from the Chemical Industry* (New York: John Wiley).

Hollerman, L. (1988), *Japan, Disincorporated: The Economic Liberalization Process* (Stanford, Calif.: Hoover Institution Press).

Huber, T. M. (1994), *Strategic Economy in Japan* (Boulder, Col.: Westview Press).

Itoh, M. (1988), 'Onshitsu no Nakadeno Seichou Kyouso [Competition for growth inside a greenhouse]', in H. Itami et al., (eds.), *Kyousou to Kakushin: Jidousha Sangyo no Kigyo Seicho [Competition and Innovation: Competitive Growth of the Automobile Industry]* (Tokyo: Toyo Keizai Shimposha).

—— Kiyono, K., Okuno-Fujiwara, M., and Suzumura, K. (1991), *Economic Analysis of Industrial Policy* (San Diego: Academic Press).

38 *Takeo Kikkawa and Takashi Hikino*

Johnson, C. (1982), *MITI and the Japanese Miracle: The Growth of Industrial Policy, 1925–1975* (Stanford, Calif.: Stanford University Press).

—— (1985) (ed.), *Industrial Policy Debate* (San Francisco: ICS Press).

—— (1995), *Japan: Who Governs: The Rise of the Developmental State* (New York: Norton).

——Tyson, L., and Zysman, J. (1989), *Politics of Productivity: How Japan's Development Strategy Works* (Cambridge, Mass.: Ballinger).

Kaplan, E. J. (1972), *Japan: The Government–Business Relationship: A Guide for the American Businessman* (Washington: US Bureau of International Commerce).

Kikkawa, T. (1991), 'Denki-jigyo-ho to sekiyugyo-ho: seifu to gyokai (The Electric Power Industry Law and the Petroleum Industry Law: Case Studies in Government–Industry Relations)', in Ryoichi Miwa and Takeshi Abe (eds.), *Kindai Nippon Kenkyu 13: Keizai Seisaku to Sangyo* (Tokyo: Yamakawa Shuppansha).

—— (1994), 'The Relationship between the Government and Companies in Japan During and After World War II', in Jun Sakudo and Takao Shiba (eds.), *World War II and the Transformation of Business System* (Tokyo: University of Tokyo Press).

—— (1995a), *Nippon Denryokugyou no Hatten to Matsunaga Yasuzaemon* (The Development of Japan's Electrical Power Industry and Matsunaga Yasuzaemon) (Nagoya: Nagoya University Press).

—— (1995b), 'Enterprise Groups, Industry Associations, and Government: The Case of the Petrochemical Industry in Japan', *Business History*, 37: 3.

Komiya, R. (1990), *The Japanese Economy: Trade, Industry, and Government* (Tokyo: University of Tokyo Press).

——Okuno, M., and Suzumura, K. (1988) (eds.), *Industrial Policy of Japan* (San Diego: Academic Press).

Limerick, P. N. (1987), *The Legacy of Conquest: The Unbroken Past of the American* (New York: Norton).

Lincoln, E. (1984), *Japan's Industrial Policies* (Washington: Japan Economic Policy Institute of America).

McCraw, T. K. (1986) (ed.), *America versus Japan* (Boston: Harvard Business School Press).

Magaziner, I. C., and Hout, T. M. (1980), *Japanese Industrial Policy* (Berkeley: University of California Press).

Mason, M. (1992), *American Multinationals and Japan: The Political Economy of Japanese Capital Controls, 1899–1980* (Cambridge, Mass.: Harvard University Press).

Myers, R., and Peattie, M. R. (1984) (eds.), *The Japanese Colonial Empire, 1895–1945* (Princeton: Princeton University Press).

Nakamura, K. (1992), ' Sangyo Seisaku to Kompyuta Sangyo (Industrial Policies and the Computer Industry)', in H. Morikawa (ed.), *Bizunesuman notameno Sengo Keieishi Nyumon* (Introduction to Postwar Business History for Businessmen) (Tokyo: Nihon Keizai Shimbunsha).

Nakamura, T. (1981), *The Postwar Japanese Economy* (Tokyo: University of Tokyo Press).

Nester, W. R. (1991), *Japanese Industrial Targeting: The Neomercantilist Path to Economic Superpower* (Basingstoke: Macmillan).

—— (1997), *American Industrial Policy: Free or Managed Markets?* (New York: St Martin's Press).

Odagiri, H., and Goto, A. (1996), *Technology and Industrial Development in Japan: Building Capabilities by Learning, Innovation, and Public Policy* (Oxford: Clarendon Press).

Okimoto, D. I. (1989), *Between MITI and the Market: Japanese Industrial Policy for High Technology* (Stanford, Calif.: Stanford University Press).

Peltzman, S. (1988), 'The Growth of Government', in George Stigler (ed.), *Chicago Studies in Political Economy* (Chicago: Chicago University Press).

Ravenhill J. (1995) (ed.), *The Political Economy of East Asia: Japan* (Brookfield, Vt.: Edward Elgar), two vols.

Samuels, R. J. (1987), *The Business of the Japanese State: Energy Markets in Comparative and Historical Perspective* (Ithaca, NY: Cornell University Press).

Sawai, M. (1990), 'Kosaku Kikai [Machine Tools]', in S. Yonekawa *et al.*, (eds.), *Sengo Nippon Keieishi, Dainikan* [Business History of Postwar Japan] (Tokyo: Toyo Keizai Shimpousha), ii.

Schultze, C. (1983), 'Industrial Policy: A Dissent', *The Brookings Review*, 2: 1 (Fall).

Sletmo, G. K., and Boyd, G. (1994), *Industrial Policies in the Pacific* (Boulder, Calif.: Westview Press).

Stiglitz, J. (1990), 'On the Economic Role of the State', in Arnold Heertje (ed.), *The Economic Role of the States* (Cambridge, Mass.: Harvard University Press).

Thurow, L. C. (1980), *The Zero-Sum Society: Distribution and the Possibilities for Economic Change* (New York: Basic Books).

Trezise, P. H. (1983), 'Industrial Policy Is Not the Major Reason for Japan's Success', *The Brookings Review*, 1: 3 (Spring).

Verdier, D. (1994), *Democracy and International Trade* (Princeton: Princeton University Press).

Vestal, J. E. (1993), *Planning for Change: Industrial Policy and Japanese Economic Development, 1945–1990* (Oxford: Clarendon Press).

Wachter, M. L., and Wachter, S. M. (1981) (eds.), *Toward a New U.S. Industrial Policy?* (Philadelphia: University of Pennsylvania Press).

Wilks, S., and Wright, M. (1987) (eds.), *Comparative Government–Industry Relations: Western Europe, United States, and Japan* (Oxford: Oxford University Press).

Wood, C. (1994), *The End of Japan, Inc.: And How the New Japan Will Look* (New York: Simon & Schuster).

World Bank (1993), *The East Asian Miracle: Economic Growth and Public Policy* (Oxford: Oxford University Press).

Yamamura, K. (1967), *Economic Policy in Postwar Japan: Growth versus Economic Democracy* (Berkeley: University of California Press).

Zinsmeister, K. (1993), 'MITI Mouse: Japan's Industrial Policy Doesn't Work', *Policy Review*, 64 (Spring), 28–35.

2

Regulatory Framework, Government Intervention and Investment in Postwar Japan
The Structural Dynamics of J-Type Firm–Government Relationships

HIDEAKI MIYAJIMA

2.1. Introduction

The rapid growth of the Japanese economy during the 1950s and 1960s (over 10 per cent of annual GDP growth) was spurred by fierce investment competition among large firms in the manufacturing sector. The investment ratio accelerated 20 per cent in the late 1950s; to 30 per cent in the early 1960s; and to nearly 35 per cent in the late 1960s—among the highest of advanced nations and far beyond prewar levels in Japan.[1] Heavy investment in plant and equipment was one of the main reasons why the international competitiveness of Japanese industries increased. Such investment led to greater productivity, the advancement of rapid import substitution, and the rapid growth of exports.

There are two contrasting historical narratives regarding the way this process occurred. One group of researchers has characterized it as the emergence of a 'capitalist developmental state' in which the state served

The author thanks Lonny Carlile, William Lozonick, and David Weistein for useful conversation regarding this topic. The author also thanks William Becker, Alice Amsden, Richard Vietor, Shigeru Matsushima, and Jim Tomlinson for helpful comment on earlier version. This work is supported by a Waseda University Grant for Special Research Project and a Ministry of Education Grant for Scientific Research.

as an effective 'pilot agency', capable of steering the private sector's investment decisions in a desired direction.[2] Other researchers characterized it as simply private-sector firms responding effectively to market incentives. The latter group believed that the incentives offered by government were not substantial enough to explain corporate behaviour, and that there was no correlation between government targeting and industrial performance.[3]

In the following chapter, a third narrative is offered—one focused on the consequences of Japan's postwar legal framework relating to antitrust policy and government intervention in the organizational structures of private corporations.[4] Rather than place the focus on either state or market, this chapter describes the evolution of the Japanese corporate system (the J-type firm) within the context of an emerging, industrial, policy-oriented developmental state, and the market opportunities in the postwar period. Analytically, it is argued that high investment was supported by the growth-oriented behaviour and long-term time horizon of J-type firms. Investment was encouraged by the emergence of an institutional setting where top managers were insulated from the short-term external pressures of the stock market and encouraged to rely on financial institutions for investment funds.[5]

Instead of only focusing on targeting and government subsidies affecting resource allocation and regulatory framework determining market structure, this chapter also looks at the role of government in establishing an institutional setting which could influence corporate behaviour. In other words, in order to discuss comprehensively the dynamic business–government interaction in the golden age of Japan, the emphasis is put on two phases of that interaction. The first clarifies the role of government, not only in solving market imperfections but in facilitating aggressive corporate strategy through industrial policy and competition policy. The second examines the regulatory framework in which the corporate system evolved, focusing on the main bank system and corporate governance structure.

Section 2 treats the impact of postwar reforms initiated by the General Headquarters of the Occupation Forces (GHQ) on corporate and industrial organization. Postwar reforms in Japan were aimed at creating a system of corporate organization based on the American model—a competitive market, dispersed ownership of corporations, and securities-based financing. However, the system that ultimately emerged in the early 1950s was a 'Japanized' version of what GHQ originally planned.

Section 3 describes the evolution of the J-firm during the 1950s, a period of extensive government regulation and intervention. I discuss capital accumulation and the effects of the Law of Compulsory Asset Capital Revaluation. Also examined in this section are three other factors that encouraged aggressive investment behaviour: promotional industrial policy (IP), antitrust policy, and debt financing made possible by a regulated financial system.

The fourth section focuses on the 1960s, a period in which IP began to decline as a consequence of trade and capital liberalization. After assessing several plans drafted by the Ministry of International Trade and Industry (MITI) and Ministry of Finance (MOF) in the early 1960s, this section discusses the drastic change in ownership structure in the wake of the stock market depression of the mid-1960s. Noteworthy here was that J-type firms behaved quite differently from how MITI and MOF intended they should. The chapter concludes with some final remarks concerning the relationship between regulatory framework and J-type firm behaviour.

Incorporated into the proceeding sections are regression analyses of the influence of industrial organization, ownership structure, and the financial system on corporate behaviour. These regressions use data about the 150 largest Japanese corporations in the years 1955, 1964, and 1972. Due to the appearance and disappearance of some companies on these lists, the total number of companies included in the three years is 202.

2.2. Postwar Reform: 'Americanization' of the Corporate System and its 'Japanization'

2.2.1. *The Impact of GHQ Policy on Corporate and Industrial Organizations*

Although significant changes in corporate and industrial organizations occurred during the command economy of the Second World War, it was the postwar reforms initiated by GHQ that were most crucial in producing a corporate system based on the J-type firm. GHQ pursued a vision of reform totally different from that of prewar bureaucrats who had tried to create what they called an 'Economic New Order' (*Keizai-Shin Taisei*). Also of importance was that Japan's postwar reform process paralleled that currently underway in the former socialist economies. As with the firms in those countries, large Japanese firms were heavily controlled and subsidized by the state, as were their stock issues. It is possible to consider Japan's postwar reforms as the first large-scale privatization experiment to establish a corporate system modelled on the American version (Aoki and Kim, 1995).

2.2.1.1. *Corporate Reorganization and Recapitalization*

The capital composition and corporate finance pattern of large firms in
prewar Japan were not particularly distinctive. Their debt-equity ratios
were low (an average of 65 per cent in 1934–6) and corporations depended
mainly on internal funds for their financial resources. However, this situation changed rapidly during the war as is shown in Fig. 2.1.

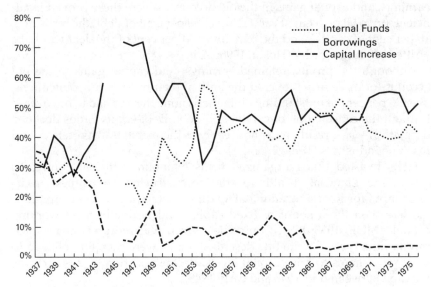

Fig 2.1 *Financial resource for investment*

From 1942 on, firms grew increasingly dependent on bank loans.
Government financial institutions (*Senji Kin'yu Kinko* [Wartime Financing
Bank]) provided a large portion of these loans. The state also guaranteed
loans from private financial institutions.

When the war ended, many Japanese firms were insolvent. In the liabilities column of the balance sheets of these firms were extremely high
levels of debt and in the assets column, huge losses of tangible assets. To
make matter worse, in 1946 the government decided to suspend payment
of huge amounts of wartime indemnities promised to the munitions companies. The losses growing out of this repudiation were estimated to
amount to nearly 20 per cent of GNE in 1946 (MOF, 1978). The procedure
adopted for reorganizing these non-financial institutions was as follows.

The process began with the government allowing companies rendered
insolvent as a result of the suspension of wartime indemnities to declare
themselves 'special account companies'. After a firm was declared a

special account company its balance sheet was divided into an 'old' and a 'new' account. Business operations were allowed to continue using the new account. The old account became the object of reorganization procedures. Once reorganization was completed, the old account was merged with the new account and the firm would then recapitalize. This process was guided by the Corporation Reconstruction and Reorganization Act of October 1946.

Debts rendered unpayable as a result of the suspension of wartime indemnities were addressed in the first instance with profits, retained earnings, and capital gains in the old account. Where these proved insufficient, up to 90 per cent of capital, up to 70 per cent of debt, the remaining 10 per cent of capital, and the remaining 30 per cent of the debt would be written off in that order (Hoshi, 1995: 325).

Although the profits, retained earnings, and capital gains in the old accounts of these firms covered the bulk of their outstanding obligations, over 30 per cent of outstanding obligations none the less had to be covered through the cancellation of capital and debt. Debt-equity ratios declined dramatically as a result, most noticeably in the metal, transportation, and machine industries (Table 2.1).

GHQ insisted that reorganized firms maintain sufficient equity. To assure the financial 'health' of the reconstructed companies, in its 'Standards for Reorganization' GHQ directed that the level of capital be 'no less than the amount of fixed capital and normally fixed working capital' (MOF, 1983: 876). Companies which had reduced their capital through the type of write-offs described above were therefore obliged to issue new shares to raise capital levels. Recapitalization of this sort was initiated between mid-1948 and early 1949.

2.2.1.2. Zaibatsu *Dissolution*

Changes in corporate governance structure were instituted by 'new bureaucrats' during the war. They did this with 'corporate controls' that were influenced by Nazi ideology and the successful economic planning of the Soviet Union. These new bureaucrats were convinced that the maximization of production required the rights of shareholders be restricted because, in their view, the risk-averse attitude of firms, caused by the overriding requirement that shareholder interests be met, was responsible for high levels of cash outflow and insufficient levels of capital accumulation. Based on this ideology, a ceiling was imposed on dividend payout ratios (up to 8 per cent) in 1940. The Munitions Companies Law of 1943 limited the rights of shareholders in ratifying the decisions of top management. In the process, power and control over the corporation shifted from shareholders to salaried managers (Okazaki, 1993*b*).

Table 2.1 *Cancellation of Equity, Revaluation of Assets and Depreciation*

(billion; %)

	A Special loss	B Cancellation ratio	C Upper limit for revaluation	D Revaluation ratio	Depreciation ratio (1)				Depreciation ratio (2)			
					1934–6	1950	1955	1960	1934–6	1950	1955	1960
Mining	40	11	104	79	1.6	3.8	6.3	6.5	1.7	4.3	6.2	7.2
Metal	113	52	105	70	3.0	1.8	4.5	7.1	3.7	3.1	5.3	7.6
Electric	60	1	⎫ 94		2.1	0.8	3.2	2.9	4.8	3.5	5.5	6.5
Other machine	27	⎭ 33	⎬	55	1.1	1.0	4.2	4.3	2.9	2.4	5.5	10.3
Transport	209	71			1.5	0.8	3.4	3.1	1.2	2.6	5.8	8.5
Chemical	50	19	97	70	6.8	1.8	4.4	5.8	7.7	4.3	6.1	7.0
Textile	47	1	101	86	4.1	1.0	4.5	5.8	6.2	2.5	5.8	6.6
Food	12	N.A	43	66	6.0	0.9	1.3	2.0	5.8	3.3	4.7	6.5
Total	576	24	682	72	4.5	1.3	3.8	4.4	5.8	3.2	5.6	6.9

Notes:
1. Total includes other manufacturing industry.
2. B is calculated as the losses cancelled out by capital/special loss (A).
3. D is calculated as the amount of revaluation implemented/upper limit (C).
4. Depreciation (1): Depreciation/Turnover.
5. Depreciation (2): Depreciation/(Asset + Asset_$t - 1$/2), Asset based on both value.

Sources: MOF (1983), xiii: 904–5; Mitsibishi Economic Research Institute, *Kigyou Keiei Bunseki* [*The Analysis of Corporate Finance*], yearly.

Further drastic changes were imposed by the postwar reforms. The view of GHQ was that dispersion of stocks to individuals (widespread ownership of securities) should be a pillar of economic democratization. GHQ believed the concentration of ownership in the hands of *zaibatsu* families and other large shareholders—which was a characteristic of the prewar system—was a major factor in Japan's militarization. The new corporate-governance structure which GHQ sought was an individual-centred, widespread-ownership system in which corporate managers would be monitored by the market as well as by boards of directors elected at shareholder meetings. Put another way, what GHQ wanted was a kind of 'market for corporate control with employee's commitment'.[6]

The procedure followed in the *zaibatsu* dissolution process began with the designation of specific firms and families as *zaibatsu* families, holding companies, and subsidiary companies. Stockholdings of designated firms and families were then transferred to the HCLC (Holding Companies Liquidation Committee).[7] The amount of shares transferred to the HCLC in conjunction with *zaibatsu* dissolution totalled 9 billion yen, or an estimated 21 per cent of the economy's capital. If one adds to this the stock-holding disposed of at that time under other programmes, a total of 14.4 billion shares, or approximately 34 per cent of the nation's total, paid-in capital were dispersed. My own analysis of the 100 largest companies of 1937 and 1955 leads me to conclude that almost half of these firms (62 out of 127) were targeted under the *zaibatsu* dissolution programme and forced to disperse nearly 50 per cent of their issued stocks (Miyajima, 1995).

The liquidation of *zaibatsu*-related stocks began in early 1948. In creating the individual-centred ownership structure, the first priority was to transfer stock holdings to a firm's employees and then to residents of the area where the company operated. No single individual was allowed to purchase more than 1 per cent of a given company's shares. At the same time, any manufacturing companies or financial institutions designated as *zaibatsu*-affiliated were prohibited outright from buying stocks of affiliated firms.

The ownership structure of Japan's largest firms was changed completely as a result of this 'democratization' of securities holdings. With nearly 70 per cent of all corporate stocks owned by individuals (Fig. 2.2), an individual-centred, widespread ownership structure emerged in place of the hierarchical, holding company-centred ownership structure of the prewar years.

Other goals of *zaibatsu* dissolution were the elimination of managers appointed by the *zaibatsu* families and the dissolution of the interlocking relationships between holding companies and subsidiary companies. The severing of personal relationships occurred primarily through the 'economic purge' of 1947, but was supplemented by the Law for Termination

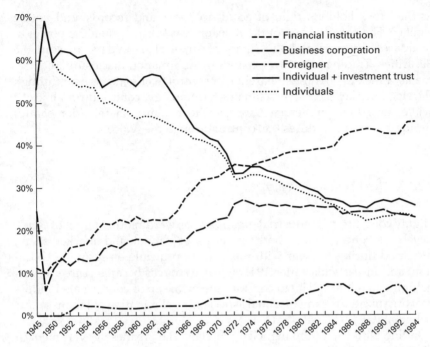

Fig 2.2 *Distribution of stockholding in all listed non-financial companies by type of investor*

of *Zaibatsu* Family Control. Approximately 2,000 former executives were purged as a result of these two measures. In the process, salaried managers replaced owner-managers on the boards of large Japanese firms.[8]

Thus, a new corporate–governance structure, modelled on the American system, emerged from the postwar reforms. Supplementing the measures that created this new structure were a series of institutional reforms designed to sustain the corporate–governance structure.

First, stock ownership on the part of financial institutions and corporations, which had been free of regulatory restrictions in the prewar period, was now severely restricted by the Anti-Monopoly Law (AML). Article 9 of the original AML outlawed the establishment of holding companies (those with 25 per cent or more of their assets in the securities of other companies) and prohibited manufacturing companies from owning the stock of other companies. Article 13 of the law limited shareholding by financial institutions to 5 per cent of a company's total stock issues. Second, the Securities Trading Act of 1948 contained various provisions which protected the rights of small shareholders. Simultaneously, an auditor system was formally introduced into Japanese firms. Third, The Commercial Law was completely revised based on the 1950 American model. GHQ guided the drafting revisions and insisted on such measures as the 'stock holder's right of access to books and records, and voting rights'.[9] The essential aim of the revision was to strengthen the power of boards of directors and the rights of small shareholders. In sum the Securities Trading Act, by expanding information-disclosure requirements, aimed to guarantee shareholder control over management through the stock market (i.e. in Hirschman's terminology, control through 'exit') while the new Commercial Law tried to enhance shareholder control through direct procedures (i.e. control through the 'voice').

2.2.1.3. Deconcentration Policy

Highly concentrated industrial organizations were another target of GHQ. Levels of concentration, both in terms of capital and market share, increased during the war with the priority principle on resource allocation, and in particular after 1941, when resources became scarce. It was natural enough for GHQ to consider the break-up of concentrated industrial organizations as an essential aspect of the elimination of Japanese war potential (GHQ/SCAP, 1951).

In line with such thinking, GHQ directed the Japanese government in 1947 to dissolve large firms through the Law for the Elimination of Excessive Concentrations of Economic Power. Initially, 325 companies were designated as targets for elimination under the law, but in the end that number was only eighteen. Still, key Japanese firms were involved, including Nippon Steel and Mitsubishi Heavy Industries. In addition, there were several instances of large firms being dissolved under the Corporate Reconstruction and Reorganization Act (Uekusa, 1979; Hadley, 1970: ch. 9). Postwar reforms contributed indirectly to the creation of a competitive market structure as well. Because the large ex-*zaibatsu* and other firms that dominated prewar industries were preoccupied with the new reforms imposed on them, independent companies minimally affected by these measures were able to use this as a window of opportunity to expand their businesses or enter into new fields.

One of the primary purposes of the Anti-Monopoly Law (AML) of 1947 was to maintain the newly created competitive market structure. It is instructive to note that the staff of the Ministry of Commerce and Industry (the predecessor of MITI) to whom GHQ delegated the drafting of the AML, simply could not understand what GHQ was asking them to do, and drafted a law modelled on the prewar law regulating cartels (The Control Law for Important Industries in 1931) which allowed cartel activities in principle but gave the government power to oversee them (MOF, 1982: 385–96). This example illustrates just how unfamiliar Japan was with the anti-monopoly concept.

The original Anti-Monopoly Law enacted in 1947 contained stricter provisions than its US equivalent. First, cartel activities were more thoroughly prohibited than in the US Sherman Act. All cartel activity was deemed prima facie illegal. Second, the law (Article 8) gave the Fair Trade Commission (FTC) the power to eliminate 'undue substantial disparities in bargaining power'. The drafting of that article was influenced by the ALCOA case of 1945 in which a large aluminium company was dissolved on the grounds that it represented a substantial disparity in bargaining power (MOF, 1981: 400–1).

2.2.2. The 'Japanization' of the American Model

Economic reform in Japan entered a new phase early in 1949. During 1948, real gross national product (GNP) recovered to 85 per cent of prewar levels (1934–6 = 100) and the rate of inflation declined from earlier peak levels. A multifaceted economic stabilization programme was then introduced. The so-called Dodge line of 1949 involved the establishment of a fixed exchange rate in place of multiple exchange rates, as well as the suspension of new loans from the RFB (Reconstruction Financing Bank). These policies had a profound impact on the operations of Japanese firms. Prior to stabilization, top management gave in to the wage demands of labour unions, expecting that wage hikes could be offset through increases in controlled prices and additional subsidies from the RFB (Okazaki, 1993). No longer able to count on soft-budget constraints of the controlled economy, they found themselves forced to reconstruct their operations on a free-market basis.

The new corporate system envisioned by GHQ ran into several critical difficulties as a result of the shift from a planned economy to a market economy. Among the biggest challenges was the stock market collapse in October 1949, precipitated by an oversupply of stocks and an increase in real interest rates. The crash affected the Americanized corporate system in two ways.

First, it made recapitalization virtually impossible. A typical example was Hitachi and Toshiba, two large electrical equipment manufacturers that suffered huge losses as a consequence of the stabilization programme. With share prices dropping below par value, both companies found they were unable to raise required capital (Miyajima, 1994). In light of the difficulty of issuing new shares in a depressed market, the Standard for Reorganization was revised in the summer of 1950 (Miyajima 1995: 384). At the same time new money for reconstruction was being supplied by the city banks.

Second, as a result of the stock market crash, top managers found them-selves dealing with the threat of takeovers. This was especially true for ex-*zaibatsu* companies, whose stock issues had been heavily liquidated; several former *zaibatsu* companies experienced hostile takeover bids. Faced with a crisis of managerial autonomy, top management teams sought to maintain stock prices through measures which mimicked 'lever-aged buyouts', technically prohibited under Japanese Commercial Law (Miyajima, 1995). Actions of this sort were particularly common in late 1949 and early 1950.

With the Japanese government pressing for measures to sustain equity prices and orders from Washington to rehabilitate rapidly the Japanese economy, GHQ backed away from its original plans for a Japanese corpo-rate system. In October 1949 the Securities Co-ordinating and Liquidation Committee indefinitely postponed the public sale of remaining *zaibatsu*-related stocks, a measure designed to alleviate the oversupply of securi-ties. At about the same time, MOF announced it would no longer give top priority to assuring individual and employee stock ownership (Miyajima 1995: 384).

Several other measures for maintaining stock prices were introduced. First, share ownership on the part of financial institutions was encouraged by the Ministry of Finance (MOF) and Bank of Japan. Second, investment trusts—the equivalent of mutual funds in the US—were introduced. Third, the original anti-monopoly statutory framework was revised. A 1949 amendment of the Anti-Monopoly Law made it possible for manu-facturing companies to hold other companies' stocks, as long as owner-ship did not substantially reduce competition. A further amendment in 1953, through a revision of Article 13, raised the ceiling on financial insti-tution ownership from the previous 5 per cent to 10 per cent (Miyajima, 1995: 384–5). As suggested by Fig. 2.2, these changes in policy led to a shift from individual- to institution-centred ownership. Cross shareholding among ex-*zaibatsu* companies also advanced in the early 1950s.

Fierce competition in product markets became a serious problem around 1952 as the Korean war boom ended. It was reported that 'excess competition' (cut-throat competition) occurred in several industries, including cotton yarn, rayon, and cement. Faced with legal restrictions imposed by the AML's provisions, MITI facilitated the creation of *de facto* cartels through the use of administrative guidance. The justification was that such collusion did not violate the AML since it was done under the guidance of MITI and therefore not voluntary (MITI, 1989).

However, it was quite clear that cartel activities were legally suspect. For instance, a *de facto* cartel in the staple fibre industry was declared a violation of the AML by the FTC. Business circles and MITI lobbied strenuously for a further revision of the AML. The upshot of this was the 1953 amendment of the AML which, along with deleting the provision proscribing disparities in bargaining power, relaxed the strict prohibitions against cartels. As a result of this amendment, cartels for depressed industries (recession cartels) and for modernization purposes (rationalization cartels) were now legal (MITI, 1988: 259–303). Together with the amendment of the shareholding articles, the revised anti-monopoly law created a profoundly modified institutional framework for the pursuit of corporate strategies.

2.3. The Heyday of Industrial Policy: The First Phase of the High Growth Era (HGE)

2.3.1. *The Promotion of Capital Accumulation Under the Law for Capital Asset Revaluation*

As discussed above, the capital composition of large Japanese firms after implementation of the Occupation reforms was characterized by low equity levels, something which GHQ did not consider desirable. The dividend payout ratio of large firms was rather high, while the depreciation ratio was very low, as is shown in Fig. 2.3.[10] Such behaviour might be characterized as oriented towards the short term and even myopic. In any event it is clear that the behaviour of large Japanese firms was quite different from what we currently conceive of as that of a J-type firm.

It is helpful here to conceive of two sets of equilibrium. One of these might be termed a 'low accumulation equilibrium', where a company maintains a high payout ratio, avoids asset appreciation, and minimizes depreciation. The second might be termed a 'high accumulation equilibrium', where a company improves its capital composition by maintaining a low payout ratio, increases the value of its assets, and enhances cash flow through depreciation. Government officials as well as business leaders considered the latter desirable, but it was the former behaviour pattern that predominated in large firms. This was natural enough under the circumstances of the time—namely dispersed firm ownership and a capital composition biased towards low equity. Under-depreciation was especially conspicuous in the machinery, metal, and chemical industries (Table 2.1).[11]

In light of such corporate behaviour, MOF and MITI instituted a series of measures designed to cause a switch from a low-accumulation to a high-accumulation equilibrium. Two special depreciation rules were introduced. One was a special depreciation allowance (a 50 per cent

Hideaki Miyajima

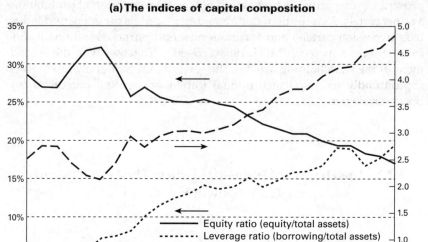

(a) The indices of capital composition

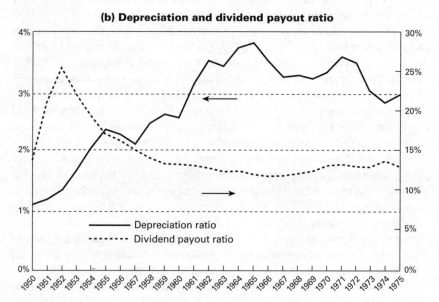

(b) Depreciation and dividend payout ratio

Fig 2.3 *Capital composition and financial behaviour of firms*

increase over three years) on designated equipment written into a 1951 revision of the Special Tax Measures Law. The second was a first-year depreciation allowance in the 1952 Enterprise Rationalization Promotion Law (which also provided an exemption from property taxes) of up to 50 per cent of the purchase price of a piece of equipment. Due to a high inflation rate, however, book values of tangible assets were considerably lower than real values (replacement prices). The resulting undervaluation of assets was a major obstacle to rapid depreciation. In response, MOF enacted the 'Law for Capital Assets Revaluation' in 1950, which was revised in 1951 and 1953. Despite this, company asset revaluation did not advance as hoped. The main reason was that the law did not stipulate the extent and magnitude of revaluation but instead left this for the company to determine. Companies preferred the lower property taxes that under-valuation made possible to the higher taxes associated with asset appreciation. According to this line of thought, asset appreciation would increase unit costs and threaten competitiveness. The increase in the capital account associated with appreciated assets would lower nominal equity ratios, lower the dividend payout ratio and, given the imperfect and underdeveloped state of the capital market, make it difficult to raise capital.[12]

Convinced that one of the reasons for the swift recovery of West Germany was its rapid depreciation policies, MOF and MITI were seriously concerned about the revaluation problem. As a result the Law for Compulsory Asset Capital Revaluation for Promoting Healthy Capital was enacted in 1954. This law outlined procedures under which companies could revalue tangible assets up to 80 per cent of their estimated value and allowed them to depreciate tangible assets on the basis of this revaluation.

It treated any increase in value as a capital gain, while at the same time limiting the payout ratio to under 15 per cent when revaluation did not occur under these rules. Finally, for companies which did revalue, it reduced corporate dividend and property taxes on those assets revalued (MITI, 1955; Toyo-keizai, 1957: 127–35).

In sum, the law provided a strong set of incentives and disincentives designed to induce companies to revalue their assets. The law appears to have been very effective. As is shown in Fig. 2.3 and Table 2.1, the depreciation ratio (depreciation divided by turnover), which was below 2 per cent in 1950–2, rose from 1954 onward while the dividend ratio began to decline rapidly beginning around 1955. Although debt–equity ratios started to increase once again after 1956 because the demand for money exceeded available internal funds, the depreciation ratio nevertheless continued to rise steadily throughout the late 1950s. The Law for Revaluation, in other words, caused a shift in company behaviour orientation, from a low-accumulation equilibrium and a short-term time horizon to a high-accumulation equilibrium based on a long-term time horizon.

2.3.2. *Government Intervention and Investment Competition*

2.3.2.1. *IP Accentuation of the 'First-Mover' Advantage*

Although direct government controls over foreign trade remained in place and several plans for industrial recovery were implemented (including the first rationalization plan for the iron and steel industries and the rationalization plan for coal mining), during the early 1950s an explicit consensus had yet to emerge on the issue of targeting new industries. Industrial policy remained a contentious issue, pitting those who favoured free trade against others who favoured autarkic development. It was only in the mid-1950s, with the publication of the 'Five Year Plan for Economic Support', that a consensus was reached among business leaders and government decision-makers on the desirability of targeting new domestic, market-based industries with the potential to become export industries (Johnson, 1982: 228–9; Kosai, 1988: 29–31). It is worth noting that this 'strategy' differed from both the 'inward oriented' import-substitution strategies commonly applied in Latin American countries and the 'outward' export-oriented industrialization strategies applied in the NIES in the 1970s.[13]

Once targeted industries were chosen, import restrictions and foreign reserve quotas began to perform a new function as mechanisms for channelling resources into targeted industries. The list of targeted industries and measures taken are summarized in Table 2.2. An early target of promotion policies was synthetic fibres. Others included the petrochemical, machinery parts, general machinery, and electrical industries. For targeted industries long-term (normally five-year) plans were drafted by councils composed of MITI officials and representatives of relevant firms. The plans outlined projections of future demand and production levels and presented corresponding investment programmes. Special promotion laws were enacted in several industries, as shown in Table 2.2.

Additionally, several promotional measures were taken *vis-à-vis* these industries: (1) preferential loans from the Japan Developmental Bank (JDB) and other government banks; (2) accelerated depreciation and reductions in corporate income taxes; (3) decreased tariffs on imported machinery; and (4) approval of foreign-technology licences.

The effect of these measures on the promotion of targeted industries was as follows. First, protective measures subsidized the set-up costs of firms in the targeted industries. Low-interest loans from JDB promoted investment in the iron and steel, shipbuilding, and machinery industries by decreasing capital costs. The spillover effect of JDB loans on private financial institutions should also be emphasized (Sawai, 1990).

Second, the information exchanged between MITI and companies in an industry during the process of drafting these plans and implementing these policies decreased the risks and uncertainty that companies faced. The long-term plans outlined by government councils also provided a point of reference for companies from which to design their own long-term plans. The late 1950s represented the first time in history that Japanese firms drafted their own long-term management plans that covered such areas as sales, production, and investment. It has been reported that in a number of prominent cases it was the Five Year Economic Development Plan of 1958 that motivated firms to draft those long-term plans (Toyo-keizai, 1961: 112–13).

It is important to note that the limited time frame of protective measures induced firms to adopt aggressive investment strategies. When Japan joined GATT, it was clear that existing restrictions of trade and capital would have to be removed within a few years. As top managers of large firms realized their companies were still small-scale and had high costs and low-quality levels in comparison with foreign competitors, they grew extremely enthusiastic about decreasing their costs within the time frame set for trade and capital liberalization (Itoh, 1988: 223–6).

Another aspect of promotional industrial policy involved quasi-fixed rules, or rules that varied from industry to industry but were implemented in an impartial and standardized manner (Murakami, 1987: 47–9). As Kikkawa and Hikino discuss theoretically in this volume, and Suzuki examines in the case of the synthetic fibre industry, companies had strong incentives to obtain subsidies by meeting the requirements stipulated in quasi-fixed rules. Because being the first to attain capacity tended to frustrate and complicate rivals' planning and implementation, there was a definite advantage to being the first in an industry to invest in large-scale plant and equipment. Also at work were lessons that top management had learned under the planned economy. During the war years, quotas were allocated in proportion to a firm's existing production capacity and its output during the preceding year. As a result, latecomers suffered smaller allotments of funds and materials than the 'first mover' and the latter tended to maintain a dominant position. It has been documented that top managers of latecomer firms regularly complained about their lesser allotments (Koyo Seiko, 1994: 83). Thus, under quasi-fixed rules, firms were encouraged to adopt growth-oriented strategies in order to attain and maintain 'first-mover' advantage.

2.3.2.2. *The Interactive Effects of the Anti-Monopoly Law and IP*

Price competition was quite fierce when the Japanese economy entered into recessions induced by tight monetary policies in the years 1954–5,

Table 2.2   *Brief Summary of Industrial Policy in Japan*

Targeted industry	1950s	1960s	1970s
Iron and Steel	50 * First Rationalization Plan 55 * Second Rationalization Plan 58 ◆ Public Sales System		70 Merger, Shin-Nihon Iron & Steel Co.
Petro-chemical	55 * Petrochemical Promotion Measures 59 Second Plan for Establishing Petrochemical Firms	64 ◆ Petrochemical Co-operation Discussion Group	
Synthetic fibre	53 * Five Year Development Plan	64 ◆ Synthetic Fibre Co-operation Discussion Group	
Automobile	55 * National Car Plan	61 Grouping Plan 65 ⊙ Finished Car	71 △
Electric machines	55 * Five Year Rationalization Plan 57 Electric Industry Promotion Temporary Measures Law		71 △ 72 ⊙ Engine

Industrial machines   56 Machine Industry Promotion Special Measures Law
                        61 Revision of Law   71 △

External environment

60 Plan for the Liberalization of Trade and Exchange
63–4 The Law for Special Industries
   64 The participation to OECD
      67 First Round of capital liberalization
         (this opened up some 50 industries,
         17 at 100% and 33 at 50%, to foreign
         participants)

Notes:
◆ Exemption of ATL, investment co-ordination
* The development plan
⊙ Abolishment of import restriction
△ Capital liberalization

1957–8, 1962–3, and 1965–6. Because requirements for gaining approval for recession and rationalization cartels under the AML were quite stringent, industries and MITI preferred to use administrative guidance in organizing cartels. The most famous example is the steel-list price system. The special laws for selected industries listed in Table 2.2 included articles exempting a relevant industry from the provisions of the AML. Cartel activities were also permitted in the export field following the enactment of the Export-Import Transaction Law in 1953 and its amendment in 1955 (MITI, 1989: 331–3).

There are two points to note here. One is that despite the spread of cartel activities in various industries, the legal framework of the AML continued to remain in place. During the 1957–8 recession, the peak business association Keidanren began to lobby for a complete overhaul of the AML. MITI drafted a new AML in 1958 modelled on the UK Restrictive Practices Act but the Diet failed to pass this amendment. Another is that the implementation of AML in Japan was quite discretionary, compared to that of the US which was based on the *ex ante* rule as shown in Chapter 6. Studies of the actual implementation of the AML suggest that surveillance over cartel activities was relaxed during recession periods and strengthened during business upturns. The evidence also suggests that recession cartels in leading industries were short lived because of the disruptive predilections of the more aggressive companies in an industry (MITI, 1989: 317–31). Thus, from a business-cycle perspective, the AML framework and MITI's industrial-organization policy functioned in a complementary manner.

This combination of the AML framework and MITI's guidance in organizing cartels encouraged companies to adopt aggressive investment strategies. Generally speaking, the higher the debt–equity ratio, the more fierce price competition becomes, because the high-interest burden puts pressure on corporations to maintain certain levels of capacity utilization. Under such circumstances, one would expect investment levels to be negatively correlated with debt–equity ratios. Top managers, however, knew or gradually learned that during recessions MITI instituted protective measures and the FTC relaxed its surveillance; for that reason they could sustain aggressive investment strategies.[14] The negative correlation between debt–equity ratios and investment levels was therefore moderated.

2.3.3. Competitive Lending in a Regulated Financial System

New investment funds were primarily supplied by the banking sector. The banking sector mediated almost all financial flows from the household to the corporate sector in an environment where savings levels were far below investment levels.[15] The dominance of financial intermediation was the result of a system in which the 'main bank' served as the largest debt holder and one of the largest shareholders of a company and therefore closely monitored client firms.[16]

While it is true that the origin of the main-bank system can be traced to the wartime period and that main banks played a significant role during postwar reconstruction, firms' dependence on borrowing decreased during the early 1950s and did not increase again until after 1956, when a new investment boom occurred (Fig. 2.1).[17] This indicates that debt financing under the main-bank system expanded under conditions different from those which had prevailed earlier.

Debt financing via the main-bank system was, in fact, facilitated by government regulation. The regulatory framework in the financial sector established during the war and the postwar reform period was composed of the following:[18]

1. The Glass Steagall-like separation of banking and securities businesses mandated by Article 65 of the Securities Transaction Act of 1948. The so-called city banks—as Japan's largest banks are known—which used to be heavily involved in the business of underwriting and brokering bonds, were no longer allowed to participate in these businesses. Regulation of international capital inflow and outflow through the Foreign Exchange and Foreign Trade Control Law in 1950 prevented foreign influence from disrupting various financial controls being applied in the domestic market.

2. The restriction of bond issuance to a small number of companies through the imposition of secured issuance (collateral requirement) and the detailed accounting criteria concerning the size and financial situation of each eligible firm. The Bond Issuance Committee (*Kisai-chosei Iinkai*) heavily regulated the amount and condition of bond issuing, taking into consideration the market situation and the balance-with-interest rate of lending. As a result, it was almost impossible for companies, especially relatively young companies with high debt–equity ratio, to raise their money by bond issuing.

3. Strict control of bank deposit rates through the Temporary Interest Rate Adjustment Law in 1947. Based on this law, MOF took the 'artificial low-interest rate policy' (to sustain the interest rate under competitive levels), from which the bank enjoyed *de facto* subsidies.[19]

Within this framework, it is important to note that the competitiveness of each city bank was conditioned by its ability to collect deposits as well as by the number and size of its client companies. This allowed main banks to collect a 'main-bank rent' from the strongest or most promising client companies (Aoki, 1994: 129–30).

Top managers at city banks recognized that selecting good client companies provided them with a huge advantage. For instance, the president of Fuji Bank suggested the following at a meeting of branch managers in 1954: 'As the economy has largely returned to normal, the accumulation of capital has made it possible for well-performing companies to improve their position and strengthen their *keiretsu* relationships [vertical *keiretsu*] . . . If a bank could establish business with these high-performance, group-affiliated firms, then this bank would strengthen its position and, at the same time, lay the foundation for growth in the future' (Fuji Bank, 1982: 797). After adopting this strategy, Fuji enlarged its screening and research divisions by dividing its screening division into first and second divisions. The first division focused on screening large clients (Aoki, 1994).

The competition for good clients among city banks, so-called 'main bank competition', was accelerated by the rivalry between ex-*zaibatsu* and non ex-*zaibatsu* banks. The ex-*zaibatsu* banks (Mitsubishi, Mitsui, Sumitomo) had easy access to a large client base, companies which had been former subsidiary firms in the prewar *zaibatsu*. On the other hand, the non-*zaibatsu* Fuji, Sanwa, and Daiichi Banks had relatively few good clients. The non-*zaibatsu* banks were in a far weaker position than the ex-*zaibatsu* banks because their clients were smaller and their business relationships were less involved.[20] The non-*zaibatsu* banks therefore tried, beginning in the early 1950s, to obtain a base of large clients for the purpose of competing with the ex-*zaibatsu* banks and obtaining economies of scale in their loan structures. The former chief of the general division of Sanwa Bank recalled that the main task of his division at that time was to figure out 'how Sanwa could compete against ex-*zaibatsu* banks', and 'with which companies Sanwa should establish business relations'.[21] This strategy in turn influenced those of the ex-*zaibatsu* banks. Through this process, debt-financing based on main-bank (*keiretsu*) financing grew in the 1950s and early 1960s.

In sum, as quasi-fixed rules of industrial policy accelerated investment, the huge demand for funds to sustain high levels of investment was met by the city banks, competing with one another for good clients under a regulated financial system. Two additional points should be noted. First, in comparison to a securities-based system, the main-bank system could better mitigate informational asymmetries between borrower and lender from which underdeveloped corporate systems often suffer. In the late 1950s, even companies like Honda and Sony which are now considered firmly established did not enjoy a good reputation in the capital market. Their main banks supplied them with large amounts of money based on their long-term relationships (Miyajima, 1996*a*). Second, as Aoki (1994: ch. 4) pointed out, the main banks tended to provide loans to client companies beyond the amount which would maximize the rate-of-return to client companies. Even when they did not have a need for it, companies had maintained a certain amount of borrowing in order to sustain their close relationships with the main bank. This reciprocal relationship was another factor raising the level of investment.

2.4. The Ebbing of IP and the Establishment of the J-Type Firm: The Second Phase of the High Growth Era

2.4.1. *The Attempt to Establish a 'New Industrial Order'*

During the 1950s, the allocation of resources in the domestic Japanese economy was effected through market mechanisms and, additionally, protective government policies allocated imports and regulated direct foreign investment. However, this system was no longer sustainable by the late 1950s. During this period Japanese exports grew at a rate twice that of all world trade. Due to particular pressure from the US, the government announced a trade- and foreign exchange-liberalization plan for the transition from protectionism to a free-trade system. The liberalization of direct foreign investment (capital liberalization) became another important policy issue after 1964, when Japan joined the OECD.

Faced with inevitable liberalization, MITI sought to redesign business–government relationships in a way that was consonant with the new era of liberalized trade and investment. MITI's vision of the industrial system and industrial organization was deemed the 'New Industrial Order'. The most central element in MITI's programme was the encouragement of production concentration through tie-ups or mergers in order to change the competition structure from one of 'excess competition' to 'workable competition'. Another MITI concern was modifying the nature of the government–business relationship so that the government could systematically intervene in the determination of prices, investment, output quality, and other variables after abolishing import restriction (MITI, 1990: 48–70).

The assumption behind this proposal was that in terms of total sales, total assets, net profit, and employment Japanese firms were too small when compared to their US and European counterparts. Therefore they had not yet reached the optimum production scale in terms of the long-run average cost. Another force behind this proposal was the existence of excess competition among firms in a given industry. MITI was convinced that these 'unusual' features in Japanese industrial organization were associated with the corporate finance patterns—for example, the predominance of financial intermediaries (Tsuruta, 1988). A draft of a Special

Industries Law based on these ideas was submitted to the Diet in 1963. The law was composed of three elements: (1) in place of a price co-ordination system, a forum would be created where representatives of government, industry, finance, and academia would plan and co-ordinate industrial activity; (2) the bulk of the financing for this system would come from the JDB, which would use its ability to guide financial flows into crucial sectors to bring about mergers and more concentrated mass production; and (3) the co-operation of private financial institutions would be enlisted for the plan under the guidance of the government financial institution, JDB (MITI, 1990).

At the same time, MOF tried to modify firm behaviour from the financial side. MOF shared the same convictions as MITI regarding the causality linking *keiretsu* financing and 'excess' competition. MOF pushed for two key items in this area during the early 1960s. First, it wanted to use regulatory authority to raise the equity ratio of large firms to at least 40 per cent. The model here was the 'conditionality' the World Bank imposed on companies to which it made loans.[22] The second was the establishment of guidelines for the corporate lending of city banks.

MOF put forward the following set of proposals at the *Kinyu Seido Chosakai* (the Council for Financial Institutions) in December 1964: (1) the establishment of a ceiling on increases in the total amount a bank could lend its large borrowers; (2) the organization of a council of city banks to determine lending policies in high-growth industries; (3) the establishment of criteria for supplying investment funds which would have to be satisfied before a city bank could provide co-ordinated loans to companies.[23]

None of these proposals was realized. The Special Industries Law did not pass the Diet despite being submitted three times during 1963–4. The main reason for this failure was the lack of support for this law outside MITI. Keidanren and the other peak business associations were wary of a renewal of strong state control. The leaders of the banking industry were opposed to the law because they were worried about government forcing them to make loans. And the FTC insisted the law violated AML principles. Given the lack of support, the ruling LDP was reluctant to pass the bill. Top managers criticized MOF's net worth–ratio regulation proposal on grounds that the proposed rules were too mechanical and inflexible to be practical (MOF, 1991: 263). As for the guidelines for city bank lending, as an executive of a city bank asserted at a meeting of the *Kinyu Seido Chosakai* (Council for Financial Institutions): 'It is difficult to determine a guideline ceiling for loans under a situation of low-equity ratios. A large amount of lending to a company might very well be necessary in order to strengthen its international competitiveness in the future.'[24]

2.4.2. The Stable Shareholder Scheme

The other major concern of both MOF and MITI was to protect Japanese companies from the takeover bids of foreign companies expected once capital liberalization occurred. In the 1950s, ownership of leading Japanese firms was still fairly dispersed and the prevailing corporate-governance structure in Japan remained characteristic of that of the market for corporate-control model. Although cross-shareholding and stable-shareholder arrangements had advanced among ex-*zaibatsu* companies, shares in most other firms were held mainly by individuals and by mutual funds (Miyajima, 1996a). Note that by the mid-1960s the regulatory framework created by postwar reforms was neutral in its effect towards—and at times even discouraging of—stable-shareholder arrangements. The percentage share held by individuals in 1963 had decreased by only 5 per cent from that of 1955. If the percentage of shares held by mutual funds is added to individuals' share, the aggregate share in 1963 actually exceeded that of 1955 (Fig. 2.2).

Given this diffuse ownership structure, it was natural for government officials and top managers of large firms to worry that foreign firms might easily take over Japanese companies. Such fears were strengthened by the stock market crash of 1962. Between the October 1961 peak and the April 1965 trough, the average share price in the first section of the Tokyo Stock Exchange (TSE) fell by nearly 50 per cent. In response, the government decided not only to support stock prices but also to use the situation as an opportunity to establish stable shareholders in leading Japanese firms. The state's formerly neutral stance towards the structure of corporate ownership, in other words, shifted to a decidedly activist one.

How did this happen? In addition to measures such as the co-ordination of capital increases by a 'Council on Capital Increase', in 1964 the government created new public/private institutions to maintain stock prices. The mission of the Japan Joint Securities Corporation (Nihon Kyodo Shoken Kabushiki Kaisha) was to maintain a floor on the Japanese market by buying up securities. Initially, this firm was financed by private banks and low-interest loans from the Bank of Japan (BOJ). The Joint Securities Corporation purchased 1.6 billion shares at a cost of 190 billion yen, but this proved insufficient.[25] Then, in January 1965, a second quasi-governmental institution, the Japan Securities Holding Association (Nihon Shoken Hoyu Kumiai), was formed. This association purchased an additional 230 billion yen in equities from investment trusts (mutual funds) and securities companies. Together, these two quasi-governmental institutions, supported by special loans from the BOJ, ultimately purchased roughly 6 per cent of all shares listed in the first section of TSE (Adams and Hoshi, 1972). This purchase was large enough to achieve the desired effect on stock prices.

The two quasi-governmental institutions systematically resold the shares they had purchased to 'stable' shareholders—that is, to financial institutions with a common *keiretsu* affiliation and to other companies that would not resell transferred shares in the short term. Some 80 per cent of the shares were resold to corporations over the ensuing five years. In effect, 'Japanese banks and firms bought more shares because the government subsidized their purchase through low-interest lending' (Weinstein, 1995).

Second, the Commercial Law was revised to make it easier for firms to stabilize their shareholders. One of the main developments was an amendment of Article 280 that allowed the board of directors of a firm to increase capital through private placements without obtaining formal approval at a general meeting of current shareholders. Private placement (third-party allocation) refers to private sales of equity, often at below-market prices, to selected persons or firms (typically directors, employees, suppliers, or distributors).[26] Another amendment made it possible for a company to restrict shareholders through provisions in the firm's articles of incorporation. The alleged reason for this amendment was to reduce the chance of foreign takeovers. It is well known, for instance, that Toyota restricted its shareholders to Japanese nationals and legal persons through a revision of its articles of incorporation (Suzuki, 1977).

As a result of such government-facilitated shareholder-stabilization programmes, there was a dramatic change in corporate ownership structure during this period, as can be seen in Fig. 2.2. Change was especially apparent in the automobile industry where the threat of foreign takeover was taken very seriously. Table 2.3 lists fifteen companies that exhibited the largest percentage increases from 1964 to 1972 in shares held by other corporations and financial institutions. It is notable that eight of them were automobile companies.

2.4.3. *Corporate Behaviour in the late 1960s*

Government intervention in the 1960s was characterized by success in promoting stable-shareholder programmes and by failure in establishing a 'New Industrial Order'. Let us now turn to the issue of changes which occurred in the system of corporate organization, focusing on mergers promoted by MITI.

Although the Special Industries Law was not passed, MITI nevertheless persevered in its effort to encourage mergers—mainly through administrative guidance. In November 1966, a memorandum was released from MITI and the FTC that relaxed the 30 per cent guideline governing

Table 2.3 *The Increase in Shareholding held by Financial Institutions and Corporations*

	Shareholding at the end of the fiscal year 1964			Increase 1957–64			Increase 1964–72		
	Financial institutions	Financial institutions and corporations	Individual	Financial institutions	Financial institutions and corporations	Individual	Financial institutions	Financial institutions and corporations	Individual
Kobe Steel	30.0	38.0	61.0	0.4	0.7	6.9	14.4	24.4	−23.7
Fuji Heavy	26.0	44.0	55.0	4.3	7.5	7.4	13.0	24.4	−24.8
Hodogaya Chemical	35.0	38.0	57.0	8.9	11.1	9.5	−0.4	25.2	−20.4
Aichi Machine Ind.	20.0	28.0	66.0	5.8	6.8	−4.1	−1.7	26.2	−20.9
Suzuki	30.0	32.0	65.0	22.1	22.4	−15.9	14.0	26.4	−25.3
Hino	32.0	48.0	50.0	−1.8	−1.6	6.4	8.4	26.7	−25.4
Nissan	51.0	59.0	40.0	18.6	20.5	−11.3	5.4	26.8	−27.4
Daihatsu	32.0	37.0	62.0	4.8	8.7	−5.0	13.9	27.3	−26.5
Toyota	41.0	53.0	45.0	11.5	15.2	−8.3	18.4	28.2	−28.3
Chuetsu Pulp	13.0	47.0	52.0	9.0	5.3	−3.2	4.7	28.3	−27.8
Nippon Synthetic Chemi	23.0	54.0	40.0	0.5	21.5	−18.2	−5.3	28.6	−24.1
Mazuda	26.0	36.0	62.0	7.5	12.1	−6.2	22.5	30.9	−38.6
Mitsui Sugar	26.0	37.0	61.0	8.6	11.7	−5.3	4.3	38.1	−39.5
Sumitomo Heavy Ind.	15.2	26.2	27.8	n.a.	n.a.	n.a.	22.3	38.3	7.5
Shimura Kako Co.	3.0	16.0	80.0	0.7	7.1	15.1	7.9	51.9	−49.1
Average (N = 202)	37.4	50.2	44.7	11.3	12.4	−6.0	−2.2	4.2	−6.5
Std	13.8	14.8	16.4	10.5	12.0	12.7	11.1	13.7	13.1

Notes:
1. Sample companies are from our own data base composed of companies which were ranked as the top 150 in 1957, 1964, and 1972. This table picks up the top 15 companies in terms of percentage change of shareholding held by financial institutions and corporations from our sample.
2. Financial institutions include the shareholding of investment trust funds (mutual funds).

Source: Companies Year Book, JDB (Japan Development Bank) Data Base.

horizontal mergers previously delineated by the FTC (MOF, 1991: 252). However, the number of mergers remained minimal during the 1960s and the concentration ratio in terms of capital actually decreased. Although the famous merger of Fuji and Yawata (to form New Japan Steel) occurred during this period, it represented the exception rather than the rule. A useful, and perhaps more illustrative counter-example, can be found in the failure—as a result of FTC opposition—of the effort to merge Oji, Jujo, and Honshu Paper, three firms that were originally created as a result of the dissolution of the prewar Oji Paper Co., during postwar reforms.

The mergers that succeeded were those occurring within the framework of a bank-centred corporate group, or *keiretsu*. After a survey of sixty-three major mergers between 1953 and 1973 (Iwasaki, 1988), four types of mergers were distinguishable:

(1) Mergers between firms belonging to the same *keiretsu* (thirty-three cases, or over half the total);
(2) Mergers between independents (fifteen cases; firms not belonging to any *keiretsu*);
(3) Mergers between (a) *keiretsu* firm(s) and (an) independent(s) (fourteen cases);
(4) Mergers in which the participating firms belonged to different *keiretsu* (only one case, that between the shipping companies Osaka Shosen and Mitsui that, contrary to all expectations, merged in the wake of a government-supported concentration drive in the shipping industry in the mid-1960s).

As this suggests, major reorganizations through mergers in Japan have occurred predominantly among firms related to one another in terms of personnel or capital; that is, those in a parent-subsidiary relationship before the merger, or firms within the same bank-centred *keiretsu* (in particular among those that had been split under the Law for the Elimination of Excessive Concentration of Economic Power).

The change in ownership structure impacted on corporate behaviour. The success of stable-shareholder programmes freed top management from stock market pressures. Evidence of this can be seen in Table 2.4 where the dividend payout ratio (DR) is regressed on the rate of equity (ROE).[27] While DR remained sensitive to ROE in the late 1950s and early 1960s, such sensitivity decreased in the late 1960s. With the exception of 1972, no correlation was detected after 1970 and R^2 declined to almost zero. A stable payout-ratio policy prevailed in large Japanese firms, along with the spread of stable shareholders.

Evidence of the change in corporate behaviour occurring after the spread of stable shareholders is found in Table 2.5 which measures the effect on investment of Tobin's q, cash flow, and other variables in accordance with a formula developed by Hoshi, Kashyap, and Scharfstein

Table 2.4   *Dividend Rate (DR) and Sensitivity of DR to Rate of Equity (ROE)*

Estimated equation: $DR = a + a_1 ROE$

Year	a_1	t-value	R^2	DR (1) %	DR (2) %
1957	51.55	1.95	0.06	15.05	15.42
1958	54.55	3.39	0.19	13.52	14.27
1959	60.12	2.51	0.10	12.47	13.51
1960	53.25	3.49	0.20	12.91	13.42
1961	73.62	4.02	0.26	12.84	13.25
1962	71.58	5.28	0.34	11.51	12.94
1963	62.91	5.28	0.33	10.11	12.51
1964	69.16	6.34	0.43	10.10	12.51
1965	41.64	6.16	0.31	10.63	12.15
1966	0.92	2.89	0.03	9.31	11.83
1967	6.65	4.68	0.09	9.75	11.93
1968	35.00	6.43	0.17	10.41	12.17
1969	8.17	3.92	0.07	10.92	12.56
1970	−0.82	−0.73	0.00	11.49	13.10
1971	−0.21	−1.56	0.00	11.43	13.30
1972	7.43	3.68	0.06	10.35	13.10
1973	0.24	1.95	0.01	10.70	13.00
1974	−3.94	−1.99	0.01	11.66	13.76
1975	0.09	0.15	0.00	10.90	13.02

Notes:
1. The sensitivity of DR (Dividend Payout Ratio) to ROE before 1964 is still tentative because of lack of data.
2. DR (1) is the average for companies from which the equation is calculated. DR (2) is the average of listed companies in the Tokyo Stock Exchange, first section.

Sources: Ministry of Finance (1978); JDB Data Base.

(1991). Here Tobin's q, the value of firm divided by net asset (see note in Table 2.5), is introduced as the proxy of the pressure of the external capital market on investment decisions. The estimation has many technical problems, and the results are therefore still tentative.[28] However, it is safe to say that although the positive influence of Tobin's q on investment is statistically significant during the first phase of the high-growth era (1957–64), it was no longer apparent in the later phase (1965–72). This is consistent with the understanding that the investment decisions of top management in the later phase of the high-growth era were shielded from external pressures in the capital market.

Companies with stable shareholders became increasingly dependent on debt financing. Despite MOF's serious concerns, debt–equity ratios increased throughout the 1960s (Fig. 2.3). This is consistent with the

Table 2.5 *The Estimation of Investment Functions: 1957–1964 and 1965–1972*

Model: $I_t = \alpha_0 + \alpha_1 K_{t-1} + \alpha_2 Tloan_{t-1} + \alpha_3 F_t + \alpha_4 q_{t-1} + \alpha_5 Y_t$

	N	K(t–1)	Tloan(t–1)	F(t)	q(t–1)	R²
1957–64	1084	0.859a	0.021	0.172a	0.034a	0.722
		(26.74)	(0.861)	(8.924)	(4.390)	
1965–72	1521	1.008a	–0.024	0.101a	–0.000	0.782
		(39.45)	(–1.216)	(10.24)	(–0.286)	

Notes:
1. Notations of variables are as follows:
    I_t: Capital investment: the increment of tangible fixed assets during the current fiscal year.
    K_{t-1}: Stock of capital: the tangible fixed assets outstanding at the end of the previous fiscal year $t-1$.
    $Tloan_{t-1}$: Borrowing: The total of borrowing oustanding at the end of the previouis fiscal year $t-1$.
    F_t: Cash flow calculated by $Dep_t + Prof_t - D_t$, where Dep, $Prof$, and D denote depreciation, net profit, and dividend, respectively.
    q_{t-1}: Torbin's q calculated by $(V_{t-1} + Debt_{t-1})/A_{t-1}$, where V_t, $Debt_t$, and A_t denote total value of firm, debt, and asset, respectively. Total value of firm is issued stock at the end of the previous fiscal year $t-1$ valued at stock market price. However, the simple average of highest and lowest price is taken as a market price instead of market price at the end of the previous year.
    $Yt-1$: Lagged production, sales plus the change in final goods.
2. All variables except q are logarithms.
3. ^{t}-value in parenthesis.
    a: Significant at 1% level.
    b: Significant at 5% level.
    c: Significant at 10% level.

Sources: JDB: *JDB Corporate Finance Data Base* (CD version); BOJ, *Economic Statistics Annual*, 1985.

investment functions shown in Table 2.5. The coefficient of cash flow (CF) decreased by almost half between 1957–64 and 1965–72, indicating that cash-flow constraints on investment were steadily mitigated. Under most circumstances, the effect of increases in debt–equity ratios is a reduction of investment levels because, by increasing risk and agency costs, capital costs are also raised. However, this did not occur in Japan, and during the time period under consideration, the effect was just the reverse.

In short, Japanese companies adopted a strategy of debt-financing under a regulated financial system and then mitigated pressures from the external market through shareholder-stabilization programmes. By adopting such a strategy they were able to realize high growth. This point can be demonstrated with a simple regression analysis in which the growth rate of firms (asset-based) is regressed on change in leverage ratio ($\triangle$B) and the per cent change in shares held by the financial institutions ($\triangle$SH-FIN). According to Miyajima (1998), the growth rate of assets is positively correlated with both $\triangle$B and $\triangle$SH-FIN. This result indicates that the more a company depended on debt-financing, the more it stabilized its shareholders and the higher the growth rate of assets. As a result, the size of companies grew large enough to satisfy MITI's original intentions. The number of Japanese firms ranked among the Fortune 500 increased from thirteen in the early 1960s to over twenty in the late 1970s.[29]

2.5. Concluding Remarks

This chapter used a 'third' historical narrative, focusing on the influence of government intervention over corporate strategy and regulatory framework over the corporate system. Let us summarize the main features and implications of this new narrative.

2.5.1. *The Impact of Postwar Reform*

To understand the business–government relationship in postwar Japan, one must note that the impact of postwar reform on industrial and corporate organization was supposed to be quite drastic compared to other defeated countries. Given significant changes in the corporate system under a wartime planned economy, postwar reforms initiated by GHQ and their Japanization gave birth to a system of corporate and industrial organization completely different from that of the prewar years.

In prewar Japan, the governance structure of large firms was characterized by the strong control of large shareholders (Okazaki, 1993*a*).[30] Corporations relied mainly on internal funds or the capital market if internal funds were not enough. Industrial organization was characterized by widespread cartel activities under a pro-cartel regulatory framework. Industrial policy implemented during the interwar period had used less financial measures, less discretionary intervention, and had a strong consideration of freedom of trade, although the ideas and measures behind prewar policy were characteristic of a developmental state (Miyajima, 1992). Given that this interaction gradually changed under the planned economy, postwar reforms—which were modelled on the American system and whose orientation was different during wartime—brought about significant changes in the business–government relationship. The newly created business–government relationship was different from the one that existed before the war, not simply a continuation and accelaration of incremental changes already established in the wartime planned economy

The above highlights the impact of postwar reform from a cross-national perspective. Despite the Allied-initiated reform process, what happened in Japan was much more drastic than what happened in West

Germany and Italy in terms of magnitude and depth of change. Berghahn (1985), for instance, chronicles the Americanization of the German economy after the Second World War but the American influence there did not extend to the corporate system.[31] The ownership structure and bank–firm relationships of West Germany did not experience the kind of crucial change seen in Japan. In this volume Plumpe points out that corporate strategy showed remarkable continuity before the Second World War. Compared to the German case of a continuous relationship between prewar and postwar economic systems in spite of discontinuous ideological relationship in economic policy, the Japanese case could be characterized as a discontinuous relationship between prewar and postwar economic systems in spite of a continuous ideological relationship with policy.

2.5.2. *Mechanism for Encouraging Investment*

This chapter has stressed that the role of government in encouraging investment in the high-growth era was quite diversified, as expected. Subsidization based on targeting not only influenced resource allocation, but also companies' strategy. Quasi-fixed rules of government intervention with targeting policy induced strategic responses among firms aiming at capturing 'first mover advantage'. The combination of the AML and MITI's policy of facilitating cartels encouraged competitive investment. As a result, the intervention and regulation, which was restrictive for competition, enhanced competition among companies.

Regulation introduced in the postwar reconstruction period also encouraged investment. The regulation was important not only because it made the industrial organization competitive, but also because it could influence the corporate system. The Special Law for Asset Revaluation transformed corporate behaviour from myopic, short-term-oriented behaviour to behaviour that was more long term. Considering the fact that firms tended to revert to their prewar behaviour, we can conclude that the impact of this law on corporate finance was not small. Aggressive investment among firms was also encouraged by the competitive lending of city banks under a regulated financial system. Another important factor was regulation concerning ownership structure. The Anti-Monopoly framework introduced during the postwar reforms was the basic framework for emerging cross-shareholding. The changing attitude of the government to shareholder-stabilization schemes was important for its extension. The prevailing shareholder-stabilized scheme in turn influenced corporate strategy through the mitigation of external capital market pressure.

2.5.3. *Dynamics of the Business–Government Relationship*

Lastly, let us summarize the structural dynamic of the business–government relationship during the golden age. As we clarified earlier, the corporate and industrial organization that emerged around the early 1950s was still the prototype of the J-type firm system. The late 1950s and early 1960s are often marked as the heyday of government intervention around which the J-type firm system evolved. As a result of process by which corporations and financial institutions looked for optimal responses to the regulatory framework, the corporate system characterized as the J-type firm gradually evolved. It was also during the 1950s that corporate behaviour particular to the J-type firm developed. In the process of learning about government discretionary intervention, corporations gradually established their highly aggressive investment behaviour.

However, this structure of government–firm interaction changed in the 1960s, when trade and capital liberalization was implemented. If we summarize the 1950s as a period when the regulatory framework and government intervention promoted the evolution of the J-type firm system, the mid-1960s and onward are characterized as a period when the J-type firm system was institutionalized and often rejected further government intervention. By the mid-1960s, the government's role in encouraging economic development through subsidization had diminished. Further, a new arrangement envisioned by MITI and MOF was frustrated by opposition from the emerging J-type corporate system. The failure of the new industrial-order plan and investment co-ordination by MITI were typical cases. The failure of intervention in bank lending by MOF was another case. In this phase, the private sector tried to be free from government intervention.

It was also in this phase that the J-type firm, supported by stable shareholders and the main-bank system, pursued increasingly aggressive investment policies which in turn led them to increase their productivity. It is safe to say that the Japanese firm system was institutionalized during this phase (Hashimoto, 1996).

In the 1970s, when external circumstances changed and the Japanese economy had a high presence in the world economy, the interaction between government and business changed again. On the one hand, the main areas of industrial policy in Japan were encouraging structural adjustment, facilitating R. & D. investment, and coping with trade friction.[32] On the other hand, the most conspicuous change concerning regulation supporting the J-type firm system was financial deregulation during the late 1970s, when financial regulation was gradually relaxed. Along with the changing pattern of corporate finance, financial deregulation changed the main bank relationships. Thus, J-type firm–government interaction entered an entirely new stage.[33]

NOTES

1. See Maddison (1989), ch. 6, and Marglin and Shor (1990), ch. 1.
2. As Chapter 1 referred, for instance, to Johnson (1982); Tyson and Zysman (1990); Nestler (1992).
3. See Trezise (1976), Okawa and Rosovsky (1983); Saxonhouse (1985); Biason and Weinstein (1993).
4. There have already been several attempts at third narratives. Itoh (1988), Komiya *et al.* (1988), and recently the World Bank (1993) tried to clarify the role of government to solve market failure and co-ordination problems, based on a theoretical framework developed by the new trade theory since Krugman (1986) and Eaton and Grossman (1986). In focusing on the reciprocal process of government and companies, this chapter follows the same line as these works, although I wish also to focus on the influence of government intervention on corporate strategy. Also important are Aoki *et al.* (1996) and Aoki (1996), which focus on the software component of economic growth, and criticize the World Bank (1993) in its premiss and overemphasis of export push strategy. In focusing on the interaction between government and the corporate system, this chapter follows the same line as these works, although Aoki focuses mainly on the role of the organizational mode in productivity, whereas I focus instead on the interdependency of industrial organization, corporate finance, and governance.
5. See Aoki (1989), Aoki and Dore (1994); for recent works in Japanese, see Hashimoto (1995, 1996).
6. GHQ's idea is not the same as the current sense of 'market for corporate control', which stresses the takeover mechanism over discipline of the top management team; see Jensen and Ruback (1983).
7. For details see Hadley (1970); MOF (1981); Miyajima (1994).
8. However, it is noteworthy that the boards of Japanese firms were mainly composed of insiders, promoted from within companies. None the less, GHQ implicitly conceived that new managers would be recruited from the external managerial market. The managerial revolution from above in Japan contained a unique characteristic, that is the predominance of insiders on the board of directors, which was in contrast to the US or UK type of two-tier structures. See in detail, Miyajima (1993: 53–82).
9. Suzuki (1977: 615–16). Suzuki, the leading researcher at the Law School at this time, pointed out that this amendment could be evaluated as the Americanization of Commercial Law.
10. This process was comparable to the German case. After currency reform, German firms were allowed wide scope to revalue their fixed assets. This provided the opportunity for very large tax deductible write-offs. Estimates of deduction from taxable income due to accelerated depreciation and other deductions and credits amounted to 8.2 per cent of total retention of the enterprise in the period 1950–4. These measures taken by the German government were supposed to be closely related to the corporate finance pattern where 87

per cent of gross investment is financed by retention including depreciation; see Corlin (1989).

11. See Keizai-dantai Rengo kai, *Keizaidantai Rengo kai Zenshi [The Pre-history of Federation of Economic Association]* (Tokyo, 1963), ii. 32–4; Toyo Keizai Shinpo-sha, *Nihon Keizai Nenpo [Annual Report for Japanese Economy]* (Tokyo, 1954), no. 3.
12. *Toyo Keizai Shin-po [Oriental Economist]*, 6 Mar. 1954.
13. As for inward and outward orientation, see Wade (1990).
14. It was initially pointed out by Nakamura (1981).
15. As for this corporate finance pattern, see Suzuki (1987) and Teranishi (1982).
16. Regarding the characteristics of the main-bank system compared to the Anglo-Saxon financial system, see Aoki and Patrick (1994), chs. 1 and 5.
17. Utilizing informational advantages based on long-term relationships, the main bank could play a significant role in corporate finance by supplying a large part of the money to a client company, and by being the manager bank of (*de facto*) syndicate loans to the firm during the reconstruction period. See Miyajima (1994: 308–15).
18. In detail, see Teranishi (1982), Ueda (1994), and Aoki (1994).
19. MOF also controlled the lending rate (the interest rate on a loan), and as a result the nominal lending rate was stabilized during the High Growth Era. However, banks could raise the effective lending rate to client companies by requiring compensating balance.
20. 'Ginko-shihai no Kyoka to *Zaibatsu* Saihensei no hoko [The Control of Banks and Direction of *Zaibatsu* Reorganization]', Shukan Toyo Keizai, 24 Oct. 1953.
21. Interestingly, Fuji and Sanwa gave priority to issuing loans to large clients, while they decided on a policy of seeking deposits from general public. Sanwa Bank was even more aggressive than Fuji Bank in placing a priority on catering to large clients because their existing client companies were limited to those in the textile industry. Sanwa focused on a 'strategy of concentrating loans on the heavy and chemical industries' in the mid-1950s (Sanwa Bank, 1974: 242).
22. In the late 1950s, when integrated iron and steel companies borrowed investment funds from the World Bank, they were requested to satisfy these conditions. For instance, see Sumitomo Metal Co. (1967).
23. In detail, see Zenkoku Ginko Kyoukai Rengo Kai [The Association of All Banking Industries], *Ginko Kyoukai 20 nenshi [The 20 Years History of Banking Industries]*, (Tokyo, 1965).
24. *Kinyu [Finance]*, Sept. 1965, 59.
25. Nihon Kyodo Shoken Zaidan (1978).
26. As a result of this revision, in order to block a third-party allocation that was proposed by the management, two-thirds of the existing shareholders would have to vote against it (Adams and Hoshi, 1972: 193).
27. This calculation follows the Way of Okawazi (1993*b*) which firstly tested the correlation between DR and ROE for the prewar (1921–36) and postwar (1961–70) periods respectively.
28. Tobin's *q* calculation in Table 2.5 is far from an ideal one, because the stock price is not appropriate and net assets are calculated without any exact estimation

of their repurchasing value. To be complete, the difference of firm should also be considered. In this regard, the result is still tentative. Table 2.5 shows the changing pattern of investment behaviour from a historical perspective.

29. Stressing the positive effect of fierce competition is misleading. Note that the fierce competition among companies under *keiretsu* outlined above were supported by external conditions, and in particular the steady expansion of demand and increasing returns on the supply side. Once these external conditions were removed, these dynamics and their impact inevitably changed. For instance, in the early 1970s there were several industries (chemicals, for instance) in which the size of Japanese firms was small compared to their US and European counterparts and in these industries the number of firms tended to exceed the optimal number from the standpoint of attaining scale economies.

30. However, their ownership structure was quite heterogeneous, ranging from the concentrated *zaibatsu* form of ownership to a more diffuse structure, like the managerial enterprise structures represented by the big cotton-spinning companies (Miyajima 1996*b*).

31. As for the criticism for Berghahn's view, see Corlin (1993).

32. As for this point, see Uekusa (1988).

33. As for this point, see Aoki (1994), Miyajima (1998), and Ueda (1994).

REFERENCES

Adams, T. F. F. and Hoshi, I. (1972), *A Financial History of the New Japan*, (Tokyo: Kodansha International Ltd.).

Aoki, M. (1989), *Information, Incentives and Bargaining in the Japanese Economy* (Cambridge: Cambridge University Press).

—— (1994), 'Monitoring Characteristics for the Main Bank System: An Analytical and Historical Overview', in Aoki and Patrick (1994).

—— (1996), 'Unintended Fit: Organizational Evolution and Government Design of Institutions in Japan', in Aoki *et al.* (1996).

—— and Patrick, H. (1994) (eds.), *The Japanese Main Bank System: Its Relevance for Developing and Transforming Economies* (Oxford and New York: Oxford University Press).

—— and Dore, D. (1994), *The Japanese Firm: The Source of Competitive Strength* (New York: Oxford University Press).

—— and Kim, H. (eds.) (1995), *Corporate Governance in the Transitional Economy: Insider Control and the Role of Banks* (Washington: World Bank).

—— Murdock, K., and Okuno-Fujiwara, M. (1996), 'Beyond The East Asian Miracle: Introducing the Market Enhancing View', in Aoki *et al.* (1996).

Berghahn, V. (1985), *The Americanization of West German Industries: 1945–1973* (Oxford: Berg).

—— —— and Okuno-Fujiwara, M. (1996), *The Role of Governments in East Asian*

Economic Development: Comparative Institutional Analysis (New York and Oxford: Oxford University Press).

Biason, R., and Weinstein, D. (1993), 'Growth, Economic Scale, and Targeting in Japan (1955–1990)', mimeo. Harvard University.

Corlin, W. (1989), 'Economic Reconstruction in Western Germany, 1945–55: The Displacement of "Vegetative Control" ', in D. Ian Turner (ed.), *Reconstruction in Post-War Germany: British Occupation Policy and the Western Zones* (Oxford: Berg).

—— (1993), 'West German Growth and Institution, 1945–90', *CEPR Discussion Papers Series*, No. 896.

Eaton, J., and Grossman, G. M., (1986), 'Optimal Trade and Industrial Policy under Oligopoly', *Quarterly Journal of Economics*, 101.

Fuji Bank (1982), *Fuji Ginko 100 nenshi* [*The Hundred Years History of Fuji Bank*] (Tokyo).

General Headquarters Supreme Commander for the Allied Nations (GHQ/SCAP) (1951), *History of the Nonmilitary Activities of the Occupation of Japan*, xxiv. *Elimination of Zaibatsu Control* (Washington).

Hadley, E. (1970), *Anti Trust in Japan* (Princeton: Princeton University Press).

Hashimoto, J. (1995),'Nihongata kigyo shisutemu no keisei [The Emergence of Japanese Type Corporate System', in T. Yui and J. Hashimoto, *Kakushin no Keieishi* [*Innovation in the Business History*], (Tokyo: Yuhikaku).

—— (1996) (ed.), *Nihon Kigyou Sisutemu no Sengo-shi* [*The Postwar History of Japanese Corporate System*] (Tokyo: University of Tokyo Press).

Hoshi, T. (1995), 'Cleaning up the Balance Sheets: Japanese Experience in the Postwar Reconstruction Period', in Aoki and Kim (eds.), *Corporate Governance in the Transitional Economy: Insider Control and the Role of Banks* (Washington: World Bank.

—— Kashyap, A., and Scharfstein, D. (1991), 'The Investment, Liquidity, and Ownership: The Evidence from the Japanese Industrial Groups', *Quarterly Journal of Economics*, 106.

Itoh, M. (1988), 'Onshitsu no Nakadeno Seicho Kyoso Sangyo Seisaku no Motarashita Mono' [The Growth Competition in the Greenhouse], in H. Itami *et al.* (eds.), *Kyoso to Kakushin* [*Competition and Innovation*] (Tokyo: Toyo Keizai Shinpo-sha).

Iwasaki, A. (1988), 'Mergers and Reorganizations', in Komiya *et al.* (1988), ch. 19.

Jensen, M., and Rubach, R. (1983), 'The Market for Corporate Control', *Journal of Financial Economics*, 11.

Johnson, C. (1982), *MITI and the Japanese Miracle: The Growth of Industrial Policy, 1925–1975* (Stanford, Calif.: Stanford University Press).

Komiya, R., *et al.* (1988) (eds.), *Industrial Policy of Japan* (San Diego: Academic Press).

Kosai, Y. (1988), 'The Reconstruction Period', in Komiya *et al.* (1988), ch. 3.

Koyo Seiko (1994), *Koyo Seiko 70 Nenshi* [*The 70 Years History of Koyo Seiko Co.*] (Osaka: Nihon Keieishi Kenkyo-Jo).

Krugman, P. R. (1986) (ed.), *Strategic Trade Policy and the New International Economics* (Cambridge, Mass.: MIT Press).

Maddison, A. (1989), *The World Economy in the 20th Century*, (Paris: OECD).

Marglin, S. A., and Schor, J. B. (1990) (eds.), *The Golden Age of Capitalism: Reinterpreting the Postwar Experience* (Oxford: Oxford University Press).

Ministry of International Trade and Industries (MITI) (1955), *Tusanshou Nenpo* [*Annual Report of MITI*] (Tokyo).

Ministry of International Trade and Industries (MITI) (1989), *Tusho Sangyo Seisaku-shi 5 Jiritsu Kiban Keiseiki (I)* [*The History of the Policies over the International Trade and Industries, iv. The Period of Economic Independence I*] (Tokyo).

—— (1990), *Tusho Sangyo Seisaku shi 10, Kodo Seishio ki* [*The History of Policies concerning International Trade and Industries, x. The Period of High Growth*] (Tokyo).

Ministry of Finance (MOF) (1978), *Showa Zaisei-shi: Shusen kara Kowa made*, xix. *Tokei* [*The Financial History of Japan: The Allied Occupation Period, 1945–52, xix. Statistical Data*] (Tokyo: Toyo Keizai Shinpo-sha).

—— (1982), *Showa Zaisei-shi: Shusen kara Kowa made, ii. Dokusen Kinshi* [*The Financial History of Japan: The Allied Occupation Period, 1945–52, ii. Anti-Trust*] (Tokyo: Toyo Keizai Shinpo-sha).

—— (1983), *Showa Zaisei-shi: Shusen kara Kowa made, xiii. Kinyu 2* [*The Financial History of Japan: The Allied Occupation Period, 1945–52, xiii. Finance 2*] (Tokyo: Toyo Keizai Shinpo-sha).

—— (1991), *Showa Zaisei-shi: Showa 27–48 nendo, ix. Kinyu 1* [*The Financial History of Japan, 1952–1973, ix, Finance 1*] (Tokyo: Toyo Keizai Shinpo-sha).

Miyajima, H. (1992), 'Japanese Industrial Policy during the Interwar Period: Strategies for International and Domestic Competition', *Business and Economic History*, 22: 272–8.

—— (1993), 'Postwar Reform in Enterprise Management: Managerial Revolution from above and the Emergence of the "Japanese-type" of Firm', *Japanese Yearbook on Business History*, 10: 53-82.

—— (1994), 'The Transformation of Prewar Zaibatsu to Postwar Corporate Groups: From Hierarchical Integrated Group to Horizontally Integrated Group', *The Journal of Japanese and International Economies*, 10.

—— (1995), 'The Privatization of Ex-Zaibatsu Holding Stocks and the Emergence of Bank-Centered Corporate Groups', in Aoki and Kim (1995).

—— (1996a), 'Bank Centered Corporate Groups and Investment: The Evidence from the first Phase of High Growth Era', *Waseda Commercial Review*, 369 (July 1997), 33–79.

—— (1996b), 'Zaikaituiho to Keieisha no Senbatsu [The Economic Purge and the Screening of the Top Manager], in Hashimoto (1996).

—— (1998), 'The Impact of Deregulation on Corporate Governance and Finance in J-type Firms', in L. Corlile and M. Tilton (eds.), *Is Japan Really Changing its Ways?: Regulatory Reform and the Japanese Economy* (Washington: Brookings Institution).

Murakami, Y. (1987), 'The Japanese Model of Political Economy', in Kozo Yamamura and Yasukichi Yasuba (eds.), *The Political Economy of Japan, i. The Domestic Transformation* (Stanford, Calif.: Stanford University Press).

Nakamura, T. (1981), *The Postwar Japanese Economy: Its Development and Structure* (Tokyo: University of Tokyo Press).

Nestler, W. (1992), *Japanese Industrial Targeting: The Neomercantilist Path to Economic Superpower* (Basingstoke: Macmillan).

Nihon Kyodo Shoken Zaidan (1978), *Nihon Kyodo Shoken Kabushiki Gaisha Shi* [*The History of the Japan Joint Securities Corporation*] (Tokyo: Kyodo Insatsu Kabushiki Kaisha).

Okawa, K., and Rosovsky, H. (1983), *Japanese Economic Growth: Trend Acceleration in the Twentieth Century* (Stanford, Calif.: Stanford University Press).

Okazaki, T. (1993*a*), 'Kigyo Sisutem [Firm System]', in T. Okazaki and M. Okuno (eds.), *Gendai Nihon Keizai Sisutem no Rekishi-teki Genryu* [*The Historical Origin of Contemporary Japanese Economic System*] (Tokyo: Nihonkeizai Shinbun-sha).

—— (1993*b*), 'Japanese Firm under Planned Economy', *Journal of Japanese and International Economies*, 7: 175–203.

Sanwa Bank (1974), *Sanwa ginko no Rekishi* [*The History of Sanwa Bank*] (Osaka).

Sawai, M. (1990), 'Kosaku Kikai [Machine Tool Industry]', in H. Yamazaki, *et al.* (eds.), *Sengo Nihone Keieishi* [*The Business History of Postwar Japan*] (Tokyo: Toyo Keizai Shinpo-sha).

Sumitomo Metal Co. (1967), *Sumitomo Kinzoku 50 nenshi* [*50 Years History of Sumitomo Metal Co.*] (Osaka).

Suzuki, T. (1977), *Shoho to tomoni Ayumu* [*The Retrospect Concerning the Commercial Law*] (Tokyo: Shoji-ho Kenkyu kai).

Suzuki, Y. (1987) (ed.), *The Japanese Financial System* (Oxford: Oxford University Press).

Teranishi, J. (1982), *Nihon no keizai Hatten to kin'yu* [*The Economic Development of Japan and Finance*] (Tokyo: Iwanami Shoten).

Tokyo Stock Exchange (1996), *Annual Securities Statistics* (Tokyo).

Toyo-keizai (1957), *Nihon Keizai Nenpo* [*Annual Report of Japanese Economy*], 97.

—— (1961), *Nihon Keiei no Kaimei* [*The Analysis of Japanese Management*] (Tokyo: Toyo Keizai Shinpo-sha).

Trezise, P. (1976), 'Politics, Government, and Economic Growth', in H. Patrick and H. Rosovsky (eds.), *Asia's New Giant: How the Japanese Economy Works* (Washingto: Brookings Institution).

Tsuruta, T. (1988) 'The Rapid Growth Era', in Komiya *et al.* (1988), ch. 3.

Tyson, L., and Zysman, J. (1990), 'Development Strategy and Production Innovation in Japan', in C. Johnson *et al.* (eds.), *Politics and Productivities: The Real Story of Why Japan Works* (Cambridge, Mass.: Ballinger).

Ueda, K. (1994), 'Institutional and Regulatory Frameworks for the Main Bank System', in Aoki and Patrick (1994).

Uekusa, M. (1979), 'Senryouka no Kigyou bunkatsu [The Dissolution of Companies under Occupation]', in T. Nakamura (ed.), *Senryo-ki Nihon no Keizai to Seiji* [*Economics and Politics under Occupied Japan*] (Tokyo: University of Tokyo Press).

—— (1988), 'The Oil Crisis and After', in Komiya *et al.* (1988).

Wade, R. (1990), *Governing the Market: Economic Theory and the Role of Government in East Asian Industrialization* (Princeton: Princeton University Press).

Weinstein, D. E. (1995), 'Foreign Direct Investment and *Keiretsu*: Rethinking US and Japanese Policy', Paper prepared for the NBER conference on 'The Effects of US Protection and Promotion Policies'.

World Bank (1993), *The East Asian Miracle: Economic Growth and Public Policy* (Oxford: Oxford University Press).

PART II

LATECOMERS

INFLUENTIAL INDUSTRIAL POLICY AND COMPETITIVENESS

3

Industrial Policy and the Development of the Synthetic Fibre Industry
Industrial Policy as a Means for Promoting Economic Growth

TSUNEO SUZUKI

3.1. Introduction

The nylon industry exhibited impressive growth, compared to the cotton and rayon industries, which began large-scale production in 1883 and 1918 respectively. Nylon production began substantially in 1951, reaching mid-growth in 1963–4 and peak growth in 1973 (see Table 3.1). Several factors contributed to the rapid post-Second World War development of nylon and other synthetic fibre industries.

In particular, government policy accelerated growth in these industries, notably the industrial policy implemented by MITI, the effective use of experience and knowledge gained during the development of the rayon industry, and the enthusiasm of private enterprise for development. When

Table 3.1   *The Annual Growth Rates of Japanese Fibres and GNP*

	Chemical fibre %	Synthetic fibre %	Nylon %	Polyester %	GNP %
1946–57	34.2	48.0	62.3	—	8.5
1958–71	10.8	23.2	20.5	30.2	10.1
1972–75	−4.6	−2.6	−3.7	0.04	2.7

Note: Chemical fibre includes rayon.

Source: Nihon Kagaku Sen'i Kyokai (Japanese Chemical Fibre Association) (1974).

discussing Japan's rapid postwar growth, people tend either to emphasize the role of MITI or that of the active involvement of enterprise (Aliber, 1963). Strangely enough, no one has yet fully examined the precise relationship between the two. This chapter will identify the different functions of each of the above and, on that basis, examine their combination. It will also look at the industrial policy which accelerated the development of Japan's postwar economy (Yamamura, 1986).

The chapter discusses the nylon industry from 1946 to 1973, focusing on two issues: setting-up problems at the inception of the industry and the regulation of investments at a high-growth stage.

Government treatment of the start-up issue encouraged positive investment in the synthetic fibre industry. In the case of new industries in particular, pioneers in the field often must produce the necessary raw materials and other goods, as well as develop distribution channels for the new product, on their own. This involves substantial investment and a corresponding increased risk. It is well known that greater risk means lower investment incentive for private companies, thus inhibiting investment levels. In the synthetic fibre industry, the government reduced this element of risk by providing pertinent information concerning potential supply and demand, etc., thereby encouraging positive investment.[1]

Government intervention through industrial policy is essential to avoid 'market failure' in such situations (Ito, 1992; Patric, 1986). As will be subsequently discussed, industrial policy regarding the synthetic fibre industry provided various forms of government support for pioneer firms during the start-up period, while also avoiding the problems by establishing a monopoly.[2]

After the Second World War, documentation shows that the government aimed to develop an advanced industrial structure by moving from 'labor-intensive industry to capital-intensive industry' (Morozumi, 1966). The government included among its standards of development an emphasis on industries which incorporated numerous related industries and created jobs (Vestal, 1993). Those falling into this category were labelled 'important industries'. Constant exchange of information was essential and consequently a system to facilitate such exchanges was developed (Corden, 1974). This was not the one-way transmission of information from government to enterprise which occurred before the war (Johnson, 1982). Rather, the content of industrial policy was tailored to the character of each industry, based on information from individual enterprises or groups representing enterprises involved in each field (Boltho, 1975). Accordingly, when considering postwar industrial policy, it is important to determine when and why the structural reorganization occurred which facilitated information exchange between MITI and important industries.

One of the first structural reorganizations taken by MITI—in consultation with business during the postwar economic revival—was to erect trade barriers. These barriers were designed to protect the domestic market and close the gap between the technical development of advanced western countries and the technical legacy of the prewar period. This gave Japanese enterprises an advantage; they could develop new enterprises by introducing foreign technology over a long-term period.

From the beginning of Japan's economic revival to its rapid-growth period, the country—which had a relatively large domestic market compared to Asian NIEs—secured a stable domestic market through its policy of restricting imports and promoting exports. At the same time, expanding exports made it possible for Japan to take advantage of economies of scale, and to continue protecting and developing new industries which emerged after the war (Itami *et al.*, 1988). A stable relationship between shareholders and businessmen and the continuity of the political party in power made it possible for government as well as business to make long-term plans (Nester, 1991).

The actual content of industrial policy was fairy representative of nations intending to develop designated important industries (Murakami, 1984). Of particular note was the long-term, low-interest financing provided by the Japan Development Bank, the preferential distribution of foreign capital for the importation of technology and raw materials, protection of the domestic market by import tariffs, and the maintenance of an oligopolistic market structure through the restriction of new participants. An organization headed by a technical official from MITI and comprised of experienced technical experts and members of pioneering firms in each field, identified and selected technologies suitable for business investment on the basis of overseas experience in advanced nations. This organization not only identified new and interesting technologies but also drew up plans for their development by defining the raw materials, the size of facilities, and the amount of capital needed (Komiya, 1990).

Another factor which contributed to the success of pioneers in the synthetic fibre industry was the availability of knowledge accumulated during the development of rayon production, and that of affiliated manufacturing companies such as textile enterprises. Without the knowledge acquired in rayon production, it is unlikely that the postwar synthetic fibre industry could have experienced such rapid growth.[3] To overlook this point is to draw the false conclusion that growth was due entirely to industrial policy.

3.2. Industrial Policy and First Movers

3.2.1. The Introduction of Industrial Policy to the Synthetic Fibre Industry

A look at imports in Japan from 1946 to 1949 shows that food and fibre materials comprised 64–90 per cent of total imports (Tsusan-sho, 1954) . In view of the shortage of foreign capital, reduction of imports and development of potential export products was a crucial issue. Synthetic fibre seemed to be the solution. Not only would its development reduce fibre imports, it would also be used to manufacture fishing nets, helping to provide fish for the Japanese people, and bring in foreign capital.

The Dodge Line was implemented in April 1949, ushering in an exchange rate of 360 yen to the US dollar. With the beginning of economic globalization, the government implemented its industrial policy in earnest. In May of the same year the Ministry of Commerce formally announced a policy titled 'The Subject of Ensuring the Rapid Development of the Synthetic Fibre Manufacturing Industry', and began promoting development activities to achieve this aim (Uchida, 1970). In the same month, the Ministry of Trade was integrated with the Ministry of Commerce and reorganized as MITI, assuming both international and domestic functions. At that point the government became actively involved in supporting development policy, a fact which clearly indicates the government's expectation that synthetic fibre would give the country a competitive edge in the international market and bring in precious foreign capital.

The Economic Stabilization Board of the Ministry of Resources in 'The Development of the Synthetic Fibre Industry' designated synthetic fibre as an important industry because of its potential for bringing in foreign capital. It requested the development of, and capital support for, basic related industries, such as those producing raw materials. Only a few advanced nations at the time were potential competitors, and if the industry were developed to a level of international competitiveness, exports could be directed at the enormous Asian market. Since the industry offered considerable potential for improving the foreign revenue situation, the policy concluded that 'if the government provides appropriate guidance during the industry's establishment, we are sure that it will, like the artificial silk and rayon industries, play a major role in the self-reliance of the Japanese economy' (Keizai Antei Honbu, 1949). To promote these industrial policies, the government provided a committee to facilitate mutual exchange of information between the government and members of different enterprises. Here ideas could be co-ordinated and put into action. Let us examine more closely the establishment and content of this forum (Noguchi, 1993).

MITI was given responsibility for promoting development of the synthetic-fibre industry (Woronoff, 1992) and in 1950 it established the *Shido-Kaigi* (Leadership Council) to replace the former *Gosei-Sen'i Konwakai* (Synthetic Fibre Association). The Council's objectives were to forecast business achievements and to create closer relations between the fibre product official of the Chemical Fibre Division of the Fibre Bureau and the raw materials officer of the Organic Division of the Chemical Department. Both were part of MITI. These activities would, in turn, facilitate the procurement of capital from financing agencies (Konwakai, 1950). Government members of the Council included Takayuki Yamamoto, Vice-Minister of MITI, a commissioner and a technical official also from MITI, the director of the Bank Bureau for the Ministry of Finance, and the director of the Loan Facilitation Department of the Bank of Japan. Members from the business community included presidents not only of companies aiming to enter the chemical fibre industry, but also of chemical companies which would supply raw materials, and the representatives of business organizations. Six sectional meetings were established under the Council, including Amilan (nylon), vinylon, Estrone (acetate), garment, nets, and industrial materials.

In addition, various tax exemptions and reductions were devised (Kagaku Gijutsu Cho, 1967). Synthetic fibre was placed in the important-product tax category in March 1950, exempting it from corporation tax. Then, in March 1951, a 25 per cent customs was put on imported synthetic fibre, while machines designated as important machinery were exempted from import duties in April of the same year. Factories in the synthetic-fibre industry were even exempted from taxes on electricity and gas. Moreover, the number of years designated as the life of machinery and facilities was reduced, and rapid depreciation rates were awarded to related businesses. Important product tax exemptions were applied to vinylon from 1950 to 1960, and to nylon from 1950 to 1958. With recognition of rapid depreciation rates, the synthetic-fibre industry was given so many tax advantages that one Treasury official claimed Toray might not have paid any taxes at all (Economisuto, 1977).

At the same time, the synthetic-fibre industry lacked the investment capital required to develop necessary infrastructure and the foreign capital required to import the latest machinery and technology from overseas. The government, therefore, through the Japan Development Bank, provided financing for infrastructure. It awarded capital loans of 4.5 million yen to Kuraray, and 1.5 million yen to Toray. The following year, it awarded another 1.25 million yen to Kuraray, 5 million yen to Toray and 3.5 million yen to Asahi-Dow.[4]

3.2.2. The Procedures of Industrial Policy

MITI permitted monopolization by pioneer enterprises during the initial set-up period in an effort to foster development. In the May 1949 meeting of the Ministry of Commerce, only one company was assigned to develop each type of fibre. Kuraray was assigned the development of polyvinyl alcohol fibre (vinylon), while Toray was assigned development of polyamide type fibre (Amilan). Each company was instructed to build a factory to manufacture an economically viable amount of their designated fibre. Other companies interested in development—including those already involved in developing other fibres—were instructed to restore or construct factories primarily for testing the viability of new synthetic fibres for manufacturing (Nihon Kagaku Sen'i Kyokai, 1974). The recognition of a single-company monopoly during the set-up period reduced initial investment risk and provided a constructive policy for procurement of raw materials. In order to ensure a supply of the materials needed for synthetic-fibre production, MITI also promoted the development of the petroleum and chemical industries.[5] The establishment of a monopoly and a system of monitoring development until each company was firmly established was at least partially the result of experience gained during the war, when development of strategic industries was targeted.

The selection of vinylon and nylon for development, and of Kuraray and Toray as the development companies, was not an arbitrary decision by MITI. The decision was made after meetings and discussions between the technical official from MITI, university researchers, and technical experts from the different companies. Kohei Hoshino, a nylon development engineer from Toray, Tsukumo Tomonari, a vinylon development expert from Kuraray, and Masahide Yazawa, an engineer responsible for vinylon development at Kanebo, all participated. Toray was assigned nylon because it was the only company already producing it. The selection of Kuraray to develop vinylon and Kanebo for viability testing was based on an evaluation of existing operating conditions in their factories and the enthusiasm and attitude of each company's management for the new enterprise.

The following evaluation by MITI was the deciding factor in the selection of Kuraray. 'Mr Soichiro Ohara [the president of Kuraray] will take on vinylon even if the fate of his company is at stake. But Itoji Muto [the president of Kanebo] would not say "even if the fate of our company is at stake" suggesting that he sees it as a side job' (Tsusan-sho, 1986). Of course there was some resistance to the Toray and Kuraray decision from Nippon Rayon in the case of nylon and from Kanebo in the case of vinylon, but this did not change MITI's policy of awarding a monopoly to pioneers in the field.

MITI subsequently approved the entry of new participants in the nylon and vinylon fields in 1953. At the same time, vinylidene chloride became a development target and the construction of optimum scale factories was promoted. Nippon Rayon entered the nylon market while Dainippon Boseki (presently Unitica) entered the vinylon field. However, although the monopolistic market structure changed to a dual monopoly, the structure continued to favour the original pioneer firms.

Through the industrial policy pursued from 1949, synthetic-fibre industries were not only able to compete against foreign imports and newcomers to the field, they also received various forms of financial support from the government. This support alone, however, was not sufficient for the development of some synthetic fibres. The problems which pioneer firms had to overcome covered a broad spectrum of the manufacturing process, from the refining of raw materials, continuous spinning, and post-spinning processing to textile manufacturing and dyeing. These companies began by using the technology and equipment developed for rayon production. However, they soon realized that rayon production experience alone was insufficient.

Development of suitable production methods was not an easy task. Everything was new—from raw materials to the type of extruder and spinning technology. Furthermore, synthetic-fibre thread had to be stretched, and the speed and strength with which it was stretched determined the quality of the thread. The thread then had to be twisted and there was no existing model to use in solving such technical problems. Even Toray, which had the greatest success, found that development was difficult. Toray began research in 1947, commencing nylon production in 1949, with a daily output of one ton. It was not until 1953 or 1954—after a five year period of trial and error—that Toray finally produced a stable filament (Toray, 1977).

After a stable filament was produced it had to be woven into cloth. Because the early looms were originally developed for rayon, they had to overcome such problems as tension and sizing for a different quality thread, as well as the occurrence of static electricity and other complications. Toray had to work with textile companies in order to solve these difficulties. The fibre makers selected textile companies which had proven themselves during the development of rayon production. The same was true for the dyeing process. But despite these measures, development was still beset with difficulties.

To begin with there was no model from which they could work. When nylon was woven with the same method used for rayon, the thread stretched too much. Moreover, in the early stages, the quality of synthetic fibres was poor and the thread often broke. However, after five or six years of earnest co-operation between synthetic-fibre makers and textile companies, a viable product was produced. Technological development and the desire to improve on the part of the textile companies were essential for the achievement of a stable fibre.

Numerous difficulties awaited the development of a dyeing process. Dyes used for natural fibres were unsuitable, as were dyes used for rayon. Nylon in particular absorbs almost no water, and consequently existing dyes could not be used. Because they had already developed a relationship with dyeing companies during the rayon period, pioneer synthetic-fibre makers were able to select the best ones to help them, yet they still experienced major difficulties. The dyeing companies studied the technology of advanced countries and experimented with different methods. Through this process they developed a type of emulsion, and with this as a base they found a way to dye nylon with an acid dye. The efforts of the Japanese dye makers finally led to a solution, but in fact it was the product of a German dye company that actually solved the problem.

3.2.3. The Growth of Nylon

The nylon market changed as quality improved. Single-filament nylon was first used as gut for fishing lines and tennis rackets, and later for toothbrushes, but it did not have a big market. The final market target was nylon as a filament in stockings, but Toray first entered the market for school and public service uniforms using nylon as a staple fibre with wool or cotton. This success was followed by exploitation of the fishing net market with nylon filament. However, fishing net manufacturers did not immediately switch over from natural fibre to synthetic fibre because of resistance from fishermen. Instead, pioneer nylon makers teamed up with net makers who had both the knowledge and desire to develop a synthetic-fibre fishing net together. They experimented repeatedly, adjusting the weaving method to improve the strength of the net. They then marketed the resulting product directly to fishermen, promoting it as rot-resistant and strong, yet lightweight, claiming that it would catch more fish than any cotton net (Shibata, 1962).

The Fishery Agency tested the nets, and the government gave fishermen an incentive to switch by providing low-interest loans for the purchase of synthetic nets, thus helping expand the market (Toray, 1954). When first movers struggled to exploit new markets the fishing net was crucial for success in business,[6] because the fishing net accounted for nearly half of nylon products as is shown in Table 3.2 (Suzuki, 1995).

The government also encouraged expansion into the uniform market. It required all members of police and fire departments to use synthetic fibre in their uniforms. Of course, the first movers themselves had taken the first

Table 3.2 *Production of Nylon Fish Nets (ton)*

Year	Production	Ratio %
1951	232	50.4
1952	568	65.6
1953	609	29.2
1954	1,007	22.0
1955	1,653	20.5
1956	2,024	13.2
1957	2,886	13.0
1958	2,633	11.4
1959	3,908	12.4

Note: A ratio is nylon nets per total nylon production.

Source: Kasen Geppo [Chemical Fibre Monthly] Aug. 1957, June 1960.

steps by going to centres of the school uniform industry, such as Kojima in Okayama Prefecture, selecting garment makers with technical ability, and making preparations for the process of producing garments. Unlike other garments, the market for school and public servant uniforms was year round rather than seasonal and offered a constant and predictable demand. This type of product was essential for a stable operation. Accordingly, it was an ideal product for synthetic-fibre companies seeking to establish regular production at a low unit cost. It was also an important market for manufacturers because of the certainty of demand. The Ministry of Education recommended that school uniforms be made of synthetic fibres.

Two factors facilitated the entrance of synthetic-fibre companies into this market. The first was the government's backup system, and the second was the fixed-quotation system. The latter was usually used when a maker was in a strong position, such as in an oligopolistic market. It guaranteed stable prices for raw materials, manufactured goods, and manufacturing companies, ensuring a stable production volume. This encouraged manufacturers to move away from using natural fibres, which were subject to price fluctuations and processing fees, and the demand for synthetic fibres increased. As the attraction of a stable manufacturing price spread, manufacturers began to seek affiliation with synthetic-fibre makers such as Toray and Kuraray. This in turn created an oligopolistic system, a result of the industrial policy that initially fostered the pioneer companies.

However, it was not the fishing net or uniform market that gave Toray incredible profits or made the company so popular with manufacturers and dealers. This was rather the result of technical co-operation between Toray and Du Pont, which enabled Toray to import a process-treatment machine. Toray then twisted the nylon filament, heat set it, and removed the twist, creating a bulky, woolly nylon which catapulted the company into the nylon sock market.

Vinylon, on the other hand, because of inferior material, did not achieve the same growth as nylon, while vinylidene chloride failed completely as a fibre material. Through the perseverance of its developers, however, vinylidene chloride found its way into the film market.

Vinylon was developed domestically by prewar research and was particularly attractive to the government because it was made from lime, which is abundant in Japan. For these reasons, MITI gave it every possible support. Due to the lack of a foreign model, however, the pioneer firm Kuraray had to solve numerous problems on its own, from technical difficulties to quality improvement and exploration of an appropriate market. Kuraray aimed to develop vinylon to the point where it would replace cotton as a staple fibre. For this very reason, vinylon was affected by price fluctuations in cotton products and was unable to achieve a stable price strategy. Even before that, Kuraray faced problems with raw materials, technology, and markets.

Not only was it a material without precedent in the world, but because it had been developed by domestic technology, Kuraray had to manufacture the raw material polyvinyl alcohol (Poval) by first obtaining carbide and acetylene. Generally, when a new material is produced, the pioneer company must produce the raw materials themselves because those materials cannot be found in the market-place. Thus, infrastructure investment is correspondingly greater and technical difficulties are also increased. For Kuraray, the greatest problems occurred in the weaving process. Once the thread was manufactured and placed on the loom, either the thread broke or the speed of weaving was too slow. Accordingly, vinylon thread not only cost more to produce, but was also unsuitable for the fashion market.

At this point, Kuraray adopted a policy known as the 'champion policy' to break into the school uniform market (Tomitaka, 1992). First it obtained backing from MITI and received permission from the Ministry of Education to put the Ministry's seal of approval on its vinylon uniforms, thereby increasing sales (Nihon Kagaku Sen'i Kyokai, 1974). School uniforms provided an assured volume of sales every year. By linking textile, dyeing, and garment-making into a single consecutive process at Kojima, Okayama Prefecture, Kuraray was able to supply a large volume of uniforms, giving it the competitive edge it needed to become a leader in the market. Kuraray adopted the same policy to break into the fishing net market. It became a leader in the production and sales of a different type of fishing net from that produced by the nylon industry. In co-operation with net makers, Kuraray manufactured and improved vinylon fishing nets, and then actively marketed them to fishermen. In these few markets Kuraray was able to establish leadership, but it never succeeded in breaking into the fashion industry because of the cold, waxy feel of vinylon fibre. The raw material Poval, however, is used as an essential sizing agent in synthetic-fibre garment-making.

As for vinylidene chloride fibre, the quality was inferior and it was impossible to find new markets outside of the fibre market. Like the nylon and vinylon markets, pioneer firms Kureha Chemicals, which spun off from the chemical division of Kureha Spinning, and Asahi Chemicals entered the fishing net field. They promoted their product by touting its non-absorption of water and heavier weight, in comparison to other synthetic fibres which shrank more easily. The major drawback of vinylidene chloride fibre, however, was shrinkage. Kureha Chemicals therefore decided to try and develop a water- and moisture-resistant vinylidene latex as well as pest-resistant nets and tents. In the end, however, they discovered an appropriate market by producing vinylidene film. This film came to be used as material for fish sausage casings, and the crisis was finally resolved (Kureha Chemicals, 1995). Asahi Chemicals also found that the best market for vinylidene chloride was not as a fibre but as a film and they developed it for the food-wrap market. Both companies established firm footholds in their respective fields.

3.3. Industrial Policy and New Entrants

3.3.1. New Entries and the Response of First Movers

Attracted by the high profits made by Toray and Nippon Rayon, other fibre companies tried to enter the nylon field. This movement was helped by the end of Du Pont's patent period. The nylon patents possessed by Du Pont expired around 1954 or 1955 and this was accompanied by the birth of new technology. The same is true of caprolactam, the raw material for nylon. Kanebo, Teijin, Kureha Spinning (presently Toyobo), and Asahi Chemicals all decided to enter the nylon field at this time.

Kanebo, judging that nylon had the potential to become a substitute for silk products, signed a contract with Snia Viscosa to introduce technology in April 1961. Teijin had already decided to switch from using rayon to nylon in the reinforced automobile tyre cords it produced. By importing caprolactam from Snia and spinning technology from the Allied Chemical and Dye Corporation, it began production in 1960. Kureha Spinning via Kureha Chemicals utilized its technical experts from vinylidene chloride development and entered the nylon field by introducing technology from Zimmer AG. Asahi Chemicals, which was already producing acrylic, aimed to add nylon as a filament to acrylic—which was mainly used as a staple fibre. It introduced caprolactam from Zimmer AG and spinning technology from the Firestone Company.

Although the expectations of each company differed, they had all been attracted to the field by impressive growth in the nylon-filament market. Moreover, they were able to get a quick start in the field and avoid export problems by introducing technology from advanced Western companies. Thus, four new entrants appeared to disturb the Gulliver-style dual monopoly of Toray and Nippon Rayon. The same phenomenon occurred in polyester.

The polyester market established by pioneers Toray and Teijin grew rapidly, due to production of such popular products as cotton blend shirts, and they were able to obtain high profits without experiencing any deficit, such as was common in the start-up period. Toyobo, Kuraray, and Nippon Rayon were the new participants in the promising polyester field.

In contrast, nobody tried to enter the vinylon market and firms already involved in vinylidene chloride worked on developing that product for the food-wrap market. In a monopolistic market, pioneer firms can make enormous profits when their product matches market needs and begins to grow. However, if the market does not respond, high profits cannot be expected, even with a monopoly. Moreover, in this type of system, the difference between successful and unsuccessful ventures rapidly becomes apparent. This encourages the entrance of newcomers to the field when they see a product with a promising future.

The strategy used in the case of nylon is a good example of the type of strategy used by pioneer firms towards new entrants in the synthetic-fibre field. At the start of the 1960s, when four new companies decided to enter the nylon field and began to import technology, the two pioneer companies delayed their efforts by regulating entry standards through the Council. At the same time, they used the extra time obtained by these delaying tactics to expand their own production plants (Uekusa and Nanbu, 1973). In 1960, when the four new participants expressed their intention of entering the field, Toray had a daily production capacity of 91 tons. By 1964, it had increased daily production to 152 tons, an expansion of 1.7 times in just four years. In the same period, Nippon Rayon doubled production. The intention of the pioneer firms was clearly to leave the newcomers behind.

Due to slight disparities in the dyeing process, Toray and Nippon Rayon had found that uneven dyeing occurred even when using the same dye and the same method. When they increased production volume, they also sought to establish standard specifications. In fact, the official product specifications which resulted replicated the product quality of that used by pioneer companies. Thus, newcomers had to conform to specifications designed for the established firms. Moreover, the increased number of pioneer firm products on the market effectively reinforced their brand names with consumers.

3.3.2. The Results of the Competition

With plant expansion, the market price of nylon dropped. Up until that time, Toray, the price leader, had maintained an almost constant market price and the two pioneer companies made high profits characteristic of a monopoly. Prior to the entry of new companies, Toray and Nippon Rayon reduced prices to keep pace with plant expansion. This was plainly intended as a blow to newcomers, who had been attracted by the high price of nylon products.

The first movers also worked to sway consumers towards their products by improving quality. On the one hand, manufacturers strove to expand the market by developing different types of processing technology, such as that for woolly nylon, while at the same time working with top makers in different fields to develop new improved products. In the case of tyre cords for example, they worked with the top maker, Bridgestone, on product development. Both these strategies successfully created a consumer preference for each product. By overcoming unfavourable synthetic-fibre characteristics such as static electricity, piling, and poor appearance, makers prejudiced consumers against the products of newcomers. Nor did they restrict development to the production side alone.

Co-operative development with machine makers and users was also promoted. Companies which used nylon or polyester as a material naturally had a close relationship with pioneer companies and relied on them for supplies. At times they even co-operated to develop new products. This resulted in a further honing of development technology, giving pioneer firms an obvious advantage over new participants. The fact that pioneer firms owned an overwhelming majority of market shares was an essential factor in their future development. Once they had increased the types of products produced, they then needed to secure production volume as quickly as possible.

New participants, on the other hand, aimed at specific markets when they entered the field, such as special markets already developed during rayon production, or markets expected to expand rapidly. The nylon and polyester markets are perfect examples of this. Since the production capacity of newcomers was limited by restrictions, the only markets which they could successfully penetrate other than their already existing product lines, were ones which had growth potential or promised high profits. As a result, pioneer firms and newcomers clashed fiercely in synthetic-fibre markets where high growth and further development were expected.

Newcomers broke into the high-profit fields of nylon and polyester by introducing foreign technology. However, they were not allowed to enter freely. Not only did they have to comply with specifications governing nylon facilities, but they also had to obtain permission to produce the raw material caprolactam. The *Sen'i-Kogyo-Setsubi Rinji-Sochiho* (Fibre Manufacturing Facilities Preliminary Measures Act) of June 1956 was revised in 1959 to place restrictions upon spinning facilities as well (Tsusan-sho, 1990). Of course, there was strong opposition to such restriction of synthetic-fibre facilities that were expecting future growth. However, these restrictions were based on MITI's belief that, in a time of increasing supply and demand for synthetic fibre, such measures were necessary for stable development. At the same time, MITI was also striving to balance this expansion with the downsizing of the natural-fibre industry and the many medium and small businesses involved in it. Regulation of synthetic-fibre facility restrictions was left to the industry while the government devised ways to implement the restrictions.

Submeetings for each type of synthetic fibre were established under the *Sen'i-Kogyo-Setsubi Shingikai* (Fibre Industry Facility Council) as a forum for self-regulation within the industry, and the Council controlled the expansion of companies on the basis of MITI's demand forecasts. If a company's proposal for expansion was approved by the Council, then MITI would recognize it. MITI drew up its demand forecasts with the intention of systematically promoting stable growth. However, MITI forecasts pointed out the gap between future demand growth and actual supply volume, and as the companies felt there was little risk involved, they all applied for expansion at the same time. As a consequence, the total amount of requests for expansion exceeded the scale determined by the forecasts, and self-regulation became very difficult, especially with competition between existing companies and new entrants.

In the spring of 1961, Toray and Nippon Rayon claimed that their previous application for expansion in the fiscal year 1962 should be recognized and that new participants in the field should start off with small plants with a daily production capacity of 5 tons. The new entrants responded that as the pioneer companies had already expanded their facilities in 1961, they should be the ones to limit expansion this time. The new entrants went on to state their desire to start at a daily production level of 15 tons, as this was an economical level for nylon facilities. The Council set up by MITI, and particularly the small subcommittees which actually made decisions concerning the synthetic-fibre industry, were chaired by a newspaper's editorial writer. Rather than being a true chairman, his real function was to present MITI's views to the business world. In many cases, a committee chair was held by the same person for a long period of time and he tended to know what views MITI wanted represented to the business world. The Council characteristically recommended that the growth of pioneer companies should not be impeded, but rather that new entrants should keep their aspirations in check, and be patient. There was therefore no change in the dominant position of pioneer firms.

3.3.3. MITI's Regulation

It was also necessary to obtain MITI's permission to introduce production technology for the raw material caprolactam. The economic scale for caprolactam production facilities was even greater than that for nylon, and therefore production required a smaller number of chemical companies than did the nylon field. Accordingly, regulation was that much more difficult. MITI only permitted one company to pursue the Snia method and one other to pursue the Zimmer method. Moreover, as a condition for obtaining a permit, technology for domestically produced products must already have been successfully put into use overseas. Where the cost of introduction was higher than usual, MITI even ordered the reduction of patent royalties. Where patent problems might occur, MITI gave instructions that the method for solving patent disputes and the responsibility for bearing the costs must be clearly written into the contract (Suzuki, 1991). This method of granting permission for introducing new technology distributed limited foreign capital for production growth by evaluating technology, avoiding risk, and reducing costs.

The Preliminary Measures Act was again revised in 1964 and the expansion or construction of new facilities was now to be regulated by a joint government and private body called the *Sestubi-Toshi Kyocho Konwakai* (Facility Investment Co-operation Association). Initially, the standards for self-regulation allowed only a fixed increase in facility capacity over a specific period of time—for example, an increase of up to 20 tons in one year. The standards also stipulated that the condition of each company—for example, capital procurement capacity, sales capability, and related manufacturing fields—must be taken into consideration, and that decisions would be based on the demand forecast from MITI for total production output of fibre. These were the main pillars of self-regulation. This method of regulating facilities, however, lacked flexibility and was therefore incompatible with economic growth. As a result of petitioning the Council and MITI, the standards for permitting the construction of new facilities were changed to allow expansion until those facilities reached an economic scale. Likewise, the standards governing additions to existing facilities were changed to 20 tons plus 10 per cent of the existing facility capacity, using existing conditions as a base. As a result of competition between pioneer companies and new entrants—and the consequent move towards expansion—facility capacity increased greatly, both for

Tsuneo Suzuki

Table 3.3 *The Extension of Plant Capacity*

	1960	1961	1962	1963	1964	1965	1966	1967
Nylon								
Toray	90.7	98.8	125.0	143.3	152.0	161.0	193.0	208.0
Nippon Rayon (Unitica)	29.5	33.0	40.0	46.9	60.0	74.0	95.0	110.0
Kanebo					15.0	29.0	34.0	50.0
Teijin					15.0	29.0	35.0	50.0
Kureha Spinning					14.0	14.0	35.0	50.0
Asahi Chemical Ind.					14.0	14.0	20.0	50.0
TOTAL	120.2	131.8	165.0	190.2	270.0	321.0	412.0	518.0
Polyester								
Toray	33.1	49.5	55.7	67.1	97.0	101.0	120.0	146.0
Teijin	30.9	64.7	64.7	79.7	98.0	101.0	120.0	145.0
Toyobo					15.0	21.0	30.0	51.0
Kuraray					15.0	15.0	30.0	45.0
Nippon Rayon (Unitica)					15.0	15.0	30.0	40.0
TOTAL	64.0	114.2	120.4	146.8	240.0	253.0	330.0	427.0

Source: Tanaka (1969).

individual companies and for the fibre industry as a whole (see Table 3.3).

This sudden expansion of facilities was sometimes accelerated by industrial policy and sometimes inhibited by it. Because decisions for self-regulation were based on MITI forecasts of demand growth, each company applied for increased facility limits and, accordingly, distribution became more liberal. Many companies then increased the number of small-scale facilities, inviting excessive competition. On the other hand, these smaller facilities were not appropriate for international competition. Pioneer companies were still given preference in facility distribution, maintaining a stable market structure.

In 1964, the facility capacity of the four new entrants in the nylon field and three new entrants in the polyester field suddenly increased. From 1960 to 1967, daily nylon production increased from 20 to 518 tons, and daily polyester production increased from 64 to 427 tons, representing an increase of about 8 times for nylon and about 7 times for polyester. The production output for nylon during the same period increased from 40,000 tons to 188,000 tons a year, while that for polyester increased from 22,000 tons to 152,000 tons a year, an increase of 4.7 times and 6.8 times respectively (see Table 3.4; Tanaka, 1969). The surplus in nylon facilities was very obvious.

Because of this surplus, the price of nylon dropped drastically. The average price of nylon thread in early 1960 was 1,242 yen/kg. but after the entry of new participants at the end of 1964 it dropped to 754 yen/kg. and in 1967 to as low as 655 yen/kg. or about half its former price. Particular attention must be given to the fact that the price of nylon dropped sharply before the four new companies entered the field. This was not just the result of plant expansion and increased supply, but rather part of the competitive strategy of the pioneer companies towards new participants. The pioneer companies expanded their facilities and also dropped the price to deal a blow to the newcomers. This was an unforeseen effect of basing the restriction of facility capacity on self-regulation.

In contrast, the smaller drop in the price of polyester was not due to a long-term supply surplus. Rather it was the result of high demand for polyester, attracting even more firms to the industry.

Table 3.4   *The Development of Nylon Production*

Year	Toray	Unitica	Teijin	Kanebo	Kureha (Toyobo)	Asahi Chemical	Total (tons)
1951	460	—	—	—	—	—	460
1952	866	—	—	—	—	—	866
1953	2,087	—	—	—	—	—	2,087
1954	4,578	—	—	—	—	—	4,578
1955	8,076	—	—	—	—	—	8,076
1956	13,500	1,834	—	—	—	—	15,334
1957	18,825	3,308	—	—	—	—	22,133
1958	19,015	4,132	—	—	—	—	23,147
1959	24,200	6,845	—	—	—	—	31,405
1960	31,436	8,865	—	—	—	—	40,301
1961	37,526	12,024	—	—	—	—	49,549
1962	42,578	15,141	—	—	—	—	57,719
1963	54,051	23,528	1,167	1,307	—	—	80,054
1964	63,822	33,356	7,463	8,821	3,446	1,449	118,866
1965	55,261	29,368	11,109	10,559	5,759	5,421	117,995
1966	66,141	33,698	12,945	12,129	11,649	8,744	146,024
1967	78,707	41,805	17,757	19,456	13,794	15,207	187,712
1968	84,361	46,355	23,166	21,650	16,440	21,373	214,607
1969	94,220	52,279	28,212	28,427	21,021	26,970	252,427
1970	110,278	59,237	38,753	35,120	25,630	32,319	303,138
1971	109,278	60,423	39,148	34,949	27,702	36,197	309,559
1972	107,683	58,453	37,216	32,750	26,768	33,927	299,188
1973	119,426	62,752	43,068	40,963	28,084	43,976	340,718
1974	98,408	56,107	39,737	33,011	24,449	39,746	293,717
1975	96,179	53,500	36,400	31,200	22,100	37,300	278,500

Sources: Toray (1977); Toyo Keizai (ed.), *Keizai Tokei Nenkan* [*Bulletin of Economic Statistics*] (Tokyo).

3.4. Stability of the Market Structure

3.4.1. Growth and Maturity

With the entry of more companies into the field, the market structure for nylon, as well as for polyester, acrylic, and vinylon, changed from a monopolistic or oligopolistic to a moderate oligopolistic structure. In comparison with the initial period when industrial policy was first implemented, market structure changed from an artificial oligopoly to a competitive market structure, and it was this that made such remarkable growth a reality.

At the same time, however, there was almost no change in the ranking system because the system of self-regulation favoured pioneer companies when it came to increasing or expanding facilities. While MITI allowed the entry of other companies into the expanding synthetic-fibre field, at the same time it approved regulation methods which were advantageous to pioneer firms.

In the development of the synthetic-fibre industry, which fell within the important-industry category, MITI first regulated market conditions to favour pioneer companies and, when the potential for growth became apparent, allowed other companies to participate. In other words, the pioneer companies initially monopolized the market and earned major profits. New participants who entered later had to seize some of the pioneer companies' share of the market in order to grow. MITI approved both the pioneer companies' monopolistic profit and the rapid self-sufficiency of newcomers (Nohara, 1968). As a result of the implementation of industrial policy, the number of new entrants was much greater in fields with obvious growth than in those with a low-growth rate. Compared with the world standard, this encouraged excessive competition among companies with smaller-scale facilities.

Looking at changes in the production output for nylon, polyester, and acrylic fibre, output clearly peaked from 1973 to 1979. Subsequently, manufacturers entered a period of maturity with little growth. If we take the production output of this period as a standard, divide the period into two parts, and take half of that value as the mid-growth point we find that nylon reached half of its peak production output in 1965 and peaked in 1973, while polyester and acrylic fibre reached their midway points in 1969 and 1970, respectively, and peaked in 1978. The average annual mean growth rate up to the mid-growth point and subsequent annual mean growth rates for each fibre are as follows: 32.1 per cent and 11.4 per cent for nylon; 37.7 per cent and 4.6 per cent for acrylic; and 31.1 per cent and 7.6 per cent for polyester (Nihon Kagaku Sen'i Kyokai, 1993). A very high growth rate of over 30 per cent was exhibited during the first half of the growth period, while a remarkably low rate was exhibited for the remaining half. This pattern is natural but the issue is the relationship between the turning-point in production growth and the entry of newcomers to the field.

New participants began operation in 1963 for nylon, in 1960 for acrylics, and in 1964 for polyester. Thus, they entered the field a few years before the turning-point. However, because new facilities were restricted by size they could not utilize the merit of scale to reduce costs. It was not until the particular fibre they were producing moved out of the growth period and into the period of maturity that they were finally able to increase their facilities and utilize the advantages of scale. Although new participants were able to make profits in the markets developed by pioneer companies,

due to competition in building and expanding facilities they were unable
to make the large profits that pioneer firms had enjoyed from increased
supply capacity and price reduction (see Table 3.5). The same is true for
acrylic and polyester.

Table 3.5   *The Ratio of Net Profit to Sales*

	Toray %	Unitica %	Teijin %	Asahi Chemical %	Kanebo %
1959 I	11.2	4.1	—	—	—
1959 II	13.2	5.7	—	—	—
1960 I	13.6	6.7	—	—	—
1960 II	12.5	6.2	—	—	—
1961 I	11.8	5.8	—	—	—
1961 II	12.3	7.1	—	—	—
1962 I	11.7	7.8	—	—	—
1962 II	11.5	8.1	—	—	—
1963 I	11.0	8.6	—	—	—
1963 II	11.3	9.7	—	—	—
1964 I	8.2	8.6	△1.89	—	—
1964 II	3.4	3.2	△3.44	△39.5	—
1965 I	1.9	2.4	△1.66	△20.2	—
1965 II	3.9	2.9	△0.75	△7.1	△3.44
1966 I	3.0	3.5	0.1	△0.3	0.4
1966 II	6.9	3.9	2.2	1.8	2.4
1967 I	9.9	4.3	4.2	3.0	4.3
1967 II	11.8	4.8	3.1	4.1	4.8

Notes: 1960 I is from Apr. 1960 to Sept. 1960; 1960 II is Oct. 1960 to Mar. 1961. △ means loss.
Source: Uekusa and Nanbu (1973: 190).

3.4.2. A Change of the Market Structure

Certainly in the nylon and polyester field, which saw rapid development,
the market share of top companies gradually decreased as a result of the
entry of new participants. In the case of nylon, the shares of the leading
company, Toray, decreased from 70 per cent to 50 per cent, even falling
below 40 per cent at one point, as a result of the entry of new companies in
1963. It is clear that fierce competition from these newcomers caused a
reduction in the leading companies' shares. However, the decline in
shares bottomed out around 1969, and stabilized with the top two companies holding about 60 per cent, and the top three companies about 70
per cent of shares (see Fig. 3.1).

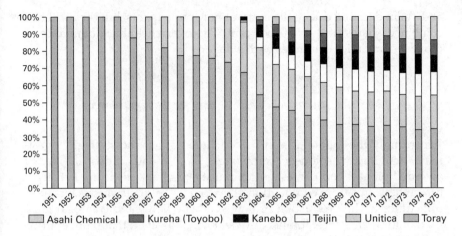

Fig 3.1 *The market structure of nylon*

Fluctuations in shares continued for a period of about five years after the newcomers entered the field, but then stopped and market shares stabilized. This reflected the growth of the nylon market. New participants entered the market just as it approached maturity and nearly ceased growing. Although growth continued, the rate was very small. There was no possibility at this point for any change in the ranking of leading companies.

By delaying the newcomers' entry into the field and by restricting their ability to increase the scale of their facilities, pioneer companies retained their dominance.[7] They could do so because new participants entered the nylon field when growth was slowing down and the market was becoming mature. In this situation there could not be a fluctuation in shares except through management error on the part of pioneer companies or through the unification of facilities among the newcomers. Nippon Rayon, encouraged by its success in nylon, entered the polyester field. But polyester fibre, unlike nylon, was mainly a staple fibre. The achievements of Nippon Rayon declined as a result of obstacles in developing a system of affiliated companies to complete the manufacturing process after spinning polyester fibre. This was a major factor in the decline of nylon shares.

In the polyester field, the shares of pioneer companies Toray and Teijin were overwhelmingly large and the gap between these companies and newcomers did not decrease as much as it did in the case of nylon. Until 1963, these two companies maintained their dual monopoly system. This was a stable dual monopoly like the one in the nylon field, where entrance into the industry was controlled by MITI and restructured by ICI patents. Moreover, as ICI and Du Pont had already entered the wool and cotton markets using polyester as a staple, the pioneers in this field were able to achieve growth without any initial debt. From 1964 the shares of Toray and Teijin declined due to the entry of new participants, but they still had combined shares of over 50 per cent. The overwhelming dominance of pioneer companies continues to this day.[8]

3.4.3. *Industrial Policy as a Reward for the First Movers*

Accordingly the following can be concluded about the strategic investment activities of pioneer companies. First of all, industrial policy awarded pioneer companies a monopolistic or oligopolistic market structure, where, free from competition, they could overcome various technical difficulties in the production of new synthetic fibres and create an ideal market for themselves. It must also be noted, however, that pioneer firms suffered many difficulties during the initial stages. Due to technical problems and delayed penetration of the market, they were burdened with quantities of unsold stock. Even Toray was rumoured to have had a management crisis.

However, with perseverance these companies obtained first-mover advantage following the success of nylon socks, polyester men's shirts, and acrylic knits. This was when the pioneer firms were finally able to garner high profits, attracting newcomers to the field.[9]

Although self-regulation of new and additional facilities resulted in a more competitive market structure, a distinct gap remained between pioneer companies and new participants. The pioneers remained at the top, while those who entered later had to be content at the bottom of the market. This point is illustrated by fluctuations in share ranking. There is a high correlation between early entry into the field and share rank, with the dominance of pioneer companies maintained throughout.

With the entry of new participants around 1963, the previous oligopolistic market structure changed to a competitive market structure, resulting in rapid expansion. As production growth levelled out from 1965 onward, the domestic market became saturated. Synthetic-fibre companies, led by the pioneer firms, began to move towards exporting. In the 1970s, around the time of the Nixon Shock and the oil crisis, there was serious expansion overseas and the synthetic-fibre industry matured.

The changes in growth described above, coupled with self-regulation of facility investment, resulted, until 1970, in a move towards a competitive market structure. Thereafter, though, the market reverted to a stable structure. This trend occurred not only in the synthetic-fibre industry but also in the Japanese economy as a whole. Newcomers who entered expecting market expansion wound up seeking an alternative source of expansion though exports. MITI, however, did not favour moving the focus of production from the domestic to the overseas market.

As mentioned earlier, synthetic-fibre makers did not manufacture thread or finish a product entirely on their own. Rather, the various processes were subcontracted to many small- and medium-scale textile, dyeing, and garment companies spread out in different regions. MITI opposed overseas expansion that might jeopardize these smaller industries, and tried to prevent the exodus of industry from Japan. As a result, Japanese synthetic-fibre production capacity suffered a relative decline. While Japan's synthetic-fibre makers were forced to restrain overseas expansion, South-east Asian synthetic-fibre makers made startling advances. The latest large-scale facilities went into operation one after another.[10]

3.5. Conclusion

Two points in this chapter are of particular importance. The first is that MITI did not perceive total competition to be correct. Instead they pursued *orderly* competition. The second is that while MITI developed and protected large companies, it also—for political considerations—strove to protect small- and medium-scale enterprises. This stance is illustrated by MITI's industrial policy.

MITI sought to establish a segregated system by dividing different synthetic fibres—including nylon, acrylic, and polyester—among synthetic-fibre makers. Moreover, in order to avoid imbalance between synthetic-fibre companies as well as between companies affiliated with the manufacture of natural fibre, it tried to maintain the stable operation of medium- and small-scale manufacturing companies. Through restricting supply, MITI provided companies with a source of reliable profit and at the same time strove to develop a system of affiliated companies, from the first step of fibre-making to the final steps of manufacturing. MITI assumed that if pioneer companies did not make a profit, others would not enter the industry and as such it would not develop. This method worked because it was implemented at a time when the Japanese economy was growing and protected from the pressures of international competition.

It was only with the development of nylon socks, polyester-cotton blend shirts, and acrylic knit sweaters that a boom occurred in the synthetic-fibre industry. Up until that point pioneer companies strove towards product improvement and development while bearing the burden of unsold goods. Naturally, they experienced many failures. In that sense new participants got a smooth ride down the path pioneer firms had created. The behaviour exhibited by MITI and pioneer companies towards newcomers can be seen as a form of compensation for the pioneers during the initial set-up period.

The first movers were able to protect their shares and maintain high profits through restrictions on facility investment. Thus, in addition to the above market incentives, MITI awarded a further incentive to those companies who took a risk and succeeded.

However, Japanese economic growth eventually slowed and even stagnated, and with the development of indigenous synthetic-fibre industries in South-east Asia, the social cost of maintaining small- and medium-sized manufacturing companies increased, and it became necessary to mobilize political power. This was the situation in the 1970s. As a result, new participants began to pursue the merits of scale by a mutual exchange of facilities and dominance shifted from natural fibre to synthetic fibre. The emphasis in development is now on materials with higher added value and the creation of a system that responds quickly to market needs. This is currently the situation in the synthetic-fibre industry.

NOTES

1. For the other industries, including textiles, see Galenson and Uekusa (1976).
2. For a theoretical analysis, see Itoh, Kiyono, *et al.* (1991), especially ch. 6, which plainly explains a setup cost.
3. Whether a company had such experiences and/or the accumulation of knowledge of the rayon industry was one of the important factors considered when deciding upon different strategies.
4. Asahi-Dow, which was established in order to produce vinyliden chloride by Asahi Chemicals and Dow Chemical in 1952, was absorbed in Ashahi in 1982.
5. This is one of the typical features of MITI's industrial policy. Co-ordination would be one of the resources which sustained the Japanese economy.
6. Nylon was, in those days, the main product for Toray from a profit viewpoint.
7. In explaining this delay, Uekusa and Nanbu (1973) claim the misleading of Kosei Torihiki Iinkai (Fare Trade Commission) as well as MITI.
8. Because first movers keep their larger market share at every stage, every company wants to rush into a new market, resulting in excessive competition.
9. The president of the company who enters into nylon production late has made that decision because, even late, entering means he gains profits. See Tomitaka (1992).
10. That the Japanese economy would eventually internationalize was one of the limitations of industrial policy in Japan. As a result MITI, fearing that local processing companies would get into difficulties, did not invite big companies to invest in foreign countries.

REFERENCES

Aliber, R. Z. (1963), 'Planning, Growth, and Competition', *Asian Survey*, 3: 12.

Boltho, A. (1975), *Japan: An Economic Survey 1593–1973* (Oxford: Oxford University Press).

Corden, W. M. (1974), *Trade Policy and Economic Welfare* (Oxford: Oxford University Press).

Economisuto (1977) (ed.), *Sengo Sangyo-shi he no Shogen*, i. *Sangyo Seisku* [*Testimony for Postwar Industrial History*, i. *Industrial Policy*] (Tokyo: Mainichi Shinbun-sha).

Galenson, W., and Uekusa, M. (1976), 'Industrial Organization', in H. Patric and H. Rosovsky (eds),. *Asia's New Giant: How the Japanese Economy Works* (Washington: Brookings Institution).

Itami, H., *et al.* (1988), *Kyoso to Kakushin: Jidosha Sangyo no Kigyo Seicho* [*Competiton and Innovation: Corporate Growth in the Auto Industry*] (Tokyo: Toyo Keizai Shinpo-sha).

Ito, T. (1992), *The Japanese Economy* (Cambridge, Mass.: MIT Press).

Itoh, M., Kiyono, K., *et al.* (1991), *Economic Analysis of Industrial Policy* (San Diego: Academic Press).

Johnson, C. (1982), *MITI and the Japanese Miracle: The Growth of Industrial Policy, 1925–1975* (Stanford, Calif.: Stanford University Press).

Kagaku Gijutsu Cho (Science and Technology Agency) (1967) (ed.), *Sen'i Shigen no Kakudai to sono Gijutsu-teki Hikei* [*The Expansion of Fiber Resources and its Technological Background*] (Tokyo: Kagaku Gijutsu Cho).

Keizai Antei Honbu Shigen Chosa-kai (The Council on the Natural Resources of the Economic Stabilization Board) (1949), 'Gosei Sen'i Kogyo no Ikusei' [Development of the Synthetic Fiber Industry]', *Shigen Chosa-kai Kankoku Dai 6 go* [*6th Report of the Resources Research Council*] (Tokyo: Keizai Antei Honbu Shigen Chosa-kai).

Komiya, R. (1990), *The Japanese Economy: Trade, Industry, and Government* (Tokyo: University of Tokyo Press).

Konwakai (1950), *Konwa-kai Gijiroku* [*Discussion Minutes*] (Tokyo: Konwakai).

Kureha Kagaku Kogyo (Kureha Chemicals) (1995), *Kureha Kagaku 50 Nen-shi* [*A 50 Year History of Kureha Chemicals*] (Tokyo: Kureha Kagaku Kogyo).

Morozumi, Y. (1966), *Sangyo Seisaku no Riron* [*The Theory of Industrial Policy*] (Tokyo: Nihon Keizai Shinbun-sha).

Murakami, Y. (1984), *Shin Chukan Taishu no Jidai* [*The Age of the New Middle Class*] (Tokyo: Chu Koron-sha).

Nester, W. R. (1991), *Japanese Industrial Targeting: The Neomercantilist Path to Economic Superpower* (Basingstoke: Macmillan).

Nihon Kagaku Sen'i Kyokai (Japanese Chemical Fibre Association) (1974) (ed.), *Nihon Sagaku Sen'i Sangyo-shi* [*The History of the Japanese Chemical Fibre Industry*] (Tokyo: Nihon Kagaku Sen'i Kyokai).

—— (1993) (ed.), *Sen'i Hando Bukku* [*The Hand Book for Fibre*] (Tokyo: Nihon Kagaku Sen'i Syokai).

Noguchi, Y. (1993), 'Economic Advisory and Planning System: Japan', in Fukui

Haruhiro *et al.* (eds.), *The Politics of Economic Change in Postwar Japan and West Germany* (Oxford: St Martin's Press).

Nohara, Y. (1968), 'Gosei Sen'i Sangyo Ikusei Taisaku no Omoide [Memories of Development Methods for the Synthetic Fibre Industry]', *Ka-sen Geppo [Chemical Fiber Monthly]* (Tokyo: Nihon Kagaku Sen'i Kyokai).

Patric, Hugh (1986), 'Japanese High Technology Industry Policy in Comparative Context', in H. Patric (ed.), *Japan's High Technology Industries: Lessons and Limitations of Industrial Policy* (Tokyo: University of Tokyo Press).

Shibata, S. (1962), *Waga Moko-kai no Kaiko [A Recollection of our Net Industry]* (Ishikawa Pref.: Ishikana-ken Gyomoko Kogyo Kyodo Kumiai).

Suzuki, T. (1991), 'Gosei sen'i [Synthetic fibers]', in S. Yonekawa *et al.* (eds.), *Sengo Nihon keiei-shi*, i [*Postwar Japanese business history*, i], (Tokyo: Toyo Keizai Shinpo-sha).

—— (1995), 'Sengo-gata Sangyo Seisaku no Seiritsu' [A Formation of Postwar Industrial Policy]', in H. Yamazaki and T. Kikkawa (eds.) *Nihonteki Keiei no Renzoku to Danzetsu [Continuity and Discontinuity of Japanese Business Management]* (Tokyo: Iwanami Shoten).

Tanaka, M. (1969), *Waga Kuni Gosei Sen'i Dokusen no Seimitsu Kenkyu [A Detailed Investigation into the Japanese Synthetic Fibre Monopoly]* (Osaka: Nihon Sen'i Kenkyu-kai).

Tomitaka, S. (1992) (ed.), *Ka-go-sen Sangyo no Sengo Hishi [The Secret History of the Postwar Synthetic Fibre Industry]* (Tokyo: Nihon Kasen Shinbun-sha).

Toray (1954), *Toyo Rayon Sha-shi [A History of Toray]* (Tokyo: Toray).

—— (1977), *Toray 50 Nen-shi [A 50 Year History of Toray]* (Tokyo: Toray).

Tsusan-sho (MITI) (1954) (ed.), *Sengo Keizai Ju-nen-shi [A Ten Year History of the Postwar Economy]* (Tokyo: Shoko Kaikan Shuppan-bu).

—— (1990) (ed.), *Tsu-sho Sangyo Seisaku-shi*, x [*The History of Industrial Policy*, x] (Tokyo: Tsusho Sangyo Chosa-kai).

Tsusan-sho Sangyo Seisaku-shi Kenkyusho (MITI Industrial Policy History Research Dept.) (1986) (ed.), *Sangyo Seisaku-shi Kaiso-roku [A Retrospective on the History of Industrial Policy]* 35 (Tokyo: Sangyo Seisakushi Kenkyosho).

Uchida, H. (1970), *Gosei Sen'i Kogyo [The Synthetic Fibre Industry]* (Tokyo: Toyo Keizai Shinpo-sha).

Uekusa, M., and Nanbu, T. (1973), 'Gosei sen'i [Synthetic fibers]', in H. Kumagai, (ed.), *Nihon no Sangyo Soshiki*, ii [*Japan's Industrial Organization*, ii] (Tokyo: Chuo Korori-sha).

Vestal, J. E. (1993), *Planning for Change: Industrial Policy and Japanese Economic Development, 1945–1990* (Oxford: Oxford University Press).

Woronoff, J. (1992), *Japanese Targeting* (New York: St Martin's Press).

Yamamura, K. (1986), 'Caveat Emptor: The Industrial Policy of Japan', in P. R. Krugman (ed.), *Strategic Trade Policy and the New International Economics* (Cambridge, Mass.: MIT Press).

4

Government and Business in Japan's General-Purpose Computer Industry

4.1. Introduction

During the computer world's roughly forty-year span—from its birth in the first half of the 1950s until the end of the 1980s when the opportunity for growth was lost—Japanese makers Fujitsu, Hitachi, and the Nippon Electric Company (NEC) were virtually alone in their tenacious pursuit of the computer giant IBM. The three Japanese makers eroded IBM's market share and subsequently acquired competitive strength internationally.

This chapter aims to clarify and analyse the government's industrial policy in terms of its effectiveness and the limits of its policy regarding competitiveness in the general-purpose computer industry in Japan.

The US Department of Commerce (1972) points out that Japan's Ministry of International Trade and Industry (MITI) played a strong and active role in the growth of the computer industry. With the exception of industry reorganization problems, the interests of MITI and computer makers were identical; computer policy was not prepared beforehand, but drawn up to solve problems as they arose. It does not analyse, however, to what extent industry policy contributed to the development of the computer industry in Japan, nor for what reasons it was able to contribute. Anchordoguy (1989) gives an excellent history and a detailed breakdown of computer industry policy in Japan, factually clarifying to what extent the policy contributed to the growth of the industry. She cites mainly cases concerning the Japan Electronic Computer Company (JECC) and a variety of joint research and development projects. Anchordoguy also calculates to what extent the JECC alleviated the computer makers' debt burden, corroborating the key role played by the computer industry policy. But she does not clarify the relationship between the effectiveness of the computer industry policy towards creating competitiveness and the distinctive character of competition in the computer industry. She also does not write about its historical changes.

This chapter draws attention to the distinctive character of, and historical changes in, general-purpose computer industry competition, clarifying the reasons why the Japanese computer industry policy was effective in creating competitiveness in the industry. I also compare the Japanese policy with American and European policies and discuss the limits of these policies.

The ideal form of competition in the general-purpose computer market came from IBM's methods for utilizing general-purpose computers. Not only did IBM offer the hardware and software required to meet the particular needs of each user, but it also offered expertise in system design and utilization methods, and service that went as far as training its users' system department personnel. Moreover, IBM brought out new machines that were dramatically superior in performance to its older models about every four years. Through rental sales it promoted a smooth transition to the new model for its users. This established the tendency for users of general-purpose computers to rely on specific makers to help them use their machines,[1] and as users acquired software developed specifically for particular tasks, they needed to be sure each new machine could operate their software. To replace those machines, other makers' computers (especially non-compatible machines) sought a superior price/performance ratio rather than compensated conversion cost. Moreover, computer performance, through the conversion of devices for logic circuits and memory, was advancing rapidly.

The above suggests the following three points regarding the competitiveness of general-purpose computers: (1) the general-purpose computer's competitive strength came to rely heavily on the maker's overall strength, including the company's reliability in developing new machines; (2) the acquisition of users early on had a long-lasting effect on competitiveness, because the size of the existing user base played an important role in the general-purpose computer market; and (3) in maintaining market competitiveness, it became necessary for computer companies to maintain an ongoing new machine development programme.

Although the first commercial computer was introduced in Japan in 1957, the following year, when IBM shipped its tube-type 650 model, NEC was quick to put out the transistor-type NEAC2201 and Fujitsu its relay-type FACOM128, followed in 1959 by Hitachi's transistor-type HITAC301. The introduction of computers in Japan sharply increased as JECC, a rental agency, started operations. In 1964 and subsequent years, the HITAC3010 and NEAC2200—products of technical tie-ups—were brought together, and the domestic machines' share of the computer market rose rapidly (Table 4.1). Those who most actively introduced computers during this market formation period were universities, government agencies, and corporate groups of companies in which each computer maker participated.

From the mid-1960s on, as the IBM 360 made its appearance and new computer application fields were being developed, the introduction of computers in Japan increased at a rate even greater than the expansion rate of overall equipment investment (Table 4.1). The domestic machine's

Table 4.1 *The General-Purpose Computer Market in Japan and JECC, 1957–1981*

Year	Annual deliveries	Percent of equipment investment[a]	Share of domestic computers	Share of JECC in domestic computers[b]
	(billion yen)	%	%	%
1957	0.15	0.01	78.1	0
1958	1.0	0.05	7.1	0
1959	2.4	0.09	21.5	0
1960	6.7	0.19	27.3	0
1961	13.3	0.27	18.3	45.8
1962	22.1	0.44	33.2	43.8
1963	43.3	0.77	29.7	45.7
1964	41.7	0.65	42.8	65.7
1965	51.5	0.82	52.2	77.0
1966	66.8	0.85	53.6	75.1
1967	108.6	1.07	47.2	71.3
1968	161.4	1.32	56.5	73.0
1969	212.4	1.36	57.5	67.6
1970	330.9	1.84	59.6	46.7
1971	350.1	1.92	58.8	42.4
1972	418.7	2.06	53.2	40.1
1973	528.3	2.00	51.4	37.4
1974	640.8	2.20	48.4	40.1
1975	614.0	2.10	55.8	36.9
1976	731.5	2.38	56.7	32.3
1977	790.0	2.42	—	—
1978	798.3	2.20	—	—
1979	834.3	2.03	—	—
1980	970.3	2.12	—	—
1981	1,009.8	2.14	—	—

Notes:
[a] Computer deliveries as percentage of overall equipment investment in private sector and public sector.
[b] Share of computers purchased by JECC in relation to domestic computers delivered.

Sources: JECC, *JECC Konpyuta Noto [JECC Computer Note]* (Tokyo), Annual; Economic Planning Agency, *Keizai Yoran [Economy Bulletin]* (Tokyo), Annual.

share of the market delivered during this period was subject to fluctuations: it increased for the most part consistently up to 1970, dropped
steeply once again between 1971—when the IBM 370 was introduced—
and 1974, and recovered again with the completion of a new domestic
series of machines that competed against the 370.

In the latter half of the 1970s Fujitsu and Hitachi were successful in developing IBM-compatible machines, and Fujitsu especially strengthened its
replacement offensive aimed at IBM users. In response to this, IBM put new
machines with significantly higher cost-performance on the market ahead
of other companies, and tried to shake itself free from the compatible-
machine makers. But Japanese makers, equipped with technical know-how
and capital, followed close behind, and as the 1980s began they assumed
superiority over IBM in hardware performance and also secured the trust of
users in their capacity to pursue IBM. As a result, IBM's share, which had
declined gradually from the latter half of the 1960s into the 1970s, dropped
steeply in the 1980s and was surpassed by Fujitsu's (Table 4.2).

Table 4.2   *Market Shares of Top Four Companies in General-Purpose Computer*
Market in Japan

Year	IBM %	Fujitsu %	Hitachi %	NEC %	Others %
1968	33.6	12.5	17.0	12.4	24.5
1971	33.2	19.6	14.7	10.9	21.6
1974	29.8	19.4	16.2	11.5	23.1
1976	29.5	20.6	15.5	13.6	20.7
1982	27.7	21.4	16.6	14.4	19.9
1984	26.0	24.7	20.5	13.2	15.6
1988	20.7	32.7	18.4	15.5	12.7

Sources: Konpyuta Eijisha, *Konpyutopia* [*Computopia*] (Tokyo), Monthly; Nikkei Konpyuta, *Nikkei
Konpyuta* [*Nikkei Computer*] (Tokyo), Monthly.

IBM's market share at the end of 1980, while it was 70 per cent in
America, 64 per cent in West Germany, 57 per cent in France, and 44 per
cent in Britain, was a low 29 per cent in Japan (Fig. 4.1). Furthermore, in
the three European countries a single domestic company was ranked
among the top four companies of each country—Siemens, CII, and ICL—
while in Japan three companies—Fujitsu, Hitachi, and NEC—continued to
hold a competitive share of the market.

Moreover, in the world market in the latter half of the 1980s, IBM's share
was eroded by Fujitsu and Hitachi, and by Amdahl, HDS, and Comparex,
who were receiving supplies of OEM—IBM-compatible machines—from
the two Japanese companies (Fig. 4.2).

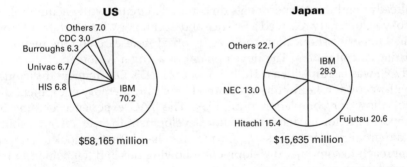

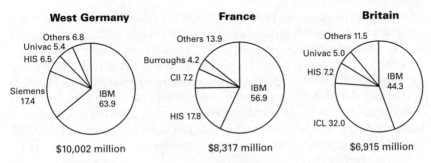

Fig 4.1 *Market share in the US, Japan, West Germany, France, and Britain*

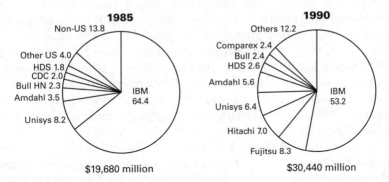

Fig 4.2 *Market share in the world, 1985 and 1990*

4.2. Government Support during the Computer Commercialization Period

The relationship between public and private groups in the Japanese general-purpose computer industry goes back to the computer trial-manufacture period. In 1952, with the co-operation of Toshiba, who had already conducted experiments on computer circuits with vacuum tubes, Tokyo University received a Science and Technology Research Fund from the Ministry of Education and was involved in research on the manufacturing of computers. The development of a Todai Automatic Computer (TAC) was begun with a completion date of 1955. But frequent difficulties with vacuum-tube circuits and cathode ray tube memory equipment did not allow for completion until 1959. The TAC experience became an opportunity for Japanese computer development to steer towards solid-state circuitry at an early stage. On the other hand, Toshiba took a cautious approach to computer development following this and fell behind in the commercialization of computers.

Computer research was begun in 1953 in the Electrical Communication Laboratory (ECL) of the Japan Telegraph and Telephone Public Company (NTT). The parametron invented by a graduate student at Tokyo University in 1954 was adopted, and in 1957 the MUSASHINO-1 (M-1) was completed. The ECL ordered the manufacture of parts and equipment needed for the M-1 from the Nihon Electronic Measuring Instruments Company, NEC, and other makers; after completion, however, it offered the technology to the four major telecommunications makers—NEC, Hitachi, Oki Electric, and Fujitsu—supporting each company's parametron computer development.[2]

As a result of this Hitachi developed a working model in 1957 and an improved version, the HIPAC101, which was exhibited at the International Information Processing Conference in Paris in 1959, where its stable operation attracted much attention. NEC completed its NEAC1101 in 1958, and in 1961 put its smallest model NEAC1201 on the market, where it was a success. And even Fujitsu, who was focused on relay-based computers, advanced the development of parametron computers. Fujitsu engaged the assistance of technical experts from the Nihon Electronic Measuring Instruments Company and completed the FACOM212 in 1959, commercialized the M-1 in 1960, and the PC-2—developed in the Takahashi Laboratory of Tokyo University—in 1962. Through the development of the parametron computer, manufacturers could acquire initial users and develop related technology and foster technical experts at the same time.

In 1952, the ETL Mark I relay-based, automatic computer was completed at the Electrotechnical Laboratory (ETL) of MITI. Manufacture of the Mark II working model, based on the Mark I, was entrusted to Fujitsu and completed in 1955. Transistor-based computer development began in 1955 in the Electronics Department, which had been established the previous year, simultaneously with the practical application of domestically produced transistors. The Mark III was completed in 1956 and the Mark IV in 1957. The ETL actively provided technical guidance to four companies—NEC, Hitachi, Hokushin Electric, and the Matsushita

Communication Industry. This resulted in the successive development of transistor-based computers—the NEC's NEAC2201 in 1958; the NEAC2203 in 1959; Hitachi's HITAC301 in 1959 and HITAC102 in 1960.

With the establishment of the Electronic Computer Specialists Committee by the Electrical Communication Society at the end of 1952, the organization of computer researchers had a very early start. In 1955 the Electronic Computer Survey Committee was established by the Radio Technology Association, with researchers from industry and universities, including user representatives, among its members. This Committee organized the joint-trial manufacture of computers by eight companies, including Toshiba, Hitachi, NEC, and Fujitsu. The Committee also surveyed, studied, and raised objections to IBM patents that were a serious problem at the time, and made various proposals, including one that proposed that Japanese computer development skip the vacuum tube and begin working from the transistor and parametron and a second that stated the need for a national policy on rental agencies. Most of these activities were handed over to the Japan Electronics Industry Development Association (JEIDA), which was established in 1958, and had a significant effect on the direction of MITI computer policy.

Communication equipment makers and electric appliance makers had already started their own computer research and development because of internal design calculation needs and the concerns of their research personnel. The transfer of technology by public research agencies to the private sector and the active exchange of information with other companies and universities supported corporate computer development and encouraged its early startup as an industry, even though it was still at the trial-manufacture stage and had a weak internal standing.[3]

The fast start of the government's protection policy is a distinctive feature of Japan's computer industry. The severe restrictions that were initially placed on computer imports and capital transactions continued into the mid-1970s. MITI, who had import approval rights, examined the possibility of substituting domestic machines and restricted imports to the utmost.[4] Also, the cabinet decision in 1963—recommending the use of domestic products in public agencies for the sake of foreign currency savings—persuaded public agencies and national universities to use domestically made computers. And this continued even after the cabinet decision was repealed in 1972, resulting in the formation of exclusive market sectors in the Japanese computer market, where domestic machines were given preference.

In 1956 negotiation on technical tie-up sanctions due to the Foreign Capital Law between IBM Japan and IBM WTC began between IBM and MITI, and negotiations on IBM's granting of patents to domestic makers followed. Although these dragged on due to the rigid stance of both parties, domestic makers who were anxious to use IBM patents facilitated a hasty agreement. Domestic makers acquired IBM patents under the same conditions, and IBM Japan was allowed to produce computers and remit profits as a special case under the Foreign Capital Law. At the same time MITI forced IBM to accept a two-year postponement to the start of its computer production in Japan. IBM also agreed to participate in a 'Conference' with MITI on machine types and production quantities for the domestic market.

The Extraordinary Measures Law for Promotion of the Electronics Industry (Electronics Promotion Law), which became the fundamental law for computer-promotion policy, was established in 1957. The Electronics Promotion Law established the financing, subsidies, and tax breaks needed for the promotion of the electronics industry. It also established exceptions to the application of the Antitrust Act for joint activities between related companies. But unlike laws that promoted other industries, the Electronics Promotion Law placed much weight on promoting technical development such as experimental research.

In the same year, the Electronics Industry Deliberation Council composed of government and private representatives and the Electronics Industry Division (renamed the Electronics Policy Division in 1969) of MITI were newly established. In 1958, the Japan Electronics Industry Promotion Association (JEIDA) was formed as an industry association in accordance with the same law. Unlike the Electronics Industry Association of Japan, whose membership included a wide range of makers centred around the consumer electronics industry, JEIDA's main members were computer and semiconductor makers and it served practical functions such as opening computer centres and displaying domestic machines. In this way, government and private organizations were set up with the aim of giving priority to nurturing the computer industry.

In April 1959 the Electronics Industry Division announced its 'Basic Policy on the Promotion of the Domestic Electronic Computer Industry', which recognized the difficulties—enormous development costs, unstable business profits, and the sharing of rental funds—involved in continuing independent development of all types of machines by private enterprises (MITI Denshi Kogyo Ka, 1959). In October of 1960 MITI conceived of a semi-public, semi-private national policy company that would rent small- and medium-scale machines and develop large-scale ones, and embarked on securing a budget.[5] But MITI's original plan was never realized because the Ministry of Finance (MOF) insisted on a plan that would concentrate total production and sales in one company, while makers demanded that their autonomy be maintained. The Ministry of International Trade and Industry formulated an alternative plan in which a rental company would be established at the joint expense of the makers—the most urgent request on the maker's side—and the Japan Development Bank (JDB) would provide financial assistance. As a result of the persuasive efforts made by

Morihiko Hiramatsu (the representative of the Electronics Industry Division Manager) towards MOF and JDB, JECC was established in August 1961. Seven companies participated in the establishment of JECC: NEC, Hitachi, Fujitsu, Toshiba, Oki Electric, Mitsubishi Electric, and Matsushita Electric. Each contributed a sum of 150 million yen.

Under the JECC system, JECC would purchase from the maker a computer ordered by an investing company at a price determined by multiplying the monthly rental fee by a fixed rate, and would rent the computer to the user. In addition, a machine cancelled by the user would be bought back by the maker at its existing value. The funds needed to maintain this system were raised from rental income, investment from investing companies, and financing from JDB and city banks. Investing companies accepted a rather large cancellation risk, and the ongoing funding supplements to JECC, as compensation for the freedom to develop new machine types and other projects.

Domestic companies began technical tie-ups with American companies to hasten the development of machines that could compete with the IBM 1401—a popular model at the time—and acquire computer development know-how that included software and input/output devices. Hitachi, after entering a technical tie-up with RCA in 1961, announced its 1401 competitor in 1962, the HITAC3010. NEC tied up with Honeywell in 1962 and domestically produced that company's H-200, which successfully replaced the 1401 because of its high cost-performance and conversion software. The company then announced the NEAC2200 in 1964. Technical agreements were also reached between Mitsubishi Electric and TRW; Oki Electric and Sperry Rand; and Toshiba and GE, and each company announced machines based on technology from their American partners. Alone among domestic makers, Fujitsu did not enter into the technical tie-up and between 1961 and 1964 it introduced a succession of independently developed new machines.

Although the Japanese computer industry had an auspicious launching in the first half of the 1960s, it lagged far behind in the development of large-scale machines. MITI devised the Mining and Industry Technology Research Association Law to grant mining and industry technology research subsidies to research associations established in 1961 by several companies. In 1962, Fujitsu, Oki Electric, and NEC established the Computer Technology Research Association, which became involved in developing 'high-performance, large-scale machines suitable to conditions in our country'. The results of this FONTAC project were the promotion of a large-scale machine at Fujitsu, and the realization that regulators were needed to bring together all parts of a joint-development project.

4.3. Computer Policy during the New Machine Development Competition Period

The System 360 unveiled by IBM in April 1964 defined the basic characteristics of general-purpose computers for the next quarter-century. IBM unified computer architecture and standardized the interface between CPU and peripheral equipment in order to produce a family of computers with versatility for both business-data processing and scientific calculations, with several models and a variety of software and peripheral equipment compatibility. Orders for the 360 far exceeded expectations, and the system—in a single stroke—made existing rental machines old-fashioned, exerting a strong impact on domestic and foreign makers. In that year, Matsushita Electric withdrew from the general-purpose computer industry because of the effects of a recession in the consumer electronics industry in Japan and JECC's increasing financial problems. And in Europe, French giant Machines Bull sold its computer division to America's GE because of financial difficulties.

In 1964 MITI made enquiries to the Electronics Industry Deliberation Council regarding a policy for improving the international competitive strength of the Japanese computer industry. The Council made several proposals: tax measures to alleviate the burden on makers to buy back cancelled machines; replenishing JECC funds; a coalition of government, universities, and private organizations to develop jointly a super high-performance computer that would set the highest standard in the world; and coalitions of companies for joint development and production. These proposals would allow domestic machines to occupy a majority of the domestic market even after the period of change expected between 1965 and 1967, and as a result two-thirds of these machines would be developed domestically.

Development was begun on a super high-performance computer (SHPC) in 1966 by the Large-Scale Industrial Technology Research and Development Programme (Large-Scale Project) of MITI's Agency of Industrial Science and Technology (AIST). The Large-Scale Project had been created to develop cutting-edge industrial technology with the co-operation of government and private organizations, funded by the national treasury. Conceived as 'research and development aimed at bringing out a commercial, large-scale machine that would be internationally accepted and be produced with domestic technology by the start of the 1970s', the project targeted a wide field that included hardware, software, logic circuits and memory devices, and input/output devices. It determined basic directions centred around ETL in MITI's AIST and entrusted development to companies and universities according to themes.[6]

Since each company had already been developing different types of computers, ETL indicated only basic performance without unifying architecture, and had proposals for Hitachi, the Nippon Electric Company, and Fujitsu; Hitachi was designated the overall manufacturer. When LSI (Large Scale Integrated-circuit) for logic circuits and IC (Integrated Circuit) memory were developed, a procedure was adopted in which several companies were designated to work on one theme, develop different technologies, and run comparison tests. Rather than have ETL's policy unilaterally enforced, efforts were made to avoid duplicate developments and to introduce competitive principles while respecting the existing state and intentions of the participating companies.[7]

In order to bring out its own data communication service, NTT, who had suspended computer development following the development of the M-1, started the DIPS (Dendenkosha Information Processing System) Project in 1968 to develop computers suitable for data communication services.[8] Although the 'three large-scale computer makers'—NEC, Fujitsu, and Hitachi—participated in this project, NTT valued 'each maker's individual technology', stopping at the unification of architecture, and it left the parts level to the discretion of each maker. Through the mediation of the Electrotechnical Laboratory, NTT accepted the wishes of the three makers to use the results of the Large-Scale Project regarding the memory hierarchical structure and the input/output interface (Tsusho Sangyo Chosakai, 1987: 95).

The Reserve for Computer Buy-Back Losses was created in 1968 as a countermeasure to increasing cancellations, enabling domestic makers to hold back a tax-free reserve of up to 10 per cent of sales made to JECC. This limit was raised to 15 per cent in 1970 and 20 per cent in 1972, and from 1970 on it could also be applied to computers sold to lease companies and other companies besides JECC.

At the same time a software industry promotion policy was added by MITI, who had established in 1969 the Electronics Policy Division (managed by Morihiko Hiramatsu) to manage computer industrial policy including software, and had established the Information-Processing Promotion Association (IPA) in 1970. This Association received government financing, subsidies, and private investment, and aimed at promoting the software industry by providing a guarantee of obligations for software companies and carrying out consignment development, purchasing, and promotional activities for programs.

What were the effects of the computer industry promotion policies of the 1960s? In response to MITI's severe import restrictions and instructions to public agencies and national universities to use domestic machines, IBM Japan put their energy into marketing large-scale machines that could not be replaced by domestic ones. As a result, the share of domestic machines in the medium-scale and small-machine market increased and the superiority of foreign machines in the large-scale machine market was maintained. An exclusive market was created in which preference was given to the use of domestic machines by government- and school-related users.[9]

The JECC contribution was also clear. In the six-year period between 1964 and 1969, when about 70 per cent of domestic machines were rented through JECC, the makers' share of responsibility for rental funds raised by JECC stopped at 10 per cent. The JDB loans had a pump-priming effect for city bank financing, and the financing these loans encouraged comprised 53 per cent of the burden.[10] The purchases made by JECC during this period totalled 245,300 million yen; when the makers themselves carried out rentals over the same 44-month period, their income was 154,300 million yen, according to estimates by Marie Anchordogy. Makers had to come up with the difference, i.e. 91,000 million yen (Table 4.3). Since the makers' portion of JECC financing was 25,200 million yen, its burden of funds was reduced to 28 per cent.

By 1971, 10,000 million yen of research and development costs had been injected into the SPHC development, which started with a total budget of 11,740 million yen (consignment cost to private sector: 9,960 million yen) (Table 4.4). It is assumed that about 8,500 million yen was paid to participating companies from budget allotments.

Research and development financial assistance provided by MITI was about 10,000 million yen, including 1,600 million yen of Mining and Industry Technology and Research subsidies—equivalent to 11 per cent of the 94,100 million yen of company research and development costs related to computers during the same period. Compared with 1972 and

Table 4.3   *Estimated Benefit of Up-Front Cash through JECC, 1964–1975*

	1964–69 (billion yen)	1970–75 (billion yen)
Under JECC rental		
Sales to JECC	245.3	621.0
Computer-trade-ins	37.7	227.8
Estimated cash flow (1)	207.6	393.2
Under own rental		
Expected rental income[a]	154.3	551.8
Computer trade-ins	37.7	227.8
Estimated cash flow (2)	116.6	324.0
Up-front cash through JECC		
(1)–(2)	91.0	69.2

Note: [a]Monthly rental income is assumed to equal 1/44 of the sales price.

Source: Anchordoguy (1989: 69–71, 83–5).

Table 4.4 *Private-Sector Investment in Computer-Related R. & D. and Government Financial Assistance* (unit: billion yen)

Year	R. & D.	Mining and industry subsidies	SHPC project	NTT DIPS project	Computer buy-back reserve[a]	New series project	NTT VLSI project	MITI VLSI project
1961	↑	0.04	—	—	—	—	—	—
1962	—	0.1	—	—	—	—	—	—
1963	11.2	0.14	—	—	—	—	—	—
1964	→	0.18	—	—	—	—	—	—
1965	→	0.12	—	—	—	—	—	—
1966	6.3	0.12	0.37	—	—	—	—	—
1967	8.4	0.09	1.19	—	—	—	—	—
1968	12.2	0.24	2.03	7.5	1.4	—	—	—
1969	17.8	0.19	2.78	7.5	2.3	—	—	—
1970	23.4	0.27	2.32	7.5	5.7	—	—	—
1971	26.0	0.73	1.33	7.5	8.2	—	—	—
1972	15.4	0.30	—	—	10.3	5.21	—	—
1973	27.1	—	—	1.67	5.6	16.66	—	—
1974	22.2	—	—	1.67	3.0	18.45	—	—
1975	30.6	—	—	1.66	5.0	13.38	6.67	—
1976	42.2	—	—	—	7.1	11.43	6.67	3.50
1977	53.9	—	—	—	4.1	—	6.66	8.64
1978	62.4	—	—	—	—	—	—	10.05
1979	—	—	—	—	3.0	—	—	6.91
1980	—	—	—	—	2.0	—	—	—

Note: [a]Reduction in government revenue due to computer buy-back reserve.

Sources: Anchordoguy (1989: 225–7, 231–44). The figures for R. & D. and the new series project are partially corrected according to the original sources: Sorifu Tokeikyoku [Statistics Bureau of the Prime Minister's Office], *Kagaku Gijutsu Kenkyu Chosa Hokokusho* [*Report on the survey of R. & D. in Science and Technology*] (Tokyo), Annual; Zeisei Chosa Kai [Tax-system Survey Committee of MOF], *Zeisei Chosa Kai Kankei Shiryo Shu* [*Collection of Documents Related to the Tax-system Survey Committee*] (Tokyo), Annual.

subsequent years—when development projects increased and government expenditure was dramatically raised—MITI's subsidies during this period were not large. But the performance of the completed SPHC system exhibited a Gibson mix of 231ns, seven times greater than the IBM 360 at the start of the project and 1.5 times greater than that of the IBM 370-165 at the end of the project. High-speed elements were also developed, such as a high-speed logic LSI with an average delay time of 1.5ns and an IC memory with an access time under 65ns, as well as buffer memory, virtual memory, multiprocessor, pipeline control, and other design elements widely adopted by subsequent large-scale computers. Additionally, a large contribution was made to improving significantly the hardware performance of subsequent domestic machines.

From the standpoint of funds, the role played by NTT was even larger. The DIPS-1 project completed a trial-manufacture machine in 1971 and a technical calculation service was started in December 1973. NTT reportedly invested 30,000 million yen up until the start of service, and twenty-two systems were introduced to expand the service network up to the end of 1976. Not only did NEC, Hitachi, and Fujitsu participate in the joint development and bear the total cost by NTT, but they also realized huge profits through the manufacture of commercial machines.[11]

The tax breaks received by the computer industry through the Reserve for Computer Buy-Back Losses were also significant, totalling 27,900 million yen between 1968 and 1972, reaching nearly 30 per cent of the 94,800 million yen of company research and development costs related to computers during the same period.

On the other hand, the software industry promotion policy did not produce the desired results. Expecting the development of SHPC basic software would be followed by independent growth, the Japan Software Company was established in October 1966 with the joint funding of Fujitsu, Hitachi, NEC, and the Industrial Bank of Japan (IBJ). It was dissolved in December 1972 after failing to realize its goals of developing a 'common language' and expanding its own business, and was subsequently hit by severe labour disputes (Uozumi, 1979: 171–3). At the IPA, moreover, although a total of 5,200 million yen in government investments and subsidies were received up until 1975, the resale and rental of software developed by the IPA consignment did not improve, failing to reach the expectations of financial institutions who had given IPA-guaranteed loans to software companies.[12]

With multilateral policy support during the high economic growth period of the 1960s and a market environment in which computer introduction was advancing more rapidly than growth in equipment investment, the domestic computer makers strove to catch up with IBM, who was the leader in both new machine development and in opening up markets. At the same time, a severe development competition was unfolding among the domestic makers themselves. NEC and Hitachi led the way in producing a series of machines in competition with the 360. They were the first to form technical tie-ups: NEC announced the NEAC2200 series based on the Honeywell H200, and Hitachi announced the HITAC8000 series, based on the IBM 360-compatible RCA Spectra 70. The FACOM230 series announced by Fujitsu was an incomplete family series with variable word-length machines and fixed word-length machines.

In subsequent development, however, Fujitsu gradually assumed superiority because it was free from restrictions imposed by technical tie-ups. The 230–5 series announced in succession by Fujitsu, starting in 1968, had reinforced on-line functions and adopted IC totally for logic circuits. In a portion of the models, attempts were made to adopt virtual memory systems, IC memory, and other leading-edge technology. NEC also introduced small- and medium-scale models that used IC between 1967 and 1969, but since the entire NEAC2200 series inherited the H200's 6-bit character architecture, it deviated from the 8-bit byte architecture that had become the standard for general-purpose computers that followed IBM 360. Hitachi, on the other hand, was late in developing succeeding machines because RCA, its technical tie-up partner, withdrew from the computer business in 1971. The HITAC 8×50 series—which had independently developed and reinforced on-line functions—was introduced after 1972.

There was also intense development competition among domestic makers in the field of large-scale machines, which lagged behind the imports. Hitachi was the first to complete a large-scale, domestic machine, the HITAC5020, in 1963. Fujitsu brought out the FACOM230-50, a commercialized version of the FONTAC, in 1966, but it was surpassed in performance by Hitachi's 5020E/F, which was completed the same year and which dominated the university and other large-scale machine markets. In response to this, Fujitsu tackled the development of a large-scale machine that would surpass the 5020F, developing the FACOM230-60 in 1968, which had completely adopted IC for logic circuits and a multiprocessor system, and which garnered high praise. Lagging behind in large-scale machines development, NEC completed the super large-scale NEAC 2200-700 in 1970. This was followed, in 1971 and 1972, by Hitachi's HITAC8800/8700, a commercialized SPHC, and Fujitsu's FACOM230-75, its top-of-the-line machine.

With such rapid new model development, the hardware performance of domestic machines caught up with IBM rapidly, and this resulted in an almost continuous rise—from 1963 to 1970—in the market share of domestic machines (Table 4.1).

4.4. Market Liberalization and Computer Policy

In July 1970, when most of the new domestic machines in competition with the IBM 360 were brought out, IBM announced its System 370. In order to inherit the expanded software assets accumulated by 360 users, the 370 used 360 architecture, confining itself to adopting a virtual memory system and other elements of 'evolutionary extension'. It also realized totally integrated circuitry, including memory, and wholesale improvement of internal processing capacity. Facing the 370's arrival, GE sold its computer department to Honeywell and in 1971 RCA withdrew from the computer market. Domestic makers were once again pressed into the development of new machines that could compete—this time with the 370.

In 1970, moreover, American requests for the liberalization of the Japanese computer market became more persistent, and both Keidanren (The Federation of Economic Organizations) and the Foreign Capital Deliberation Council agreed that 'computers should also be liberalized', opposing the computer industry. Since MITI also resisted this, liberalization of the computer market did not occur that year. When the decision on the categories included in the fourth liberalization of the capital market was reached in 1971, the offensive and defensive stances of the Foreign Capital Deliberation Council and MOF and MITI were continued. In July of that year, Prime Minister Eisaku Sato instructed MITI minister, Kakuei Tanaka, to prepare a concrete plan for computer industry liberalization. Tanaka invited leaders of six domestic companies to come together and talk about the support measures desired by the computer industry. He then decided to liberalize computer imports in stages, starting in 1972, with a three-year grace period for capital transactions. At the same time, he tried to establish an implementation policy for special accounts and formulated other measures aimed at development subsidies for domestic machines.[13]

In April 1971, after MITI formulated the Extraordinary Measures Law for the Promotion of Particular Electronics Industry and Machinery Industry, integrating promotion policy for the electronics industry and the machinery industry, it called on computer makers to group together for the development of machines that could compete against the IBM 370. As a condition for subsidies, MOF emphasized the reformation of the six-company system, but the companies were slow to respond. In August of the same year a Special Account for Promotion of Computer Industry plan was prepared by MITI, who worked hard to form groups among the six domestic makers.[14] This resulted in the announcement of tie-ups formed first by Fujitsu and Hitachi in October, followed by NEC and Toshiba, and then Mitsubishi Electric and Oki Electric in November. Six domestic makers consolidated into three groups. The special account was not recognized by MOF; instead, the Subsidies for Development of New Series Computers was set up and given a budget of 34,100 million yen for a three-year period beginning in 1972 (JECC, *Kokusan Denshikeisanki Nyuze*: 23 Feb. 1972; 18 Dec. 1972).

Fujitsu decided that in order to branch into foreign markets it would be necessary to achieve compatibility with IBM general-purpose machines, which were the world's *de facto* standard. The company invested in, and did joint development work with, the Amdahl Company, set up by Gene Amdahl, the designer of the 360, after he resigned from IBM because of a difference of opinion about new machine development. Fujitsu then formed a tie-up with Hitachi, who had developed the IBM 360-compatible HITAC8000. The tie-up of the two companies, however, was premissed on 'identical architecture', with models allotted to and separately developed by both companies. As for Toshiba and NEC, their tie-up resulted from the introduction of HIS technology because Honeywell had purchased the GE computer business and set up Honeywell Information Systems, Inc. (HIS). In the case of Mitsubishi Electric and Oki Electric, who had already joined together to produce and sell computer-related products, Mitsubishi Electric was responsible for CPUs and Oki Electric for peripheral devices.

The three groups each formed their own technology and research associations,[15] and from 1972 to 1976 MITI gave these associations 57,100 million yen for new computer development, 4,500 million yen for peripheral equipment development, and 3,500 million yen for IC development—a total of 65,100 million yen in subsidies. This was about half the 137,500 million yen of computer-related research and development costs of the industry. With a subsidy rate of 50 per cent in principle, these subsidies were awarded on a priority basis—according to the ability of each company to bear financial responsibility, and they were ordered as follows: Fujitsu and Hitachi, NEC and Toshiba, and Mitsubishi Electric and Oki Electric.[16] As a result, each group in turn announced a new series to compete with the IBM 370 beginning in 1974.

In Japan, computer imports and capital transactions were fully liberalized in December 1975; after that, however, the hardware performance of domestic machines often outstripped that of IBM machines (Table 4.5). Fujitsu' s M-Series, which was compatible with the IBM 370, was cheaper and performed better, and had been geared towards IBM users. After its introduction to the market, it successfully replaced IBM machines.

At the same time IBM was restricted by the existence of massive amounts of software accumulated by 360/370 users and kept its 370 architecture for a long period of time, partially due to its failure in developing the new FS (Future System) machines. The FS machines' aim was the conversion of architecture, and IBM submitted internal documents that

Table 4.5   *Characteristics of the Large Models of IBM, Fujitsu, Hitachi, and NEC*

Announced	Model	Company	Processor LSI		Main memory		Max MIPS[a]	
			Gates per chip	Delay-time per gate	Device	Access-Time	UP[b]	MP[c]
Nov. 1974	M-180	Hitachi	130	1.2ns	4 Kb DRAM	150ns	3.2	5.8 (2)
Nov. 1974	M-190	Fujitsu	100	0.7ns	4 Kb RAM	100ns	4.1	7.4 (2)
Mar. 1975	370/168-3	IBM	12	1.7ns	2Kb SRAM	320ns	2.5	4.4 (2)
Apr. 1976	ACOS900	NEC	200	0.7ns	16Kb DRAM	200ns	n.a.	n.a. (2)
Mar. 1977	3033	IBM	37	1.0ns	4Kb DRAM	285ns	5.1	8.6 (2)
Jan. 1978	M-200	Fujitsu	100	0.7ns	16Kb DRAM	150ns	6.8	12 (2)
Sept. 1978	M-200H	Hitachi	550	0.7ns	16Kb DRAM	100ns	6.9	12 (2)
Sept. 1980	ACOS1000	NEC	200/1200	0.5/0.9ns	64/256Kb DRAM	150ns	n.a.	n.a. (4)
Nov. 1980	3081	IBM	704	about 1.5 ns	16Kb DRAM	312ns	7.7	25 (4)
Feb. 1981	M-280	Hitachi	550/1500	0.45/0.35ns	64Kb DRAM	120ns	13	24 (2)
May 1981	M-380	Fujitsu	1300	0.35ns	64Kb DRAM	150ns	16	28 (4)
Feb. 1984	308X-X	IBM	n.a.	n.a.	64Kb DRAM	312ns	8.2	28 (4)
Feb. 1985	3090	IBM	n.a.	0.4ns	64Kb DRAM	n.a.	15	50 (4)
Nov. 1985	M-780	Fujitsu	10000	0.18ns	256Kb SRAM	55ns	34	110 (4)

Notes:
[a] MIPS: million instructions per second.
[b] UP: unit process.
[c] MP: multi-processor (the numbers in parentheses are the maximum number of processors).
Source: Nikkei Konpyuta, 15 Oct. 1990.

included development data to the courts, because of an antitrust suit that will be described later.

From these court documents, Japanese makers learned that one-megabit level VLSI (very large scale IC) chips would be used in IBM's next-generation computer FS to be available in the 1980s, and joint development of a VLSI through JEIDA and other agencies was moved forward (Aida, 1992: last vol., 356–7; Tateishi, 1993: 280–1; Tarui, 1984: 142).

With the co-operation of Fujitsu, Hitachi, and NEC, NTT started development of a 64K-bit VLSI memory in 1975 with a three-year schedule and a planned budget of 20,000 million yen. That development was successful in 1977 due to the photolithography method.

In April 1976 MITI had Fujitsu, Hitachi, NEC, Mitsubishi Electric, and Toshiba set up the VLSI Technology Research Association, organizing the joint development of a VLSI needed for the next generation of computers. In determining the membership of this VLSI Project, MITI did not approve of the participation of Oki Electric, who had not fulfilled commercialization obligations, a condition for receiving previous subsidies for development of the new series.

This new project aimed at developing, by 1979, micromanufacturing technology for line widths of 0.1–1 micron (sub-micron), which would be needed for one-megabit level VLSI, and a total of 72,000 million yen (including 30,000 million yen of government subsidies) was invested. The Joint Laboratory, which consisted of research members from the five participating companies and ETL, was in charge of the development of 'common and fundamental' technology focused on micromanufacturing technology. Two group laboratories—the Computer Development Laboratory (CDL), established by Fujitsu, Hitachi, and Mitsubishi Electric, and NEC-Toshiba Information Systems (NTIS), a NEC-Toshiba joint corporation—handled the development of process technology, testing technology, and devices related to the computer architecture of each company (Tarui, 1984: 144; JECC, 1980: 145).

This was the first attempt to bring technical experts from competing companies together in one place, and it yielded results. Various new semiconductor manufacturing devices were developed, starting with the electron beam exposure system, which gave especially high resolution from a photolithograph and, in 1980, a 256K-bit VLSI memory was produced.

To summarize, post-liberalization computer development in Japan aimed at securing competitive superiority over IBM machines that were expected to appear in the future market, unlike former development aimed at existing IBM machines. By carrying out joint-development projects, such as that typified by the VLSI, concurrent with the independent development of companies, domestic makers overtook IBM in semiconductor technology, which had become the corner-stone of computer hardware. Around 1980, Japanese semiconductor manufacturing technology led the world in high-speed, high-density manufacturing. As a result, Japanese general-purpose computers gradually expanded their superiority in hardware performance, overtaking IBM (Table 4.5).

4.5. Concluding Remarks

At the start of the computer-industry policy in Japan, during the initial market-growth period in the latter half of the 1950s, a system of market protection and financial support to development and sales was arranged. One of the factors that prompted the Japanese government to develop the industry (i.e. MITI) was the launching—*en masse*—of the computer industry in the late 1950s by major communication-equipment makers and electric-appliance makers. In addition to this were the existence of a strong sensitivity to American electronics technology, chiefly among Japanese electronics engineers, stemming from the experience of defeat in the Second World War; the active exchange of information with other companies and of overseas-based information through groups such as the Electrical Communications Society and the Radio Technology Association; and the transfer of technology to the private sector by MITI's Electrotechnical Laboratory and Electrical Communication Laboratory of NTT (a public corporation until 1985).

A second distinctive feature was that industrial policy consistently followed IBM, and policies were continually evolved to match changes in the competitive climate that accompanied the introduction of new IBM machines. This took place once Japanese computer makers had accepted IBM's methods of using, developing, and marketing general-purpose computers. The 'threat from IBM'—of its giant-firm status and the cyclical appearance of new epoch-making machines—forcibly gave a basis to domestic computer development policies and environment, and forced a gathering of a wide array of support from government (including NTT), bureaucracy, and the private sector.

The third feature was that concrete policy contents were determined and influenced by opinions in the computer industry that had been sifted through JEIDA, or after consideration of the intentions of each company, but were not the unilateral initiative of the government. Respect for the independence of computer makers, information exchange among public and private sectors, and efforts to form mutual agreements are recognized in the establishment of the JECC, management of the joint-development project, and the restructuring of the computer industry. Then, as the ascendancy of the top three companies—Fujitsu, Hitachi, and NEC—gradually became clear, the government's aid policies were concentrated on these particular companies. Accepting the results of market competition, MITI avoided intervention that would distort market relations.

Thus Japanese computer policy had a significantly different personality from policies in Europe and America. In Europe a large number of small-scale companies flooded the market (Britain), major companies were slow to start (Germany's Siemens), or quickly reached a standstill (France's Bull). The British, French, and German governments started to develop their domestic computer industries for the first time in 1967, three years after the announcement of the IBM 360.[17] Thereafter the European governments, having accepted foreign capital investment from IBM and others, adopted a 'national champion' strategy. That strategy concentrated subsidies, loans, and public procurement on a consolidated maker made up of weak computer makers (Britain's ICL and France's CII) or a traditional large company that was lagging behind in computer development (West Germany's Siemens).

This resulted in weakened incentives to improve competition among companies that received aid. Moreover, Unidata, which was a joint establishment of three EC countries (CII, Philips, Siemens) aimed at competing with IBM, collapsed due to policy changes and the pull-out of participating companies, plus changes in government ruling parties, industrial policy that lacked cohesion, frequent policy changes regarding the nationalization of computer companies, aid objectives, and so on.[18]

In the United States until 1981, when copyright laws were amended to protect software, and 1982, when the Department of Justice withdrew its antitrust suit against IBM, US computer-industry policy was consistent and rested on maintaining a competitive environment by restricting the activities of IBM.

IBM came to accept the introduction of clear-out sales, the onerous supply of patents (the consent decree of 1956), and the separation of software prices from hardware prices (the unbundling of 1970). Furthermore, in the 1970s, IBM was sued in succession by the Department of Justice and its competitors. Fearing the outcome of the suit that accompanied continual requests by the Justice Department to split up the company, IBM gradually assumed a conservative business posture.[19] Also during this period, IBM was restricted by the accumulation of IBM 360/370 software and kept its 370 architecture for a long period of time, but because there were no intellectual property rights until the 1981 copyright law amendments, use of the company's information could not be restricted. As a result, the direction of IBM's new machine development became predictable even for competitive makers, and the rise and rivalry of compatible makers, especially the Japanese, was permitted.

Computer policy in Japan, in conjunction with domestic and foreign market conditions, helped improve the competitive strength of domestic machines. The quick start of Japanese policy went hand in hand with the desire for industrialization of the large electronics companies, kick-starting the computer industry and helping domestic makers acquire the initial users that would become their base for future competition. The continuous and multilateral aid policies aimed at IBM, coupled with the quick growth of the domestic market and the creation of a domestic machine priority market, alleviated the burden on domestic makers and concentrated their efforts on technical development with clear targets. Technical development competition that continued over a long period was beneficial to the major Japanese electronics companies, who could use top science and engineering graduates and plan their continuous, long-term employment.

The government's market protection policy allowed the import of foreign machines in business applications not handled by domestic machines, and in the 1970s the market liberalization schedule was determined. This caused competitive pressure from foreign machines to be exerted on domestic makers. Government aid dispensed through the JECC consisted only of rental-fund loans, and order-taking had to be done by domestic makers themselves. Even in the case of joint-development projects carried out with government subsidies, the development of new machines that would compete in the market was the responsibility of each maker. These conditions accelerated the competition between domestic makers.

The government, as is evident from the case of Oki Electric in the VLSI project, monitored the efforts of companies granted subsidies, and prevented inefficiency in the industrial policy. As a result, industrial policy functioned very effectively in the area of hardware development, where makers could clarify and focus on targets.

On the other hand, industrial policy regarding the software industry did not yield expected results, and this was due to a variety of reasons. For a long time IBM offered software and hardware in packages, and in a world of general-purpose computers where users developed their own particular software it was difficult to develop and sell it packaged. Even after the software price was separated from the hardware price, software products were not readily recognized as independent products in Japan, and independent software companies not subcontracted to hardware makers had difficulty in growing.[20] In such an era the fact that the government's aid policy towards the software industry could not yield results comes as no surprise.

The fundamental reason, however, lies in the characteristics of software itself—in its remarkable diversity and the necessity for fast responses to market needs. Therefore, it is extremely difficult to clarify and focus on targets, as in the case of hardware, and government policy results cannot be effectively monitored. The value of software products is determined after the fact, by daily evaluation on the market; it is not an easy target for industrial policy, which determines aid based on previously clarified targets.

In conclusion, I will comment on the historical boundaries of the Japanese computer-industry policy. Computer-industry policy, which began and ended with pursuit of IBM, pushed the actions of domestic companies in one direction and framed the entire industry. The companies who received policy aid basically invested the majority of their resources in the development of large-scale, general-purpose computers—similar to IBM. They received computer architecture from IBM or their tie-up partners, and the bulk of their development effort went towards improving the design of logic circuits and memories, and developing leading-edge semiconductor elements.

The computer policy's concentration on existing makers went hand in hand with the absence of venture capital in Japan, impeding the birth of new, innovative computer makers. As a result, the Japanese computer industry, along with IBM, was late in riding the downsizing wave created in the US in the second half of the 1980s by venture businesses specializing in personal computers, workstations, and semiconductors.

Needless to say, the Japanese government was not the only one late to notice the sudden downsizing trend in the world's computer market (see Fransman, 1995: 184–5). Furthermore, the assertion that industrial policy led the direction of Japan's computer industry exaggerates the role of industrial policy. But industrial policy did force Japan's computer industry to unite in one direction—that of following IBM. Industrial policy in Japan was one of the reasons that the computer industry was able to pursue IBM—and the historical boundary of that policy became apparent in the computer world's turnover period.

NOTES

1. A 1962 survey in America showed that 92 per cent of users who had used a previous computer ordered their second computer from the same manufacturer as the first. A survey of 1971 orders showed that 82 per cent of IBM customers who ordered a new computer remained with IBM. See Brock (1975: 51).
2. For details regarding the relationship between the initial computer development performed by Japanese makers and the Electrical Communication Laboratory and Electrotechnical Laboratory, refer to related essays intermittently appearing between vol. 16, no. 2 (Feb. 1975) and vol. 19, no. 8 (Aug. 1978) of Joho Shori Gakkai.
3. For details regarding the machine development of each maker in the Japanese

general-purpose computer industry and competitive conditions between makers, see Nakamura (1995: 243–78).

4. If domestic machines could substitute for import machines from the standpoint of design specifications, the import applications were not approved by MITI. See Konpyuta Eijisha [Computer Age], Apr. 1973, 21. And even if IBM PCS (punched card system) users submitted import applications for the IBM 1401 to MITI, one to two years would be required for approval. See Kaneda (1994: 65).

5. At the time the conception of a national policy company consisted of 2,000 million yen of capital funds (one-half government expenditure) and 2,000 million yen of loans (financial investment, interest: 6.5 per cent). See Hiramatsu (1961).

6. In the development of the Super High-Performance Computer, research development items that had to be consigned were divided into sixteen, and, in addition to Hitachi, NEC, Fujitsu, Toshiba, Mitsubishi Electric, Oki Electric, and Toko, participants in the development included Tokyo University, JEIDA, and the Japan Software Company, which had been established for the development of the machine's software by the joint investment of Fujitsu, Hitachi, NEC, and the Industrial Bank of Japan. See MITI Kogyo Gijutsuin (1972: 201).

7. Development was entrusted to the different methods of each company: logic circuit packaging technology to NEC, Hitachi, and Fujitsu, and memory IC to NEC and Fujitsu. See MITI Kogyo Gijutsuin (1972: 8).

8. For more details regarding the progress of the DIPS development, see NTT (1978), middle volume, 676–83.

9. According to the JECC (1970), the domestic machine share of the base amount of installations was 88.8 per cent of government department installations (government, related agencies, and other public organizations) and 95.9 per cent of university installations (universities, high schools, and other schools).

10. Of the total funds of 252,200 million yen that were required in the period 1964–9, JECC raised 25,200 million yen in capital increases and 133,400 million yen in loans centred around 46,500 million yen from the Japan Development Bank. See JECC (1973: 50–1).

11. According to Yukio Mizuno, who was in charge of the Information Processing Department of NEC, 'We were helped a great deal by DIPS. Not only was everything we made guaranteed to be sold, but we also got the newest technology.' See Shimoda (1984: 115).

12. Between 1970 and 1978, IPA spent about 10,000 million yen in the development of about 70 programs, with very little return from rentals to users of the developed programs or from sales. Also, throughout the 1970s, IPA guaranteed loans amounting to only about one-tenth to one-half of what it was authorized to guarantee. See Anchordoguy (1989: 128–30).

13. For details regarding the course of computer industry liberalization, see Konpyuta Eijisha , Oct. 1971, 10, and Tateishi (1993), last volume, 182–92.

14. In MITI's plan of that time, tariff increases on computer-related products were a source of revenue, and the plan incorporated a special account of 157,000 million yen for a five-year period between 1972 and 1976, centred around 99,000 million yen of Subsidies for Development of New Series Computers. But this became 139,000 million yen at the stage of the request to MOF (JECC, 20 Dec. 1971; Konpyuta Eijisha, Oct. 1971, 10; Jan. 1972, 39).

15. Fujitsu and Hitachi formed the Super High-Performance Computer Development Technical Research Association, NEC and Toshiba set up the New Series Technical Research Association, and Mitsubishi Electric and Oki Electric established the Super High-Performance Computer Technical Research Association.

16. According to Toshiba, NEC received about 23 per cent and Toshiba about 15 per cent of the total subsidies given to the three groups (Toshiba Denshikeisanki Jigyobu, 1989: 118). As for the distribution among the three groups, it is estimated that Fujitsu-Hitachi received under 50 per cent, NEC-Toshiba over 40 per cent, and Mitsubishi Electric-Oki Electric over 10 per cent (Uozumi, 1979: 142).

17. For more details regarding computer development and related policies in Europe, see Flamm (1987, 1988).

18. Jim Tomlinson comments on the British computer industrial policy as follows. 'As regards foreign investment by multi-national companies, the British view was that this was an unambiguous "good thing" on both balance of payments and import of technology ground, but there was no attempt to regulate the transfer of technology, apart from general exhortation by government, . . . The reliance on a single national champion must be related to the absence of a strong commitment to the virtues of competition in Britain, and the parallel belief in the benefits of scale for national efficiency' (Tomlinson, 1996).

19. For more details regarding IBM suits brought by the Department of Justice and competing makers and the effects of these suits on IBM, see Brock (1975: 155–80), and Ferguson and Morris (1993).

20. On the distinctiveness of the Japanese software industry Martin Fransman notes: 'This pattern of usage in Japan—with mainframes dominating long-term, obligational relationships between vendors and users, and proprietary computer systems—had important implications for Japanese software industry and the software market.' According to OECD, the ratio of customized to packaged software in 1985 was 0.31 in America, 0.61 in Germany, and 0.67 in Britain respectively, while in Japan the figure was 9.95 (Fransman, 1995: 184–5).

REFERENCES

Aida, H. (1992), *Denshi Rikkoku Nihon no Jijoden [The Autobiography of Japan, A Nation Established by Electronics]* (Tokyo: Nippon Hoso Kyokai).

Anchordoguy, M. (1989), *Computers Inc.* (Cambridge, Mass.: Harvard University Press).

Brock, G. W. (1975), *The US Computer Industry* (Cambridge, Mass.: Ballinger).

Ferguson, C. H., and Morris, C. R. (1993), *Computer Wars* (New York: Times Books).

Flamm, K. (1987), *Targeting the Computer* (Washington: Brookings Institution).

—— (1988), *Creating the Computer* (Washington: Brookings Institution).

Fransman, M. (1995), *Japan's Computer and Communications Industry* (New York: Oxford University Press).

Hiramatsu, M. (1961), 'Nihon Denshi Keisanki Kabushiki Gaisha ni tsuite [Japan Electronic Computer Company]', *Denshinkyo Kaiho [JEIDA Bulletin]*, 15 (Tokyo, Sept. 1961), 2–5.

Japan Electronic Computer Company (JECC) (1970), *Wagakuni Denshikeisanki Jitsudo Chosa [Survey of Working Computers in Japan]* (Tokyo), Mar.

—— *Kokusan Denshikeisanki Nyuzu [Domestic Computer News]* (Tokyo), Monthly.

—— (1973), *JECC Junenshi [Ten-Year History of JECC]* (Tokyo).

—— (1980), *JECC Konpyuta Noto 1980 [JECC Computer Notes 1980]* (Tokyo).

Joho Shori Gakkai (Information Processing Society), *Joho Shori [Information Processing]*, (Tokyo), Monthly.

Kaneda, H. (1994), *NEC Konpyuta Hattatsu no Monogatari [The NEC Computer Development Story]* (Tokyo: NEC Creative).

Konpyuta Eijisha [Computer Age], *Konpyutopia [Computopia]*, (Tokyo), Monthly.

MITI Denshi Kogyo Ka [Electronics Industry Division] (1959), 'Denshi Keisanki Kokusanka ni taisuru Kihon Hoshin [Basic Policy Regarding Domestic Production of Computers]', in Nihon Denshi Kogyo Shinko Kyokai (JEIDA), *Denshinkyo Kaiho [JEIDA Bulletin]*, 1 (Tokyo, May 1959), 18–19.

MITI Kogyo Gijutsuin [Agency of Industrial Science and Technology—AIST] (1972), *Ogata Purojekuto ni yoru Chokoseino Denshikeisanki [Super High-Performance Computer Project as Large-Scale Project]*, (Tokyo).

Nakamura, K. (1995), 'Konpyuta Sangyo—Hanyoki no Kokusai Kyosoryoku [The International Competitive Strength of General-Purpose Machines in the Computer Industry], in H. Takeda, (ed.), *Nihon Sangyo Hatten no Dainamizumu [The Dynamism of Japanese Industrial Development]* (Tokyo: Tokyo Daigaku Shuppankai), 243–78.

Nikkei Konpyuta Sha [Nikkei Computer], *Nikkei Konpyuta [Nikkei Computer]* (Tokyo), Monthly.

NTT (1978), *Nihon Denshin Denwa Kosha Nijugomenshi [Twenty Five-Year History of NTT]* (Tokyo).

Shimoda, H. (1984), *IBM to no 10 nen Senso [The Ten-Year War with IBM]* (Tokyo: PHP Kenkyujo).

Tarui, Y. (1984), *IC no Hanashi [The Story of IC]* (Tokyo: Nippon Hoso Shuppan Kyokai).

Tateishi, Y. (1993), *Hasha no Gosan [Miscalculations of the Winner]* (Tokyo: Nihon Keizai Shinbunsha).

Tomlinson, J. (1996), 'Comment on Kiyoshi Nakamura "Government and Business in Japan's General-Purpose Computer Industry" ', 23rd Fuji Conference comment paper.

Toshiba Denshikeisanki Jigyobu [Toshiba Computer Business Department] (1989), *Toshiba Denshikeisanki Jigyoshi [The History of Toshiba Computer Business]* (Tokyo).

Tsusho Sangyo Chosakai [International Trade and Industry Survey Committee] (1987), *Ogata Purojekuto no Ayumi [The Course of the Large-Scale Project]* (Tokyo).

Uozumi, T. (1979), *Konpyuta Senso [Computer Wars]* (Tokyo: Seiya Shoten).

US Department of Commerce (1972), *Japan, The Government-Business Relationship: A Guide for the American Businessman* (Washington).

5

Early Postwar Industrial Policy in Emerging Economies
Creating Competitive Assets or Correcting Market Failures?

ALICE H. AMSDEN

5.1. Introduction

Industrial development may be understood as a process either of correcting market failures or of creating competitive assets (resources that add value to raw labour power). This chapter develops a competitive assets approach to late industrialization using the postwar cotton textile industry as an example. Given similar industrial policies but different social constraints, latecomers in East Asia tended to out-perform those in Latin America and India in the social construction of such assets. Japan was a pioneer in social construction, honing an effective business–government relationship, although it started with more advanced competitive assets than its neighbours at the time of international opening.

5.1.1. Understanding Intervention

Four questions about postwar late industrialization promote an understanding of the role of industrial policy.

1. Why was there so much government intervention in the first place? The East Asians in particular were hostile to interventionism politically given their rivalry with communist regimes in China and North Korea.

Why did governments in Taiwan and South Korea (hereafter just Korea) interfere economically none the less, and why did they do so starting with their labour-intensive leading sector, cotton textiles? After the removal of 'distortions' by means of real exchange-rate devaluations and the introduction of a duty drawback system (access to imported inputs at world prices) in the mid-1960s, why did governments in both countries continue to protect the home market, provide greater incentives to exports, and subsidize long-term capital formation? The removal of 'distortions' should, in theory, have allowed Taiwan and Korea to compete in textiles at international prices.

2. Why were there differences in the degree of intervention among East Asian countries, all suffering presumably from the same market failures (imperfect knowledge, underdeveloped capital markets, and so forth)? Government policy tended to be more *laissez-faire* in Hong Kong than in Taiwan and Korea. Why was the Hong Kong textile industry competitive in world markets without the government's help?[1]

3. Why did India, Brazil, and Mexico not emerge as major international players in the postwar cotton textile industry? They failed to do so despite having more experience in this industry than Taiwan and Korea (India and Mexico had pre-modern textile industries and Brazil began developing textiles in the late nineteenth century, whereas textile production for the market did not emerge in Korea and Taiwan until the late colonial period).[2]

4. Why was industrial policy generally more successful in East Asia than in Latin America or India?

5.1.2. *Competitive Assets and Production Costs*

In the competitive assets approach, answers to these questions run along the following lines.

1. Interventionism in Taiwan and Korea, even in textiles, was large because a low-wage advantage was offset by the disadvantage of few competitive assets and consequently, low productivity. Their governments had a choice, therefore. They could either lower real wages further (depreciating the exchange rate)[3] or subsidize competitive asset creation in various forms until productivity rose sufficiently to equalize domestic and international unit production costs.

2. The government could intervene less in Hong Kong than in Taiwan and Korea because Hong Kong's competitive assets were relatively great and/or its social constraints were relatively small.

3. Due to social constraints (fear of labour redundancy), the textile industries of India, Brazil, and Mexico were not radically modernized after the war; there was relatively little investment in competitive assets such as new physical plants, equipment, or technological capabilities. Without a modern production capacity, exporting was highly problematic.

4. Industrial policy in East Asia was generally more effective than in India or Latin America because the social construction of competitive assets proceeded according to different principles. Subsidy allocation in East Asia—including Japan—tended to involve reciprocity and performance standards, whereas in India and Latin America it tended to take the form of 'giveaway'.

Competitive assets are resources, capabilities and their organization that add value to raw labour power. Hence, they raise the level and rate of change of 'value added' (wages + profits) per worker, or $(w + \pi)/e$.[4] As indicated in Table 5.1, some competitive assets are endowed or inherited (such as pre-modern manufacturing experience); others are internal to the firm (such as specific skills and technological capabilities); and others are external to the firm (such as infrastructure and inter-firm information networks).

The absence of competitive assets lies at the root of industrial backwardness, which is defined as a state where industries commonly regarded as the comparative advantage of low-wage countries cannot operate profitably because domestic productivity levels are below world levels. Specifically, the low-wage advantage of poor countries is offset by their low-productivity disadvantage. Therefore, domestic costs of production (we focus on marginal or unit costs, MC_D) exceed international prices, P_I: $P_{Ii} < MC_{Di}$.

If, under these cost conditions, international and domestic prices are equal ($P_{Ii} = P_{Di}$), production is not profitable. The inability to compete internationally (at home or in export markets) even in the most allocatively correct labour-intensive industries is the major initial reason why governments intervene in the economies of late industrializers— economies devoid of competitive assets in the form of novel proprietary technology. They deliberately distort domestic costs and prices in order to cover the expenses of learning until firms acquire the competitive assets (including capital) necessary to compete at world prices.

During the new entrant's long learning period, its domestic unit production costs may be expected to exceed international unit production costs; hence, its prices and those prevailing in the international market must also differ for firms to produce at a profit. The social construction of competitive assets, then, involves the emergence of business enterprises (typically hierarchically managed in mid-technology industries[5]) and the interaction between those enterprises and government to raise productivity and bridge a profitability gap during relatively long break-even

Table 5.1 *Competitive Assets*

---

1. Nationally-Endowed or Inherited
   A. Raw materials
       manufacturing-related/unrelated
   B. Manufacturing experience
       pre-modern
       colonial
       émigré
   C. State bureaucratic experience
       pre-modern
       colonial
       émigré
2. Internal to Domestic Firms
   A. Entrepreneurial capabilities
       project execution skills
       access to capital
   B. Managerial capabilities
       production/distribution
   C. Engineering capabilities
       innovation/product development
   D. Worker-related capabilities
       quality control
3. External to Domestic Firms
   A. Infrastructure
       physical
       education
   B. Foreign investment
   C. State bureaucratic capabilities
       (same as 2[A–D])
   D. Inter-firm networks

---

periods with various public and private subsidies. Examples are protection of export incentives and preferential credit in the case of government, and cross-subsidization of different industries or products in the case of diversified firms. The long-term disequilibria of catch-up in the absence of proprietary technology may be represented as follows: $MC_D > MC_I$; $P_D = P_I$.

Finally, at the technological frontier, firms aim to create new industries and transform the entire set of existing industries by investing in science-based proprietary know-how to create knowledge-based monopolies. The first mover[6] that succeeds in commercializing a technological breakthrough in industry h is rewarded with a cost advantage: $MC_{Dh} < MC_{Ih}$.[7]

Given that the costs of the first mover are lower than those of would-be competitors, if international prices are higher than domestic prices

$(P_{Ih} > P_{Dh})$, then the first mover gains world market control. If international and domestic prices are equal $(P_{Ih} = P_{Dh})$, then it earns extra surplus.

Thus, in the learning/production approach, industrial development involves parallel movements of building business enterprises, accumulating competitive assets and graduating from one set of distortions ($MC < P$) to another set, an industrial path that is very different from that predicated on market-oriented approaches. These view industrial development as a progression towards increasingly perfect markets (Pareto optimality, zero transactions costs, or the absence of market failure), as indicated in the following section.

5.1.3. *Market Failures and Comparative Advantage*

In the orthodox market-failure approach,[8] answers to the previously stated questions about government and economic development run along the following lines.

1. There was substantial government intervention in developing countries due to interventionism before the war, an ideology of interventionism after the Second World War, and a need to satisfy the demands of interest groups. If market forces had been allowed to operate, allocatively correct, labour-intensive industries such as cotton textiles would not have required government support.

2. Hong Kong's government intervened less than Taiwan's and Korea's because it was committed to a *laissez-faire* policy regime and, because of its colonial status, was relatively immune from interest-group politics.

3. India, Brazil, and Mexico failed to emerge as international players in the postwar cotton textile industry because of their governments' bias over subsidies in favour of selling in domestic, rather than in export, markets.

4. Industrial policy was more successful in East Asia than in India and Latin America because there was less of it and it was more trade oriented (see, for example, World Bank, 1993).

All the market approaches to industrial development share the ultimate theoretical ideal of perfect markets as the companion of advanced economic development. They also share a common set of assumptions which guarantee (tautological one might argue) that if markets *are* working perfectly (and countries are pursuing their comparative advantage), economic growth is assured. For example, if growth is nil then by definition the explanation must lie in market distortions ('failures' or 'imperfections'). Thus, at the heart of comparative advantage theory is the idea that backwardness is rooted in market imperfections, although this approach does not acknowledge the need for government intervention. Such imperfections are expected to vanish if governments merely get out of markets altogether and allow them to function freely.

Government-induced imperfections have the effect of raising domestic prices above world prices——the barrier to development lies in too-high prices of exchange rather than in too-high firm-level production costs.[9] Thus: $P_{Di} > MC_{Di} = MC_{Ii} = P_{Ii}$.

The excess of domestic prices over domestic costs typically has one of two causes, both government related: an overvalued exchange rate (whose effect is to raise labour costs by international standards) and/or product market monopoly power. To cover relatively high product prices in the interests of profitability, governments provide trade protection to industries with the most powerful interest groups. Instead of 'learning tariffs' (or infant industry protection) as in the competitive assets approach, there are simply 'interest group tariffs' in the orthodox market view (Baldwin, 1969).

If, in this view, markets are free of distortions, then the most efficient level of production costs in any industry is determined by the country with the greatest comparative advantage. Its production costs determine international costs ($MC_{Di} = MC_{Ii}$) and there is an international competitive equilibrium ($MC_{Ii} = P_{Ii}$). Thus, any supply-side production problems are assumed away—in theory low-wage countries inevitably have the competitive edge in labour-intensive industries because productivity in these industries is assumed to be the same everywhere.[10] The assumption of a ready supply capacity, whether for export or domestic consumption, is central to market approaches such as those of Krueger (1984) and Bhagwati (1972). Their preoccupation is not on how to create a viable production capacity in industrializing countries, which is taken for granted, but rather on how to get exchange prices right, to achieve an efficient balance between exports and domestic sales.

Competition among firms in comparative advantage economics is seen to drive the process of catch-up, as well as life, at the world technological frontier. Distortions in the form of monopoly profits ($P > MC$) are squeezed out of the system and prices and marginal costs are equalized, even in high-technology industries. Catch-up itself involves countries pursuing sequentially higher stages of comparative advantage. Thus, industrial development is viewed as a shift of resources from less to more productive uses.

Table 5.2 summarizes the major differences introduced thus far between the learning and orthodox market approaches to industrial development. Regarding initial conditions, the root of backwardness in the learning approach is the set of skills (even in labour-intensive industries) that is too primitive to achieve productivity levels and production costs competitive

Table 5.2 *The Market and Learning Approaches to Industrialization*

Market	Learning
1. *Initial conditions* (i-type industry): $P_D > MC_D = MC_I = P_I$ .... domestic distortion .... same technology .... competitive equilibrium	$P_I < MC_D$ .... low productivity If $P_I = P_D$ no production
2. *Catch-up process* (m-type industry): $P_D = MC_D = MC_I = P_I$ Removing distortions	$MC_D \neq MC_I; P_D \neq P_I$ Subsidizing learning
3. *Technological frontier* (h-type industry): $P_D = MC_D = MC_I = P_I$ Absence of distortions	$MC_D < MC_I$ First Mover D's advantage If $P_I > P_D$, world market control If $P_I = P_D$, extra surplus

Notes:
P_D: Domestic price.
P_I: International price.
MC_D: Domestic marginal (unit) cost.
MC_I: International marginal (unit) cost.
Industry types: i = low-skill, labour-intensive; m = mid-technology; h = high technology.

with those of more industrialized countries. In the comparative advantage approach, government-related distortions (support of monopolies, overvalued exchange rates) raise domestic prices above world levels and prevent otherwise cost-efficient, labour-intensive industries from competing globally.

Fig. 5.1 summarizes the differences in the two approaches as they apply to the example of cotton textiles.

Assume there is only one production factor—labour—and that real wages and the price of foreign exchange move in tandem. Then a backward country at (B) is one with higher unit-labour costs (W/Y) than the prototype at (A) for any conceivable set of potential export goods. While A may have higher wages (W/L) than B, it also has higher productivity (L/Y). On net its productivity advantage offsets its factor price disadvantage. Competitiveness under these circumstances can be attained by the backward country through one of two means: either by a reduction in wages (a movement from B to C) or by an increase in productivity (a movement from B to D).[11]

In the case of postwar textiles, point A in Fig. 5.1 represents Japan and point B represents Taiwan and Korea. In positive terms, the competitive assets approach explains countries at point B due to a shortage of technological capabilities, for instance, capability to influence firm-specific

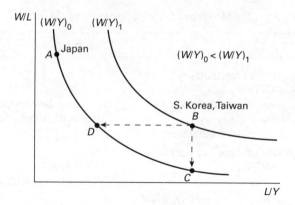

Fig 5.1 *Subsidizing learning or cutting real wages*

productivity (the ability to mix raw cotton, to set the speeds and feeds of machinery, to repair fabric flaws, and so forth). In normative terms, the competitive asset approach says countries at point *B* should use industrial policy to promote enough learning to raise productivity in the long-term, moving from *B* to *D*. The market approach explains countries at point *B* in terms of previous government interventions, that kept wages too high, the exchange rate too low, or prevented knowledge from flowing to domestic firms from overseas. It says countries at point *B* should, therefore, lower real wages (devalue), moving from *B* to *C*.

Almost all latecomers after the Second World War chose the risky option of long-term productivity growth, but with varying degrees of success.

5.2. Cotton Textiles: East Asia

It was the textile industry which saw the start of postwar industrial policy in East Asia.[12] Despite its labour intensity, this industry was a training ground for later government economic interventions in more skill-intensive or heavy industry. Cotton textiles——initially spinning and weaving and then later clothing——became the leading sector in Korea, Taiwan, Hong Kong, and later Thailand. Why governments intervened at all in this industry and why they intervened more in Taiwan and Korea than in Hong Kong is the issue addressed in this section. International organizations such as the World Bank have proposed Hong Kong as a successful model for emulation by the poorest countries (World Bank, 1993).

Moreover, the populations of Korea and Taiwan were relatively well educated and both countries had adequate physical infrastructure (by developing country standards) because of American foreign aid in the 1950s. Despite this, their governments found it necessary actively to promote the early textile industry.

The reason the Taiwan and Korean governments intervened with tariff protection, subsidized investment credit, export incentives, and import substitution of synthetic fibres is that the textile industry in the mid-1960s could not compete at market-determined production costs against the textile industry of Japan.

Japanese industry was considered the most efficient in the world at the time. Furthermore, both Taiwan and Korea imposed restrictions on direct foreign investment, fearing Japanese takeover of local textile companies.[13] Foreign investments were subject to stringent export requirements which effectively restricted their location to export processing zones.

Because low wages do not necessarily result in low-wage costs, wages per unit of production (unit-labour costs) rather than wages, should be considered as the basis for international comparisons of competitiveness. Such a comparison runs up against a number of difficult measurement problems, some involving productivity and others involving wages. Accurate productivity differences across countries depend on the specific textile product and on the stages of integration included in the comparison, which vary from company to company. Some textile products require different proportions of inputs (such as labour and raw materials) and consequently may exhibit different costs per unit. Wage measures need to be industry specific because, in the 1950s and 1960s, the average level of textile wages compared with the average level of all wages tended to be higher in developing countries than in industrialized economies (GATT 1966). Moreover, wage differences depend on the exchange rate. If the rate is overvalued—usually due to some form of government interference— then domestic costs are also inflated by international standards and competitiveness is undermined. In fact, to the extent that developing countries could not compete internationally in textiles after the Second World War (as depicted by B in Fig. 5.1), the market solution was to allow exchange rates (wages) to depreciate, until unit labour costs fell sufficiently to achieve competitiveness (a point like C in Fig. 5.1). With this short-term, free-market solution, there was no need for industrial policy.

Bearing in mind these measurement problems, some international cost comparisons for unbleached cotton sheeting in the early 1960s are presented in Table 5.3. In this low-quality, high-volume market segment, Japan had lower unit costs (per yard) than either India, the Phillipines, or Hong Kong. Japan's hourly textile wages (in 1959) at $0.17 exceeded those of either India, at $0.12, or Hong Kong, at $0.10, but Japan's higher labour productivity offset this disadvantage (United States Senate, 1961).

142 ｜ Alice H. Amsden

Table 5.3 *Production Cost of Unbleached Cotton Sheeting in the United States, Japan, India, and Hong Kong (US cents per linear yard)*

	United States 1960		Japan 1960		India 1960		Hong Kong 1963	
	Costs per yard	% of total costs	Costs per yard	% of total costs	Costs per yard	% of total costs	Costs per yard	% of total costs
Total Costs	14.6	100	11.4	100	11.3	100	14	100
Cotton Cost	8.4	57.5	7.8	68.6	5.6	49.8	7	50
Labour Cost	3.9	26.8	1.7	15.1	2.5	22.1	2.1	15
All Other Cost	2.3	15.7	1.9	26.3	3.2	28.1	4.9	35

Sources: US Department of Commerce, *Comparative Fabric Production Costs in the United States and Four Other Countries* (Washington: Government Printing Office, 1961), table 8, p. 21; and GATT, *A Study On Cotton Textiles* (Geneva: GATT, 1966).

The 'other costs' in Table 5.3 depend on such factors as the cost of raw materials and inputs such as land, water, and power; the age of plant and equipment; utilization rates; and tax rates. As a proportion of total costs, these 'other' costs were lowest in the United States. Still, Japan had a total cost advantage over these three competitors, although actual trade flows would also depend on transportation costs, tariffs, and additional selling costs. The cost disadvantage for Hong Kong is especially telling given its free-market policies. Presumably its exchange rate was 'right' but even so, it could not compete against Japan at market-determined production costs. How, then, did textiles become Hong Kong's leading sector without government support?

5.2.1. Minimalism: Hong Kong

The answer lies in the different constraints that Hong Kong faced. We define a constraint as a condition (permissive or repressive) that impinges on the social construction of a competitive asset and is beyond a country's ability to control or alter substantially in the short run through capital investment. Examples are cultural norms, income distribution, international political autonomy, regional economies, and membership in (or exclusion from) political arrangements such as trade pacts. One permissive constraint that Hong Kong enjoyed was membership in the British Commonwealth, which enabled Hong Kong to partake of Commonwealth Preferences throughout the 1950s and early 1960s. Given these Preferences (which effectively enabled Hong Kong to increase its selling price and hence value added per worker, or 'productivity'), Hong Kong's textiles did not have to compete directly against those of Japan in the markets of Commonwealth members, including Great Britain. In 1963 textiles accounted for 44 per cent of Hong Kong's total exports. The United Kingdom absorbed as much as 54 per cent of the textile export total (compared to 30 per cent by the US).[14]

An influx of Asian textiles (especially from Hong Kong, India, and Pakistan) into the markets of high-wage countries soon created demands for protectionism. This resulted in an agreement under the auspices of GATT whereby the textile exports of low-wage exporting countries were subject to quotas (GATT, 1966). The allocation of these quotas partially depended on first-mover advantages, or existing market share. Hong Kong was one of the earliest postwar Asian textile exporters. This was due to its political stability, access to finance, and overseas Chinese entrepreneurs, who brought extensive textile manufacturing and marketing experience with them from China. Therefore, Hong Kong received favourable quota treatment: 'Hong Kong possessed larger export quotas than Taiwan and South Korea, and especially other LDCs' (Ho and Lin, 1991: 277). Ironically, one of Hong Kong's major competitive assets derived precisely from a type of international cartel arrangement which the country's economic philosophy deplored.

Hong Kong was able to buttress its international competitiveness in manufacturing with virtually no government assistance (save the provision of mass subsidized housing) because it could regulate a flow of cheap labour from mainland China. By contrast, Korea and Taiwan maintained tight immigration policies. Thus, while labour markets were free from trade union pressures in all three countries until the late 1980s, Hong Kong also benefited from immigration.[15] Finally, Hong Kong thrived with a free-market policy due to its early entry into clothing manufacture. When Taiwan and South Korea were in political disarray due to war in the 1950s, and investing in cotton spinning and weaving at a time when people in the domestic market made their own clothes or had them made by tailors, Hong Kong was establishing its clothing industry. Thus, Hong Kong's leading sector was not cotton spinning and weaving but rather apparel manufacture. As early as 1961 exports of clothing from Hong Kong exceeded exports of textiles whereas the reverse was true in Korea. As late as 1987, clothing accounted for roughly one-third of Hong Kong's exports (Ho and Lin, 1991). The manufacture of apparel is considerably more labour-intensive than the manufacture of textiles. Therefore, international competitiveness depends relatively more on low wages in apparel production than in upstream textile manufacture, whose total unit-cost determination is more sensitive to productivity and non-wage costs. Total labour requirements per dollar of output in Hong Kong were roughly twice as great in clothing than in textiles, while total capital requirements per dollar of output were approximately three times as great in textiles than in clothing.[16]

By virtue of its small size as well as trade orientation, Hong Kong's export concentration was extreme and rose rather than fell as per capita income increased in the period 1963–71 (Lin, Mok, et al., 1980). With a large share of industrial activity devoted to apparel manufacture in a tiny economic unit, Hong Kong's need for industrial policy in the form of either trade protection or subsidized credit was negligible. Instead, the government could focus its attention on immigration policy and land use policy, including subsidized low-income housing, as noted earlier.

The only other comparable case of free-market industrialization is Switzerland—another small, trade-oriented economy that enjoys outstanding competitive assets, particularly innovative ones, along with exceptionally low wages by European standards (Crouzet, 1972). In light of these competitive assets, both countries represented special cases, rather than an alternative model to the industrial policy approach to catching up.

5.2.2. *Maximalism: Korea and Taiwan*

By comparison with Japan or Hong Kong in the 1950s and early 1960s, Korea and Taiwan brought only low wages to compete in world markets. Given that both Korea and Taiwan tended to have overvalued exchange rates during this period, it is difficult to estimate their true international cost competitiveness. In 1959, hourly wages in their textile industries were estimated to be roughly one-third of what they were in Japan (United States Senate, 1961).

Very rough estimates of labour productivity, throughout the 1970s, suggest that Korea and Taiwan were only one-third as productive in textiles as Japan. Therefore, at the very bottom end of the market, both countries may have had equal average costs to those of Japan. Nevertheless, other costs, such as for electricity and capital, are likely to have been higher. Productivity for textile products other than gray goods, particularly those that required dyeing and other finishing steps, is almost certain to have been considerably lower.[17]

This productivity disadvantage persisted in spite of a long learning period for textile manufacture that began during the colonial period, and extensive technology transfers provided by textile machinery sellers beginning in the 1950s.[18] Machinery makers such as Platt (UK), Howa and Enshu (Japan), and Picarol (Belgium) sent their agents to Korea and Taiwan to set up new equipment and to troubleshoot erratic problems. In effect, technology transfer in the textile industry was 'turn-key', and foreigners all but ran the major mills initially. Yet productivity was still relatively low.

In the 1950s, US AID targeted many of its subsidized non-project loans to the textile industry (Hong, 1979). For their part, the Korean and Taiwan governments were sensitive to the textile industry's needs, both because of its importance in the economy and because of its politically powerful industry-wide association (for Korea, see Kim, 1966).

In a preview of industrial policy in the 1960s, textile manufacturers were given protection from foreign imports as well as from Japanese foreign investors interested in establishing production in former colonies. When over-capacity emerged in the late 1950s to the early 1960s, an array of export incentives were made available to textile manufacturers (as well as to other industries).[19]

Workers' demands were also checked by martial law and repression of trade union activity. Real wages were further depressed by recurrent exchange rate devaluations, undertaken partly as a consequence of pressure from US AID. For instance, the Korean won was devalued by 50 per cent in 1961, from 65 to 100 won for the dollar in January, and from 100 to 130 won for the dollar in February (Frank, Kim *et al.*, 1975). The result, according to the Economic Planning Board, was inflationary because the price of imported raw cotton jumped, and this jump affected the production costs of all cotton products and the price of cotton yarn. In turn, a consequence of inflation was real wage decreases. The rate of growth of price-deflated earnings was 0 per cent in 1962, −5.2 per cent in 1963, and −5.8 per cent in 1964 (Frank, Kim *et al.*, 1975: 222). Yet despite these measures—or because of them—the economy continued to stagnate rather than become internationally competitive.

Under continued pressure from Washington, both Korea and Taiwan 'liberalized' their economies around 1965. Ironically, this was the start of their industrial policies, because restructuring tipped the balance towards greater interventionism. Liberalism took the form of duty drawbacks (rebates for tariffs paid on imported inputs used for exports). Certain deposit rates were also temporarily raised in an effort to increase savings (all banks were state owned). Nevertheless, trade restrictions tended to be increased. Between 1963–7 and 1968–72, average tariff rates in Korea rose from 30 per cent to 64 per cent for yarns, 75 per cent to 98 per cent for certain fabrics, and from 49 per cent to 89 per cent for other types of fabrics (Hong, 1979: table B16). Export incentives were made much more generous. Finally, long-term investment credits were targeted to specific industries and even firms.[20]

Aided by rapidly rising wages in Japan, after 1965 Korea's and Taiwan's textile exports soared and productivity rose. Yarns (kg.) per employee in Korea increased from 20.62 in 1965 to 30.95 in 1971; fabrics (m.) per employee rose in the same time period from 87.1 to 108.8 (Kim, 1980: 231). In terms of Fig. 5.1, after 1965 government strategic policies to increase international competitiveness became strongly committed to moving from *B* to a point like *D* rather than *C*.[21] In 1967, the Korean government became first among the late industrializers to establish a Ministry of Science and Technology (the Taiwan government soon followed suit). This symbolized a long-term commitment to build assets related to technological capabilities.

5.3. Latin America and India: Limitations of Industrial Policy

Postwar latecomers outside East Asia introduced industrial policies that were quite similar to those of latecomers inside East Asia. Politics everywhere also tended to be authoritarian, although the strength of organized labour varied. Yet economic performance in non-East Asian countries—especially in Latin America—did not equal that in East Asia. We attribute this difference to variations in *policy implementation* and effectiveness in creating labour-intensive leading sectors, especially textiles.

Because all emerging economies, including Argentina, Brazil, Chile, Mexico, India, and Turkey had no ready, internationally competitive supply capacity after the Second World War—either for export or import substitution—their industries had to be created anew or modernized. This process was attempted through measures that typically included trade protection, preferential credit, and export incentives. Outside East Asia export incentives were usually introduced slightly later, after the first energy crisis of 1973, and for social reasons the exchange rate (real wages) could not be devalued as much or sustained at as low a level, which made exporting manufactures more difficult.[22]

The inferior economic performance of the non-East Asian latecomers has been attributed by economists to poor export behaviour *tout cour*. To appreciate all the reasons behind the non-East Asian export deficiency, it is helpful to understand why the latecomers failed to become major textile producers. This failure is significant because the textile industry has few obvious competitors in its ability to generate foreign exchange and political stability, by giving large numbers of people—workers as well as small entrepreneurs—a chance to raise their incomes. Why was the textile industry not relatively more successful after the Second World War in Argentina, Brazil, Chile, and Mexico (referred to below as Latin America), especially since Latin America has a longer textile manufacturing history than East Asia and Latin American industry was generally more advanced?

The importance of textiles in total manufacturing output in prewar Latin America is suggested in Table 5.4. By 1955 the net value of manufacturing per capita was at least 50 in major Latin American countries but less than 15 in Asia (see Table 5.5).

5.4. First-Mover *Dis*-advantage?

The mechanized Latin American textile industry began in the late nineteenth and early twentieth centuries (earlier in Mexico's case). Most machinery was first imported from Europe—predominantly England, Germany, and France, and after the First World War from the United States. The industry benefited from tariff protection (sometimes designed to raise revenues rather than promote industrialization) and market-driven currency depreciation (Platt, 1973). The Great Depression caused further currency depreciation and natural protection. During the Second World War the advanced countries diverted resources from textile to wartime manufacture, providing Latin America, in theory, with an opportunity to gain market share. Theory, however, did not translate into practice.

Alice H. Amsden

Table 5.4 *Share of Textiles and Apparel in Total Manufacturing Output of Brazil, Mexico, Argentina, and Chile for Selected Years*

	Share of textiles/apparel in total manufacturing output %
Brazil	
1919	38.3
Argentina	
1914	9.6
1925–9	9.8
Chile	
1914	20.4
1929	23.4
Mexico	
1930	29.5

Sources: Data for 1914 (Chile and Argentina) adapted from Victor Bulmer-Thomas, *The Economic History of Latin America Since Independence* (Cambridge: Cambridge University Press, 1994), 138. All other data adapted from Frederick Stirton Weaver, *Class, State, and Industrial Structure: The Historical Process of South American Industrial Growth* (Greenwich, Conn.: Greenwood Press, 1980), 102.

Table 5.5 *Net Value of Manufacturing per capita, Latin America and Asia, 1955*

Country	Net value of manufacturing per capita
Asia	
Indonesia	10
Korea (Rep.)	8
Philippines	13
Thailand	10
Latin America	
Argentina	145
Brazil	50
Chile	75
Columbia	45
Mexico	60
Peru	25
Venezuela	95

Source: Alfred Maizels, *Industrial Growth and World Trade* (Cambridge: Cambridge University Press, 1963), 35.

After the war textiles became a decreasing share of manufacturing output and employment. The largest Latin American countries were self-sufficient, but the region as a whole became a net importer of around 9 per cent of total textile consumption (mostly of rayon and other synthetic fibres) (ILO, 1963).

Apart from exchange rate-related problems, the main factors behind the Latin American textile industry's fate were low productivity and costs. Low productivity was caused by old or inappropriate equipment, the small size of plants, and operating deficiencies. According to one estimate of obsolescence, 'if an old, well-organized spinning and weaving factory acquire[ed] modern equipment and re-adapt[ed] its organization to the new machinery, it would more than double labour productivity' (UNECLA, 1951: 6).

A large share of machinery in Brazil and Mexico—Latin America's major textile producers—had been bought in the 1920s and early 1930s, and had not been replaced or reconditioned since. This was due to shortages of new machinery and capital during the war. Capital markets, especially in Brazil, were not geared to long-term lending for manufacturing investments; producers in the 1950s were even having trouble financing working capital for raw materials. Borrowing abroad was made more risky by exchange rate instability, and only Chile had relatively new equipment.

Thus, even if the exchange rate environment had been more export friendly, a beginners' curse in the form of old equipment was partly to blame for the textile industry's woes.

Exchange-rate devaluation could conceivably have made Latin America's wage rates more internationally competitive, but given the region's considerably higher postwar per capita income than that of East Asia, devaluation might not have been adequate to equalize the labour cost component.[23]

Still, Latin America does not appear to have been all that uncompetitive *vis-à-vis* Asia in the early 1960s. The available data are very rough and from more than one source, but suggest a measure of parity between Brazil and India on the one hand and Chile and Hong Kong, on the other, in cotton and labour costs per unit of output. An index based on the US (= 100) for costs of cotton and labour (1960/1) to produce a yard of unbleached cotton sheeting is as follows:[24]

US	100
Japan	78
Brazil	94
Chile	125
Hong Kong	123
India	99

Brazil's advantage lay mostly in its lower unit costs of cotton (Brazil was a major cotton-producing country) while Chile's disadvantage lay in higher unit costs of both cotton and labour.

Costs of capital, electricity, and other items would have made the decisive difference in Asian and Latin American cost competitiveness in third markets, and both sets of countries required strong measures to improve productivity *vis-à-vis* Japan. Nevertheless, industrial policies in Brazil and Mexico left the restructuring of the textile industry more or less to the private sector. Targeted industries in Brazil, for example, focused on other resource-based sectors in which Brazil had a comparative advantage, such as pulp and paper, iron and steel, and petrochemicals. But, given the alternatives, the private sector—including domestic and foreign investors—did not appear to find the textile industry a very exciting financial prospect. For one, the unions in Argentina, Chile, and Mexico had considerable political and organizational power. For another, to modernize the textile industry would have involved immediate reductions in employment—the estimate for reconversion of a large textile mill in Brazil was a 40 per cent labour force cut (UNECLA, 1963). As a result, there was little enthusiasm in the government to target textiles for restructuring.

When the major Latin American textile producers did start to introduce modernization programmes (beginning in the 1960s and running until the 1980s), they may have been too late to catch up with their East Asian competitors. Between 1968 and 1974, the annual growth rate of output in the textile sector was 5 per cent in Argentina, 4 per cent in Brazil, −0.3 per cent in Chile, 8.5 per cent in Mexico, and 22 per cent in Korea. The annual growth rate of labour productivity was roughly 4 per cent in Argentina, 0 per cent in Brazil, −1.4 per cent in Chile, 5 per cent in Mexico, and 14 per cent in Korea (UNIDO, 1979: 236–7).

The same constraint, related to governmental fears of unemployment amidst unequal income distribution, impeded the modernization of textile mills in India, whose competitiveness with East Asia in the early postwar period initially appeared respectable. The failure of the Indian textile industry to export was partially the result of the large size of its domestic market and price factors.

Price competitiveness was seriously affected by sharp increases in the cost of raw cotton, rising labor costs, and relatively old capital equipment. Secondly, the pressure of domestic demand coupled with the relative attractiveness of the home market reduced the exportable surplus. The devaluation of the rupee in June 1966 did little to improve competitiveness or make exports more attractive because given the withdrawal of previous export incentives, its net effect was negligible. (Nayyar, 1973: 19)

But the failure of the Indian textile industry to become export oriented was also related to its failure to modernize:

Apart from these price factors, Indian textiles were not sufficiently competitive in world markets owing to their relatively poor quality. Although modernization of the textile industry would have led to the requisite quality improvement, it would have resulted in a considerable reduction in employment. The introduction of automatic looms on a wide scale was therefore not possible in view of the welfare implications of such a policy. (Nayyar, 1973: 19)

In the absence of modernization, exporting was beside the point.

5.5. Policy Implementation

The relative success of industrial policy in East Asia compared to other late-industrializing countries is evident in mid-technology industries as well as in labour-intensive industries. The social construction of competitive assets, not least of all the creation of hierarchically managed firms and related technological capabilities, was given greater attention and proceeded more smoothly than elsewhere.[25] In addition, the implementation of industrial policy was more effective.

Given an absence of proprietary technologies and other competitive assets comparable to those enjoyed by latecomers in the nineteenth century, industrial policies in postwar emerging economies cut far deeper into free market forces than in earlier North Atlantic experience. The deeper the intervention, the more problematic the implementation. Generally the East Asians did better at implementation than other latecomers. The *proximate* reason for this related to differences in the principles governing subsidy allocation. Deeper reasons were historical and structural. In East Asia, subsidies tended to be exchanged for concrete performance standards that were monitored by a capable bureaucracy. The principle governing subsidy allocation was one of reciprocity. Outside East Asia subsidies tended to be allocated without attached conditionality. The principle governing subsidy allocation was one of giveaway (Amsden, 1989).

This is not to say that other countries did not attempt to introduce reciprocity, a case in point being the Indian cotton textile industry in the early 1960s. Replacement of old machinery by new required large amounts of foreign exchange and placed a burden on the balance of payments. At the time, the Indian textile industry's imports of raw cotton exceeded its exports of finished products. But in 1962 'the Government permitted replacement of plain looms by automatic looms as an export promotion measure; subject to the conditions that the mills undertook to export 50 per cent of such production and gave a guarantee towards this obligation' (Nayyar, 1973: 10).

Nevertheless, the response of the textile industry was indifferent because '(1) producers were not willing to guarantee such a high proportion of exports, and (2) they could not raise adequate financial resources necessary for the replacement of old machinery. Apart from the intensely competitive nature of the world market, the incentive to export was impaired by the relative attractiveness of the home market' (Nayyar, 1973: 10). It was also insufficient, by comparison, with incentives provided in East Asia, which included preferential finance for modernization.

The Brazilian government also attempted to impose performance standards on business in exchange for subsidies. From the 1950s until the 1980s, long-term investment credit for industry came almost exclusively from a state-owned development bank, BNDES. An examination of BNDES's contracts with its clients reveals performance standards requiring that borrowers reach a minimum scale of output, hire professional managers, and have insured access to certain inputs, depending on the industry (Amsden and Behr, 1995). In almost no case, however, were performance standards tied to exports, as they were in East Asia.

Big business groups in Korea (*chaebol*) have been self-disciplined to the extent that they have competed fiercely with one another, despite the fact that group affiliates are expected to buy from each other if no better product is available from 'outside' firms.[26] Nevertheless, after 1975 intergroup competition in Korea was enhanced immeasurably by the government. Each *chaebol* tried to qualify to establish a general trading company—which promised large profit-making opportunities—by meeting tough government performance standards regarding minimum export volume and number of export products. Only in the early 1990s, at the government's instigation, did groups even begin to co-operate in technology sharing.

Under Japanese colonialism all banks in Korea (and Taiwan) were state owned. After a brief interlude in the 1950s, when, at the insistence of American aid advisers, state commercial banks were divested to private owners (better described as speculators), they were swiftly renationalized by the military government of Park Chung Hee. Banks in Taiwan during this period never succumbed to privatization. With nonbank financial institutions still relatively weak, the Ministry of Finance has maintained tight control over all forms of credit, giving the government enormous leverage over the private sector (Amsden and Euh, 1993). For instance, by regulating the financial portfolios and size of non-bank financial institutions, and by retaining power to investigate their financial irregularities, the government can still effectively determine the price of credit.

In addition, the Ministry of Finance and the Economic Planning Board (now merged into the Ministry of Finance and Economy) have disciplined companies by means of price controls in the name of curbing monopolistic abuses and dampening inflation. As late as 1986 the prices of 110 commodities were under government guidance, including flour, sugar, coffee, red pepper, electricity, gas, steel, chemicals, synthetic fibres, paper, drugs, nylon stockings, automobiles, and televisions. While such surveillance formally ended with liberalization after 1987, key oligopolies are still subject to government price surveillance.

In the case of automobiles, for example, foreign cars were not seen on Korean roads and Korean cars were not seen on foreign roads for thirty years. All the same, the industry's leader—the 90 per cent locally owned Hyundai Motor Company—became the first late-industrializing automobile maker to export to Europe and the United States. The industry was induced to cut costs and thereby raise profits because automobile prices were, and continue to be, supervised by the government. Typically, Korean automobile companies have been allowed to set the price of a new model above world prices, which helped them recoup fixed investment. Automobile companies are then pressured to keep prices down, which has induced them to improve productivity and quality. Between 1974 and 1991 average prices of Korean automobiles in real won *fell* for small, medium, and large models.

The most important performance standard imposed by the government on subsidy recipients has pertained to exports. The government protected Korean industry from foreign competition but at the same time forced it to meet export targets determined jointly by business and government, thereby bridging the dichotomy between export-led growth and import substitution. Targeted firms and industries were given subsidized credit and access to foreign exchange, but at the same time they were prevented from engaging in capital flight. Legislation passed in Korea in the 1960s stipulated that any illegal overseas transfer of $1 million or more was punishable with a minimum sentence of ten years' imprisonment and a maximum sentence of death. Companies were allowed to import foreign technology but they were pressured to build their own technological capabilities, being constrained by the Ministry of Science and Technology to import the same technology only once and at the lowest possible cost. Firms were permitted to exploit their labour, and working hours were among the longest in the world. But they had to invest in labour training (or pay a tax to finance government training programmes). Local firms were always given the advantage over foreign firms, and the government used the threat of foreign entry to elicit good performance.

Most of all, firms were disciplined informally, in the form of bureau chiefs in the Ministry of Finance, Ministry of Commerce and Industry, and Economic Planning Board telephoning company CEOs or top managers and lecturing them on appropriate behaviour. This ranged from buying locally made inputs, introducing specific foreign technologies, investing (or not) in new capacity (all capacity expansions required government approval), diversifying export markets, and improving product quality.

Such arm-twisting was facilitated in Korea by the fact that the same small set of companies operated in multiple industries. The group form of business, moreover, made discipline easy because the performance of a single conglomerate could be judged on multiple counts; only if a group succeeded in one industry would it be rewarded by the government with a licence and credit to enter yet another industry.

Thus, discipline of business by government took various direct and indirect forms, including stimuli to competition associated with the formation of general trading companies, price controls, credit allocation conditionality, performance standards attached to subsidies, and informal 'administrative guidance'.

The importance of state discipline over big business was appreciated by Korean President Park Chung Hee, along with his keen appreciation (some would say to a fault) of the central role of big business in catching up. He writes in his book, *Our Nation's Path*:

One of the essential characteristics of a modern economy is its strong tendency towards centralization. Mammoth enterprise—considered indispensable, at the moment, to our country—plays not only a decisive role in the economic development and elevation of living standards, but further, brings about changes in the structure of society and the economy. . . . Therefore, the key problems facing a free economic policy are coordination and supervisory guidance, by the state, of mammoth economic strength. (Park, 1962: 228–9)

The ability of the government to discipline subsidy recipients meant that a long-term approach to profit maximization could be adopted. Oligopolistic sectors were supported for lengthy periods, but ultimately became competitive internationally.

5.6. Japan as Pioneer: Reciprocity

Japan was the pioneer of the late-industrializing model in which competitive assets are socially constructed through a process that involves a reciprocal relationship between government and business (largely in the form of diversified business groups such as the *zaibatsu*). I would argue that major elements of this model arose even in latecomer countries that were not directly influenced by Japan, such as Brazil and Mexico.

These countries, like Japan, had to catch up without the initial competitive asset of products and processes (proprietary technologies) that had played an important role in the catch-up experience of the North Atlantic countries after the First Industrial Revolution (Hikino and Amsden, 1994). The model that arose among latecomers in East Asia, however, bore an even closer resemblance to the model in Japan. That resemblance existed because Japan had either colonized such countries, had invested in them, or had competed against them (in some cases, such as China, since the late nineteenth century). Thereby Japan's influence spread throughout the region.

An example of the reciprocal principle operating in postwar Japan concerns the machine tool industry. In exchange for protection of certain types of machine tools in the 1970s, Japanese machine tool builders were committed to devoting half their total output to advanced machine tool types by a specified date. How general reciprocity was in the allocation of subsidies in Japan, however, remains an open empirical question. It may be that reciprocity was not borrowed from Japan by other East Asian countries but was instead invented by them, especially Korea. Reciprocity may have been a response to their need for even greater government intervention than Japan found necessary, because of their fewer initial competitive assets.

5.7. Conclusion

I have tried to argue that late industrialization is a process that uses industrial policy for the purpose of socially constructing long-term competitive assets rather than deconstructing market failures. Although more empirical and theoretical work is required to develop the competitive assets approach, I would argue that the empirical evidence largely supports such an approach when the four questions raised at the beginning of this chapter are considered:

1. There was substantial government intervention in postwar latecomer countries because even labour-intensive industries (cotton textiles were the example) could not compete at market-determined production costs because of a shortage of competitive assets that created low productivity. Rather than continuing to decrease real wages (depreciate the exchange rate) to create competitiveness, governments instead chose the long-term option of supporting businesses in order to enable them to acquire technological capabilities and thereby raise productivity.

2. Hong Kong's labour-intensive industries could compete internationally without much government support (save subsidized housing) because its membership of the British Commonwealth spared it the need to compete against Japan and generous export quotas from an international export cartel secured it foreign markets. Ironically, Hong Kong benefited from the very market imperfections (trade arrangements) its economic philosophy deplored.

3. India, Brazil, and Mexico did not emerge as major postwar international players in the cotton textile industry because of their relatively large domestic markets and unequal income distribution. These made it difficult for their governments to back efforts to modernize textile capacity since it was feared that modernization would create massive labour redundancies.

4. Industrial policy in East Asia tended to be more effective than in other latecomer countries because the social construction of assets was better. In particular the social principles governing subsidy allocation were superior—reciprocity in East Asia, giveaway elsewhere.

NOTES

1. The government's help was not inconsequential, however, because all land in Hong Kong (its scarcest resource) was (and remains) government owned. Land policy enabled the government to finance an excellent system of physical infrastructure and also to subsidize workers' housing.
2. For India, see Chandavarkar (1994), Kiyokawa (1983), Matsui (1968), and Mehta (1953); for Brazil, see Stein (1957); for Mexico see Thomson (1989) and Thomson (1991); and for Korea, see Eckert (1991).
3. For the theoretical equivalence under reasonable assumptions of exchange-rate devaluation and real-wage reduction, see Krugman and Taylor (1978).
4. Where w = wages paid, π = profits earned, and e = number of workers employed. Value added is measured as either the sum of wages and profits (the value which the firm adds to the inputs it purchases from outside) or as the value of final output, which is roughly the product of final selling price times quantity sold minus the value of purchased inputs (purchased input price times purchased input quantity). Therefore, the magnitude of value added is influenced by both productivity effects and final price effects. Resources, capabilities, and their organization that reduce $(w + \pi)/e$ may be thought of as competitive liabilities.
5. Mid-technology industries are characterized by non-science-based technology, growing international demand, incremental technology improvements, and more capital and skill intensity than low-technology industries. They include transportation equipment, machinery, fabricated metals, rubber, paper, non-industrial chemicals, and certain electronic products (non-assembly operations in production and commodity products such as lower-end semiconductors). Low-technology industries include apparel, textiles, and primary metals.
6. For the distinction between inventor, pioneer, and first mover, see Chandler (1990).
7. We ignore quality innovations and assume that such breakthrough lower

domestic costs relative to international costs. In fact, quality innovations may be just as important as (or more important than) cost innovations.

8. There is not one but several market-failure approaches to economic develop-ment. One of the most perceptive emphasizes market failures due to imperfect information, see Stiglitz (1989). The one we analyse is the most influential and orthodox, which regards market distortions (failures or imperfections) as gov-ernment created and, therefore, resolvable simply by getting the government out of the economy. For a discussion of market failures, see Bator (1958) and Ledyard (1987).

9. Although high exogenous exchange prices, such as the foreign exchange rate, may raise firms' costs.

10. 'Technology' in an industry is assumed to be the same everywhere although the definition of a technology allows factor proportions to vary such that a labour-abundant country may use a labour-intensive technique but the same 'technology' as a capital-abundant country that uses a more capital-intensive technique.

11. A reduction in real wages is usually formulated in terms of a foreign exchange devaluation (we assume the two to be identical). The two are identical theoreti-cally under reasonable assumptions (Krugman and Taylor, 1978). That is, in theory a decrease in the price of domestic currency for foreigners is accomplished by a decrease in the domestic price of labour. There is also abundant empirical evidence for the postwar period that this is the case (Helleiner, 1994). Exchange rate devaluations may result in a lower rate of profit rather than a lower wage rate, although this is much less likely. For simplicity we focus in this chapter on the reduction of wages (and the price of land) to achieve international competi-tiveness and do not introduce the complications of exchange rate movements.

12. 'East Asia' in this context refers to latecomers other than Japan.

13. This fear in Korea intensified after the renewal of diplomatic relations with Japan in 1965. Taiwan loosened its restrictions on foreign investment after the United States recognized China in 1972.

14. [(OECD), 1965 #392], 62 and 72.

15. By the 1990s, per capita income in Hong Kong was roughly twice that of South Korea, suggesting that the *average* wage level was also higher. But wage dis-parities across different sectors were probably greater as well, as suggested by Hong Kong's much more unequal income distribution than South Korea's (Amsden, 1992: table 5.2).

16. The data are for 1970 (Lin, Mok, *et al.*, 1980: table 6.7); factor-intensity estimates for Korea may be found in Hong (1979).

17. For an estimate of productivity differences in textiles in Japan, Korea, and Taiwan in the mid-1960s, see Woo (1978). Even in the early 1970s value added per worker in textile manufacture differed dramatically. Kuznets (1994) estimates that at prevailing exchange rates, value added per worker in Korea was only 35.9 per cent as great as in Japan in 1970 and 36.1 per cent as great in 1977 (82).

18. The South Korean textile industry began under Japanese colonialism. One of the leading enterprises was Korean owned, and received minor subsidies from the Japanese government (Eckert, 1991). Many of the firms that were modern-ized in the 1950s (there were twelve major integrated spinning and weaving companies) originated as Japanese properties before the war (Kim, 1966).

19. See Frank, Kim, *et al.* (1975) and Liang and Liang (1982).
20. These long-term investment credits were often targeted to export-oriented industries, but do not get counted as an export subsidy. Therefore, estimates of export subsidies (and thus, estimates of real effective exchange rates) are biased downwards.
21. Around 1965 the textile industries of Korea and Taiwan also began to be transformed by the worldwide substitution of synthetic fibres for cotton fibres. Among other advantages, such substitution raised product quality and increased the effectiveness of exchange rate devaluations by reducing dependence on imports. Both governments were proactive in providing subsidies to domestic firms to begin production of synthetic fibres.
22. For an excellent account of Brazil, see Fishlow (1972). For India, see Nayyar (1973).
23. For a more general discussion of Latin America's international labour cost competitiveness, see Mahon (1992).
24. For the first four countries, see UNECLA (1963). The numbers for India and Hong Kong are extrapolated from Table 5.1 in relationship to the numbers for Japan. As Table 5.3 suggests, total costs in Japan are 78 per cent of those in the US. This is the same index number relationship between Japan and the US noted above. Nevertheless, the above comparison, unlike Table 5.3, excludes 'other costs.'
25. This major point deserves more attention than is possible here. See Amsden forthcoming) for a more thorough analysis.
26. The following discussion on Korea is based on Amsden (1996).

REFERENCES

Amsden, A. H. (1989), *Asia's Next Giant: South Korea and Late Industrialization* (Oxford and New York: Oxford University Press).
—— (1992), 'A Theory of Government Intervention in Late Industrialization', in L. Putterman and D. Rueschemeyer, *State and Market: Rivalry or Synergy?* (Boulder, Col.: Lynne Rienner).
—— (1996), 'Korea: Enterprising Groups and Entrepreneurial Government' , in Alfred D. Chandler, Jr., F. Amatori, and T. Hikino, *Big Business and the Wealth of Nations* (New York: Cambridge University Press).
—— (forthcoming), *The Rise of the Rest, 1850–2000: Late Industrialization Outside the North Atlantic Economies*.
—— and Behr, J. (1995), 'Performance Standards in the Allocation of Preferential Credit in Brazil', mimeo, MIT.
—— and Euh, Y.-D. (1993), 'South Korea's 1980s Financial Reforms: Good-bye Financial Repression (Maybe), Hello New Institutional Restraints', *World Development*, 21: 3. 379–90.

Baldwin, R. E. (1969), 'The Case Against Infant-Industry Tariff Protection', *Journal of Political Economy*, (May/June), 295–305.

Bator, F. (1958), 'The Anatomy of Market Failure', *Quarterly Journal of Economics*, 351–79.

Bhagwati, J. (1972), *Trade Policies for Development: The Gap Between Rich and Poor Nations* (Bled, Yugoslavia: Macmillan).

Chandavarkar, R. (1994), *The Bombay Cotton Textile Industry, 1900–1940* (Cambridge: Cambridge University Press).

Chandler, A. D., Jr. (1990), *Scale and Scope: The Dynamics of Industrial Capitalism* (Cambridge, Mass.: Harvard University Press).

Crouzet, F. (1972), 'Western Europe and Great Britain: 'Catching Up' in the First Half of the Nineteenth Century', in . A. J. Youngson, *Economic Development in the Long Run* (London: George Allen and Unwin), 98–125.

Eckert, C. J. (1991), *Offspring of Empire: The Koch'ang Kims and the Colonial Origins of Korean Capitalism* (Seattle: University of Washington Press).

Economic Planning Board (1962), *Economic Survey* (Seoul).

Fishlow, A. (1972), 'Origins and Consequences of Import Substitution in Brazil', in L. E. DiMarco, *International Economics and Development: Essays in Honor of Raul Prebisch* (New York: Academic Press).

Frank, C. J., Kim, K. S., *et al.* (1975), *Foreign Trade Regimes and Economic Development: South Korea* (New York: NBER).

General Agreement on Tariffs and Trade (GATT) (1966), 'A Study on Cotton' (Geneva).

Helleiner, G. K. (1994) (ed.), *Trade Policy and Industrialization in Turbulent Times* (New York and Oxford: Oxford University Press).

Hikino, T., and Amsden, A. H. (1994), 'Staying Behind, Stumbling Back, Sneaking Up, Soaring Ahead: Late Industrialization in Historical Perspective', in R. R. William, J. Baumol, and Edward N. Wolff, *Convergence of Productivity: Cross-National Studies and Historical Evidence* (New York and Oxford: Oxford University Press), 285–315.

Ho, Y.-P., and Lin, T.-B. (1991), 'Structural Adjustment in a Free-Trade, Free Market Economy', in H. Patrick, *Pacific Basin Industries in Distress: Structural Adjustment and Trade Policy in the Nine Industrialized Economies* (New York: Columbia University Press).

Hong, W. (1979), *Trade, Distortions and Employment Growth in Korea* (Seoul: Korea Development Institute).

ILO (1963), *Textile Industry and World Growth* (Geneva).

Kim, J. B. (1966), 'The Korean Cotton Manufacturing Industry', Ph.D. diss., University of Berkeley, Calif.

Kim, Y.-B. (1980), 'The Growth and Structural Change of the Textile Industry', in C. K. Park, *Macroeconomic and Industrial Development in Korea* (Seoul: Korea Development Institute), iii.

Kiyokawa, Y. (1983), 'Technical Adaptation and Managerial Resources in India: A Study of the Experience of the Cotton Textile Industry from a Comparative Viewpoint', *Developing Economies*, 21.

Krueger, A. O. (1984), 'Trade Policies in Developing Countries', in R. W. Jones and P. B. Kenan, *Handbook of International Economics* (Amsterdam: North Holland).

Krugman, P., and Taylor, L. (1978), 'Contractionary Effects of Devaluation', *Journal of International Economics*, 8. 445–56.

Kuznets, P. W. (1994), *Korean Economic Development: An Interpretive Model* (Westport, Conn.: Praeger).

Ledyard, J. O. (1987), 'Market Failure', in J. Eatwell, M. Milgate, and P. Newman, *The New Palgrave Dictionary of Economics* (London: Macmillan), iii. 326–8.

Liang, K.-S., and Liang, C.-I. H. (1982), 'Trade and Incentive Policies in Taiwan', in K.-T. Li and T.-S. Yu, *Experiences and Lessons of Economic Development in Taiwan* (Taipei: Academia Sinica).

Lin, K.-S., Mok, V., *et al.* (1980), *Manufactured Exports and Employment in Hong Kong* (Hong Kong: Chinese University Press).

Mahon, J. E. J. (1992), 'Was Latin America Too Rich to Prosper? Structural and Political Obstacles to Export-Led Industrial Growth', *Journal of Development Studies*, 28 (Jan.), 241–63.

Matsui, T. (1968), 'On the Nineteenth-Century Indian Economic History—A Review of a "Reinterpretation" ', *Indian Economic and Social History Review*, 5:1 (Mar.).

Mehta, D. S. (1953), *The Indian Cotton Textile Industry: An Economic Analysis*, G. K. Ved for the Textile Association.

Nayyar, D. (1973), 'An Analysis of the Stagnation in India's Cotton Textile Exports During the 1960s', *Oxford Bulletin of Economics and Statistics*, 35:1. 1–19.

Park, Chung Hee (1962), *Our Nations Path: Ideology for Social Reconstruction* (Seoul: Dong-A.).

Platt, D. C. M. (1973), *Latin America and British Trade, 1806–1914* (New York: Harper and Row).

Stein, S. J. (1957), *The Brazilian Cotton Manufacture: Textile Enterprise in an Underdeveloped Area, 1850–1950* (Cambridge, Mass.: Harvard University Press).

Stiglitz, J. E. (1989), 'Markets, Market Failures, and Development', *American Economic Review*, 79:2. 196–203.

Thomson, G. P. C. (1989), *Puebla de Los Angeles: Industry and Society in a Mexican City, 1700–1850* (Boulder, Col.: Westview Press).

—— (1991), 'Continuity and Change in Mexican Manufacturing, 1800–1870', in J. Batou, *Between Development and Underdevelopment: The Precocious Attempts at Industrialization of the Periphery, 1800–1870* (Geneva: Librairie Droz), 255–302.

United Nations Economic Commission for Latin America (UNECLA) (1951), *Labour Productivity of the Cotton Textile Industry* (New York).

—— (1963), *The Textile Industry in Latin America* ii. *Brazil* (New York).

United Nations Industrial Development Organization (UNIDO) (1979), *World Industry Since 1960: Progress and Prospects* (New York).

United States Senate (1961), *Hearings before a Subcommittee of the Committee on Interstate and Foreign Commerce* (Washington: Government Printing Office).

Woo, K. D. (1978), 'Wages and Labor Productivity in the Cotton Spinning Industries of Japan, Korea, and Taiwan', *Developing Economies*, 16.

World Bank (1993), *The East Asian Miracle: Economic Growth and Public Policy* (Oxford: Oxford University Press).

PART III

PRIME MOVERS

ANTITRUST POLICY WITH INSIGNIFICANT INDUSTRIAL POLICY

6

Postwar US Antitrust Policy, Corporate Strategy, and International Competitiveness

WILLIAM H. BECKER

6.1. Introduction

The United States did not adopt explicit industrial policies in the postwar period. This is not to say that the American government failed to affect the behaviour of business. Indeed, the Great Depression of the 1930s and the Second World War had markedly increased the power of the government in Washington over economic activity, with important consequences for corporate enterprise.

But once the conflict ended there was little public support for a continuation of wartime's direct government micromanagement of industry. Instead, the experiences of war and depression prompted a more general approach to the economy, towards a reliance on macroeconomic Keynesian policy and liberalized international trade. There were, however, important exceptions. The independent regulatory agencies established or strengthened in the 1930s over banking, securities, transportation, broadcasting, telecommunications, and energy continued their work in the early decades of the postwar period. Another exception involved defence-related industries. Because of Cold War national security needs the federal government continued to fund substantial research and development efforts in the high-tech industries of aeronautics, jet propulsion, nuclear energy, electronics, and computers. The US Department of Defense and agencies concerned with energy were the major purchasers of products resulting from this research.

Antitrust policy proved to be an exception, too, and received increased attention in the postwar period. Indeed, Congress strengthened antitrust law in 1950 by adopting the Celler–Kefauver Act. The law was passed at a time when the Truman administration (1945–53) had filed an unprecedented number of antitrust suits against major corporations. Based on the 1950 legislation, the Eisenhower administration (1953–61) announced new guidelines for mergers in 1955. The government's strong antitrust stance in regard to mergers during both Democratic and Republican administrations demanded the attention of corporate strategists in the 1950s and 1960s.

This chapter addresses the theme of the 23rd Fuji Conference—the interrelationship between government policy (that is, for the purposes here, antitrust policy), business behaviour, and international competitiveness—by focusing attention on several questions. What was the antitrust tradition in the United States? Why was there a continued commitment to an antitrust policy after the war? Why and how did the antitrust policy and its use by government officials change in the postwar period? To what degree did the antitrust policy affect the strategic behaviour of large-scale enterprise in the decades following the Second World War? What role did this altered behaviour play in the international competitiveness of major businesses in key industries?

In answering these questions, this chapter argues that the impact of the government's pursuit of an antitrust policy did not uniformly influence corporate strategy, nor were its consequences always the government's intent. As such, it is difficult to attribute to antitrust policy sweeping, direct consequences for the competitiveness of particular American enterprises and their related industries during the postwar period.

This is not to say that the antitrust policy was unimportant. In the postwar years it helped shape the strategic options of corporate managers. But it channelled, rather than directed, corporate behaviour. As a policy, it was never so rationally enforced that it provided corporate leaders with only one possible strategic option, nor were business strategies regularly adopted only because of the antitrust policy. It was only one part of the environment influencing top executives who formulated corporate strategy. For firms in some industries the antitrust policy profoundly influenced corporate strategy; in others the influence was considerably less.

In any event, antitrust policy in the postwar years provides a significant example of the unusual ways in which business and government interacted in the American political economy. Partisan political considerations influenced the adoption of antitrust law and the way in which different presidents chose to apply it. The internal organizational dynamics of the agencies created to administer the antitrust policy also influenced decisions on when and in what industries antitrust laws would be employed. The antitrust policy also points up the importance of the legal profession in the American political economy.

The federal courts, in particular the Supreme Court, defined and redefined what was and was not permissible under the antitrust laws. Private antitrust attorneys served as intermediaries between their corporate clients and the government. The most prominent among them were key figures in the 'community of expertise' or 'issue network' that focused its professional work on antitrust policy in the postwar period (Heclo, 1978: 103–4). They closely followed the government's filing of suits, court opinions, and the work of legal theorists and academic economists on antitrust subjects.

Together, this community of experts took part in the debates that reshaped theories about antitrust policy. By the 1970s an influential group of academics on the law and economics faculties at the University of Chicago had challenged the basic premises of the antitrust tradition. During the presidency of Ronald Reagan (1981–9) their ideas provided the intellectual justification for the political decision virtually to abandon antitrust as a major tool of government policy.

6.2. Antitrust in Perspective

In 1950 the US Congress strengthened the country's antitrust laws by passing the Celler–Kefauver Act, sometimes referred to as the anti-merger act of 1950. The new legislation was passed in the midst of a highly partisan political debate about the influence of big business in the economy, and about the need to protect consumers and small businesses from the concentrated power of large-scale enterprise. The original antitrust legislation, the Sherman Antitrust Act of 1890, had passed Congress under similar circumstances.

After the adoption of that legislation in 1890, government officials viewed antitrust as law enforcement. Indeed, the Sherman Act was a criminal statute. Congress had hoped to achieve desirable economic outcomes by having the government's executive branch enforce the law through the adversarial proceedings of the courts. Individual enterprises could also bring suit against competitors for violating the 1890 antitrust statute. If successful, the injured party could recover damages, a private legal remedy designed to make enterprises obey the law.

During the century that followed, the government's decision to bring a suit was often a political matter decided by presidents and their advisers. The latter included the Attorney General (the chief law enforcement officer of the federal government) and, after 1933, the Assistant Attorney General in charge of antitrust. In that year Congress established a separate Antitrust Division in the federal Department of Justice under an Assistant

Attorney General. The new division grew in staff and resources in the postwar period and became an important influence in how and when antitrust suits were brought (Eisner, 1991: 23–5, 58–69).[1]

The federal courts have also played an important role in enforcing and defining antitrust. Because the parties in an antitrust suit frequently appealed against the decisions of lower federal courts, cases often reached the Supreme Court. Because the 1890 Sherman Act stated its objectives in broad and vague language, that body had a continuing part to play in defining the meaning of the law. As the makeup of the court changed with deaths and retirements over the years, new justices revisited antitrust doctrine. As a result, the Supreme Court continued to play a key role well into the postwar period—which it has jealously guarded—in defining what was and was not legal under antitrust legislation.

Antitrust enforcement, therefore, has not been the preserve of professional civil servants applying objective standards to achieve the goals of a well-articulated public policy. Enforcement of the antitrust laws has depended heavily on judicial, political, and bureaucratic opinion. Thus, changing presidential administrations, the makeup of the Supreme Court, and the internal dynamics of the Antitrust Division have influenced the enforcement of antitrust laws. 'Indeed', as one student of antitrust legislation has observed, 'enforcement of the antitrust laws has been sporadic, and to some degree, idiosyncratic' (Fligstein, 1990: 192–3).

The uncertainty, vagueness, and complexity of the law forced corporate leaders to rely on law firms that specialized in antitrust litigation. As early as 1900, major law firms in New York and Chicago had partners who almost exclusively had an antitrust practice. By the 1950s one of the best attended meetings at the annual gathering of the American Bar Association was of specialists in antitrust law. Meetings of the ABA's antitrust section provided a venue for the interaction between corporate and governmental antitrust legal specialists.

The latter included officials and staff from the Justice Department and the Federal Trade Commission (FTC), as well as high-ranking congressional staff members who advised members of Congress on antitrust matters. By the 1960s academic economists and legal theorists took part in these meetings and published in specialized antitrust journals (Eisner, 1991: 98–9; Fligstein, 1990: 212–14).

When the government began to prosecute an antitrust policy more aggressively in the 1940s and 1950s, attorneys in private practice at major law firms became important consultants to business leaders on the antitrust implications of business strategy. On behalf of their corporate clients, these attorneys often solicited unofficial opinions from the justice department about the legality of planned mergers (Eisner, 1991: 23–4).[2]

Private antitrust attorneys thus served as important intermediaries between government and corporation. Their value was enhanced if they had served—as many did—in the Justice Department or FTC for a few years before taking lucrative positions in private law firms as antitrust specialists. There was also some movement in the other direction. In the postwar years key officials in the Antitrust Division were drawn at times from among prominent private practitioners of antitrust law (Eisner, 1991: 87; Fligstein, 1990: 213–14).

Whether in government or private practice, antitrust attorneys took part in the intense and partisan debates that led to the first piece of postwar antitrust legislation—the Celler–Kefauver Act of 1950. The legislation strengthened a weakness originally contained in the Clayton Antitrust Act of 1914. This piece of legislation, and the Federal Trade Commission Act of the same year, had been designed to clarify some of the ambiguities in the original Sherman Act of 1890. The Clayton Act outlined more specifically what the government considered to be illegal anti-competitive practices. The Federal Trade Commission Act established an independent agency to define and prosecute anti-competitive practices (Eisner, 1991: 23–5; Fligstein, 1990: 93, 96).

Section 7 of the Clayton Act forbid an enterprise from gaining control of a competitor by buying shares in its business. As interpreted by the courts, however, the Clayton Act did not prevent acquisitions by merger or the outright purchase of another firm's physical assets. For decades, proponents of rigorous antitrust enforcement saw this as a serious weakness in the law. It seemed to allow firms to grow larger by merger, without the likelihood of prosecution under existing antitrust laws (Eisner, 1991: 23–5; Fligstein, 1990: 25, 77).

The political partisanship that accompanied the 1950 legislation was not unusual. Indeed, the original antitrust legislation (the Sherman Act) had emerged in 1890 following more than a decade of sharp public debate over the proper relationship between concentrated economic power and a democratic polity. Political partisanship also accompanied the antitrust prosecutions of the early 1900s. Business leaders objected to the sensationalized manner (public news conferences) in which some of the government's antitrust suits were announced (see Freyer, 1992; Lamoreaux, 1985; and Sklar, 1988).

Of more importance, conflicting and contradictory decisions handed down by the Supreme Court in the early decades of the century made corporate planning difficult. At times the Court seemed to oppose all combinations designed to create large-scale enterprise. At other times, however, it would allow some, as long as they were 'reasonable'. What constituted reasonableness ensured a continued role for the federal courts in antitrust matters, but became a source of further uncertainty among business leaders (Sklar, 1988: 137–48).

By 1920 the Supreme Court had provided what proved to be a definitive decision on antitrust law. In breaking up American Tobacco and Standard

Oil in 1911, the justices had set a new standard for judging the legality of corporate behaviour. That is, violations of the antitrust law turned on whether the offending party *intended* to harm its competitors. Did it try to force competitors out of business by price wars or 'predatory pricing'(Sklar, 1988: 137–48)?

The Supreme Court reaffirmed this interpretation based on intent in its 1920 decision in a case against United States Steel brought by the government. At the time, US Steel controlled substantial percentages of basic and fabricated steel capacity. The court stated that size (judged by value of assets or market share) did not matter *per se*. Instead, the crucial legal test remained the behaviour and intentions of corporate managers *vis-à-vis* their competitors. Intent was a concept well suited to a body of legislation and judicial opinion concerned with enforcing the law. It was something that judges, prosecutors, and attorneys could form judgments about, based on documentary evidence gained from corporate files and the testimony of witnesses under oath (Freyer, 1992: 188–91; Sklar, 1988: 150–1).

During the 1920s, the government reduced the number of antitrust prosecutions compared to the previous decade. Most cases involved smaller enterprises who had continued to engage in horizontal cartel behaviour. Antitrust enforcement remained comparatively slack for much of the 1930s. Indeed, many believed that price deflation in the 1930s had been brought on by an excess of competition in the 1920s. Moreover, the administration of Franklin D. Roosevelt (1933–45) in effect suspended enforcement of the antitrust laws in the early 1930s (see Table 6.1).

Through the National Recovery Administration (1933–5) the government encouraged industrial collusion. The NRA allowed industries to fix prices and reduce production to increase profits. Increased profits, the scheme hoped, would then lead to higher levels of investment and hence recovery. Not surprisingly, the NRA—based on dubious economic reasoning—did not work as planned. Following an adverse ruling by the Supreme Court about the NRA's constitutionality, Roosevelt abandoned it in 1935, less than two years after its founding (Hawley, 1966: 166).

In 1938 the Roosevelt administration returned to antitrust enforcement. The year before, an already slow economic recovery stalled. Deterioration in major economic indicators (unemployment, industrial output, business bankruptcies) suggested the return of the worst conditions of the depression. Roosevelt administration officials believed that the largest enterprises in oligopolistic industries contributed to the slow pace of recovery. Because of their market power, big businesses operated at reduced levels of employment and investment, while still enjoying adequate returns on the assets they employed (Bain, 1956; Hawley, 1966: ch. 20).

In public, Roosevelt adopted a more political, partisan explanation. Big business, he argued, withheld investment because of its opposition to his plans for reform and recovery. In 1938, the president appointed a high-

Table 6.1 *Cases Brought by Department of Justice*

Year	Number	Year	Number	Year	Number	Year	Number
1920	11	1928	11	1936	9	1944	25
1921	26	1929	10	1937	8	1945	25
1922	22	1930	3	1938	13	1946	43
1923	10	1931	5	1939	38	1947	33
1924	16	1932	11	1940	82	1948	56
1925	14	1933	9	1941	105	1949	35
1926	11	1934	8	1942	74	1950	60
1927	21	1935	4	1943	38	1951	55

Source: Fligstein (1990: 168).

profile special study board—the Temporary National Economic Commission—to investigate the dimensions and consequences of concentration in American industry. Its task was to propose measures to strengthen the existing antitrust laws and to identify industries in which enterprises seemed to be violating those laws.

At the same time, the administration substantially increased funding and staffing for the Antitrust Division. Included in the expansion of the division was the hiring of several staff economists who were assigned to assist in the review of potential suits. The Antitrust Division markedly increased the numbers of cases; many of the suits were accompanied by intense publicity (see Table 6.1). In 1941, a record was reached with the filing of 105 suits; from 1918 to 1928, the annual average had been about ten (Eisner, 1991: 80–3; Fligstein, 1990: 167–8).

When the United States entered the Second World War, the Roosevelt administration deferred antitrust prosecutions. High-profile suits complicated the government's relations with large-scale enterprises needed for the war effort. By the end of the war, 100 of the country's largest industrial corporations were operating 75 per cent of the government-financed plants for the war effort (McQuaid, 1994: 12–15).

After the war, Roosevelt's successor, Harry S. Truman (1945–53), revived antitrust prosecutions. In 1948 as the Democratic party's candidate for president, Truman attacked the anti-competitive practices of big business in his campaign for re-election. His surprise victory, along with his party's winning a majority in both houses for control of Congress, was followed by an intensified antitrust campaign against 'bigness' in industry. In the five years after the war, the Department of Justice filed 167 antitrust suits. Included in this number were cases against at least 50 of the 100 largest industrial corporations. Major firms subjected to a challenge included DuPont, A.T. & T., US Steel, ALCOA, General Motors, the major meat-packing companies, and several firms in the tyre and petroleum industries (Fligstein, 1990: 170, 197).

In this charged political atmosphere, the Truman administration co-operated with Democrats in Congress to strengthen the antitrust laws. The result—following well-publicized hearings—was the Celler–Kefauver Act of 1950 that tightened the provisions of the 1914 Clayton Act regarding horizontal and vertical mergers. The act stated that 'no corporation . . . shall acquire the whole or part of any of the assets of another corporation engaged also in commerce, where . . . the effect of such acquisition may be substantially to lessen competition, or tend to create a monopoly'. This provision formed the basis for postwar prosecutions of mergers, which became the major activity of the Antitrust Division and the FTC (Eisner, 1991: 23–4; Fligstein, 1990: 173–90; Neale & Goyder, 1980: 181–6).

By the time Congress passed the Celler–Kefauver Act, however, the principles upon which the government based antitrust prosecutions had already undergone a change. The new thinking had resulted from the studies of the Antitrust Division in the late 1930s. Economists on the staff of the Antitrust Division were central to the development of new principles. Their ideas had been influenced by accepted interpretations of industrial economics at the time. They focused on market structure as the foundation for determining whether antitrust law was violated, instead of management's intent to employ monopolistic practices against competitors. The staff economists argued that market structure was directly connected to corporate behaviour and performance. Dominant firms in highly concentrated industries were therefore almost automatically suspect. Under these principles of what was called a Structure-Conduct-Performance (SCP) analysis, large enterprises dominant in their industries were likely to be guilty of administering prices and limiting production in order to reduce competition and increase profits (Eisner, 1991: 77, 100–10).

The federal courts first accepted an SCP interpretation in a decision against ALCOA (*United States* v. *Aluminum Co. of America*) in 1945. Intent to monopolize, the government argued, was implied in the company's long-time market dominance. Linking structure to conduct in this case also made the government's task easier by reducing the need of direct evidence for intent to monopolize (Eisner, 1991: 76–85, 100–3).

By the 1960s and 1970s, the SCP precepts had won over most legal and judicial practitioners of antitrust legislation. But appeals to economic analysis invited scrutiny by academic economists and legal theorists. Beginning in the 1960s and increasingly in the 1970s, adherents to a new school of industrial organizational economics offered a potent criticism of the SCP approach to antitrust legislation. Referred to as the Chicago School—because key legal and economic theorists were on the faculty of the University of Chicago—these scholars challenged the links among structure, conduct, and performance. Leading proponents of the Chicago

School maintained that in essence the market itself would punish those who acted in ways contrary to economic rationality, that is, to the efficient employment of assets to maximize profits. The only role the Chicago School saw for invoking an antitrust policy was to prevent price-fixing. By the end of the 1970s, their ideas had virtually won over the expert community of antitrust specialists.[3]

By then, too, a majority on the Supreme Court had come to accept the new mode of thinking propounded by the Chicago School. During the Reagan administration (1981–9), the head of the Antitrust Division himself was a prominent convert to the Chicago School analysis. As a result, the 1980s witnessed a significant decline in the number of antitrust cases brought by the government (Eisner, 1991: 100–10).

While antitrust theorists engaged in a rigorous debate about first principles, the actual enforcement of antitrust laws was carried out much as it had always been prior to the 1980s. Most heads of the Antitrust Division in the postwar years spoke about the need for well-articulated guidelines for enforcing antitrust legislation. Some produced such documents. But none of them stayed in the job long enough to carry through with a series of prosecutions consistent with such pronouncements. In fact, cases against major firms were often taken up in response to complaints from competitors (see Table 6.2). These cases were not the result of some larger strategy of antitrust enforcement (Eisner, 1991: 126–35).

Table 6.2 *Private Antitrust Cases*

Year	Number
1960	228
1965	472
1970	877
1975	1,375
1980	1,457
1985	1,052

Source: Kovaleff (1994: ii. 659).

In any event, most of the antitrust cases filed by the Justice Department in the postwar years under the Celler–Kefauver Act were brought against firms that had formed horizontal mergers. These routine cases had always represented the bulk of antitrust prosecutions. The Celler–Kefauver Act made it easier for the government to win such cases (Eisner, 1991: 86–7; Fligstein, 1990: 196).

The professional publications of antitrust lawyers and the business press—and, one assumes, the private consultations between attorneys and clients—warned corporate executives against horizontal and vertical

mergers. Mounting a defence in an antitrust prosecution was time con-
suming and could seriously disrupt corporate planning. It also could
prove expensive. In 1958, for example, the government won its first major
case against a large vertical merger under the Celler–Kefauver Act (*United
States* v. *Bethlehem Steel*). Bethlehem Steel acquired Youngstown Sheet &
Tube in 1957. Bethlehem was ranked second among steel producers and
Youngstown sixth. Bethlehem, located on the east coast, acquired
Youngstown to enter the midwestern market for steel. Following the
court's adverse decision, Bethlehem entered the midwestern market by
building a major plant near Chicago. The latter strategy cost the company
more than the original acquisition would have done. Similarly,
International Telephone & Telegraph, a leading conglomerate firm, made
three major purchases of companies in 1968. In 1969, the government filed
suit, and after three years of legal manoeuvring, ITT consented to divest
some of its acquisitions before the case reached the Supreme Court. This,
too, proved an expensive decision for ITT (Eisner, 1991: 207–11; Greer,
1992: 225, 232).

6.3. Antitrust and Corporate Strategy in Postwar America

What impact, then, did the Celler–Kefauver Act of 1950 and the prosecutions initiated by the Antitrust Division have on corporate strategy in the
postwar period? In the 1960s and 1970s observers believed that data on
merger activity indicated a fairly direct link between antitrust policy and
corporate behaviour (see Table 6.3). These data also suggested that
antitrust policy had important unintended consequences. Instead of slowing mergers the new law and government antitrust policy seemed to be
the driving force in an unprecedented merger movement in the 1950s and
1960s, a period of time in which related (diversified) and unrelated (conglomerate) mergers increased (Adelman, 1961: 236–54; Mueller, 1977:
315–47; Stigler, 1966: 225–58).

   Some of the largest corporations in the United States implemented
diversification strategies by putting together unrelated mergers. They
acquired new businesses in both distantly related and unrelated lines of
business. In these same years a few enterprises adopted explicit strategies
of conglomeration, which took diversification a step further. That is, corporate leaders made it the focus of their enterprise to acquire numerous
unrelated businesses by merger. These enterprises remained part of conglomerates so long as they produced satisfactory financial returns. When
they did not, they were sold, 'divested' in the parlance of the time.

Table 6.3 *Number of Mergers over $10 Million*

Type of merger	1951–5	1956–60	1961–5	1966–70	1971–7
Horizontal	59	82	78	77	133
Vertical	20	36	52	51	35
Related	55	98	143	326	163
Unrelated	20	41	52	186	163
Number of mergers	154	257	325	640	494

Source: Fligstein (1990: 195).

In any event, the links between the government's filing of antitrust suits and the number and nature of mergers seemed apparent. Between 1940 and 1947 there had been 2,062 mergers worth $1 million or more; between 1948 and 1953 the number dropped to 58. This change followed the government's filing of suits against major corporations after the war and Democrat Harry Truman's unexpected victory in the presidential election of 1948 (Fligstein, 1990: 195).

The numbers of mergers began to pick up in the early 1950s and led, in the following decades, to one of the longest merger movements in American history. During American involvement in the Korean war (1950–4), the government backed off on antitrust prosecutions for much the same reason as it had during the Second World War (the need for a close working relationship with key industries producing war-related goods). The election of Republican President Dwight D. Eisenhower in 1952 also seemed to promise a less interventionist government than had been the case under Truman (Fligstein, 1990: 197–8).

By 1955, however, the Eisenhower administration (1953–61) had begun to file antitrust suits as merger activity increased. Indeed, Eisenhower took the issue of antitrust enforcement from the Democrats and identified it with the Republican's commitment to free markets. During Eisenhower's two administrations, the Department of Justice filed over 300 antitrust suits.

In the bulk of these cases in the 1950s (and in the 1960s as well) the government prosecuted horizontal and vertical mergers much more frequently than mergers of firms in distantly related and unrelated industries. This was the case, even though through the 1960s horizontal and vertical mergers made up a smaller percentage of the total number of mergers.

Between 1951 and 1956, 86 per cent of the mergers challenged under the Celler–Kefauver Act were horizontal and vertical, even though they made up only 51 per cent of mergers in those years. By the end of the 1960s (1966–70), 81 per cent of the suits under the Celler–Kefauver Act were filed against horizontal and vertical mergers, although they represented only

19 per cent of mergers valued at over $10 million at the time (Kovaleff, 1980: app. A).

In short, the largest number of mergers was among unrelated businesses, those prosecuted the least under the antitrust laws. These statistics suggest a strong link between corporate behaviour and antitrust policy.

Yet, was an antitrust suit, or even the threat of one, enough to induce top management to alter corporate strategy? In some cases the answer is apparently yes. Frequent consultations between the Antitrust Division and attorneys representing corporate clients must have dissuaded executives against vertical or horizontal acquisitions. Acquisitions in distantly related or unrelated markets clearly would pose less risk.

But to gain a fuller perspective of the impact of antitrust enforcement on corporate strategy, it is necessary to examine the larger context in which executives made decisions to diversify. To be sure, the government's enforcement of antitrust laws shaped options and channelled corporate behaviour in certain directions. Between 1951 and 1977 almost all enterprises with assets of $1 billion or more undertaking horizontal or vertical mergers faced an antitrust suit—127 out of 136 (Fligstein, 1990: 203).

Nevertheless, strategic decision-making was the result of numerous influences, both from inside and outside the corporation. The mix of pressures changed from enterprise to enterprise, and from time to time in the same enterprise. Most corporate executives were clearly influenced by the prospect of antitrust prosecutions. But there were others.

From inside the corporation, the interests of stockholders—a key element in the structure of corporate governance in the United States—were an important influence on corporate strategists in the postwar period. Despite the division between owners and managers, in practice and in law managers could not ignore their stockholders. There might have been agency problems in the American system, but ultimately the basic interests of stockholders had to be addressed (Donaldson, 1994: 24–8).

In the postwar period, stockholders in the highest income categories preferred long-term growth to short-term gains. Comparatively high personal income tax rates inclined stockholders towards capital gains over dividend income. In 1952, only 4.2 per cent of the population—among the wealthiest people in the country—held stocks. In that year households held 91 per cent of corporate equities; financial institutions held only 7 per cent. While the holdings of financial institutions increased in the next decades, households (for the most part those of wealthy individuals) still held the bulk of corporate equities. (In 1960 the percentages were 87 per cent for households and 11 per cent for financial institutions; in 1970 the percentages were 79 per cent and 17 per cent.) Wealthy stockholders preferred capital gains to dividend income because in the 1950s those in the highest tax brackets faced a 70 per cent tax rate (Blair and Uppal, 1993: 26–7; Chandler, 1994: 16–17, 21; Donaldson, 1994: 29).

This preference posed an essential challenge to management. Mature companies with stable technologies which were dominant in their markets found it harder to increase market share as time went on. Industries included in this group were textiles and apparel; rubber and plastics; stone, clay, and glass; primary metals; fabricated metal products; engines, farm, and construction machinery; and transportation equipment.

The rate of growth of dominant firms in established markets tended to reflect that of their industries as a whole. In the early postwar years, this was not a serious issue because of the dominance American firms had in a world recovering from war. By the mid-1960s, however, mature industries had excess capacity, a problem exacerbated by competition from firms in an economically recovered Europe and Japan. By the later 1970s, US manufacturing was operating at less than 70 per cent capacity and rates of corporate profit registered a significant decline from the 1950s. The automobile, steel, and textile industries were particularly troubled.[4]

In these circumstances, the government's antitrust policy limited options. Acquisition of firms in the same industry, especially for large companies, invited prosecution or at least troublesome delays from the Justice Department. Of course acquiring competing firms in a slow-growing industry was not necessarily a good strategic option in any event. Thus, depending on the industry, in the 1960s and 1970s unrelated diversification proved a more attractive option than before (see Table 6.4). Nevertheless, vertical integration and overseas expansion remained the most common strategy among the largest industrial corporations (Donaldson, 1994: 28).

Table 6.4 *Strategies of Largest 100 Industrial Corporations, 1919–1979*

Strategy	1919–29	1929–39	1939–45	1948–59	1959–69	1969–79
Vertical	52	72	81	85	74	71
Related	13	15	20	35	56	53
Unrelated	—	—	—	8	11	22
Multinational	41	54	62	64	77	92

Note: For each decade, the total is larger than 100 because firms entered and left the category of the 100 largest. Also, there is overlap between multinational and other strategies.

Source: Fligstein (1990: 145).

Armco Steel—the forty-third largest US manufacturing company in terms of assets in 1948—provides a good example of a firm following a strategy of diversification. By the late 1950s the effects of the postwar boom for steel had worn off. At the same time, inexpensive aluminium substitutes for steel and increasing labour difficulties convinced top management that, even if steel were not exactly a dying industry, they had to find other places to invest. At first, they modernized their steel-making operation to reduce costs and increase efficiency. They then invested in a related industry, by purchasing a major producer of oil field equipment. Armco began to produce the tubular steel used in pipelines. In the 1960s they also acquired a major producer of non-metallic materials. By that time management had also moved into financial services and, in the 1970s, the company moved into the equipment-leasing business (Donaldson, 1994: 31–4).

Management at Armco and other diversifying firms financed their strategies through retained earnings. As such, top managers followed decades of corporate practice by retaining significant proportions of earnings for reinvestment. Strategists preferred this internal capital market to cash obtained through the sales of new equities. The latter would have reduced earnings per share, a standard measure of corporate performance at the time.[5]

Diversification strategies promised corporate leaders the growth needed to produce the capital gains preferred by stockholders in high-income tax brackets. They also held out the prospect of reduced risk and greater stability, as corporate leaders invested earnings in businesses with different market cycles. Risk reduction was attractive to a generation of corporate leaders who had begun their careers in the depression of the 1930s, in the midst of shrinking industrial markets and financial collapse. Diversification simply appeared to managers as a prudent way to manage corporate resources (Donaldson, 1994: 28–31).

Moreover, diversification was not a radical departure from past practice. It had developed during the depression and the Second World War. In the 1930s, industrial corporations had moved into new lines of business to cope with declining sales in core markets. Managers in industries as different as food processing and petroleum sought new—and usually related—product markets by diversification. Under the pressure of the Second World War, however, some businesses diversified into totally unrelated business activities.

Thus, General Mills, a leading producer of flour and prepackaged baking goods, produced ordnance during the war under government contract. The success in this effort predisposed management to diversify in the postwar period. In the 1950s and 1960s, General Mills acquired companies that produced household appliances, chemicals, and electronic products for the military (Bernstein, 1987: 61–70; Donaldson, 1994: 91–3; Fligstein, 1990: 144–60; Winter, 1993: 55–79).

In addition to the success of past experience with diversification, the promise of long-term, low-risk growth held other attractions for managers. It allowed them to make generous contract settlements with organized union employees while holding out the prospect of assured long-term employment. More generally, diversification strategies built loyalty among the corporation's managerial ranks. Managers at all levels could look forward to increasing pay and benefits while participating in unusual ventures which opened up new career paths (Donaldson, 1994: 24–8).

Top managers who succeeded in achieving high levels of growth through diversification strategies could look to their peers for approval. Growth became the measure of corporate achievement, even beyond short-term profitability, in the first two postwar decades. Graduate schools of management and the business press routinely extolled the wisdom of such strategies and lauded those successful in pursuing them (Donaldson, 1994: 26–8, 32, 34).

But not all industries had enterprises that utilized strategies of diversification to meet managers' and stockholders' interest in growth. In the high-tech industries producing pharmaceuticals, electronic components, computing equipment, scientific instruments, aircraft, and aerospace products, top managers followed a different strategy to achieve the benefits that growth brought to enterprises in mature industries (Chandler, 1994: app. C; Hall, 1994: 121–31).

Corporate strategists in high-tech enterprises sought growth by intensifying investment in promising technologies. Many of the new technologies of the postwar period—computers, jet propulsion, aeronautics, antibiotics, television, nuclear power—had advanced because of substantial government support during the Second World War and then during the Cold War that followed (see Table 6.5). By the 1950s, however, enterprises involved in these high-tech industries, even though the government

Table 6.5 *Funding for Research and Development, 1955–1990* (millions of 1982 dollars)

Year	Total funds	Federal government		Industry	
		Amount	%	Amount	%
1955	22,760	12,923	0.54	9,282	0.41
1960	43,648	28,191	0.65	14,591	0.33
1965	59,351	38,532	0.65	19,384	0.33
1970	62,405	35,636	0.57	24,851	0.40
1975	59,883	30,986	0.62	26,679	0.45
1980	73,255	34,557	0.47	36,065	0.49
1985	102,462	46,870	0.46	52,252	0.51
1990	110,470	48,591	0.44	56,757	0.51

Note: Aside from the federal government and industry, universities, colleges, foundations, and non-profit organizations provided the balance of R. & D. funds.

Source: Mowery (1995: 166).

continued to provide them with R. & D. funds and markets, also sought commercial outlets to ensure satisfactory levels of growth. Corporate leaders built or enhanced research operations and invested in human capital by hiring highly trained scientists and engineers. That is, they invested in the organizational and human capabilities needed to transform new technologies into marketable products (Chandler, 1994: 36–9; Flamm, 1988: 64, 84–5).

International Business Machines provides a good example of a company that expanded its sales of computers beyond the government market that funded its initial development of computing technology and machines. In the mid-1950s the company substantially increased funding for R. & D. into commercial applications of main frame computers. These investments eventually paid off for IBM, as its well-established marketing capabilities enabled the company to outdistance competitors for the business computer market. The strategy helped launch the computer revolution and provided IBM with decades of unmatched growth and profit (Flamm, 1988: 82–7; Usselman, 1993: 1–35).

Pharmaceutical manufacturer Merck, Sharpe & Dohme provides a good example of a high-tech enterprise that commercialized antibiotics that were developed in conjunction with the government during the Second World War. Before the war Merck produced fine chemicals for pharmaceutical manufacturers and individual pharmacists. It began serious pharmaceutical research in the 1930s. Thus, it was prepared to take advantage of the discoveries about antibiotics advanced by government-supported research during the Second World War. It was also well positioned to benefit from the postwar boom that brought about the widespread use of mass-produced antibiotics. Merck acquired Sharp and Dohme in 1953, a manufacturer of prepackaged drug products, to give the company marketing capabilities both in the United States and overseas.

Merck also invested heavily in combining and expanding the research laboratory operations of both companies. While it diversified operations into some related product areas, its major focus from the 1960s on was the development and commercialization of new therapies (Sturchio and Galambos, 1991: 18–32; Galambos with Sewell, 1995).

These two examples underscore how, in the prosperous first decades of the postwar era, top managers focused on finding suitable investment outlets for high rates of earnings. This was as true of enterprises in mature industries as those engaged in high-tech areas. The former diversified its investments while the latter intensified them. As such, it is not unreasonable to conclude that the strategists of enterprises located in high-tech industries were not as influenced by the antitrust policies of the federal government as those in mature industries. High-tech strategies focused inward on the more intensive use of resources rather than outward on acquiring enterprises in unrelated activities.

6.4. Antitrust and International Competitiveness

What role did antitrust policies have in the international competitiveness of American enterprises? To begin with, one must observe that the source of a firm's competitiveness is an issue that has generated an enormous, controversial body of literature. Even so, antitrust policies *per se* had not assumed a large place in the thinking of those Americans most concerned about competitiveness in the 1970s and 1980s.[6]

There were a few exceptions. M. E. Porter in his widely read book *The Competitive Advantage of Nations* (1990: 662–4) applauded antitrust policies for increasing the competitiveness of enterprises in the domestic market. As a result, firms were positioned to enhance their advantages, which made them more competitive with foreign enterprises. Members of the Chicago School took a different approach. An antitrust policy prevented efficiency-seeking strategies by discouraging vertical mergers. Indeed, the latter might have reduced costs, which would have positioned firms to better meet foreign competition.

Nevertheless, diversification was the important link between competitiveness and antitrust legislation. What has most concerned those interested in competitiveness were the consequences of diversification and the resulting restructuring of firms in the 1970s and 1980s (Blair, 1993). Thus, the significance of antitrust legislation to international competitiveness depends on how much weight one assigns to diversification as a result of the antitrust policy.

Diversification represented a major change in the management of large American enterprises. The multidivisional managerial structure (M-form) pioneered by DuPont and General Motors in the 1920s had become common by the end of the 1940s among large industrial enterprises. As large as these enterprises were, most of them remained in similar lines of business. Top managers removed themselves from the daily operations of the business to focus on allocating resources and assessing the performance of divisions by return-on-investment (ROI) criteria. Even so, top executives still had the opportunity to interact with the middle-level managers responsible for the day-to-day operations of each division. They continued to learn from each other about the direction and problems of the enterprise. As a result, decisions at the top could be based on specific knowledge of the firm's products and processes. Continued learning, and the familiarity of upper with middle management, were important parts of the enterprise's organizational capabilities (Chandler, 1994: 18–19).[7]

Diversification into distantly related and unrelated businesses, however, gave corporate leaders managerial responsibilities in industries in which they were unfamiliar. At the beginning of World War II, the largest industrial corporations managed (at the maximum) ten different divisions. By the end of the 1960s, large enterprises might manage four times that number, and the largest even more. Many of these divisions themselves were large, producing several different product lines, increasing the complexity of the overall operation (Chandler, 1994: 18–19).

ROI became the tool by which top management controlled vast enterprises. Corporate leaders could only know their diverse enterprises in abstract statistical terms. Chief executives had little familiarity with the markets and technological characteristics of the many divisions of newly created vast enterprises. As sophisticated as the budgetary, control, and managerial systems were in overseeing such operations, close experience with the products and processes of numerous divisions was almost impossible (Baldwin and Clark, 1994: 110–43; Chandler, 1994: 17).

The consequences were clear. Firms heavily involved in the diversification common to mature industries tended to be less competitive internationally than those high-tech firms that avoided the strategy. In a recent analysis of competitiveness, A. D. Chandler assembled data on the changing global market shares of the twelve largest international firms in key industries between 1960 and 1986. He found that American firms located in high-tech industries retained larger proportions of global market share over time than those located in mature industries. This was especially true in pharmaceuticals; computers and office equipment; and aircraft and aerospace.

American firms in these industries had the largest global market shares in 1960 and 1986. In the mature steel industry, in contrast, the loss of position was striking. In 1960 American steel producers had 74 per cent of the global market; in 1986 it was 16 per cent. Changes in automobiles and trucks were less sharp, but still important, as global market share went from 83 to 50 per cent between 1960 and 1986 (Chandler, 1994: 24, 67 (table B).[8]

To be sure, there was a significant level of government support for R. & D. in the high-tech industries (DiFilippo, 1990). Then, too, the government was an important customer for the output of numerous high-tech enterprises throughout the postwar period. Even so, by the 1950s firms in high-tech industries were focused on commercializing their technologies, rather than engaging in broad strategies of diversification.

The corporate restructuring that began in the 1970s and accelerated in the 1980s provided another link between diversification and antitrust. The restructuring of these years grew out of the failures of the diversification strategies of earlier decades.

Restructuring's consequences depended heavily on how it was undertaken. Most of the restructuring that occurred was initiated by management itself. When divestiture and new mergers were part of the restructuring, they tended to be among firms in related industries and were considered friendly. That meant they were initiated by one of the merging parties in a co-operative manner. Those firms that restructured to correct for overdiversification by lowering costs, increasing productivity, and refocusing management on core organizational capabilities, made efficiency gains and presumably positioned themselves the better to meet foreign competition (Hall, 1994: 114–29; Healy, Palepu, and Ruback, 1990).

Restructuring produced the most negative consequences when it was the result of hostile takeovers. When threatened by the prospect of a hostile takeover, management often defended itself by adopting drastic measures. Frequently, such defences resulted in much higher levels of debt, followed soon after by reductions in investment of all kinds, including short-run R. & D. expenditures. Hostile takeovers, however, were confined for the most part to firms in a few industries, the most important of which were petrochemicals, rubber, stone, clay, and glass. Thus, negative consequences were not widespread (Blair and Schary, 1993: 149–204; Chandler, 1994: 43–57; Hall, 1994: 132–4).

In short, diversification as a rule did not prepare enterprises for foreign competition. The firms that have done best in international markets tended to be found in high-tech industries and enterprises located there were not among the major diversifiers. Firms that best responded to the negative consequences of diversification were those that undertook their own restructuring (de-diversification). They fared better than those forced to do so by transaction-oriented corporate raiders. Those warding off raiders and hostile bids increased debt to protect sitting managements. Whether such defences were successful or not, they tended to reduce R. & D. and other capital expenditures, at least in the short run. In the face of an increasingly competitive environment, as Chandler has observed, 'when it was critical to enhance products and skills and to improve facilities, such resources were too often dissipated or even destroyed' (Chandler, 1994: 57).

6.5. Conclusion

It can be said in summary that during the last century an antitrust policy in the United States has often been linked to partisan politics. The original antitrust legislation in 1890, as well as the initial antitrust campaign of the government in the early twentieth century, were part of highly charged public debates about the power of big business in the economy. For almost two decades after this first antitrust campaign had run its course, the government was relatively indifferent to enforcing antitrust laws. At the end of the 1930s, however, interest increased largely for reasons of partisan political advantage. The government enlarged its enforcement capabilities and launched a major antitrust campaign. The Second World War deflected this effort at strict enforcement, but following the war the Truman administration revived the campaign. Congress got involved by strengthening the antitrust law in 1950.

For the following three decades, the government actively enforced the antitrust laws. The bulk of antitrust prosecutions were directed at horizontal mergers. By the 1980s, that policy had run its course. In the 1980s, the administration of Ronald Reagan virtually abandoned antitrust prosecutions. This policy reversal was part of another partisan development, the desire of the Reagan administration to reduce the role of the federal government in the economy.

The politically motivated changes of the 1980s were justified in theoretical terms by reference to a well-developed body of economic and legal criticism. While an antitrust policy has primarily been a matter of law enforcement and politics, from the 1930s on there has also been a sustained theoretical legal and economic debate. Until the 1970s, most proponents of antitrust legislation argued that the structure of an industry determined the conduct of firms, with major (often negative) consequences for economic performance. In the 1970s, however, the Chicago School effectively challenged this structural analysis. These economic and legal theorists argued that efficiency gains should be the criteria by which proposed business behaviour was judged. By that standard they argued against the employment of most antitrust law.

Despite the politics and theoretical arguments, corporate strategists in the postwar era had to operate in an environment influenced by antitrust prosecutions. The latter channelled corporate decision-making by limiting options or increasing the risks of following certain kinds of strategy.

From the mid-1950s to the 1970s, the government—often using the strengthened antitrust legislation of 1950—prosecuted those engaged in horizontal and to a lesser degree vertical mergers. In consequence, corporate strategists avoided the possibility of antitrust prosecutions by engaging in unrelated or conglomerate mergers or enhancing multinational operations. In examining these diversification strategies it was clear that antitrust was not the only factor influencing the behaviour of top corporate management. Diversification satisfied the interests of stockholders in long-term, low-risk growth and also allowed management to meet the needs of other stakeholders in the business.

In high-tech industrial enterprises, corporate strategists were less likely to adopt diversification strategies. There, managers could meet the needs of the firms' various stakeholders by investment in the commercialization of technologies, a process in which corporate resources were used intensively to advance corporate capabilities.

In the 1970s and 1980s the impact of antitrust legislation on the international competitiveness of American firms was linked to the consequences of earlier diversification strategies. By the end of the 1960s, two decades of growth and high levels of profits had come to an end. At the same time, foreign competitors were beginning to make inroads into the markets of enterprises in a number of key industries. Highly diversified firms performed badly in these changed circumstances. In retrospect, diversification ill-prepared many firms for changing circumstances, especially increasing foreign competition during and after the 1970s. By that time, however, a major restructuring was under way. For many enterprises, restructuring produced efficiency and productivity gains, which prepared them to meet increasing foreign competition. Those firms restructured as the result of hostile takeovers often ended up with increased debt, reduced capital, and reduced R. & D. expenditures. As such, they were not as well prepared to meet foreign competition. High-tech firms that had not, as a rule, followed diversification strategies remained among the most competitive American enterprises in international markets.

NOTES

1. The head of the Federal Trade Commission—an independent federal agency charged with maintaining competition—might also be involved in such decisions. The FTC was a considerably weaker agency than the Antitrust Division.
2. The value of these interchanges became so obvious that Congress made pre-approval of mergers a requirement in the Hart–Scott–Rodino Antitrust Improvements Act of 1976.
3. Leading proponents and their works were Richard A. Posner, *Antitrust Law: An Economic Perspective* (Chicago: University of Chicago Press, 1976); Robert H. Bork, *The Antitrust Paradox: A Policy at War With Itself* (New York: Basic Books, 1978); and George J. Stigler, *The Organization of Industry* (Homewood, Ill.: Richard D. Irwin, 1968).
4. For a comparison of the economic difficulties of the 1970s to the 1930s see M. A. Bernstein (1987: 207–16).
5. Equity was used when it could be exchanged for assets in a merger. The new assets produced returns more quickly than funds invested in new plant and equipment. In that way, equity to purchase assets was less likely to harm earnings per share (Donaldson, 1994: 28–9).
6. For a good statement of the issues involved, see J. Zysman and L. Tyson (eds.), *American Industry in International Competition: Government Policies and Corporate Strategies* (Ithaca, NY, 1983). Also see O. L. Graham, *Losing Time: The Industrial*

Policy Debate (Cambridge, Mass., 1992) for a discussion of the issue of competitiveness as the result of a failed attempt to institute an industrial policy for the United States.

7. Chandler prepared his essay for a study underwritten by the United States Council on Competitiveness and the Harvard University Graduate School of Business Administration. Published separately as part of this project was M. E. Porter, *Capital Choices: Changing the Way America Invests in Industry* (Washington, 1992).

8. Chandler cautions on the need for care in using these data. They do not represent the share of the largest among all competitors, only a representation of the performance of the largest twelve. Still, he found the assembled data the most compelling available about the consequences of diversification and technological endowments for international competitiveness.

REFERENCES

Adelman, M. A. (1961), 'The Antimerger Act, 1950–1960', *American Economic Review*, 51. 236–54.

Bain, J. S. (1956), *Barriers to New Competition* (Cambridge, Mass.).

Baldwin, C. Y., and Clark, K. B. (1994), 'Capital Budgeting Systems and Capabilities Investments in U.S. Companies after the Second World War,' *Business History Review*, 68. 110–43.

Bernstein, M. A. (1987), *The Great Depression: Delayed Recovery and Economic Change in America, 1929–1939* (New York: Brookings Institution).

Blair, M. M. (1993) (ed.), *The Deal Decade: What Takeovers and Leveraged Buyouts Mean for Corporate Governance* (Washington: Brookings Institution).

—— and Schary, M. A. (1993), 'Industry-Level Pressures to Restructure', in Blair (1993).

—— and Uppal, G. (1993), *The Deal Decade Handbook* (Washington: Brookings Institution).

Chandler, A. D. (1994), 'The Competitive Performance of U.S. Industrial Enterprises since the Second World War', *Business History Review*, 68. 1–74.

DiFilippo, A. (1990), *From Industry to Arms: The Political Economy of High Technology* (Westport, Conn.: Greenwood Press).

Donaldson, G. (1994), *Corporate Restructuring: Managing the Change Process From Within* (Boston: Harvard Business School Press).

Eisner, M. A. (1991), *Antitrust and the Triumph of Economics: Institutions, Expertise, and Policy Change* (Chapel Hill, NC: University of North Carolina Press).

Flamm, K. (1988), *Creating the Computer: Government, Industry, and High Technology* (Washington).

Fligstein, N. (1990), *The Transformation of Corporate Control* (Cambridge, Mass.: Harvard University Press).

Freyer, T. (1992), *Regulating Big Business: Antitrust in Great Britain and America 1890–1990* (New York: Cambridge University Press).

Galambos, L., with Sewell, J. E. (1995), *Networks of Innovation: Vaccine Development at Merck, Sharp & Dohme, and Mulford, 1895–1995* (New York: Cambridge University Press).

Greer, D. (1992), *Business, Government, and Society* (New York: Prentice Hall).

Hall, B. H. (1994), 'Corporate Restructuring and Investment Horizons in the United States, 1976–1987', *Business History Review*, 68. 121–31.

Hawley, E. W. (1966), *The New Deal and the Problem of Monopoly* (Princeton: Princeton University Press).

Healy, P. M., Palepu, F. G., and Ruback, R. S. (1990), 'Does Corporate Performance Improve after Mergers?', NBER Working Paper 3348 (Cambridge, Mass.).

Heclo, H. (1978), 'Issue Networks and the Executive Establishment,' in King (1978): 103–4).

King, A. (1978) (ed.), *The New American Political System* (Washington).

Kingdon, J. (1984), *Agendas, Alternatives, and Public Policies* (Boston).

Kovaleff, T. P. (1980), *Business and Government During the Eisenhower Administration: A Study of the Antitrust Policy of the Antitrust Division of the Justice Department* (Athens, Oh.).

—— (1994) (ed.), *The Antitrust Impulse*, 2 vols. (Armonk, NY).

Lamoreaux, N. R. (1985), *The Great Merger Movement in American Business, 1895–1904* (New York: Cambridge University Press).

—— and Raff, D. M. G. (1995) (eds.), *Coordination and Information: Historical Perspectives on the Organization of Enterprise* (Chicago: University of Chicago Press).

McQuaid, K. (1994), *Uneasy Partners: Big Business in American Politics* (Baltimore, Md.: Johns Hopkins University Press).

Mowery, D. C. (1995), 'The Boundaries of the U.S. Firm in R&D', in Lamoreaux and Raff (1995).

Mueller, D. C. (1977), 'The Effects of Conglomerate Mergers: A Survey of the Empirical Evidence', *Journal of Banking and Finance*, 1. 315–47.

Neale, A. D., and Goyder, G. G. (1980), *The Antitrust Laws of the U.S.A.: A Study of Competition Enforced by Law* (New York: Cambridge University Press).

Porter, M. E. (1990), *The Competitive Advantage of Nations* (New York: Free Press).

Sklar, M. J. (1988), *The Reconstruction of American Capitalism, 1890–1916: The Market, the Law, and Politics* (New York: Cambridge University Press).

Stigler, G. J. (1966), 'The Economic Effects of the Antitrust Laws', *Journal of Law and Economics*, 10. 225–58.

Sturchio, J. L., and Galambos, L. (1991) (eds.), *Values and Visions: A Merck Century* (Rahway, NJ: Merck and Co.).

Usselman, S. W. (1993), 'IBM and Its Imitators: Organizational Capabilities and the Emergence of the International Computer Industry', *Business and Economic History*, 22. 1–35.

Winter, S. G. (1993), 'Routines, Cash Flows, and Unconventional Assets: Corporate Change in the 1980s,' in Blair (1993).

7

Competition and Industrial Policy in Britain, 1945–1973

JIM D. TOMLINSON

7.1. Introduction

This chapter will develop three themes about British competition and industrial policy from the end of the Second World War to OPEC 1.

First, the weakness of domestic competition policy was coupled to a high level of international protection until the 1960s. This has led to the common view that British industry languished in a non-competitive environment, with disastrous consequences for long-run competitiveness (Allen, 1979; Caves, 1968; Crafts, 1988). However, this picture is oversimplified because of the large-scale entry of multinational (especially American) firms into Britain which competed with British-owned firms in many key sectors. The policy of welcoming multinationals is an unduly neglected feature of British policy affecting the level of competition in the economy.

Second, Britain failed to develop a coherent relationship between competition and industrial policy. Competition policy was slow to develop, partly because of the idea that the main basis for industrial efficiency was economies of scale and related technical development, *not* the existence of competition. Throughout most of this period industrial policy was characterized by a lack of co-operative and consensual relationships between government and business. Business was highly politicized and therefore especially resistant to attempts by Labour governments (1945–51, 1964–70) to pursue active policies of industrial intervention. But even under the Conservatives, business seems to have resisted any limited attempts at a

I am grateful to members of the Fuji conference, and especially Professor Etsuo Abe and the editors of this volume, for helpful comments.

greater governmental role, except in the case of 'rescues' of companies in declining sectors (Hall, 1986).

Third, while Britain did have a peculiar and arguably unhelpful policy mix during this period, we should be careful about exaggerating its importance for industrial performance. The relationship between policy and performance will be illustrated in a discussion of the car industry in the last section of the chapter.

7.2. Competition Policy

Prewar Britain certainly had a very weak commitment to competition policy, a position often unfavourably contrasted with the US and its antitrust policies that dated from 1914 and before. This difference partly reflected the fact that in an open economy, with very few restrictions on imports before 1931, the structure of industry remained highly fragmented. Few sectors found it possible to sustain cartels or other restrictions on competition. It was politically significant that the kind of populism which was an important factor in the American situation never gained a foothold in Britain. As a response to the Great Depression, after 1931 the imposition of trade controls coincided with a policy of (mainly indirect) government encouragement of restrictive arrangements by firms (Freyer, 1992; Mercer, 1991).

During the war and early postwar years, this approach to industry was questioned both inside and outside of government. The shifting attitudes of business itself were important to this questioning. The most detailed study of British antitrust policy emphasizes the impact of business, in a manner parallel with Kolko's famous analysis of the evolution of American industrial policy (Kolko, 1963; Mercer, 1995). While much of this argument is persuasive, I suggest that in understanding the development of competition policy (and industrial policy more generally) it is important to look at the ideology and calculations of the governing parties and the effects of business pressure.

The political commitment to an expansionary, full-employment economy embodied in the bipartisan 1944 White Paper on employment policy, led to a revival of interest in competition amongst economists, civil servants, and some politicians. But neither of the main political parties regarded competition as central to their economic programmes.

On the Labour side, there had long been the view that industrial efficiency should be seen very much in 'productionist' terms, largely as a function of technology and scale. This was linked with a general hostility towards market forces, seen as leading both to instability and 'anarchy' in the workings of the economy.

There were arguments in the party on such issues, and in the 1920s, for example, one minority strand of opinion called for a much more positive approach to markets (Thompson 1994). In the 1930s, some of Labour's economists coupled a movement towards Keynesianism with an enthusiasm for markets and competition at the microeconomic level (Durbin, 1985). But Labour's policies in the 1930s showed a continuing commitment to the view that 'rationalization' of industry, especially through nationalization, was the key to efficiency. The operation of market forces was seen as having failed to generate the necessary rationalization of industry in the 1920s. Overall, the perceived success of wartime planning tended to reinforce such attitudes (Brooke, 1992: ch. 6). There was a minority view, pressed by Gaitskell, that competition should be encouraged (Freyer, 1992: 241–50; Mercer, 1995: 56–60). Labour's 1945 election manifesto included a commitment to introduce controls on monopoly, but this reflected more a *political* hostility to big business than a conversion to the virtues of competition.

In 1945 Labour was extremely concerned with rectifying the perceived inefficiencies of the British economy. For the majority of the party, industrial efficiency was to be sought primarily by various forms of public regulation, including nationalization and the establishment of Development Councils. Behind both of these lay the idea that the route to efficiency lay through amalgamations or co-operation to achieve scale economies previously blocked by the fragmented-ownership structure of British industry. Alongside these policies were more specific initiatives aimed at raising the competence of management and improving the technological level of British industry. Once again, enhanced competition was not regarded as a vital issue (Tiratsoo and Tomlinson, 1993; Tomlinson, 1993).

On the Conservative side, it is important to note that the party had never been wholeheartedly committed to economic liberalism (except in its enthusiasm for private property). Scepticism about the benefits of competition and market forces had been reinforced by the competitive problems of British industry from the late nineteenth century and then by the interwar slump. By the 1930s the party had become strongly protectionist, and arguments on domestic policy tended to focus on the extent to which government would be directly involved in the emerging 'corporatist' arrangements, rather than whether such arrangements were desirable (Ritschel, 1992: 57–64). As with Labour, there was a small minority group within the Conservative Party who, by the end of the war, were disillusioned with 1930s-style restrictionism (Cockett, 1995: ch. 2).

After their election victory in 1945, Labour introduced the first legislation on monopolies in 1948. However, this Act did not make monopoly illegal *per se*, but established a Commission to judge the balance of public interest where a monopoly position existed. In addition, the Commission relied on a government department both to supply cases for investigation, and to decide what to do with the conclusions from such investigation. In large part the Commission was fatally weakened by very limited support for what it was trying to do, and the focused hostility it aroused from employers who were effective in 'capturing' the Ministries concerned (Mercer, 1995: chs. 5, 6).

More effective policy did not come about until the 1956 Restrictive Practices Act, which allowed judicial judgment on collusion between firms, and resulted in a much tougher pro-competition stance than under the 1948 Act. This piece of legislation did *not* reflect a very strong commitment to competition by the Conservative government, which had come to power in 1951. Rather it reflected industrialists' hostility to the form of the 1948 Act, with its independent commission, which many industrialists regarded as influenced too heavily by the ideas of economists (Mercer, 1995: ch. 7). However, there was some growth in government support for competition as the economy seemed set on an expansionary path. In particular, the question of Britain's relationship with other Western European countries was increasingly influenced by the idea that increased competition could redress economic failings (PRO, 1956*a*).

Competition policy remained highly controversial in the Conservative Party up until its loss of office in 1964. After the 1956 Act there was a wave of mergers, and this led to pressure on the government to legislate on the issue. Equally, there were growing complaints about Retail Price Maintenance, which Labour had nearly abolished before it left office in 1951. Internal struggles within the Conservative government delayed action into the early 1960s, and only legislation concerning RPM was actually passed (in 1964), while the proposals to reform monopoly and merger law came too late to be enacted before the 1964 election. This sudden burst of activity on the competition front followed Britain's rejected attempt to join the EEC, which many Conservatives at the time embraced as a way of 'shaking up' British industry to bring it out of its perceived sleepiness (PRO, 1963*a*).

When they came to power in 1964 Labour enhanced competition policy by the 1965 Monopolies and Mergers Act, which toughened the provisions against monopoly while retaining the basic assumptions of previous legislation. It also introduced new provisions concerning mergers, though the legislation was clear in its view that only a minority of mergers were potentially harmful to the public interest. That was the last significant legislative change in this area in the period under review. Under both parties the movement towards a more vigorous antitrust policy was halting. Neither of them was driven by a strong ideological commitment to competition as the key source of efficiency, even at the end of this period. But policy is never just a matter of the ideology of the governing party, and in this field it was very much affected by business attitudes (Mercer, 1995: *passim*). Another factor shaping policy which deserves some attention is the impact of the US.

The US enthusiasm for antitrust legislation as a component of the 'gospel of productivity' it tried to export to Western Europe in the early postwar years is well known (Maier, 1987: ch. 3). In the defeated enemy countries of Germany and Japan the victorious Americans sought to frame pro-competition laws similar to those at home. This was done primarily to combat what they saw as the basis of territorial expansionism in monopolistic concentrations of economic power, and the results of these policies have been much analysed (Berghahn, 1986). In Western Europe generally the story was different, both because the US was dealing with its Allies, and the focus of attention was the economic, rather than political, aspects of antitrust legislation.

Both these points applied to Britain, of course. Anglo-American discussions of the desired role of competition in the postwar period went back to the middle of the war, arising from discussions about postwar commercial policy (Gribbin, 1991: 143–5). While firm conclusions were slow to emerge from these discussions, they did, for example, stimulate extensive studies of cartel arrangements by the Board of Trade (Elliott and Gribbin, 1977: 345–6). The initial concern of these discussions was international cartels but it quickly became apparent that it was very hard to disentangle international cartel operations from domestic cartels and other restrictive arrangements. In 1944, the White Paper on employment policy set out the case for seeing monopolies as incompatible with an expanding, fully employed economy. This kind of argument had domestic origins which predated the Anglo-American discussions, so the impact of the US should not be exaggerated. It seems likely that American propaganda did, however, reinforce the trend on the British left to be hostile to cartels and the like on largely *political* grounds, even if it aroused further business opposition to such ideas (Mercer, 1995: 72–6).

Neither the American loan to Britain in 1946 nor Marshall Aid involved explicit commitments on Britain's part to pursue an antitrust policy. Therefore, the link between American enthusiasm for Britain to act on this issue and the 1948 Monopolies and Restrictive Practices Act was indirect. There were domestic forces at work which made some kind of legislation almost inevitable. Nevertheless, British policy on this question seems to have played some role in many of the discussions in the late 1940s on economic policy between the two countries. The European Co-operation Administration—the body set up to administer Marshall Aid—seems to have regarded change in Britain in this area as an important component of the reforms needed to raise the country's efficiency. The London office of the ECA reported in 1949 on the scale of restrictive agreements in Britain, suggesting they played a significant part in raising the costs and prices of

British goods in both home and overseas markets. The report said, 'Until this basic problem is attacked, the whole technical assistance program, not only in England but in continental Europe as well is basically compromised' (NRA, 1949a: 4).

This report came a year after the 1948 Act, and reveals substantial American scepticism towards that legislation. The newly created Monopolies Commission, it was suggested, 'is little more than window-dressing meant to silence those zealots who from time-to-time say that the government is not doing an effective job in coping with restrictive practices' (NRA, 1949a: 7).

This scepticism was based not only on the well-known differences between American and British legislation. It was also predicated on the British desire for an investigative body which would make a judgment on the effects of any monopoly situation it found, without any presumption that such monopolies were against the public interest. In addition, it was recognized that vigorous pursuit of this stance would be inhibited by the Monopolies Commission's small staff of twelve, whereas, 'In the US we consider ourselves woefully understaffed with 280 people in the antitrust division and 200 professionals in the Federal Trade Commission' (NRA, 1949a: 7).

Large-scale economic aid from the US to Britain ceased in 1950, but it was under the Mutual Security legislation—which followed Marshall Aid—that the most explicit attempt was made to tie financial help to Britain's pursuit of antitrust measures. These provisions were embodied in the Benton–Moody amendments to the Mutual Security Act, under which relatively small amounts of economic aid could go to countries in receipt of military aid. The recipients pursued three stated objectives. These were 'a) to increase the participation of private enterprise in resources development; b) to discourage restrictive business practices, and to encourage where suitable competition and productivity; and, c) to encourage free labour unions' (NRA, 1952). The MSA (successor to the ECA) and the American government agreed that only the second of these applied to Britain, but in the ensuing attempts to persuade the Conservative government to take this clause seriously the divergence of attitude on this issue between the two countries became apparent.

In responding to the Benton–Moody proposals the Conservative government emphasized that the 1948 Act expressed a bipartisan view of monopolies and their treatment. 'Monopolies are neither good nor bad in themselves: the task of the Commission is to examine all aspects of monopolies and recommend reforms'(PRO, 1953a). When Senator Benton visited London it was stressed to him how unwise it would be to use American money to try to change British attitudes on such topics: 'If the programme were presented as an overt attempt to change attitudes there would be a tremendous rumpus' (PRO, 1953b).

Keen to acquire American money, the British authorities responded to the Benton–Moody proposals by putting forward a broad programme of research and activities, within which research on monopolies was only a small part. In this approach they seem to have gained support from some MSA representatives in London, who regarded the views of Washington as too paternalistic. One particular proposal from the US which aroused scorn in London was for University Chairs in Restrictive Practices, an idea successfully deflected into funding for Chairs in Industrial Engineering (PRO, 1952a; PRO, 1953c).

Because of Britain's sensitivity that it should not appear to bend its knee to American wishes, the terms of Britain's bid for Conditional Aid eventually went to the cabinet. In outlining the proposed bid the Chancellor of the Exchequer said 'it was not possible for HMG to go any further towards fulfilling the anti-monopoly conditions because of the accepted policy of the empirical approach'. In the cabinet some distaste was expressed for the idea of accepting the American conditions at all, but it was generally agreed that a bid for the money on the terms proposed be made, as long as supervision of the day-to-day spending of funds was not required (PRO, 1952b).

The end result of much huffing and puffing on the issue was a series of academic analyses of restrictive practices in a number of British industries, whose effects—while perhaps not entirely trivial—were hardly world-shaking (Mercer, 1995: 173). Overall, the US role in shaping British antitrust policy seems to have been quite small. It was perhaps most apparent at the end of the war when there was a coincidence of *political* hostility towards monopolies, rather than in later attempts to alter the British equivocation on the economic principles of free competition.

Finally, it must be noted that competition policy had complex effects on the competitive environment. In particular, the 1956 Act seems to have encouraged the emerging trend towards merger and amalgamation which, by the late 1960s, gave Britain a highly concentrated industrial structure by international standards (Elliott and Gribbin, 1977: 355–60; Hannah, 1983: ch. 10).

7.3. Protection in Britain

Britain in the 1940s and 1950s remained a relatively protectionist country, and this eroded only towards the end of the following decade. The policy was essentially bipartisan, as both parties accepted the rhetoric of 1940s American economic internationalism, but regarded movement in that direction as inescapably slow for an economy with as weak a balance of payments as the British. But the shape of this protectionism was not guided by current industrial concerns. Instead, the pattern of protection reflected the events of the 1930s, rather than any assessment of the post-war needs of British industry. The relaxation of protection was mostly related to balance of payments concerns (and international politics) rather than industrial policy (Oulton, 1976; PRO, 1959*a*).

Balance of payments considerations allowed the Attlee government to reduce protection against non-dollar imports from the late 1940s, and this process continued into the 1950s. Helped by favourable movement in the terms of trade, the balance of payments position eased. This easing included the dollar position, as the postwar dollar shortage proved not to be the permanent problem envisaged by many in the 1940s. The competitive shortcomings of British industry became more and more apparent in the 1950s, but this was registered largely in declining shares of export markets rather than growth in import penetration, which remained low in manufacturing. Britain was slowly moving from the traditional pattern of swapping manufactured exports for imported food and raw materials, to the present pattern of relying on both exports and imports of manufactures. Where import penetration did rise sharply, as in cotton textiles, this did lead to major political pressures for protection, but this was not the common pattern of concern with trade before the 1970s (PRO, 1956*b*; PRO, 1959*b*). Pressure on British protectionism arose from a commitment to the American design for a liberalized international economy, which, given the strength of the British commitment to the Atlantic Alliance, always figured high in discussions of British trade policy. Britain therefore made concessions on this issue to assuage American feelings, though the pace of liberalization generally fell short of American hopes (PRO, 1960–3).

The major change in attitudes towards trade began with the movement towards Western European integration, which Britain had initially spurned, but which, from the late 1950s, came to be seen as a possible solution to Britain's political and economic dilemmas. Britain first tried to get 'the Six' to limit their ambitions to a free-trade area, thus allowing Britain to become a member on its own terms. When this failed EFTA was created, very much as a second best, and shortly afterwards Britain began its initially unsuccessful attempts to enter the EEC (Howell, 1962). Though the calculations behind this change of heart were complex and involved many political rather than economic judgements, part of the economic argument which persuaded the government was that EEC entry would increase the competitive pressure on British companies and consequently improve their performance. Certainly, by the early 1960s, this was commonly asserted by proponents of British membership (PRO, 1964).

The Kennedy Round of GATT 1964–8 initiated a big reduction in Britain's level of protection, despite the emergence of 'fundamental disequilibrium' in the balance of payments at this time. After a short period of increased protectionism (import surcharges) in 1964–5 this disequilibrium was dealt with first by deflation, and then in 1967 by devaluation. A return to an earlier era of long-run protectionism no longer seemed viable; the government treated the trend towards liberalization as irreversible (Beckerman, 1972: 17–18).

The rapid erosion of protection from the late 1960s was the most important change in the competitive environment in the postwar period. It led to a sharp rise in import penetration, from around 10 per cent in the mid-1960s to almost 25 per cent by the middle of the 1970s (Williams *et al.*, 1983: 112). There was no balancing expansion of exports, and thus began the period of chronic crisis in the British balance of payments. However, it remains mysterious why the competitive performance of British industry was so poor in the face of this import competition, even in sectors which had seen substantial competition in the domestic market from multinational firms. While the important role of multinationals—mainly American in this period—in the British economy has long been recognized, the implication of their presence for the competitive environment has received rather less attention.

Britain had welcomed American multinationals since the late nineteenth century, and only briefly—in the 1890s and just after the First World War—had this stance been politically contentious (Mackenzie, 1902). As a major overseas investor, Britain could see the benefits of free flows of capital, and also the immediate benefits to the balance of payments. Although prior to 1939 British governments had not taken positive steps to encourage capital inflows, the postwar Labour government more actively encouraged such inward investment, especially for balance of payments reasons but also where it was believed the inflow would lead to increased efficiency. In 1949 the Chancellor of the Exchequer, Stafford Cripps, told the American European Co-operation Administration that American investment would be welcomed as long as it either improved Britain's dollar position or made 'a significant contribution to the United Kingdom's industrial efficiency by the provision of foreign know-how and techniques not otherwise available'.

Jones is probably right to say that the British government at this time was clearer about the balance of payments aspect of American investment than the efficiency impact. Nevertheless, the policy of welcoming such investment, as well as the incentive offered by Britain's high level of protection, did have a significant impact. The volume of such investment rose substantially in the 1940s and 1950s (Jones, 1900; NRA, 1949*b*).

Dunning's pioneering study of American multinationals, published in 1958, emphasized the favourable environment for such investment in the immediate postwar period, and calculated that by 1955 it totalled $941 million in manufacturing alone, $1,200 million invested in all sectors of the

British economy, and just under 60 per cent of total US direct investment in Europe. This American presence was concentrated in a few sectors such as oil refining, pharmaceuticals, industrial instruments, and cars. This investment continued to grow into the 1960s, so that Britain remained the most important recipient of US direct investment right through the 1960s, with total investment reaching $9,638 million by 1972 (Dunning, 1958: chs. 1, 2; Dunning, 1993: 172).

In sum, during the period from 1945 to 1973 Britain slowly evolved a more active antitrust policy. There was some convergence with American policy in this period, as emphasized by Freyer (1992), though British legislation continued to regard both monopolies and mergers as possible objects of investigation rather than undesirable *per se*. In the case of mergers the ambivalence of government was especially marked. Beginning in the 1950s, the rise of takeover activity stimulated fears about the growth of monopolistic concerns, while the emerging weaknesses of the British economy led to a belief that concentration and rationalization of firms to develop 'national champions' was desirable. This tension in policy was to continue throughout the period.

7.4. Industrial Policy

British industrial policy in the postwar decades is difficult to summarize partly because there were major changes over time, and partly because there was never a single Ministry or agency responsible for such policy or whose activities could be said to define the contents of that policy. It has long been common in discussions of postwar Britain to say that enthusiasm for short-run Keynesian macro management led to the neglect of industry by governments of all political colours (Hall, 1986). But without disputing the importance accorded to macropolicy in Britain, the idea that this crowded out industrial policy appears open to revision, certainly for the Labour governments of the period and perhaps for the Conservative governments as well.

The industrial policies of the Attlee government of 1945–51 responded to two imperatives. One was improving the balance of payments from the disastrous legacy of war, the other was the need to improve the overall efficiency of British industry, perceived by the government to be suffering from serious long-term deficiencies. These two concerns were not easily reconciled. In conditions of strong demand for British exports, where dollars were not available to many potential purchasers of American goods and competitor producers like Germany and Japan were temporarily out of the running, export expansion was largely supply constrained. What could be made could be sold. This did not provide the ideal atmosphere for encouraging long-term changes to production and selling methods. Profits were high, markets easy, and much hay was made while the sun shone.

In addition, employers were generally hostile to the government's attempts to change business behaviour, and given the government's reliance on the private sector for exports the leverage it could exert was limited (Tomlinson, 1996: ch. 13). The government took a number of initiatives to improve industrial efficiency in the private sector, such as setting up the British Institute of Management, encouraging research and development by such bodies as the National Research and Development Corporation, giving investment incentives, and expanding the supply of trained labour. It tried less successfully to improve 'human relations' in the private sector by encouraging the creation of Joint Production Committees, the appointment of personnel managers, and tripartite development councils. These measures accompanied the major programme of nationalization. This programme, which occurred in the late 1940s, was motivated largely by the belief that only through public ownership could the impediments to rationalization—put on companies by private ownership—be removed (Millward and Singleton, 1995). Thus nationalization fitted in with the 'productionist' attitudes about efficiency evident in the prewar period. Hence in Labour's eyes, public ownership was seen as an alternative to competition as a way of improving efficiency in the economy.

In the immediate postwar years industrial policy aimed at expanding the output of particular sectors operated mainly via the allocation of materials, especially iron and steel. This successfully raised the export ratios in a number of industries while there was still a sellers' market, but it had a controversial impact on the long-run performance of the industries concerned. (This point is returned to in the discussion of cars in the section below.) Alongside these physical measures of planning went financial mechanisms which attempted to give priority to export sectors, both by the regulation of new issues and the pattern of bank advances. The impact of the controls of new issues seems to have been small, but control of the pattern of bank advances is more controversial. Traditionally it is argued that British governments did not use such controls effectively, for example, in contrast with France (Hall, 1986). Such a conclusion seemed to be correct in the immediate postwar years, when physical controls were more important. In the longer term, Hannah has argued, the pattern of bank advances was significantly tilted towards manufacturing, which was what the government wanted (Hannah, 1995). If true this implies that industrial policy was effective in achieving its aims, as effective under the Conservative governments after 1951 as the Labour government before that.

From 1951 these physical allocation mechanisms were largely abolished, the priorities of government policy become less obvious, and the parameters of industrial policy more obscure. However, we can distinguish three significant facets of such policy; those aimed at improving the performance of the whole of industry (Crosland, 1949: 117–26), those aimed at particular sectors of the economy (which we can divide into low-tech declining sectors and high-tech sectors), and those aimed at affecting the location decisions of industry.

The Attlee government was keen to raise the investment rate from the abysmally low levels reached in the war, when, at its worst, net investment was negative. One mechanism was the tax incentives to investment introduced in 1945. These were to become a permanent feature of postwar policy. Their precise form and value varied frequently, both because of controversy about their effectiveness and their role as short-term regulators of demand in the economy. Under the Attlee government any impact they may have had was outweighed by the impact of the physical controls.

Initially these controls were extremely ineffectual, and up to 1947 far more investment projects were started than the economy had the physical resources to complete. Thereafter investment was cut back, as the government strove to get on top of excess demand. Investment cuts of the late 1940s led some to suggest mistakenly that the Attlee government gave a low priority to investment (Barnett, 1995); in fact, it rose substantially in this period, from about 10 per cent to 15 per cent of GDP (Feinstein, 1972: tables 39, T36).

The major constraint on investment in this period was the availability of iron and steel, for which the main competing use was embodiment in exports. These two priorities jostled each other, and left private consumption way behind; between 1946 and 1952 exports rose by 77 per cent, investment by 58 per cent, and private consumption by 5.9 per cent (Cairncross, 1986: 24).

Under the Conservatives the importance of investment in the rhetoric of policy was increased by an emphasis on growth, and the contemporary belief that investment level was the key to growth rates. But the Conservatives abandoned the physical controls on investment, and sought to encourage its expansion through tax breaks and by regulating the overall level of demand. As well as using investment incentives, they sought to use income tax to raise the rate of return on investment. However the pre-tax rate of return started to trend downwards in the 1950s, and the income tax cuts of the period did no more than offset this decline, so post-tax returns remained stable (King, 1975).

The use of demand management to influence demand and hence investment, has been the cause of much controversy. When the first wave of postwar analyses of British economic 'decline' came out in the late 1950s, it was popular to blame this type of macro-management and the stop-go cycle it generated for depressing the investment rate in Britain (Shonfield, 1959). However this explanation should be treated with caution. Cycles in the level of activity were no greater in Britain than elsewhere in Western Europe in this period, so it is not readily apparent why they should have had such an adverse affect on investment (Whiting, 1976). On the other hand, it seems likely that the prolonged 'stop' in policy between 1955 and 1958 did have a significant effect in depressing investment during those years.

However, probably more important than these cyclical aspects was the fact that for all their enthusiasm for investment, the Conservatives also wanted to be the party of consumption, the party that would free the British consumer from the shackles of postwar austerity. They gave a much higher priority to raising consumption than the Attlee government. Between 1950 and 1960, by contrast with the preceding period, exports rose by £8.1 billion, investment by 12.8 billion, and consumers expenditure by 26.8 billion. In the 1960s, though the cycles in activity were larger, both export and investment performance were much better than in the 1950s, and consumption absorbed much less of the expansion in output (Cairncross, 1992: 93, 153–7).

Along with the rhetorical commitment to increasing investment went an emphasis on increasing general industrial efficiency by means of agencies such as the British Institute of Management and the British Productivity Council. Both of these originated in the Attlee period, the BPC being the continuation of the Anglo-American Council on Productivity. The goal of both these organizations was to professionalize British management and to improve its practices in such areas as cost accounting, production engineering, and marketing. Both bodies received financial aid from the government but relied for their success on firms buying their proffered services. By and large this take-up was very limited, and this is indicated by the continued financial crises they suffered and governmental agonizing over how much money should be spent in the face of employers' indifference (PRO, 1956–61).

A similar pattern of indifference by a majority of firms is evident in the reaction to the government's attempts to improve 'human relations' by such methods as the appointment of personnel officers and the encouragement of joint production committees (Tiratsoo, 1995). Overall, though there were exceptions, British firms were slow to change their practices in the directions urged by 'progressive' management thinkers and by government.

Industrial policy is usually thought of as involving government attempts to privilege particular sectors of industry. In this period, such policies were pursued at both ends of the spectrum—the low-tech labour intensive and the high-tech.

At the low-tech end the major private sector recipients of government support were shipbuilding and cotton. Shipbuilding was deemed important both because of the strategic aspect of the industry and its concentration in regions of relatively high unemployment. The issue of protection did not arise here because the basic problem of the industry was its loss of export markets. Very considerable sums of money were spent, perhaps £200 million in 1970 prices between the mid-1960s and mid-1970s, in a largely unsuccessful attempt to stem the industry's decline. In cotton the government refused to block the inflow of cheap imports because most of these originated from Commonwealth countries. Instead it offered the industry a subsidized re-equipment scheme, which, however, was not taken up by as many companies as anticipated and again failed to stem the industry's decline (Mottershead, 1978: 461–71; Singleton, 1991; Thomas, 1983).

In both these cases an important motive for government action was regional unemployment, which had been addressed by policy in the 1940s, had faded from the agenda in the early 1950s, and had emerged again at the end of that decade. Regional policy involved both a defence of existing employment and attempts to encourage growing industries to locate in areas of relatively high unemployment, this latter policy being particularly marked from the beginning of the 1960s (Parsons, 1986: ch. 5). The effects of this latter policy are controversial, and are returned to in the discussion of the car industry below.

Many of the industries nationalized in the 1940s soon emerged as declining industries in the 1950s, and any account of industrial policy must give importance to how this decline was managed. The decline in demand for items such as coal and rail transport soon led to a deterioration in their financial position, and poor financial performance became characteristic of most of the British public sector. Loss-making in this sector can be regarded as equivalent to subsidies in the private sector, yet the position is rather more complicated than such easy generalizations may allow. Financial losses by public corporations were not simply a result of commercial failure, but also of the government use of those industries to pursue anti-inflationary policies, leading to prices being held down (Millward, 1976).

Financial performance is therefore not a good measure of productive performance in these industries. To a large extent because of massive labour shedding—especially in coal and the railways—the productivity record of the nationalized sector in this period is not inferior to that of the private manufacturing sector (Millward, 1992). There were undoubtedly difficulties with the whole approach to the nationalized sector in the 1950s and 1960s, but it is important not to conflate their performance in these decades with that in the quite different circumstances of the 1970s and 1980s.

At the high-tech end of the industrial spectrum, the government's intervention mainly took the form of support for R. & D. activity. It is important to put this policy in an appropriate context. In the literature on British industrial decline it is a commonplace to blame inadequate levels of R. & D. activity for a large part of that decline (Smith, 1986). But recent work by Edgerton has sought to question that view. He argues that, at least until the late 1960s, Britain was second only to the United States as an R. & D. spender, whether measured in absolute terms or relative to GDP. He points out that misleading impressions have been given because so much of British R. & D. was (and is) concentrated in a few sectors—such as pharmaceuticals and chemicals and, more importantly, because so much of it is in military or strategic areas rather than what is normally designated 'civilian R. & D.' (Edgerton, 1994).

The implication of this view may be that the problem with British R. & D. has not been an inadequate level of expenditure but a misdirection in spending. This in fact was argued many years ago by Peck, when he noted how much of British manpower and money was engaged in R. & D. in sectors such as military-oriented electronics, aircraft, and nuclear power, where the chances of significant commercial benefits for a relatively small country like Britain were small (Peck, 1968). This point may be put the other way round; what Britain lacked, and what the government failed to encourage, was a large enough R. & D. effort in the kind of mid-tech areas such as electrical and mechanical engineering, machine tools, etc. For a country of Britain's size mid-tech industries were likely to yield much better commercial returns. The reason for the obsession with areas such as aircraft and nuclear power may be seen as a combination of 'great power' pretensions on the part of government, and a widespread view that 'big science' was the way to economic advance, rather than the more mundane activities involved in developing technologies in the mid-tech industries (Coopey, 1993).

It is difficult to summarize British industrial policy in the period from 1945 to 1973. There was no clear ideology of such policy during this period. Both Labour governments in these years were more 'interventionist' than the Conservatives, and both gave a higher priority to raising efficiency than is often appreciated. But these political distinctions should not be exaggerated. From the late 1950s, with the dawning realization of Britain's relative decline, the Conservatives attempted to spur industry to greater efficiency. They focused on the labour market and aimed at improving education and training and the mobility of the workforce. These policies coexisted rather uneasily with an increasing emphasis on competition as a route to efficiency, which had been gradually growing in the 1950s, but which was spurred in part by the failure to gain entry to the EEC.

As declinism gained ground in British policy during the 1960s and early 1970s, both parties became more inclined to regard industry as requiring a 'shake-up', both from direct government action and from enhanced competition. The tensions in this combination were probably at their height in the late 1960s, when the liberalization of trade led to a bid to create 'national champions' to compete in world and domestic market. At the same time a competition policy was reinforced, especially with respect to mergers, by the 1965 Act. Usually these tensions were resolved in favour of allowing mergers, as the naïve doctrines about the benefits of scale-for-efficiency continued to hold sway (Mottershead, 1978: 477–8).

7.5. The Impact of Policy on the Car Industry

The British car industry has been the object of a great deal of scholarly inquiry, its recent decline commonly being treated as a paradigm of Britain's overall industrial difficulties (Church, 1994; Foreman-Peck *et al.*, 1995; Williams *et al.*, 1987). This chapter makes no attempt to add to the general analysis of the industry's history, but rather treats it as an example of the issues involved in assessing Britain's competition and industrial policies.

The first question to be addressed is the industrial significance of the development of postwar competition policy. The major car companies themselves were never the object of investigation by the Monopolies Commission, though component suppliers were. Laws against resale price maintenance were significant for an industry which had traditionally been a strict enforcer of its retail price structure (Johnson-Davies, 1955). Under the 1948 Act a company supplying more than one-third of the domestic market could be referred to the Commission, and from the time of its creation in 1952 BMC was in such a position continuously (see Table 7.1).

But the idea of referring the company to the Commission never seems to have been discussed in government circles (Mercer, 1995: ch. 6). This is not surprising, as it seemed clear that the company faced stiff competition from other producers in Britain, of which the most important by far was Ford. Not until the end of the period were imports a factor (Table 7.2). Table 7.1 shows how the industry became increasingly oligopolistic over this period, with only four significant mass producers of cars by the early 1970s. But the figures do not suggest any cosy collusion between these firms: though short-run price competition was limited, there were vigorous attempts to improve market share by competition in model design and quality. As Rhys (1972: 316) summarized the position at the end of the period:

Although short-run price competition is absent, the motor car market is nevertheless a highly competitive one. There is no question of monopoly, and despite the

Table 7.1 *Shares of Total Car Output In the Postwar Period*

	BMC %	Standard %	Ford %	Rootes %	Vauxhall %	Others %
1946	43.4[a]	11.5	14.4	10.7	9.0	11.0
1950	39.4[a]	11.1	19.2	13.5	9.0	7.8
1955	38.9	9.8	27.0	11.4	8.5	5.4
1960	39.5	11.2	26.8	10.0	9.1	3.4
1965	38.2	6.5	29.5	10.6	12.8	2.4
1970	48.1[b]	—	27.3	13.3	10.8	0.5

Notes:
[a] Austin and Nuffield merged in 1952.
[b] Includes Jaguar and Rover.
Source: Rhys (1972: 312).

small number of significant domestic producers, little evidence of oligopolistic practices. Competition between domestic producers and between home and foreign car makers is intense. So although the car market is not 'perfectly' competitive it is nevertheless highly competitive.

Rhys's reference to competition from foreign-car producers reflects the fact that at the end of the 1960s import penetration in cars took off, from levels below 5 per cent of the market to over a quarter by the time of OPEC 1 (Table 7.2). This shift largely reflected two factors: the reduction in tariffs under the Kennedy Round of GATT and the extraordinary boom in domestic demand unleashed by the Conservative government's expansionary monetary and fiscal policy after 1970 (Blackaby, 1978: 52–74).

The liberalization of trade in cars followed a long period of high protection in the industry. In fact, cars were one of the 'pioneer' protected indus-

Table 7.2 *Import Penetration in the Car Industry*

	Imports as a percentage of new car registrations
1965	5.2
1966	6.5
1967	8.3
1968	8.3
1969	10.4
1970	14.3
1971	19.3
1972	23.5
1973	27.4

Source: Williams *et al.* (1983: 280).

tries in Britain, gaining a 33.3 per cent nominal tariff under the Mckenna duties of 1915, and hanging on to it (except for a brief period between 1924 and 1945) throughout the interwar and postwar years. Oulton calculated that prior to the Kennedy Round cuts the effective rate of tariff protection for British cars was 41.5 per cent, falling slightly to 36.3 per cent if the effects of taxes are taken into account. This was one of the highest rates of protection of a major industry, and even after the Kennedy Round (implemented in July 1968) the rate remained at 21.2 per cent (Oulton, 1976: 77–87).

It is difficult to account for this high level of protection. Oulton stresses the inertia in the tariff structure in postwar Britain, and how it reflected the pattern established in the 1930s rather than postwar considerations. He finds no statistical evidence that factors such as the level of import penetration, absolute size, or capital intensity of an industry affected the pattern (Oulton, 1976: 69–72). The evidence from public records does not suggest any great pressures to maintain high protection of the car industry. On the contrary, at the time of widespread discussion of Britain's trade relations with Western Europe in the late 1950s, the industry was more sanguine than the government about its ability to survive a liberalization of trade in that region (PRO, 1959–60).

One consequence of this protectionist stance was the encouragement of foreign producers to establish production facilities in Britain. An important reason for the establishment of Ford at Dagenham at the end of the 1920s was the Mckenna duties (Church, 1994: 7). Britain was the biggest centre of European-car production by American multinationals throughout the 1950s and 1960s.

Several authors have assessed the welcome given by British governments to American car companies. Hodges and Wilks concentrate on the 1970s, but Reich takes a much longer-term view and draws stronger conclusions (Hodges, 1974; Reich, 1990). In his account, Britain's welcoming attitude—essentially to Ford—is contrasted with that of postwar West German governments. This contrast is argued largely to account for the divergent fortunes of each country's main indigenous car producer, BMC and Volkswagen respectively. This argument suggests that the British government had seriously damaged the industry by their policies of welcoming the multinationals. Yet how persuasive is this argument?

Reich sees the British government not just treating multinationals on equal terms with indigenous producers, but effectively favouring them. He details how Ford, in both World Wars, aided the war effort and in so doing gained favour and influence with the government. Reich also discusses the maintenance of good relations, though less intimately after the Second World War. The claim that Ford and Vauxhall were actually *favoured* over domestic producers relies on two specific arguments. First is that they did better than domestic producers during the steel allocations of the late 1940s (Reich, 1990: 97, 265). However, while Reich is right to

contradict Dunnett's view that the Attlee government imposed an ener-
vating 'equal misery' on all producers in the steel allocations (a point
returned to below), his argument that Ford gained special favour seems
doubtful. Tiratsoo has shown that multinationals were *not* particularly
favoured in his account of how the British-owned Standard Motors persuaded the government to grant favours by seeming to be a plausible
'national champion' (Dunnett, 1980; Tiratsoo, 1992).

Reich's second argument is that British and foreign-owned firms faced
differential threats from nationalization. The British owners, he argues,
saw widespread nationalization in the late 1940s and 'feared they would
be next'. By contrast, he suggests, the American companies 'did not face
the same fear of impending nationalization. Multinationals may face such
a threat in the Third World, but they generally do not in a liberal state'
(Reich, 1990: 265, 266).

This perceived differential threat had important behavioural consequences. In Reich's view it largely accounts for the high levels of distributed profits in British-owned companies, as they tried to make hay while
private ownership allowed them to do so. American companies, by contrast, retained and invested much more of their profits and accumulated
the higher levels of capital assets which became one of source of comparative success later (Reich, 1990: 265–7).

Certainly the issue of nationalizing the car industry had been a live one
in Labour Party circles since the 1930s. But the chances of this occurring
were always very slim. It never formed part of an official Labour Party
commitment. The reasons against public ownership were clearly spelled
out in a party document in 1948, which noted the unemployment consequences likely to result from any rationalization of a nationalized car
industry. On the other side it noted how important the industry was to the
export drive and how that role would be threatened by nationalization.
The report therefore came out against any public ownership of the industry (Bowden, 1995).

The government was also very conscious of the industry's role in the
export drive, and, though it urged improvement on the industry, it both
publicly renounced any intention to nationalize and worked hard at con-
ciliating its leaders. For example, it responded fully to the SMMT request
that the 1947 Transport Act should explicitly rule out any role in constructing road vehicles for the newly created Transport Commission
(Bowden, 1995: 108–9). A car producer in the late 1940s would have had to
have been paranoid indeed to have felt that nationalization was a likely
policy to be pursued by the Attlee government. The low-investment policy is much better explained by other factors than a threat of public ownership, a point returned to below.

Dunnett has been the most critical of those who blamed the government
for the demise of the British car industry. His strongest criticisms are

threefold (Dunnett, 1980). First, as noted above, that the policy of steel allocations in the early postwar period was harmful. Second, that the impact of the macroeconomic stop-go policies in the 1950s and 1960s was seriously damaging to the industry. Third, that regional policy from the early 1960s increased the costs of manufacturing cars to a significant degree. Each of these criticisms is open to substantial doubt.

The steel allocation argument is that the Attlee government, keen to get output and exports at almost any cost, distributed the steel so as to keep all producers going: '. . . the steel quota system, in striving to be fair, effectively froze industrial structure . . . [and] frustrated the forces of the market operating to achieve a needed rationalisation and standardisation of the industry' (Dunnett, 1980: 35–6).

There are a number of problems with this argument. Most generally it should be noted that the steel allocation system ran only for a relatively short period, from 1945 to 1954, too short a period to account for a significant part of the industry's problems. Second, it is not obvious that untrammelled competition would necessarily have led to the disappearance of the less efficient in the postwar period; with demand and profits so buoyant conditions were ideal for the survival of almost any producer. Most important, however, is that in fact the government *did* discriminate between companies in the allocation of steel and other resources where it believed a company had good prospects. This is the point emphasized by Tiratsoo (1992) in his detailed account of the Attlee government's relationship with the Standard car company. His argument is not that Standard was necessarily deserving of such favours, though from the perspective of the late 1940s the company looked a better bet than it did with hindsight. Tiratsoo says the government was quite willing to discriminate where it thought such a strategy appropriate.

At this time the government did not put a lot of emphasis on mergers in its policies for the car industry. This reflected the fact that by contemporary standards the industry was already quite concentrated, with five companies having over 70 per cent of the output. Rather, in line with contemporary analyses of the industry, they emphasized the need for standardization, both of the industry's cars and the components used in them (PEP, 1950). The second argument made by Dunnett and other critics of the government is the impact of stop-go policies on the stability of demand in the industry. The effects of these policies seem to be exaggerated both in general and in relation to the car industry. In general terms research has shown that fluctuations in output in Britain in the 1950s and 1960s were no greater than in other, more rapidly growing, Western European economies. The impact on the car industry of stop-go was undoubtedly exacerbated by the use of hire purchase terms as a weapon in the macroeconomic armoury, with disproportionate impact on the demand for consumer durables like cars. But Silberston (1963) has shown how the effects of changes in income are much more important than changes in hire purchase terms in the variations in the demand for cars.

On the more general impact of stop-go, Jones and Prais found that fluctuations in demand were as great in West Germany and the US as in Britain. They stressed that 'there is no doubt that car production is much more variable than is industrial production as a whole (in Britain it is about five times as variable). But that appears to be an inescapable characteristic of this industry, and is a result of the product being relatively durable, and its purchase postponable, much as other capital goods' (Jones and Prais, 1978).

Finally, there is the question of regional policy. From the early 1960s the government strongly encouraged car producers to undertake proposed expansion in areas of high unemployment, and all the major companies did so in the early 1960s. Dunnett (1980: 76–81) argues that this policy raised production costs and was also harmful because it brought into the workforce a more militant element that further hampered the industry's performance. Church (1994: 59) suggests that 'there is no dispute over the adverse effects' of this policy, though he notes that they are 'unquantified' (93). But it is possible to dispute these adverse effects by pointing out that there were benefits as well as costs to companies locating in areas of high unemployment. Wages were 20–5 per cent lower in such areas, such as the North-West and Scotland, in comparison with the Midlands or the South-East where most of the car firms were originally located (Silberston, 1963: 265).

Indeed a major reason for this policy of regional dispersion was the government's belief that excessive expansion of employment in the more buoyant regions was a potent cause of wage inflation (PRO, 1963b). It may be objected that if these wage differences were not offset by productivity differences, and therefore profits were higher in the areas of high unemployment, firms would have located there without need of government inducement. But such an argument ignores the fact that managerial preference rather than relative profits has been an important source of location decisions in Britain, so that leaving such decisions to 'the market' may not lead to the most profitable locations (Heim, 1988).

The argument is that evidence that the governments of the 1950s and 1960s were guilty of serious sins of commission in their relations with the car industry is limited. As regards sins of omission, it is clear that, in principle, the government could have initiated a much more rigorous antitrust policy or reduced tariffs quickly to bring about a more competitive environment. But encouraging the multinationals to locate in Britain (partly as a result of the tariff) meant there was nevertheless a high level of competition in this sector.

Of course there are other aspects of the industry's environment which could have been affected by government action. An obvious example is industrial relations. Much of the literature about the decline of the car industry has focused on these relations. Certainly, from the 1960s these relations deteriorated, and interruptions of work became frequent. However, there is now much evidence showing that, poor as they were, industrial relations were probably not crucial to the industry's postwar difficulties. From different perspectives this has been argued by Marsden *et al.* (1985), Tolliday (1988), Willman and Winch (1985), and Williams *et al.* (1987). As Tolliday argues, the crisis in the industry in the 1960s 'was *not* primarily the result of industrial relations problems. In fact, it was management's misreading of their problems and their systematic privileging of the labour question over other issues that resulted in serious errors and distortions of performance and in significant part disabled them from confronting the real problems of the industry' (1988: 68).

A more complex question is that of the industry's investment strategies. It seems well established that BMC differed from both of the American multinationals in respect to investment, with an emphasis on minimum investment to 'patch and mend' production facilities, rather than the wholesale recasting undertaken by Ford and Vauxhall. Some have suggested that this was a typical example of 'short-termism' in Britain, geared to maximizing and paying out as dividends, as much as possible (Williams *et al.*, 1983). Others, notably Lewchuk (1987), have seen this strategy as deriving in turn from the failure of British firms to follow a 'Fordist' strategy of mass production, mainly because of the constraints of the British industrial relations system.

Tolliday has powerfully criticized this argument, pointing out that, certainly until the 1960s, unions were weak in the car industry, and management was not forced to adopt a low-investment strategy by union pressure. On the contrary, he argues, the strength of management encouraged them to go for labour-intensive methods. Similarly, as he points out, the piecework payments system which is at the centre of Lewchuk's criticism was not unambiguously inferior to the daywork system pursued by Ford. One of the peculiarities of industrial relations in the car industry was the extent to which the much-abused shop steward under the piecework system found himself in the role of 'progress chaser', trying to maintain his members' wages (Tolliday, 1988: 70–1).

In sum, it looks as though the particular strategy pursued by the British-owned car industry in the 1950s and 1960s was largely the result of factors internal to the firm and unaffected by the government. The industry was subject to competition from the American multinationals, but this did not provide enough of a stimulus to prevent the loss of competitive power, which became catastrophic when firms were then subjected to rapidly rising demand and foreign competition.

7.6. Conclusions

Britain's industrial policy in this period is in marked contrast to that of other countries, including Japan. In the latter case the most striking institutional difference was the absence of any body in Britain remotely comparable to MITI, and the reasons for this have been explored elsewhere (Tomlinson, 1997). While Japan combined protectionism with the encouragement of competition between domestic producers, Britain combined high protection and weak antitrust legislation during most of this period. However, and again unlike Japan, this was coupled to an unusually encouraging attitude towards inward direct investment, which significantly increased competition in major manufacturing sectors. The picture of British industry languishing in a stagnant, protectionist backwater should therefore be seriously modified. The car industry is a classic case where competition was not a sufficient condition for the maintenance of levels of efficiency comparable to international competitors.

REFERENCES

Allen, G. C. (1979), *The British Disease* (London: Institute of Economic Affairs).

Barnett, C. (1995), *The Lost Victory* (London: Macmillan).

Beckerman, W. (1972), *The Labour Government's Economic Record 1964–70* (London: Duckworth).

Berghahn, V. (1986), *The Americanization of West German Industry* (Leamington Spa: Berg).

Bowden, S., 'The Motor Vehicle Industry', in Millward and Singleton (1995).

Blackaby, F. T. (1978), 'Narrative', in F. T. Blackaby (ed.), *British Economic Policy, 1960–74* (Cambridge: Cambridge University Press), 52–74.

Brooke, S. (1992), *Labour's War: The Labour Party During the Second World War* (Oxford: Oxford University Press).

Cairncross, A. (1986), *Years of Recovery: British Economic Policy 1945–51* (London: Methuen).

—— (1992), *British Economic Policy Since 1945* (London: Methuen).

Campbell, J. (1993), *Edward Heath: A Biography* (London: Cape).

Caves, R. E. (1968), 'Market Organization, Performance, and Public Policy', in R. E. Caves (ed.), *Britain's Economic Prospects* (Washington: Brookings Institution).

Church, R. (1994), *The Rise and Decline of the British Motor Industry* (London: Macmillan).

Cockett, R. (1995), *Thinking the Unthinkable: Think Tanks and the Economic Counter-Revolution* (London: Fontana).

Coopey, R. (1993), 'Industrial Policy in the White Heat of the Scientific Revolution', in R. Coopey, S. Fielding, and N. Tiratsoo, *The Wilson Governments 1964–70* (London: UCL Press), 102–22.

Crafts, N. (1988), 'The Asessment: British Economic Growth over the Long Run', in *Oxford Review of Economic Policy*, 4, pp. i–xxii.

Crosland, C. A. R. (1949), 'The Movement of Labour in 1948, Part I', in *Bulletin of the Oxford University Institute of Statistics*, 11.

Dunnett, P. (1980), *The Decline of the British Motor Industry: the Effects of Government Policy, 1945–79* (Beckenham: Croom Helm).

Dunning, J. (1958), *American Investment in British Manufacturing Industry* (London: George Allen and Unwin), chs. 1, 2.

——— (1993), *The Globalization of Business* (London: Routledge), 172.

Durbin, E. (1985), *New Jerusalems: The Labour Party and the Economics of Democratic Socialism* (London: Routledge, Kegan Paul).

Edgerton, D. (1994), 'British Research and Development Since 1900', *Journal of European Economic History*, 23. 49–67.

Elliott, D., and Gribbin, J. (1977), 'The Abolition of Cartels and Structural Change in the UK', in A. Jacquemin and H. W. de Jong, *Welfare Aspects of Industrial Markets* (Leiden: Instituut voor Bedrüfskunde).

Feinstein, C. H. (1972), *National Income, Ouput and Expenditure of the UK* (Cambridge: Cambridge University Press).

Foreman-Peck, J., Bowden, S., and Mackinlay, A. (1995), *The British Motor Industry* (Manchester: Manchester University Press).

Freyer, T. (1992), *Regulating Big Business: Antitrust in Great Britain and America 1880–1990* (Cambridge: Cambridge University Press).

Gribbin, D. (1991), 'The Contribution of Economists to the Origins of UK Competition Policy', in P. de Wolf, *Competition in Europe* (Dordrecht: M. Nijhoff), 143–5.

Hall, P. (1986), *Governing the Economy* (Cambridge: Polity).

Hannah, L. (1983), 'British Industrial Policy, 1945–1995: Effective but Inefficient Intervention?', in L. Hannah, *The Rise of the Corporate Economy* (London: Methuen).

Harris, N. (1972), *Competition and the Corporate Society* (London: Methuen).

Heim, C. (1988), 'Government Research Establishments, State Capacity and Distribution of Industry Policy in Britain', *Regional Studies*, 22. 375–86.

Hodges, M. (1974), *Multinational Corporations and National Governments: A Case Study of the UK Experience* (Farnborough: Saxon House).

Howell, D. (1962), 'Expanding Prosperity', in L. Beaton, *Principles in Practice* (London).

Johnson-Davies, K. C. (1955), *The Practice of Retail Price Maintenance with Special Reference to the Motor Industry* (London: Iliffe).

Jones, D., and Prais, S. (1978), 'Plant Size and Productivity in the Motor Industry: Some International Comparisons', in *Oxford Bulletin of Economics and Statistics*, 40. 131–52.

Jones, G. (1990), 'The British Government and Foreign Multinationals before 1970', in M. Chick, *Governments, Industries and Markets* (Aldershot: Edward Elgar).

King, M. (1975), 'The Profits Crisis: Myth or Reality?', *Economic Journal*, 85.

Kolko, G. (1963), *The Triumph of Conservatism: A Re-interpretation of American History 1900–1916* (New York: Free Press).

Lewchuk, W. A. (1987), *American Technology and The Motor Vehicle Industry* (Cambridge: Cambridge University Press).

Mackenzie, F. A. (1902), *The American Invaders* (London: H. W. Bell).

Maier, C. (1987), *In Search of Stability* (Cambridge: Cambridge University Press).

Marsden, D., et al. (1985), *The Car Industry: Labor Relations and Industrial Adjustment* (London: Tavistock).

Mercer, H. (1991), 'The Monopolies and Restrictive Practices Commission 1949–56: A Study in Regulatory Failure', in G. Jones and M. Kirby (eds.), *Competitiveness and the State in Twentieth Century Britain* (Manchester: Manchester University Press).

—— (1995), *Constructing a Competitive Order: The Hidden History of British Anti-Trust* (Cambridge: Cambridge University Press).

Millward, R. (1976), 'Price Restraint, Anti-inflation Policy and Public and Private Industry in the UK 1949–73', *Economic Journal*, 86.

—— (1992), 'The Nationalized Industries', in M. Artis, and D. Cobham, *The Economic Policies of the Labour Government 1974–79* (Manchester: Manchester University Press).

—— and Singleton, J. (1995) (eds.), *The Political Economy of Nationalisation in Britain 1920-50* (Cambridge: Cambridge University Press).

Monopolies and Mergers Commission (1963), *Lucas Industries*, BPP XVI.

Mottershead, P. (1978), 'Industrial Policy', in F. T. Blackaby (ed.), *British Economic Policy, 1960–74* (Cambridge: Cambridge University Press).

NRA (1949a), RG469/392, ECA Subject Files box 21. ECA London to.

—— (1949b) RG469/392, ECA Mission to UK, box 7, Cripps to Bilsland, 18 Oct.

—— (1952) 469/1409, ECA Mission to UK, Office of Director box 22, 'Mission proposals Concerning the UK Program Under Benton/Moody Amendments', 16 Feb.

Oulton, N. (1976), 'Effective Protection of British Industry', in W. M. Corden and G. Fels (eds.), *Public Assistance to Industry* (London: Macmillan).

Parsons, D. W. (1986), *The Political Economy of British Regional Policy* (London: Routledge).

Peck, M. (1968), 'Science and Technology', in R. E. Caves *Britain's Economic Prospects* (Washington), 448–84.

PEP (1950), *Motor Vehicles: A Report on The Industry* (London).

PRO (1952a), T235/134, 'Conditional Aid', 22 July.

—— (1952b), CAB128/25, Cabinet Minutes, 11 Sept.

—— (1953a), T235/134, L. Radice to P. Shillott, 'Conditional Aid', 22 Aug.

—— (1953b), T235/134, 'Note of Conversation with MSA reps.', 13 Oct.

—— (1953c), T235/135, Sub-Committee on Technical Assistance, 16 Aug.

—— (1955–61), BT258/272, 'BPC: Conditions For Grant in Aid'.

—— (1956a), CAB 134/1231, *Economic Policy Committee* , 'Plan G and The Moment in British History', 23 Aug.

—— (1956b), PREM11/5155, Eden to Macmillan, 24 Feb.

—— (1959a), CAB134/1682, *Economic Policy Committee*, 'Dollar Liberalization by the UK', 3 Apr.

—— (1959b), PREM11/5155, Macmillan to President of Board of Trade, 25 Oct.

—— (1959–60), T230/485, *Committee on the Future Prospects of The Motor Industry*.

—— (1960–3), CAB 134/1852-4, *Economic Steering (Europe) Committee*, Minutes and Memos.

—— (1963*a*), CAB 134/1698, *Economic Policy Committee*, 'Economic Policy After Brussels', 4 Mar.

—— (1963*b*), T171/608, Budget Papers, draft budget speech, Apr.

—— (1964), CAB 134/1808, *Economic Policy Committee*, 'The Kennedy Round', 20 Apr.

Reich, S. (1990), *The Fruits of Fascism* (Ithaca, NY: Cornell University Press).

Rhys, D. G. (1972), *The British Motor Industry: A Survey* (London: Butterworth).

Ritschel, D. (1991), 'A Corporatist Economy in Britain? Capitalist Planning for Industrial Self-Government in The 1930s', *English Historical Review*, 106. 57–64.

Shonfield, A. (1959), *British Economic Policy Since the War* (Harmondsworth: Penguin).

Silberston, A. (1963), 'H.P. Controls and the Demand for Cars', *Economic Journal*, 73. 32–53.

Singleton, J. (1991), *Lancashire on the Scrapheap* (Oxford: Oxford University Press).

Smith, K. (1986), *The British Economic Crisis* (Harmondsworth: Penguin).

Thomas, J. (1983), in Williams *et al.*, (1983).

Thompson, N. (1994), 'Hobson and The Fabians: Two Roads to Socialism in The 1920s', in *History of Political Economy*, xxvi. 203–20.

Tiratsoo, N. (1992), 'The Motor Car Industry', in H. Mercer, N. Rollings, J. Tomlinson, *Labour Governments and Private Industry: The Experience of 1945–51* (Edinburgh: Edinburgh University Press).

—— (1995), 'British Management since 1945', paper to the Institute of Contemporary British History.

—— and Tomlinson, J. (1993), *Industrial Efficiency and State Intervention: Labour 1945–51* (London: Routledge).

Tolliday, S. (1988), 'Competition and the Workplace in the British Automobile Industry', *Business and Economic History*, 17. 63–77.

Tomlinson, J. (1993), 'Mr. Attlee's Supply-Side Socialism', *Economic History Review*, 46. 1–23.

—— (1994), *Government and the Enterprise Since 1900: The Changing Problem of Efficiency* (Oxford: Oxford University Press).

—— (1996), *Democratic Socialism and Economic Policy: The Attlee Years* (Cambridge: Cambridge University Press).

—— 'British Industrial Policy through a Japanese Mirror: Why No MITI in Britain?', in E. Abé and T. Govruish (eds.), *Japanese Success? British Failure?* (Oxford: Oxford University Press).

Whiting, A. (1976), 'An International Comparison of the Instability of Economic Growth', *Three Banks Review*, 66. 26–46.

Wilks, S. (1984), *Industrial Policy and the Motor Industry* (Manchester: Manchester University Press).

Williams, K., Williams, J., and Thomas, D. (1983), *Why are The British Bad at Manufacturing?* (London: Routledge).

—— —— and Haslam, C. (1987), *The Breakdown of Austin Rover* (Leamington Spa: Berg).

Willman, P., and Winch, G. (1985), *Innovation and Management Control: Labour Relations at BL Cars* (Cambridge: Cambridge University Press).

8

Regulation American Style, 1933–1989

RICHARD H. K. VIETOR

8.1. Introduction

Government regulation of business in America has reflected a unique mix of policies and institutional arrangements. In Europe, Japan, Canada, and Latin America, combinations of state-owned enterprise and discretionary administrative supervision were the normal forms of governmental control of business. In the United States, by contrast, semi-autonomous bureaucracies with formalized procedures and close judicial oversight developed detailed control over a substantial segment of private enterprise. With access to the world's largest market, most domestic firms did not worry about international competition—and nor did public policy. In fact, one of the central points of this chapter is how different postwar America was from most other countries, in terms of industrial policy. It really did not have any. Its policies were primarily regulatory, formulated to stabilize and serve the domestic market.

Government regulation in the United States, moreover, has generally not been an affirmative public act, primarily because the citizenry has been so suspicious of central government authority. In political debate, proponents of regulation have felt compelled to argue that some sort of market or managerial failure justified regulatory intervention. These include what economists call externalities (such as environmental effluents), informational problems (such as consumer-product labelling), public goods (airwaves or a sound banking system), the presence of natural monopoly (in which one firm has lower unit costs than two or more firms at any level of output), and anti-competitive behaviour (price discrimination or collusion). Yet, quite often the impetus for federal regulation came from business managers seeking to mitigate 'excessive' domestic competition, macroeconomic instabilities, perceived structural problems (such as depleting resources) or even political interference (from local legislatures or popular movements).

A considerable body of scholarship has been devoted to analysing economic regulation.[1] The literatures of economics and political science have provided some useful explanatory models for specific industries at certain times. These models are often inadequate for explaining the evolution of regulation as a political-economic system affecting a wide range of industries over a long period of time. Historical interpretations, while dynamic, are rarely used to explain how regulation works or what it actually does.

Broadly speaking, there have been three theoretical approaches to explaining regulation: a public-interest model, a 'capture' or private-interest model, and organizational models. In the public-interest view, to which most scholars once subscribed, economic regulation is a relatively altruistic response by government to undesirable business conduct — some sort of 'market failure'. This is a normative approach in the sense that the origins and results of regulation are taken at face value as serving the public interest.[2] The private-interest theories, which have all but superseded the public-interest approach, were first developed by political scientists in the 1950s. In these early versions, regulation intended to serve the public interest was subverted by a process of 'capture', in which private interests gained influence or control over regulators (Bernstein, 1955).[3] In more extreme versions of the capture model, regulatory origins are even attributed to the private interests of the firms to be regulated. The abandonment of public-interest theory was exemplified by Gabriel Kolko, a historian writing in the Marxist tradition in 1963, and by George Stigler, an economist and member of the Chicago School, writing in 1971.[4] Eventually, these simple capture theories were elaborated to embrace a variety of private interests, competing in the political market-place for influence or votes (see Buchanan, 1968; Noll, 1989; Peltzman, 1976). Overlapping the public-interest and capture theories are various bureaucratic and organizational explanations that attribute motive, process, and outcome to individuals and organizational factors within regulatory bureaucracies. These models tend to be qualified and pragmatic, based on analysis of diverse regulatory circumstances or first-hand experience. They explain regulatory policy industry by industry and agency by agency, through intellectual traditions, entrepreneurial skills, and the political ambitions of key regulators.[5]

This chapter presents the recent history of economic regulation in a framework that relates regulation to changes in market structure, political interests, and the behaviour of firms. At the heart of this model is the idea of *market structuring*—a non-normative interpretation that focuses on the impact of regulation on the structural characteristics of markets. In this view, government regulation of any sort shapes market structure, and large-scale changes in regulation can affect markets decisively. Through this market-structuring process, regulation powerfully affects the behaviour of business firms, and, in turn, generates economic interests that compete analogously in the political arena to effect further changes in public policy. Under diverse circumstances, regulation can help or hurt either regulated firms, their customers, or any particular subgroups (e.g. suppliers, substitutes, competitors) within the market. Over time, this regulatory interaction between business and government has also been shaped and defined by broad changes in technology, macroeconomic conditions, and political values.

This chapter is organized into four parts that highlight the evolution of regulatory policy in America. The first part deals with the age of regulation, from the Great Depression until the late 1960s. During this period the federal government imposed economic regulation of entry, price, and competition in nearly 20 per cent of the national economy. After the Second World War these new regulatory systems were expanded and elaborated, shaping the industries that comprised the national infrastructure and fostering development and integration in a relatively noncompetitive environment. Because US markets were so large, however, these regulatory regimes largely affected domestic, rather than international, competition.

Section 8.3 will deal with the forces of regulatory reform and deregulation that evolved after the late 1960s and bore fruit as a massive programme of deregulation, legislated during the era of President Jimmy Carter (1977–80). In a series of legislative initiatives undertaken in just three years, barriers to domestic competition in oil, gas, electric power, banking and securities, telecommunications, airlines, railroads, and trucking were removed or substantially redirected. Among the causes of these changes were the deterioration of economic performance in the United States and new pressures from international competition.

A third section is devoted to looking in some detail at the deregulation of telecommunications. Here, I examine AT&T's adjustment to partial deregulation, especially as it related to its international competitiveness in the switching-equipment business. After 1982, the divested AT&T struggled for five years to define a new and partially international strategy. Finally, after 1987, it began to implement a strategy designed to make it the dominant data distributor in the United States and a major equipment vendor internationally by the year 2000.

In Section 8.5, I examine the results of deregulation in the decade of the 1980s, when government-managed competition and market-oriented controls emerged as the basis for a period of consolidation and economic growth. Since America was the first country to deregulate significantly its infrastructure businesses, we can perhaps learn some lessons about the effects of the deregulatory process.

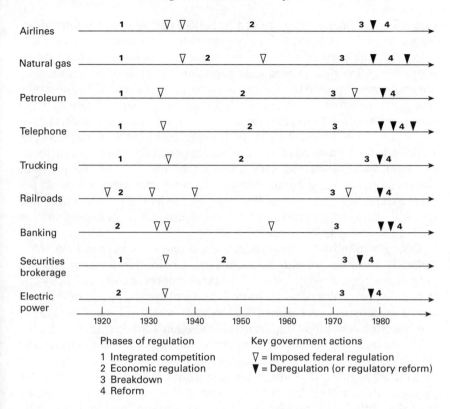

Fig 8.1 *Era of economic regulation*

Fig. 8.1 generally depicts the four phases of government intervention in the microeconomy, for nine industries, from the 1920s to the late 1980s. In this part, too, we can draw some conclusions about the effects of regulation on industry structure and the behaviour of firms.

8.2. The Age of Regulation

Prior to the onset of the Great Depression in 1929, the economy of the United States had grown quickly for almost a decade. 'A concentrated flowering of investment opportunities' in technologically new industries—natural gas, petroleum and automobiles, telephone, trucking and airlines—had led the way (Gordon, 1951: 194). But as each of these improved systems came into conflict with established infrastructure and expanded nationally, they created jurisdictional, price, and entry problems with which only the federal government could cope.

In 1929, this burst of growth was rudely interrupted by depression—a deep depression that seemed to last indefinitely, and for which the only apparent reasons were the failure of markets, big business, and competition. Gross national product (GNP) fell at an unprecedented rate (−8.6 per cent per year) for four years, and then limped along for another five. Investment ceased, especially in the infrastructure. Prices fell 25 per cent. Dividends were suspended, bond payments delayed, and insolvencies by the thousands swept the very sectors that had driven the previous decade's impressive growth. Worst of all, unemployment rose to 25 per cent. Productivity growth halted and the federal budget, which had recently averaged surpluses of $810 million annually, collapsed into an average deficit of $2.2 billion (1929–37).

'Changes in industrial conditions', wrote one economist in 1936, 'have seriously undermined faith in laissez faire. Choice in the matter of social policy now appears to lie between the preservation of competition by law (a paradoxical policy of social control) and state participation in the exercise of the already concentrated economic authority' (Burns, 1936: 523).

In the six years following Franklin Roosevelt's inauguration in March 1933, the federal government constructed a regulatory state, eventually combined with a vigorous attack on monopoly. The new administrative programmes emerged gradually, at first from the associationalism of the previous decade, but increasingly from Roosevelt's own pragmatism, from the clutter of liberal ideas touted by his advisers, and from efforts by big business to enlist government in the stabilization of markets (Brinkley, 1989: 85–121).[6] No important sector was overlooked: agriculture, manufacturing, finance, utilities, transportation, and natural resources all came in for direct or indirect state intervention.

Preoccupied as they were with low prices and surplus output, New Dealers set out to cartelize agriculture and manufacturing. Roosevelt was willing to take drastic measures, but he insisted on voluntary and decentralized controls, following the model of the Hoover administration. Congress passed the Agricultural Adjustment Act in May 1933, and the National Industrial Recovery Act in June. The Agricultural Act allowed the Secretary of Agriculture to set prices and limit output by entering marketing agreements with farmers and distributors. Although held unconstitutional by the Supreme Court in 1936, a second Act passed by Congress in 1938 allowed acreage restrictions and minimum prices that became the basis of US agricultural policy. The National Industrial Recovery Act, to establish codes of fair competition (e.g. setting minimum prices), was also overturned by the Supreme Court in 1935.

The more durable parts of New Deal regulation were focused industry by industry, as indicated by Table 8.1. Banking, where the crisis was deep-

Table 8. 1 *New Deal Economic Regulation*

Financial Services
    Banking Act of 1933 (Glass-Steagall)
    Securities Act (1933)
    Securities Exchange Act (1934)
    Banking Act of 1935

Telecommunications
    Communications Act of 1934

Transportation
    Emergency Railroad Transportation Act (1934)
    Air Mail Act of 1934
    Motor Carrier Act (1935)
    Civil Aeronautics Act of 1938
    Federal Maritime Act (1938)
    Transportation Act of 1940

Oil, Natural Gas, and Electric Power
    Connally Hot Oil Act (1935)
    Public Utility Holding Company Act (1935)
    Natural Gas Act of 1938

Retail and Wholesale Distribution
    Robinson-Patman Act (1936)
    Miller-Tydings Act (1937)

est, was the point of departure. When Roosevelt was inaugurated, the nation's financial assets lay in ruin: thousands of banks, brokerage firms, investment trusts, and insurance companies had failed. The President immediately declared a nationwide bank holiday and got Congress to pass the Banking Act of 1933. This law, including the Glass-Steagall Act, tightened branching restrictions, created federal deposit insurance, imposed interest-rate ceilings on deposits, empowered the Federal Reserve Board to set reserve requirements, and decoupled commercial banking from investment banking.

This Act divided federal regulatory authority among three institutions. The Office of Comptroller of the Currency would continue to supervise national banks. A new Federal Deposit Insurance Corporation would not only insure deposits (through members' contributions), but would also regulate state-chartered banks that did not join the Federal Reserve System. And the Federal Reserve would regulate bank holding companies as well as state-chartered member banks. This structure was fraught with regulatory gaps, administrative inefficiencies, and jurisdictional rivalry among the agencies. For the next half a century, it left each group of banks with a specialized segment of the market, serving separate customer groups with slightly different products in restricted geographic regions. What little competition remained was based on service, not price. Fig. 8.2 depicts graphically how the fragmented, regulation-defined industry structure and product-service markets were served by each type of financial institution.

To manage the equity side of the business, the Roosevelt administration enacted the Securities Act of 1933 and created the Securities Exchange Commission (SEC) in 1934. Financial disclosure for issuers of new corporate securities was the fundamental concept. With the securities industry's grudging support, Congress required corporate issuers of new securities to register all offerings and publish a prospectus. Investment bankers underwriting the sale would be criminally liable for its accuracy. To limit speculative fervour, the law also required a twenty-day 'cooling-off' period between registration and sale. The Securities Exchange Commission received broad authority and flexible rules, which contributed to its relative success over the next few decades (McCraw, 1984).[7]

Once financial markets were stabilized, the Roosevelt administration turned its attentions to problems in communications, power, and transportation.

For the Bell Telephone System, the Great Depression was a setback though not a calamity. During the 1920s, AT&T had grown by acquiring hundreds of independent local telephone companies, tying them together with its long-distance monopoly into a nationwide network with 80 per cent market share. It manufactured all of its own equipment at its Western Electric subsidiary and led the nation in electronics research at the Bell Labs. Between 1929 and 1931, though, subscribership dropped 25 per cent and usage 36 per cent. AT&T was forced to lay off 150,000 employees.

In the spring of 1934, a special investigative panel commissioned by Congress to study holding companies issued its report on telecommunications. 'The telephone business', concluded the panel, 'is a monopoly . . . it is supposed to be regulated.' Yet, 'regulation, particularly by the federal government, ha(s) been nominal'. The panel recommended a major overhaul, including the codification of all federal legislation in the areas of telephony, telegraphy, and broadcasting. It proposed the creation of a new Federal Communications Commission (FCC). With the Roosevelt administration's support, legislation to this effect (the Communications Act of 1934) passed quickly and without controversy since the Bell System did not actively oppose it (US Congress, 1934).

The Communications Act created a seven-member Commission, to be appointed by the President. The Commission was vested with extraordinary powers. In the telephone sector, it would supervise rates, facilities, consolidations of companies, equipment purchases, research, and accounting standards. In the broadcast area, it would allocate frequencies and license broadcasters by region, levels of power, and category of

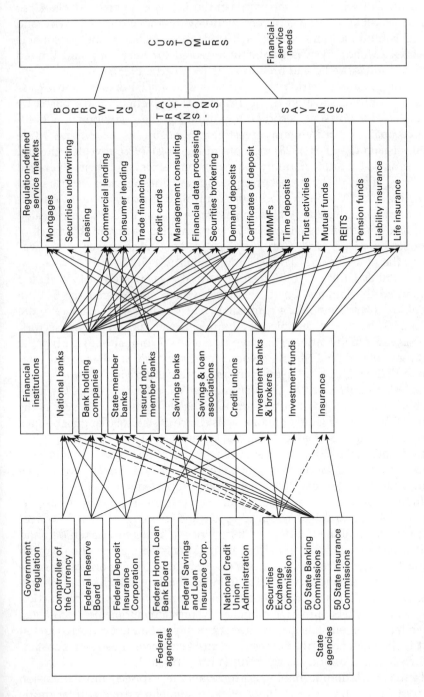

Fig 8.2 *Regulation-defined financial-service markets*

content. The objective, in the words of the Act, was 'to make available, so far as possible, a rapid, efficient, nationwide and worldwide wire and radio communications service with adequate facilities and reasonable charges'. Monopoly was implicitly accepted for telephony and limited competition for radio and broadcasting (Schwartz, 1973).

In the gas and electric power industries, financial distress and excess capacity only aggravated the jurisdictional problems already posed by interstate transmission, vertical integration, and the development of holding companies. An immense investigation, begun by the Federal Trade Commission (FTC) in 1928 and continuing until 1935, revealed the full scope and structure of utility holding companies and their leveraged finances. A few of the largest groups, such as Cities Service, Electric Bond and Share, and Middle West Utilities controlled as many as ninety operating subsidiaries in thirty states. In gas transmission, FTC studies revealed that fifteen companies controlled 73 per cent of capacity; in the distribution sector, 85 per cent. Concentration in the electric power sector was about the same (Federal Trade Commission, 1934–5).

The Public Utilities Holding Company Act was passed in 1935. Title I contained the famous 'death sentence', which empowered the SEC to break up interstate holding companies. The Commission reviewed more than 2,000 holding companies of all kinds. In the gas and electric sectors, the SEC eventually ordered the divestment of 417 companies. Title II of the Act reorganized the Federal Power Commission (FPC) and gave it regulatory jurisdiction over interstate transmission of electricity.

In 1938 Congress passed the Natural Gas Act, extending the FPC's jurisdiction to interstate gas transmission. Although Congress did not specify the form of regulation for either industry, its choice of statutory language—'just and reasonable' rates tied to the 'actual legitimate cost of property'—pushed the Commission to adopt the state utility model of cost-of-service, ratebase, rate-of-return regulation. Unfortunately, this method would prove more complicated and less effective when applied at the federal level.

In the petroleum sector, federal authority was constrained by the apparent intrastate nature of oil production and refining. When the Great Depression combined with new discoveries in Texas to weaken demand and strengthen supply, oil prices fell to 25 cents per barrel. The financial impact of such prices finally drove oil companies to support the passage of a Market Demand Act in Texas in 1932. This law, which other oil-producing states soon emulated, authorized pro-rationing of production based on forecasts of market demand. To provide enforcement of illegal, interstate shipments, the federal government passed the Connally Hot Oil Act in 1935. Henceforth, domestic oil markets and prices were substantially stabilized until the early 1970s (Vietor, 1984a: 21–6).

In transportation, technological innovation conspired with depression to weaken the financial viability of railroads. Not only did total traffic decline (by almost 50 per cent), but substitutes diverted a significant share of the railroads' freight and passenger traffic. Passengers increasingly turned to automobiles, buses, and even airplanes for intercity transport. Important railroad cargoes, such as oil and chemicals, were diverted to lower-cost pipelines while high-value, short-haul freight went to intercity trucking. As more than a hundred of the nation's railroads sank into receivership, the Interstate Commerce Commission (ICC) was unable to respond effectively.

Congress made several efforts to deal with this situation. The Emergency Transportation Act of 1933 changed the basic rate formula that the ICC had used since 1920. Instead of tying rates to asset value and earnings to a fixed nationwide target, the new law encouraged the Commission to set rates pragmatically, considering their effects on traffic movement and intermodal competition. In 1935 Congress passed the Motor Carrier Act to bring interstate trucking under federal control. Support for this regulation came not only from the railroads and the ICC, but also from state regulators who could not control interstate traffic and from some large trucking companies that wanted protection from price-cutting and hit-and-run entry by small truckers. Under this Act, the Commission set minimum rates and granted certificates of convenience, route by route and product by product. In the Transportation Act of 1940, Congress charged the ICC 'to provide for fair and impartial regulation of all modes of transportation': rail, barge, truck, and pipeline. A 'co-ordinated' intermodal transport system was ostensibly designed to protect the railroads (Transportation Act of 1940).[8]

In aviation—an infant industry barely active by the mid-1920s—competition had been intense from the outset. Before airframes and engines were sufficiently developed for passenger service, mail carriage was the principal commercial activity. But poorly designed federal subsidies encouraged underbidding for routes and pricing below costs. Walter Brown, the Postmaster-General in the Hoover administration, sought legislation that would give him greater discretion to award routes and set rates. The McNary–Watres Act of 1930 incorporated most of Brown's objectives.

Brown promptly organized a cartel, giving key routes to the largest carriers (American, United, and TWA), and dividing the rest among six other firms. For the next few years, the system grew rapidly, with the big three developing into vertically integrated holding companies. In 1934, however, a congressional investigation precipitated a scandal by exposing Brown's cartelized system. Congress promptly enacted a new regulatory law, banning vertical integration and giving the ICC control of entry. This, in turn, led to intense price competition and 'irresponsible campaigns of mutual destruction'. After a federal aviation commission recommended a new form of regulated competition that would curtail point-to-point competition while encouraging better service, Congress finally passed the

Civil Aeronautics Act of 1938. A five-member Civil Aeronautics Board appointed by the President received broad authority to grant certificates of public convenience, approve or amend tariff rates and set mail rates, control mergers and acquisitions, control methods of competition, and gather and disseminate operating and financial information. In effect the old cartel, with most of the same participants, was resurrected.

From the late 1930s until the late 1960s and early 1970s, economic regulation shaped most aspects of market structure in these industries. High-quality, widely available service, secure contractual arrangements, and stable pricing were the main objectives—and indeed accomplishments—of federal regulators.

In banking and financial services, the market was atomized. Multiple federal and state regulators chartered and regulated particular types of commercial banks, thrifts, mutual funds, investment banks, credit unions, and insurance companies. By 1980 nearly 50,000 financial institutions managed more than $3.8 trillion in financial assets (Federal Reserve System, 1985). Markets were segmented, with each type of financial product limited to one or two categories of firms. Assets (loans) and liabilities (deposits) were closely regulated. Competition was limited to non-price services: free gifts, free checking accounts, free parking, and as many branch offices as possible. Failures were rare.

Stabilization was the focus of communications regulation. The FCC approved AT&T rules that prevented interconnection of 'foreign' (non-Bell) equipment and encouraged nationwide average pricing. Under pressure from state regulators, it allowed a growing share of local telephone-plant costs to be allocated to long distance for rate-making purposes. As Bell technology drove down the costs of long-distance transmission, prices were held relatively steady. This created a sizable cross-subsidy from long-distance users to local-service subscribers, encouraging the rapid spread of a 'universal' telephone service.[9] The Bell System guaranteed high-quality service, equitably priced. The network, right down to its sturdy, uniformly black leased telephones, was an engineer's dream. There was no such thing as discount service or a cheap phone. In exchange, the FCC allowed healthy profits and prevented competitive entry.

Natural gas markets and industry structure were stabilized by the early 1950s. Wartime construction of interstate trunk pipelines and postwar expansion of urban distribution systems resulted in a huge network of regional monopolies. The FPC awarded relatively few new certificates for competitive entry into established markets, and the SEC completed its restructuring of industry ownership in the early 1950s.[10] The new industry structure had three parts. Production was done by some two dozen integrated oil companies plus hundreds of independent producers; interstate pipelines were operated by 115 firms; and local distribution was handled by 900 public utilities (Federal Power Commission, 1954).

In 1954 the Supreme Court extended the FPC's jurisdiction to natural gas prices at the wellhead. The Commission's subsequent efforts to enforce 'just and reasonable' rates were bogged down in impossibly complex procedures for allocating costs and determining rate base. Regulators first tried firm-by-firm proceedings, then regional rate-setting, and finally nationwide rate cases to set prices according to 'vintage' (year of discovery). In real terms, natural gas prices were effectively frozen at their mid-1950s level. Inevitably, low gas prices relative to those of alternative fuels stimulated demand, but were not high enough to stimulate replacement supplies. The huge inventory of reserves discovered in the late 1940s was gradually drawn down (Vietor, 1984*a*).

For air passenger service, the Civil Aeronautics Board early designated sixteen 'trunk carriers' to serve major urban markets. For forty years, until 1978, the CAB prohibited any trunkline entry at all. Typically, point-to-point routes were allocated to two or three carriers at a time, with identical tariffs and terms of service. In the early 1950s, a handful of local carriers were encouraged to offer regional service to smaller communities, so long as they did not undercut the fares of trunk carriers. Mergers were discouraged unless financial problems threatened a carrier. Pricing was simple, with standard coach and first class fares. Ticket sales were mostly direct, through independent travel agents or at the airport. Competition took the form of service rivalry: newer aircraft, more frequent non-stop departures, fancier meals, movies, guaranteed reservations, free baggage handling, and elaborate on-board entertainment (Caves, 1962; Fruhan, 1972; Richmond, 1961). Despite rising overhead costs, productivity gains from technological innovation were sufficient to hold prices steady in real terms until the late 1960s (Civil Aeronautics Board, 1972). For long distances, air travel in passenger miles surpassed those of rail and bus services by the 1950s and even for shorter intercity hops by the 1960s.

Taken together, the New Deal regulatory initiatives constituted a vast new public-policy regime of microeconomic stabilization. Direct price and entry competition was curtailed or eliminated from most industries deemed 'affected with the public interest'. Prices were generally tied to historical average costs: lower-cost, high-volume services cross-subsidized smaller, higher-cost consumers. Sales, marketing, and distribution remained relatively simple, as rivalry was limited to non-price services. Industry structure, as it existed right after the Second World War, was held more or less constant.

8.3. Breakdown of the New Deal Regulatory Order, 1968–1983

Many of the same types of change that stimulated economic regulation in the 1930s disrupted and eventually shattered the established regimes of New Deal economic regulation in the 1970s and early 1980s.

Underlying macroeconomic and political conditions framed the broad context of regulatory change. Real economic growth slowed abruptly after 1968 (from 4.3 per cent to 2.2 per cent annually); inflation accelerated and interest rates more than tripled. After the devaluation of the dollar in 1971 and the first oil shock in 1973, the US economy was fundamentally weaker than it had been during the thirty years prior to 1968. Excess industrial capacity, low productivity growth, and high unemployment accompanied the inflation and high interest rates.

Table 8.2 *US Basic Economic Conditions: Selected Indicators*

	1938–68 (% change)	1968–83 (% change)
Real GNP growth (per year)	4.3	2.2
Inflation (GNP deflator)	3.8	7.0
Interest rate (average 3 mo. treasury)	2.0	7.4
	1948—68 (% change)	1968–83 (% change)
Labour productivity growth (per year)	3.3	1.2
Average federal deficit (billions)	$3.1	$58.3

Source: Economic Report of the President, 1973, 1991.

The New Deal regulatory systems had been developed over thirty years, in the context of a strong, non-inflationary macroeconomy, very different from that prevailing in either the 1930s or the 1970s. Regulatory methods and rules were predicated on constant or falling real costs and prices, and steadily rising demand. When these macroeconomic conditions changed in the late 1960s, latent problems with regulation were suddenly apparent: over-capitalization, debt leverage, a bias towards excess capacity, high costs, and cross-subsidized pricing schemes.

With the Vietnam War going badly, with the economy stagnating and inflation apparently unmanageable, with the nation's energy supply seemingly held hostage by OPEC, and with political malfeasance touching the White House itself, people simply lost faith in government. The intellectual and political legitimacy of government economic intervention established during the Great Depression, and embodied in New Deal policies, had been thoroughly eroded by the mid-1970s.

For a brief time, an odd combination of political interests supported deregulatory reform. This impetus started with consumer activists such as Ralph Nader and liberal politicians, such as Senator Edward Kennedy, who believed that most regulation had been captured by the regulated industries. In the mid-1970s, these forces were joined by moderate critics of government bureaucracy and by industrial-organization economists who studied regulation and advised the administrations of Presidents Ford and Carter (Derthick and Quirk, 1985: 29–57). In the early 1980s, these interests came to be dominated by anti-government conservatives and Chicago School economists who viewed market outcomes as preferable to government controls and who generally supported the Reagan administration.

Technological innovation was a third factor that helped precipitate regulatory change. By making substitutes available, dissolving product-market distinctions, increasing capacity, and lowering entry costs, innovations changed the economic characteristics upon which regulations were premissed. Wide-bodied jets, automated teller machines, microwave transmission, digital switching, and nuclear power are examples of innovations that had these effects. Eventually, when regulators could no longer contain the economic pressures created by such innovations, they were forced to give way.

Regulatory failure also contributed to deregulation. When pressures from these other sources developed, regulatory bureaucracies invariably found it difficult to adjust. In telecommunications, for instance, they failed to understand the problem of opening entry while maintaining cross-subsidies. In the case of airlines the regulators did respond, but made matters worse by extending conventional principles to inappropriate extremes. And in the face of natural gas shortages, regulators tried to raise prices and provide incentives, but simply became gridlocked by the weight of their own adjudicatory and administrative procedure.

Policy entrepreneurship was a fifth source of change. In both the public and private sectors individuals who understood the consequences of regulatory failure—or at least saw opportunities for change—used the courts, the regulatory arena, and legislative reform to drive the process of change. Bill McGowen, the chairman of MCI; Alfred Kahn, chairman of the Civil Aeronautics Board; James Schlesinger, Secretary of Energy; and Todd Connover, the Comptroller of the Currency, are all good examples.[11]

8.3.1. Airline Deregulation and Political Entrepreneurship

Air transport was the first industry in which the New Deal regulatory regime was overturned, and the only industry to date in which the regulatory agency itself was disestablished. The impact of airline decontrol was so quick and dramatic that it provides a lens for understanding the same forces at work more gradually in the other industries. The airlines' customary problem with excess capacity worsened in 1969. Fare increases, deliveries of very expensive wide-bodied aircraft, and slower macroeconomic growth all contributed to a gathering crisis. Load factors declined, fuel and labour costs rose, and increased debt at rising interest rates all combined to swamp the gains in productivity that previously had held fares down. To make matters worse, regulators responded to the situation by condoning capacity cartels. They grounded brand-new 747s, imposed a moratorium on new route authority, and jacked up fares. When passenger growth stagnated because of a recession, return on equity for most companies declined to a level less than half that of unregulated businesses (Jordan, 1973: 184–203; US Congress, 1975: 145–6).

In 1975, Senator Edward M. Kennedy and his staff counsel Stephen Breyer orchestrated a highly publicized series of hearings on the airline industry, which succeeded in attracting political attention to the broader issues.[12] And, just at this time, Jimmy Carter campaigned for the presidency on a platform that promised regulatory reform. After taking office in 1977, Carter appointed Alfred Kahn, a professional economist and an evangelist for marginal-cost pricing, to chair the Civil Aeronautics Board. Kahn moved boldly to encourage open entry, low-cost service and price competition in specific markets (Vietor, 1984*b*). These successful experiments encouraged Congress to pass the Airline Deregulation Act of October 1978.

Although Congress had intended an orderly five-year phaseout, there came a tidal wave of competition that surprised everyone: first entry, then price cutting, then route abandonments, and restructuring by incumbent carriers. By mid-1980, competition was wide open and brutal. New airlines sprang up everywhere, with leased aircraft, non-union labour, low overheads, no-frills service, and names such as Midway, New York Air, and People Express. They entered the intercity routes where prices generally exceeded costs and where the potential for traffic growth was greatest. Fares not only declined in real terms in these dense markets, but even for city pairs with little or no competition. By 1987, more than 90 per cent of all standard fares were discounted in some way.[13]

Major trunk carriers eventually restructured, each with different route plans, fleet composition, marketing and service concepts, and labour relations. After forty years of regulatory protection, their rigid cost structures were unsustainable in the face of competition. Inefficient aircraft were grounded. Maintenance, operations, and training facilities were central-ized. Employment was reduced, wages lowered, and previously accept-able work rules renegotiated.

The most important operational change was the shift by all major carri-ers to a 'hub-and-spoke' route design. Direct flights between individual city pairs were drastically reduced and most flights were funnelled through one or two huge centres. Computerized reservation systems, already important, became the key to winning and maintaining market share. Price-sensitive customers were offered an array of discounted seats, adjusted daily by reservations computers to match demand. Advanced boarding passes, comfortable lounges, free trips, and up-grades to first class maintained the loyalty of frequent business travellers. By concen-trating operations and raising utilization rates, this entire system facili-tated cost reduction through economies of scale and scope. The real cost-per-passenger-mile of airline travel fell by nearly 30 per cent between 1981 and 1988.

Over the course of the 1980s, demand for air travel rose rapidly, yet safety appeared unaffected. Quality of service deteriorated, however, measured by delays and complaints. The industry was substantially restructured (see Fig. 8.3), with significantly higher concentration levels nationally, one- or two-firm dominance at every major hub, and a dra-matic failure rate among new entrants (Department of Transportation, 1987: 64–5).[14] Industry profitability, on average, all but disappeared.

8.3.2. Natural Gas and Regulatory Failure

In the gas industry regulation failed in a fundamental way after the New Deal: it actually produced a shortage of natural gas. Late in 1968 the American Gas Association sent a warning to the FPC that prices were too low to sustain an adequate supply. Ironically, this critique came from an organization of distributors and transmission companies that had always opposed higher wellhead prices.[15] But it was too late. Real prices had declined for nearly a decade, stimulating demand but discouraging exploration for new supplies. Net additions to reserves declined in the 1960s for the first time since the Second World War, and prices in unregu-lated intrastate markets rose beyond the regulated price by a growing margin (Vietor, 1984a: 157–60, 196–8, 270).[16] Pipeline companies announced 'curtailments' of gas deliveries under long-term contracts. By 1977, these curtailments exceeded 15 per cent of nationwide demand.[17]

Desperate transmission and distribution companies now launched a series of high-cost gas-development projects, such as imported liquefied

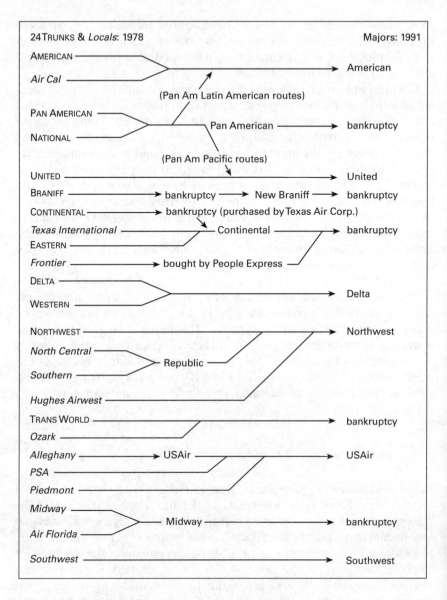

Fig 8.3 *Consolidation of trunk and local airlines prior to deregulation*

natural gas (LNG), coal gasification, and an Alaskan gas pipeline. These projects made sense only in a rate-based, regulated world, however, and all were eventually abandoned. Attempts by regulators to alleviate distortions in supply, price, and demand were frustrated by several factors: institutional inertia, procedural barriers, and the rhetoric of consumer advocacy. When the FPC departed from its traditional 'just and reasonable' criteria in 1969 in an effort to raise prices, it clashed with judicial precedent and ran into a barrage of opposition.[18] Eventually, the Commission turned to rate-setting on a nationwide basis, in which rate-based assessment and cost allocation made little sense. By 1976 this approach managed to push 'new gas' prices closer to the thermal-equivalent price of oil, but it did not significantly affect the overall supply or demand for natural gas.

Congress, meanwhile, first addressed the gas shortage in 1971, but made no substantial changes. Although it was now obvious that the original Act of 1938 had been inappropriately extended by the Supreme Court to wellhead price regulation, the oil shock of 1973 suddenly confused the issue. Producers attacked price controls while consumer activists attacked 'windfall profits' and blamed shortages on a conspiracy of the oil companies that produced gas and petroleum jointly. Distributors and transmission companies regarded all legislative reform proposals with ambivalence. Political gridlock persisted until 1978, when Congress finally approved the Natural Gas Policy Act (NGPA), as part of President Carter's broader National Energy Act. Under this complicated legislation, price controls on new gas would be phased out 'fairly'. Congress designated nine new categories of gas, from different sources, well depths, and vintages—each with a different price schedule. 'Old' gas would remain regulated indefinitely, but the deepest, highest-cost gas could now sell at market prices (US Congress, 1978).

As might have been predicted, pipeline companies immediately bid up the price of new gas. The oil shock of 1979, meanwhile, doubled the price of gas substitutes and stimulated panic buying. Pipeline companies now signed 'take-or-pay' contracts, agreeing to pay producers very high prices even if they could not take the gas. There was little consideration of demand elasticity. But after a few years high prices did stimulate increased production, conservation, and—when oil prices fell after 1982—substitution. By 1985 spot-market gas prices were falling freely. Pipeline companies could not sell enough gas, while distributors, consumers, and their political representatives were outraged at paying above-market—albeit contractual—prices.

Now under intense but conflicting pressures from producers, pipeline companies, distributors, state regulators and consumers, the Federal Energy Regulatory Commission (FERC, as the former FPC was now called) fumbled towards further regulatory reform. First, the FERC allowed gas distributors to back out of long-term purchase contracts. It encouraged 'contract carriage' in which pipeline companies were allowed to carry gas for distributors that purchased it directly from a producer. New rates were developed that separated the charges for the fixed and variable costs of gas transportation (FERC, 1984). This stuck the pipeline companies with 'take-or-pay' liabilities measured in billions of dollars (Interstate Natural Gas Association of America, 1988: 2). To cope with the situation the FERC issued Order 436 in 1985, a landmark ruling under which interstate pipelines that intended to transport third-party gas (which producers were now willing to sell directly to distributors at lower prices) would be required to do so on a non-discriminatory basis. To provide equal access to buyers and sellers, pipeline companies would have to 'unbundle' their gas sales business from their gas transport business, each with separate tariffs. Most producers accepted these terms grudgingly, as they would help them to escape their long-term supply contract and compete for new business. FERC also substantially deregulated most old gas (FERC, 1985).

Order 436 pushed the entire American gas industry further into becoming a general industry. In less than two years, the proportion of gas sold and transported by interstate pipelines fell below the portion that was merely transported. As short-term gas purchase markets developed, brokers and independent marketers sprang up everywhere. Mergers, divestitures, and acquisitions effected a thorough restructuring of the industry, much like that in airlines.[19] Here, too, costs were reduced, systems were streamlined, and earnings weakened. But unlike the new regime in airlines, this new situation did not amount to more deregulation. Rather, it was a new form of asymmetrically regulated competition.

8.3.3. *Financial Services and the New Economic Context*

American-style banking regulation worked well enough from the late 1930s to the late 1960s, as long as high rates of economic growth, low inflation, and low interest rates prevailed. Banks, thrifts, brokers, and mutual funds all prospered. But in the late 1960s, when large federal deficits required Treasury financing, a credit crunch ensued. Short-term rates exceeded Regulation Q, the Federal Reserve's ceiling on deposit interest (Cox, 1966: 121). The result was disintermediation: the bypass of traditional financial institutions in the exchange of funds between lenders and borrowers.

As short-term interest rates on deposits exceeded long-term earnings from fixed-rate loans, banks—and especially thrifts—experienced a decline in deposits and a squeeze on margins. More serious bouts of disintermediation and mismatch between earnings from fixed-rate loans and the cost of deposits at higher market rates followed in 1970, 1974, 1979, and 1981 (Cargill and Garcia, 1985: 81–4). In 1981, there was a shift of several hundred billion dollars from depository institutions to less-regulated investments such as money-market funds and treasury bills. Meanwhile, slower economic growth and a decline in the national savings rate intensified competition for market share in financial services. The demise of fixed exchange rates and the petro-dollar imbalances following the oil shock of 1973 helped internationalize American financial markets and institutions. Large borrowers gained access to foreign markets, while foreign banks entered US markets. Government deficits and the oil shocks of 1973 and 1979 aggravated inflationary pressures, forcing nominal interest rates to new heights.

In this environment of incipient competition, technological developments in information processing and telecommunications offered new opportunities to reduce costs and stimulate revenues. Applications began in bank operations, where reader/sorter document processors and mainframe computers revolutionized record-keeping and transactions processing. Improvements in digital transmission facilitated electronic funds-transfers and created cost savings and new services for multibranch networks. By the early 1980s, the new technology had reached out into the distribution channels. With the development of automatic teller machines, point-of-sale terminals, and 'smart cards', up-to-date technology became essential to competitiveness in banking (Goodman, 1986: 181–93; Lawrence and Shay, 1986: 53–92).

By changing the basic conditions of supply and demand, the new macroeconomic and technological circumstances strained the prevailing regulatory structure. Where regulations were most binding, or where loopholes were most inviting, aggressive firms devised means of breaching product and geographic constraints. Beginning in the early 1970s, innovative managers at Citibank devised negotiable certificates of deposit. Mutual banks in Massachusetts created the NOW account (Negotiable Order of Withdrawal) to compete with commercial banks for checkable deposits. Merrill Lynch developed a Money Market Mutual Fund to capture savings deposits when market interest rates exceeded Regulation Q.

Meanwhile, new organizational innovations such as bank holding companies, 'non-bank banks' (firms that made loans or took deposits, but not both), and loan production offices were used to circumvent the market and product boundaries devised by regulators. And these loopholes opened both ways. While they allowed banks to escape restrictions, they also helped non-bank financial companies to penetrate lucrative and hitherto protected banking markets. By the late 1980s financial incomes for the ten largest non-financial firms, the six largest non-bank financial companies, and the five largest bank holding companies were about equal (Davidson, Lynch, and Vietor, 1985).

Despite these economic and entrepreneurial pressures, politicians were extremely slow to accept reform. Not only did the American public have an abiding distrust of concentrated financial power, but vested interests were unusually well organized and politically influential. The provisions of the Glass–Steagall and McFadden Acts still protected thousands of inefficient and uncompetitive firms. Fragmented regulatory bureaucracies jealously guarded their jurisdictions. Eventually, though, the disintermediation and mismatch so devastated the thrift industry that Congress was forced to act. In 1980, with the support of most bankers, it passed the Depository Institutions Deregulation and Monetary Control Act (DIDMCA). Deposit-interest ceilings (Regulation Q) were phased out. Commercial banks were allowed to offer interest-bearing NOW accounts. Federally chartered thrifts received new freedoms from product and geographic restrictions, and the deposit insurance ceiling was raised from $40,000 to $100,000.[20]

But DIDMCA was not enough. In 1981, as the economy plunged into recession with record-high interest rates, a wave of failures gripped the savings and loan industry. Congress seemed to panic and hastily passed the Garn–St Germain Act. This Act provided easier and wider access to funds, especially money-market deposit accounts at market rates. It also allowed thrifts unprecedented freedom to make loans for commercial real estate and construction and to buy low-grade bonds.[21] Supervisory oversight, meanwhile, was curtailed by a presidential administration determined to unleash 'private enterprise'. In combination, these measures proved to be a colossal mistake.

At the state level, restrictions on branching, interstate banking, and financial-service diversification came increasingly under attack. The resulting changes were motivated not so much by free-market sympathies as by the threat of insolvency that was forcing regulators to loosen restrictions and allow strong firms to buy out weaker ones. Size, scale, scope, and diversity were increasingly the best, and perhaps only, hedges against financial risk.

The consequences of these state and federal changes were extraordinary. Competition among financial institutions to attract deposits and make loans quickened. As prices fell towards marginal costs or below, banks were forced to cut costs and charge their customers openly for services formerly provided 'free'. With commercial banks under credit pressure from bad oil loans and dubious sovereign loans to developing countries, thrifts had a clear field to embark on a lending spree, with deposits now subsidized by federal insurance. From 1983 to 1987, credit flowed freely from savings and loans into markets no one else would serve. The result was a financial catastrophe—a savings and loans crisis that would cost taxpayers between $300 and $400 billion to resolve.[22]

A wave of consolidations of failing thrifts and failing banks followed. Out of necessity, McFadden Act restrictions on interstate banking quickly collapsed. Money centre banks became much larger and a new group of 'super regional' banks, with assets in the tens of billions, emerged

(Rhoades, 1985: 29–36).[23] By the end of the 1980s, the whole New Deal structure in banking was near the point of collapse. A system of regulated competition had taken its place, not unlike the system in the natural gas and telecommunication industries. But, because the vested interests were so complex, Congress would continue to have difficulty restructuring the regulatory system first established in 1933.

8.3.4. Technology and Telecommunications

In the late 1960s, AT&T's end-to-end monopoly in electronic voice communication began to unravel under pressure from technological innovations. On both the supply and demand sides of the business, new technological opportunities changed cost characteristics. Both FCC and AT&T found it increasingly difficult to maintain either prevailing restrictions on entry or the cross-subsidies that had facilitated universal service.

In long-distance transmission, microwave technology originally developed for radar during the Second World War reduced the costs of entry for point-to-point systems providing a service between cities. As early as 1959 the FCC had allowed large users to build their own such systems (FCC, 1959). Before long, entrepreneurs found that they could resell telephone circuits to small users at prices far below those charged by AT&T, with its burden of overheads and cross-subsidies. The first licence to such an entrepreneur was issued in 1969 to Microwave Communications Inc. (MCI), headed by William McGowan. Within a decade, MCI and others had built networks of private line services. By manipulating tariffs and leasing lines from AT&T, they had succeeded in offering long-distance service to the public at retail prices below those charged by AT&T itself (FCC, 1969).[24] Although regulators opposed this all-out competitive entry, by then it was an accomplished fact, sustained by the courts.

In equipment, the process was similar. AT&T's prohibition on interconnection of non-AT&T equipment broke down in the late 1960s under pressure from innovation and entrepreneurship. First the Carterfone, a device that connected field-mobile radios to the telephone network, forced its way through the courts and into the AT&T system (FCC, 1968). As electronic equipment made with transistors and integrated circuits destroyed the economies of manufacturing electro-mechanical equipment, a flood of non-Bell products swamped the market. These included telephone sets, PBXs (switching systems located on customers' premises), answering machines, and facsimile machines. By 1980, the FCC acknowledged the new reality and deregulated terminal equipment altogether.

Regulatory barriers between computing and communications likewise gave way to innovation. The convergence of data processing and switching technologies overwhelmed the boundaries drawn by the Justice Department in the antitrust settlement of 1956, when it left AT&T whole but excluded it from the computer business. In 1971, the FCC tried to enforce this separation by a new definition of terms, regulating data processing only when it was incidental to the function of switching a phone call. When that effort failed the commission took a different tack, distinguishing in 1980 between 'basic' and 'enhanced' services and forcing AT&T to keep these activities organizationally separate. Not until 1986 did the FCC finally concede that AT&T's business could not be kept separate from computing (FCC, 1971).[25]

Through the mid-1980s, only the local-exchange segment remained fully regulated and generally closed to competitive entry. In 1982 the Justice Department and AT&T settled a major antitrust suit begun eight years earlier. In that suit, the government accused AT&T of using its market power at a local-exchange level to prevent competition in long-distance services and the sale of equipment. In the settlement, AT&T agreed to divest its twenty-two local-exchange operating companies, which were then reorganized into seven regional holding companies, each with $10 to $14 billion in assets (Temin and Galambos, 1987).[26]

The federal court that supervised the settlement divided the telephone market into 161 regions (LATAs, or local access and transport areas). Only the regional operating companies and other independent telephone companies could provide intra-LATA service. But the regional Bell companies could not compete in inter-LATA (long-distance) markets, nor manufacture equipment, nor provide 'enhanced' services with information value added.[27]

The problem of open entry into the long-distance market was aggravated divestiture. Through an historic system of jurisdictional separations, long-distance revenues subsidized local-exchange rates. Over the years, as the cost of long-distance services dropped and the costs of the local-exchange infrastructure rose, settlements between AT&T and the National Association of Regulatory Utility Commissioners had allocated 26 per cent of local fixed costs to long distance (although long-distance calls accounted for only 7.9 per cent of total usage). With divestiture, a system of 'access charges' was established in which the amount of local fixed costs recovered from long distance was (very gradually) reduced. AT&T thus made huge payments to the local bell companies, for 'access', but these were somewhat reduced over the course of a decade (although not nearly as much as cost-based pricing warranted). AT&T's rates, therefore, could be lowered substantially, which allowed it to compete more effectively with MCI and other new entrants (Davidson & Vietor, 1985: 2–23).

By the time these changes were fully implemented in mid-1986, nearly a dozen companies such as MCI and Sprint competed with AT&T in the long-distance market. In terminal equipment, AT&T's market share had

US West
Mountain Bell
Northeastern Bell
Pacific Northwestern
Bell

Pacific Telesis	**Bell South**	**Ameritech**	**Bell Atlantic**
Nevada Bell	Southern Bell	Ohio Bell	New Jersey Bell
Pacific Telephone	South Central Bell	Indiana Bell	Bell of Pennsylvania
		Michigan Bell	Diamond State Telephone
	Southwestern Bell	Illinois Bell	Chesapeake & Potomac
		Wisconsin Telephone	Telephone Companies (4)

NYNEX
New England Telephone
New York Telephone

Fig 8.4 *Geographic reorganization of regional Bell holding companies*

dropped to below 40 per cent in most product lines. Even in central office equipment, such as digital switches and fibre-optic transmission systems, such multinational firms as Northern Telecom, NEC, Siemens, and Ericsson provided stiff competition for AT&T (Vietor and Yoffie, 1993: 129–92).

Despite all this rivalry, telecommunications remained a regulated market. Changes in regulatory form and scope were spreading in many states, but public utility commissions still controlled key aspects of entry and exit, service, price, and rate of return. The federal court supervising the consent decree in the AT&T case controlled the activities of the Bell operating companies. And the FCC was more active than ever, regulating AT&T's long-distance tariffs, access to its circuits, and the new rules for 'open architecture' in local networks. Here, too, regulated competition, as opposed to total deregulation, had become the new policy norm.

8.4. AT&T: Strategy for a Less Regulated Market

For AT&T, this increasingly competitive yet asymmetrically regulated market structure posed daunting strategic problems. In its core long-distance business MCI and Sprint were only supervised by the FCC, not regulated on a rate-of-return basis. In the market for business products and services, AT&T was especially hampered by the separate-subsidiary requirement of Computer Inquiry II. AT&T Communications, the long-distance arm of the company, had to operate with virtually no ties to AT&T Technologies, which provided terminal equipment. Thus, equipment such as PBXs and computers could not be offered jointly with telecommunications services. And, in central-office equipment, AT&T Network Systems faced several challenges: to meet the technical requirements of equal access; to catch up with Northern Telecom's lead in digital central-office switches; to satisfy the demands for new features and functions from its now fragmented and independent customers—the regional Bell companies; and to establish a sales presence in major foreign markets.

Overshadowing all this day-to-day friction was the issue of structural restrictions in the Modified Final Judgment. No sooner were the regional Bells divested than they began petitioning the court for waivers to expand their services. By 1987, when the court had agreed to review the judgment's restrictions, most of the regional companies had formulated strategies to expand beyond the limits of plain old local access and transport. The very prospect of relief from the restrictions and much less congressional legislation created a relationship of potential competition.

Two CEOs struggled with this changing regulatory environment at AT&T, but with little strategic success. Charlie Brown, the man responsible for the 1982 divestiture settlement, was able to manage the short-term transition, but little more. James Olson, his successor, started to reorganize the company late in 1986, identifying three broad strategic goals: (1) to defend the core business (long-distance services and network equipment sales); (2) to establish a position in 'data networking'; and (3) to become a global force. At the same time Olson reorganized the company to fit this framework, with an End-users Organization, AT&T Technology, and AT&T International.

Cost control was part of the rationale for these changes. In 1986 AT&T had announced a force reduction of 30,000 people and wrote off $3.2 billion for asset revaluation and facilities resizing. With continuing network modernization these efforts yielded a 10.8 per cent reduction in costs for 1987. Although this cheered Wall Street in the short run, it was only a start if AT&T were to become competitive. In the policy arena, AT&T faced two issues of strategic importance: review of the MFJ restrictions and 'price caps'—a new alternative to rate-of-return regulation. AT&T's political effectiveness on these issues was vital to its future earnings.

On the revenue side, AT&T adopted a vigorous advertising campaign (featuring actor Cliff Robertson) in an effort to achieve brand recognition as a long-distance company and win customers based on premium-quality service. This initiative, enhanced by credit card promotions, volume discounts, and subscriber inertia was quite successful. Over the next thirty months, as customers made their choices, AT&T retained about an 84 per cent market share.

In 1987, the Justice Department was preparing for its first, triennial review of the Modified Final Judgment. Various Bell companies were petitioning to remove one or more of the MFJ restrictions, and AT&T realized it was in no way ready to compete. It launched a vigorous political defence of restrictions, based on continuing 'bottlenecks' in all markets. Although it won, the company realized that it would have to adopt a different way of thinking about competition in the future (Huber, 1987).

The second threat came from Dennis Patrick, a new chairman of the FPC who supported 'price caps' as a more competitive and cost-effective alternative to rate-of-return regulation. The idea—adopted from England— was to regulate price directly, rather than earnings, in order to avoid the inefficiencies of rate-of-return regulation. By tying long-distance prices to productivity gains, sellers (AT&T) and buyers (customers) could split the benefits of effective competition. In early 1989, after more than a year of intense lobbying by all parties, the FCC adopted a price-caps formula with which AT&T could live. Henceforth, its long-distance rates—on average— would have to decline annually by 3 per cent to match anticipated productivity gains. AT&T, though, could exceed its authorized rate of return if it managed to cut costs or increase productivity by more (FCC, 1987).[28]

While contesting these regulatory issues at home, AT&T was learning through painful experience that Asian and European regulatory systems were at least as complicated and posed awesome barriers to entry. In Japan, AT&T had tried to sell switches directly to the Japanese phone company Nippon Telephone and Telegraph, but lost out to Northern Telecom, the only foreigner allowed into that segment. It did form joint ventures in Taiwan and Korea that began selling central office equipment throughout Asia. In Europe, a 1983 joint venture with Phillips to build equipment in the Netherlands developed slowly, as did a PC deal with Olivetti, and smaller ventures with Telefonica (Spain), SGS (Italy), and NKT (Denmark).

AT&T's initial global strategy prior to the late 1980s was to sell all products in all major regions of the world, relying on direct sales, a few joint ventures, and indirect sales through local partnerships and distributorships. 'AT&T had been a monopoly,' recalled one AT&T executive in Tokyo, 'and we believed that everyone in the world must want AT&T products' (Vietor and Yoffie, 1993: 170). Throughout Europe and Asia, AT&T was getting beaten in contract after contract due to poor execution, the separation of its own operating units, failure of its joint-venture partnerships, hastiness, and, especially, lack of political savvy.

In 1988, Robert Allen succeeded James Olson as chairman of AT&T after Olson's unexpected death. Finally, the strategy began to change. In March 1989, Allen announced a more decentralized organization to cut costs and 'strengthen customer relationships'. The plan designated nineteen semi-autonomous business units and twenty-four divisions. The latter were support or sales organizations that were required by contract to sell their services internally to the business units. The business units, representing each major AT&T product line, were given supposedly firm responsibilities for meeting net-income levels. Drastic though this was, Allen cautioned that 'if employees focus solely on the organizational changes, they are missing the point'. The point was to help 'our people get closer to their customers' (Allen, 1988).

Now AT&T articulated an aggressive strategy of generating 25 per cent of its revenues outside the United States. Despite its earlier missteps, its overseas sales by 1988 were $980 million—representing 20 per cent annual growth. AT&T's most notable success was a victory over Siemens, Alcatel, and Ericsson in 1989 to win a contract with Italtel, Italy's state-owned telecommunications company. The Italtel deal demonstrated international learning and more maturity on the part of AT&T. By 1990, AT&T's international equipment sales exceeded $1.5 billion, a sixfold increase in four years.

8.5. The Drift Towards Regulated Competition

Forty years of economic regulation deeply affected the structure and organizational capabilities of the major firms in each industry. These effects, however, became clear only with the benefit of hindsight, particularly after some degree of deregulation. All four of the dominant companies I studied (American Airlines, El Paso Natural Gas, AT&T, and BankAmerica) in my recent book, *Contrived Competition: Regulation and Deregulation in America*, were driven by 'service values' (Vietor, 1994). That is, service standards rather than operational efficiency *per se* (as measured by such conventional yardsticks as return on assets), defined managers' strategic goals and career incentives. Partly as a consequence, all the firms had high-cost structures relative to what they were able to achieve in response to deregulation.

Under regulation, labour costs were higher and productivity lower than they proved to be under deregulation. All four firms turned out to have excess capacity in plant and equipment. To deal with the process of regulation, these firms had employed a strikingly high number of lawyers, lobbyists, tariff specialists, and public affairs managers. The more regulated the industry, the larger and more important were these functions for the individual firms.

Most importantly, regulation had reached into the core of these businesses by shaping their operating systems. AT&T's hierarchical, redundant network and durable telephone equipment, American Airlines' fragmented, point-to-point route structure and diverse fleet, BankAmerica's 1,000-plus branch network, and El Paso's huge gathering system, were all products of their regulatory circumstances. Not surprisingly, large parts of these structures proved untenable under competitive rivalry.

Economic regulation had also inhibited the development of some business functions that are common in competitive firms. Marketing and distribution channels were severely underdeveloped. For the most part they were limited to brand advertising and direct sales. Strategic pricing, product-line differentiation, and market segmentation by customer characteristics were rudimentary or non-existent. If customers wanted an airline ticket, they went to the airport or possibly to an independent travel agent. If one wanted a telephone, one leased it from AT&T. To get natural gas, a large user negotiated a long-term supply contract with the El Paso firm, with everything bundled together. If a borrower wanted a loan, no matter if it were for real estate, an automobile, a child's education, or a small business startup, he or she went to the local branch of BankAmerica and talked with a loan officer. In all four industries and companies, price was seldom a factor and prices among competing firms customarily were exactly the same.

Deregulation obviously affected all of these business characteristics. The less gradual and more thoroughgoing the change, the greater the impact, especially on the firm's bottom line. Thus in airlines, American Airlines was driven to huge losses ($20 million a month) within eighteen months of the Airline Deregulation Act of 1978. In natural gas, where deregulation was gradual and partial, El Paso limped along, making semi-coordinated adjustments over the course of a decade. For BankAmerica, the pattern was complicated by its location in California and by the bank's unique statewide branch system. As the California economy boomed and competition remained minimal, the early effects of deregulation scarcely touched BankAmerica. These conditions lulled its management into complacency, requiring a much more severe—in fact, near-fatal—adjustment in the mid-1980s. After MCI's entry into the long-distance telephone market in 1975, AT&T watched its market share and profit margins shrink for more than a decade before its competitive response finally made a decisive difference.

Successful adjustment to deregulation entailed first-mover advantages. Where management recognized weaknesses quickly, saw the need for strategic adjustment accurately, and implemented organizational changes effectively, it could seize a lasting advantage in the newly competitive market. Of course, this combination of responses was unusual. Among my four cases, American Airlines is the best example of such a response. Robert Crandall, American's chief executive, immediately grounded inefficient aircraft, laid off redundant employees, and reorganized the firm's route structure into a more efficient hub-and-spoke network. He and his management also recognized the importance of strategic pricing and of new distribution channels, especially computerized reservation systems. They educated their employees intensively about the need for work flexibility and higher productivity. No other airline saw all these factors so quickly, recognized its own weaknesses and strengths so accurately, or implemented the necessary changes so ruthlessly and effectively.

In El Paso's case, management was quick to recognize some problems, but not others. The company curtailed its high-cost gas purchases earlier than other firms in the industry, but did not attend expeditiously to its excess plant and high operating costs. It was quick to embrace new regulatory initiatives, even when they were obviously inequitable. El Paso trusted regulators to mitigate inequities and implement reforms efficiently. When this did not happen, the firm's management was forced to reassess its strategy repeatedly, not making the kind of long-term progress that it needed to remain dominant in the industry.

At BankAmerica, new management had a positive strategy for deregulation in 1981, but even then it did not fully realize the severity of the bank's weaknesses. Even when the then chief executive officer Sam Armacost recognized these problems, he and his staff were too slow in implementing the necessary cost-cutting, credit controls, technological modernization, and change in corporate culture towards a more market-oriented organization. Only several years later, when driven to near failure under extremely difficult economic circumstances, could the bank finally make the necessary changes. In the end, however, its strategic adjustment to deregulation did prove successful.

AT&T, by far the largest and least competitive of the four firms, adjusted most gradually with repeated strategic false starts and revisions. The company's immense physical plant (network, manufacturing, real estate, imbedded equipment), its hierarchical structure, and the Bell System's culture of lifetime employment, together posed overwhelming barriers to change. Cost-cutting proved very difficult. So did reorienting employees to the goal of responding to customers' needs. As the market was resegmented by deregulation, AT&T struggled to implement a strategy of vertically integrated 'information movement and management' on a global scale. AT&T continued to earn healthy returns, but it remains unclear whether the new strategy is feasible as a long-term plan.

What is clear is that for all four of these firms—and just as surely for their competitors—regulatory change intimately affected every significant aspect of corporate strategy and structure. The responses of the firms contributed to the market-structuring process of regulation itself. Their

actions helped shape supply and indirectly affected demand. Throughout
the whole era of deregulation, these firms engaged vigorously in the political process, trying to steer the direction of regulatory change in ways that
would hurt them least. Among the four firms, AT&T experienced the single worst political loss (divestiture), but also the largest regulatory successes later (reductions of its access charges, maintenance of competitive
restrictions on the Bell operating companies at least until 1995, and international expansion).

We now have in place all of the essential pieces of a conceptual framework for analysing and understanding economic regulation. At the heart
of this dynamic model, as mentioned at the beginning of this chapter, is
the idea of *market structuring*. Through this market-structuring process, in
which any degree of government regulation affects the characteristics of
the market, it also affects the behaviour of business firms. For a regulated
firm the business environment comprises two parallel contexts: the regulation-defined market-place and the political arena of vested interests that
reflect those market relationships. A regulated firm, to be effective, needs
strategies that will enable it to compete (or, in the case of a monopoly,
enable it to operate effectively) in both the regulated market and the political arena. Those strategies must be complementary and reinforcing.
Broader changes, in technology, macroeconomic conditions, and political
values underlie the entire process.

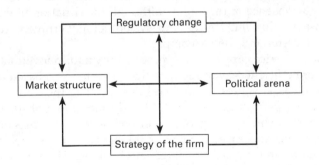

Fig 8.5 *Market-structuring process*

Viewed from this perspective, monocausal interpretations of regulation
make little sense. For both the onset of economic regulation in the 1930s
and the revision or removal of regulation in the 1970s and 1980s, changing
basic economic conditions and political values played a major role. Only
within that context is it worth discussing public or private interests, market failures or regulatory failures. What we see historically is that market
conditions, often affected by existing regulatory policies, gave rise to political pressures for regulatory change. These pressures usually included

elements motivated by the public interest, by bureaucratic considerations, and by competing private interests. Regulated industries did not usually capture the regulatory process, but they did influence it. In both the 1930s and the 1970s firms played an important role in the processes of regulatory reform and market-structuring, yet rarely was this a controlling role.

This historical and institutional framework can usefully inform both public policy and business decision-making. A strikingly obvious observation from a policy perspective is the extraordinary dynamism of markets—even when regulated—and the constant difficulty regulators have in keeping up with market shifts. In each of the industries I studied, regulatory regimes which sought industry stabilization responded poorly to technologically induced economic changes and also to the exercise of political entrepreneurship. Changes in basic macroeconomic conditions had a significant impact on regulation within particular industries and as a more general political phenomenon.

Finally, we can see from these histories the limits to regulation. At least within an American context of private property and due process, regulation can distort market structure only so far before economic and competitive pressures begin to undermine the regulatory process itself. The New Deal experiment in economic regulation, which lasted nearly forty years, was largely over by 1980. Since about 1983, when the drive towards deregulation petered out, it has been generally replaced by regulated competition. The overall picture in the mid-1990s became characterized not so much by the absence of regulation, although the situation in the airlines came close to this, but by a new system of government regulation designed to foster and control competition.

In principle, price caps linked to productivity and innovation certainly seem a more efficient way to regulate than do rate cases based on historical costs and asset values. Open access does address the conflict between inherently competitive gas production and more oligopolistic interstate gas-transport business, and provides incentives to keep costs and prices at a minimum. And in commercial banking almost no one can argue against market interest rates or interstate banking. These reforms make sense for customers as well as for the international competitiveness of US banks.

But the new systems of regulated competition that have thus far evolved in natural gas, telecommunications, and banking still have a number of serious problems. Policies such as Order 436 in gas, price caps in telecommunications, or the requirements of the 1989 Financial Institutions Reform Act in the savings and loan sector are extremely complex and require more bureaucrats and lawyers than ever to administer. Any division between regulation and competition, moreover, requires firms to make detailed and inevitably static cost allocations. And some services have been segmented into socially undesirable categories.

But what has changed most is the New Deal's fundamental premiss that competition was the problem. Now it is viewed as the solution. Yet since neither consumers nor firms are entirely pleased with the outcomes, it remains uncertain whether, in the end, this new policy regime will prove more durable than its predecessor.

NOTES

1. For surveys of this literature, see Horwitz (1989), McCraw (1975), Mitnick (1980).
2. Social and political historians, for the most part, subscribe to this perspective. For example, see, Hawley (1966), Hays (1957), Hofstadter (1955).
3. For failed pluralism, a variant of this approach, see Lowi (1969), McConnell (1966).
4. Among historians, Gabriel Kolko is the most noted proponent of this view; among economists, George Stigler. See Kolko (1963), Stigler (1971).
5. For examples, see Anderson (1981), Breyer (1982), Derthick and Quirk (1985), McCraw (1984).
6. See also Hawley (1966) and Higgs (1987).
7. See also Loss (1961).
8. Transportation Act of 1940, quoted in Clair Wilcox, *Public Policies Toward Business* (Homewood, Ill., 1960), 660.
9. For more detailed analysis of this pricing system, see Sichter (1981), Vietor (1989).
10. Under Section 11 of the Public Utilities Holding Company Act, the SEC reviewed registrations for 929 utilities (electric and gas). By 1954, it had forced the divestment of 417 companies, including 158 gas utilities with assets of $158 million (Securities and Exchange Commission, Annual Reports, 1951–4).
11. For a more detailed discussion of policy entrepreneurship, see Coppin and High (1991), 95–9.
12. US Congress (1975), Committee Print, 145–6.
13. Bailey, Graham, and Kaplan (1985), 54–66; also Joedicke (1988).
14. Of at least 18 new entrants in the major routes between 1979 and 1985, 16 failed or were acquired. In the commuter airlines segment, 48 of the 50 largest firms were tied to majors through joint marketing arrangements, or were acquired.
15. W. M. Jacobs to Lee White, 16 Dec. 1968, reprinted in US Congress, House, Interstate Commerce Committee, Subcommittee on Communications and Power, Natural Gas Act of 1971 (92nd Cong., 1st Sess.), 139.
16. See also American Gas Association, *Gas Facts 1979* (Arlington, Va., 1980), 6.
17. Demand here is taken to be the supply that had previously been ordered under long-term contracts. Meanwhile, natural gas production itself peaked in 1973, at 22.5 trillion cubic feet (tcf). By 1986, it had fallen to 17.4 tcf.

18. For the major examples of these efforts, see FPC, 'Pipeline Production Area Rate Proceeding', Opinion No. 568, 42 FPC 738 (1969), aff/d *City of Chicago* v. *FPC*, 458 F. 2d 731 (1971); *PSC of New York* v. *FPC*, 511 F. 2nd 338 (1975).
19. Cambridge Energy Research Associates (1988); also, Energy Information Administration (1986).
20. Pub. L. No. 96-221, 94. Stat. 132. For analysis of these provisions see Loring and Bruncy (1985), 347–54.
21. Pub. L. No. 97-320, 96 Stat. 1501. For analysis, see Richard Fischer *et al.* (1982).
22. Federal Home Loan Bank Board (1990). For analyses of the causes of these problems, see Carron (1982) and Balderston (1985).
23. See also Board of Governors of the Federal Reserve System, *Annual Statistical Digest, 1987* (Washington, 1988), 211; Edwin B. Cox, *Bank Performance Annual, 1988* (Boston: Warren, Gorham & Lamont, 1989), 232; and FDIC, *Statistics on Banking, 1988* (Washington, 1989).
24. See also Coll (1986), 51–2, 83–5, and *MCI Inc.* v. *FCC*, 580 F.2d 590 (D.C. Cir.), cert. denied, 439 US 980 (1978).
25. See also Second Computer Inquiry, 77 FCC 2d 384 (1980) and FCC, Docket No. 85-229, 'Report and Order', Third Computer Inquiry, 16 June 1986. At this time, AT&T entered the computer business directly, competing with IBM, Digital, and other companies.
26. See also Tunstall (1985) and Vietor (1989), supra n. 41.
27. *US* v. *AT&T*, C.A. No. 82-0192, 'Modification of Final Judgment', 24 Aug. 1982.
28. See also *Communications Week*, 20 Mar. 1989, 1, 52.

REFERENCES

Allen, R. (1988), 'A Direction for AT&T'.

Anderson, D. D. (1981), *Regulatory Politics and Electric Utilities* (Boston: Auburn House).

Bailey, E. E., Graham, D. R., and Kaplan, D. P. (1985), *Deregulating the Airlines* (Cambridge: MIT Press), 54–66.

Balderston, F. (1985), *Thrifts in Crisis* (Cambridge, Mass.: Ballinger Publishing).

Bernstein, M. (1955), *Regulating Business by Independent Commission* (Princeton: Princeton University Press).

Breyer, S. (1982), *Regulation and its Reform* (Cambridge, Mass.: Harvard University Press).

Brinkley, A. (1989), 'The New Deal and the Idea of the State', in S. Fraser and G. Gerstle, *The Rise and Fall of the New Deal Order, 1930–1980* (Princeton: Princeton University Press), 85–121.

Buchanan, J. (1968), *The Demand and Supply of Public Goods Economics* (Chicago: Rand McNally).

Burns, A. R. (1936), *The Decline of Competition* (New York: McGraw-Hill), 523.

Cambridge Energy Research Associates (1988), *Natural Gas Trends* (Cambridge, Mass.).

Cargill, T., and Garcia, G. (1985), *Financial Reform in the 1980s* (Stanford, Calif.: Hoover Institute Press), 81–4.

Carron, A. S. (1982), 'The Plight of the Thrift Institutions' (Washington: Brookings Institution).

Caves, R. E. (1962), *Air Transport and its Regulators* (Cambridge, Mass.: Harvard University Press).

Civil Aeronautics Board (1972), *CAB Handbook of Airline Statistics* (Washington).

Coll, S. (1986), 'The Deal of the Century' (New York: Atheneum).

Coppin, C. A., and High, J. (1991), 'Entrepreneurship and Competition in Bureaucracy: Harvy Washington Wiley's Bureau of Chemistry, 1883–1903', in J. High (ed.), *Economic Regulatory: Theory and History* (Ann Arbor: University of Michigan Press), 95–9.

Cox, Jr., A. H. (1966), *Regulation of Interest Rates on Bank Deposits* (Ann Arbor: University of Michigan Press), 121.

Davidson, D., Lynch, J., and Vietor, R. (1985), *Regulation and Competition in Commercial Banking*, (HBS Case Services, No. 9-385-247, Boston), exhibit 3, 35.

—— and Vietor, R. (1985), 'Economics and Politics of Deregulation: The Issue of Telephone Access Charges', *Journal of Policy Analysis and Management 5* (Fall), 2–23.

Department of Transportation (1986, 1987), *Air Carrier Monthly Traffic Statistics, 1986, 1987* (Washington).

—— (1987), *Air Transport World* (Washington), 64–5.

Derthick, M., and Quirk, P. (1985), *The Politics of Deregulation* (Washington: Brookings Institution), 29–57.

Energy Information Administration (1986),'Pipeline Mergers and Their Potential Impact on Natural Gas Markets', *Natural Gas Monthly* (Feb.) pp. xxi–xliv.

Federal Circuit Court (1959), *Above 890 Mc.*, 27 F.C.C. 359.

—— (1968), *Carterfone* 13 F.C.C. 2d 606.

—— (1969), *Microwave Communications, Inc.*, 18 F.C.C. 2d, 953.

—— (1971), *Regulatory & Policy Problems Presented by the Interdependence of Computer & Communications Services & Facilities*, 28 F.C.C. 2d 267.

Federal Communications Commission, CC Docket 87-313 (1987), 'Notice of Proposed Rulemaking' 21 Aug.

Federal Energy Regulatory Commission (1984), *Final Rule*, Docket No. RM83-71, Order No. 380, 25 May.

—— (1985), *Order 436*, Stats. & Regs. 30,665 (Nov.), 31,467; 50 *Federal Register* 42,408 (18 Oct.).

Federal Home Loan Bank Board (1990), *Annual Report 1989* (Washington).

Federal Power Commission (1954), *Statistics of Natural Gas Companies, 1954* (Washington).

Federal Reserve System Board of Governors (1985), *Flow of Funds* (Washington).

Federal Trade Commission (1934–5), *Summary Report of the Federal Trade Commission to the Senate of the United States . . . On Economic, Financial, and Corporate Phases of Holding and Operating Companies of Electric and Gas Utilities*, vols. 68–9a, 72a (Washington).

Fischer, R., *et al.*, (1982), 'The Garn-St. Germain Depository Institutions Act of 1982: What's in It for You?' (Arlington, Va.: The Consumer Bankers Association).

Fruhan, W. (1972), *The Fight for a Competitive Advantage* (Boston: Harvard Business School).

Goodman, L. S. (1986), 'The Interface Between Technology and Regulation in Banking', in A. Saunders and L. J. White, *Technology and the Regulation of Financial Markets* (Lexington, Mass.: Lexington Books), 181–93.

Gordon, R. (1951), 'Cyclical Experience in the Interwar Period: The Investment Boom of the Twenties', the National Bureau of Economic Research, *Conference on Business Cycles* (New York), 194.

Hawley, E. (1966), 'The New Deal and the Problem of Monopoly' (Princeton: Princeton University Press).

—— (1981), 'Three Facets of Hooverian Associationalism: Lumber, Aviation, and Movies, 1921–1930', in T. K. McCraw (ed.), *Regulation in Perspective* (Boston: Harvard Business School), 99.

Hays, S. P. (1957), 'The Response to Industrialism' (Chicago: University of Chicago Press).

Higgs, R. (1987), *Crisis and Leviathan* (New York: Oxford University Press), 159–95.

Hofstadter, R. (1955), *The Age of Reform: From Bryan to F.D.R.* (New York: Knopf).

Horwitz, R. B. (1989), *The Irony of Regulatory Reform* (New York: Oxford University Press).

Huber, P. (1987), *The Geodesic Network* (Washington: US Department of Justice).

Interstate Natural Gas Association of America, Policy Analysis Department (1988), 'The Unrelenting Take-or-Pay Problem: Year-end 1987 Exposure and Costs' (Washingto).

Joedicke, R. (Shearson Lehman Brothers) (1988), 'Airline Analyst's Handbook', 12 Sept.

Jordan, William A. (1973), 'Airline Capacity Agreements Correcting a Regulatory Imperfection', *Journal of Air Law and Commerce*, 39. 184–203.

Kolko, G. (1963), *The Triumph of Conservatism: A Reinterpretation of American History, 1900–1916* (New York: Free Press).

Lawrence, C., and Shay, R. P. (1986), 'Technology and Financial Intermediation in Multiproduct Banking Firms: An Econometric Study of U.S. Banks, 1979–1982', in C. Lawrence and R. P. Shay, *Technological Innovation, Regulation, and the Monetary Economy* (Cambridge: Ballinger Books), 53–92.

Loring, H. H., and J. M. Bruncy (1985), 'The Deregulation of Banks', *Washington and Lee Law Review*, 42: 2 (Spring), 347–54.

Loss, L. (1961), *Securities Regulation* (Boston: Little, Brown), i. 23–64.

Lowi, T. J. (1969), *The End of Liberalism* (New York: Norton).

McConnell, G. (1966), *Private Power and American Democracy* (New York: Knopf).

McCraw, T. K. (1975), 'Regulation in America: A Review Article', *Business History Review*, 49. 159–83.

—— (1984), *Prophets of Regulation* (Cambridge, Mass.: Harvard University Press), 162–76.

Mitnick, B. (1980), *The Political Economy of Regulation* (New York: Columbia University Press).

Noll, R. (1989), 'Economic Perspectives on the Politics of Regulation', in R. Schmalansee and R. D. Willig. (eds.), *Handbook of Industrial Organization* (New York: Elsevier), ii. 1254–89.

Peltzman, S. (1976), 'Toward a More General Theory of Regulation', *Journal of Law and Economics*, 19: 2. 211–40.

Rhoades, S. A. (1985), 'National and Local Market Banking Concentration in an Era of Interstate Banking', *Issues in Bank Regulation* (Spring), 29–36.

Richmond, S. B. (1961), *Regulation and Competition in Air Transportation* (New York: Columbia University Press).

Schwartz, B. (1973) (ed.), *The Economic Regulation of Business and Industry: A Legislative History of U.S. Regulatory Agencies* (New York: Chelsea House), iv. 2374–95.

Sichter, J. W. (1981), 'Separations Procedure in the Telephone Industry: The Historical Origins of a Public Policy' (Cambridge, Mass.: Center for Information Policy Research).

Stigler, G. (1971), 'The Theory of Economic Regulation', *Bell Journal of Economics and Management Science*, 2,: 1. 3–21.

Temin, P., with Galambos, L. (1987), *The Fall of the Bell System* (New York: Cambridge University Press).

Tunstall, W. B. (1985), 'Disconnecting Parties' (New York: McGraw-Hill).

US Congress (1934), 'Report on Communications Companies', part III, no. 1, *House Report No. 1273* (73rd Congress, 2nd Session) (Washingto), ix, xii.

—— (1975), Senate Judiciary Committee, Subcommittee on Administrative Practice and Procedure, *Civil Aeronautics Board Practices and Procedures—A Report* (94th Congress, 1st Session), Committee Print (Washington), 145–6.

—— (1978), 'The Natural Gas Policy Act of 1978', *Senate Conference Report No. 95-1126* (95th Congress, 2nd Session) (Washington).

Vietor, R. H. K. (1984*a*), *Energy Policy in America Since 1945* (New York: Cambridge University Press), 21–6.

—— (1984*b*), *Chicago-Midway (A): Alfred Kahn and the CAB*, HBS Case Services, No. 9-384-156 (Boston).

—— (1989), 'AT&T and the Public Good: Regulation and Competition in Telecommunications, 1910–1987,' in Stephen Bradley and Jerry Hausman (eds.), *Future Competition in Telecommunications* (Boston: HBS Press), 27–105.

—— (1994), *Contrived Competition: Regulation and Deregulation in America* (Cambridge, Mass.: Harvard University Press).

—— and Yoffie, David (1993), 'Telecommunications: Deregulation and Globalization', in David Yoffie (ed.), *Beyond Free Trade* (Boston: HBS Press), 129–92.

PART IV

FOLLOWERS

INSIGNIFICANT ANTITRUST POLICY WITH LITTLE INFLUENCE OF COMPETITIVENESS ON COMPETITIVENESS

9

The State and Enterprise in the German Economy after the Second World War

WERNER PLUMPE[1]

9.1. Introduction

The economic history of the Federal Republic of Germany, during the 1950s and 1960s (Abelshauser, 1983) in particular, appears to be marked by two peculiarities.[2] First, economic power increased rapidly, to an extent and at a pace unexpected after the destruction of war. The economic consequences of war were overcome by the mid-1950s and West Germany had decisively crossed the threshold to affluence by 1960 (Glastetter, Högemann, and Marquardt, 1991). Second, the years from 1949 to 1966 were marked by a severe conceptual break within state economic policy. The era of the *Wirtschaftswunder*, the economic miracle, was at least in the public's opinion, also the era of *Wirtschaftsliberalismus*, an economic liberalism which seemed radical in the German context.

During these years the tradition of state intervention and of markets dominated by cartels and agreements was broken (Giersch and Paqué, 1993). The parallel occurrence of the economic miracle and economic liberalism rapidly turned into a causality. Especially in the government's description of economic policy,[3] the economic liberalism of the 1950s was presented as the engine of postwar growth. Popular for a long time, this proposition is still often put forth today. Not surprisingly, it proved, on further examination, to be far too simple. Research on the economic history of this period has revealed that the state did indeed intervene in the economy (Hagemann, 1984; Jakli, 1990), but other factors which encouraged rapid growth were present at the end of the war and this growth is no longer to be seen as the result of a liberal economic policy (Abelshauser,

1983). Furthermore, state intervention in capital formation and investments, for example, followed long-practised corporatist patterns: hence Erhard's economic miracle becomes merely a myth, albeit a very effective one (Abelshauser, 1984: 285–318).

This critique has itself drawn criticism, as indeed any evaluation of economic policy concepts may become a point of contention,[4] and this chapter examines in detail the causes of the economic miracle and its preconditions in order to evaluate the state's significance in economic development generally and for business strategy in particular. An ambivalent picture will be drawn. While the state withdrew from direct economic intervention after 1949 (with important exceptions), at the same time its significance for economic reconstruction cannot be overemphasized. Above all, the significance of government action lay as much in the creation of a competitive framework, the general support of private capital formation, and the promotion of a global orientation within industry, as in guaranteeing important normative factors (economic peace, anti-communism, social partnership).

In the 1950s and early 1960s direct economic intervention was limited to overcoming restrictions in capital formation and to propping up deficit areas (agriculture after 1955, the coal industry after 1958–9) (Abelshauser, 1987b; Jakli, 1990; Priebe, 1985). This neo-liberal policy orientation amounted to a conceptual break with Nazi political practice.[5] It had significant consequences for strategies chosen within West German industry—companies were practically forced into the world market, albeit in favourable conditions. This was a challenge companies readily accepted, given that the move to autarky after 1933 had not necessarily been freely followed. Moreover, this move did not lead to a break with world markets.[6]

The argument in this chapter follows various stages. I begin with a sketch of the economic development of the 1950s and 1960s and proceed to a presentation of the concept and practice of *Soziale Marktwirtschaft* (Haselbach, 1991; Nicholls, 1994). The significance and quality of state intervention during economic reconstruction will then be discussed using the example of Investment Aid for the Ruhr Area *(Investitionshilfe für die Ruhr)* (Adamsen, 1981). Here the still widespread gaps in existing research on postwar West German economic history will be noticeable (Kramer, 1991). Although highly contentious, the economic history of West Germany has not been sufficiently analysed; microeconomic studies which provide a detailed analysis of company strategy under the economic miracle are especially lacking (Stokes, 1994b: 233–52).

A number of terms must be clarified before discussing actual developments. Whereas in its English usage the term 'industrial policy' has a rather comprehensive meaning, the German term *Industriepolitik* merely denotes direct state intervention in the manufacturing industry. However this does not apply to state policy before the mid-1960s, apart from a few minor exceptions.[7] On a regional level, though, the picture is a different one. Some *Länder* (federal states) pursued a very active industrial and regional policy and were not shy of direct economic intervention. In this sense the term *Industriepolitik*, and the concept of the direct acceptance of state responsibility for the industrial development it denotes, are not suited to an analysis of the federal government's economic policy after 1949. This has rarely been asserted. Simon Reich's linking of the economic success of the early Federal Republic to guidelines set down in the Nazi era and to a systematic industrial policy on the part of the federal government (Reich, 1990) has also found little support.[8] As has already been emphasized, this does not mean that the role of state economic policy in postwar reconstruction should be discounted, but it is an indication that it requires careful analysis. It seems that international competitiveness and the production capability within West German industry were strong enough to allow for an international role. After 1949 the issue became how to create a setting within which West German industry was able to thrive.[9]

9.2. Economic Development of West Germany, 1945–1949 and 1966–1967

There is general agreement within economic research that the West German economy's postwar cycle lasted from the founding of the Federal Republic until the 1960s. Abelshauser speaks of the 'langen fünfziger Jahren' (Abelshauser, 1987*b*), the long 1950s, which ended in 1966; Giersch *et al.* suggest three phases (Giersch, Paqué, and Schmieding, 1993)—a phase of spontaneous growth from 1949 to 1960, a phase of directed growth from 1960 to 1973, and a phase of deceleration and stagnation between 1973 and 1989. In the international context, the economic development of West Germany appears as in the terms shown in Table 9.1. The rate of West German economic growth also fell continuously. While the annual growth of the gross domestic product (GDP) was between 5 and 15 per cent until 1960, it fell to under 5 per cent during the 1960s. In 1966–7 GDP diminished (Borchardt, 1976: 724 ff.). Despite the downward trend, growth rates were impressive. Capital stock was fully utilized at a rate of over 100 per cent during the first half of the 1950s, remaining between 97.5 per cent and 100 per cent until the mid-1960s. The high unemployment rate after currency reform was reduced by the mid-1950s; from that point on full employment, and even a labour shortage, dominated until 1974. Although capital stock was fully utilized, pressure on inflation remained low; between the Korean Boom and the end of the 1960s the inflation rate

Table 9.1 *Average Annual Growth Rate of GDP (US, Japan: GNP), 1950–1989*

	1950–60 %	1960–73 %	1973–80 %	1980–89 %
West Germany	8.2	4.4	2.2	1.9
France	4.6	5.6	2.8	2.1
Italy	5.6	5.3	2.8	2.3
United Kingdom	2.8	3.1	0.9	2.7
United States	3.3	4.0	2.1	3.0
Japan	8.8	9.6	3.7	4.2

Source: Giersch, Paqué, and Schmieding (1993).

remained between 1 and 4 per cent (Giersch, Paqué, and Schmieding, 1993). The years between 1950 and the end of the 1960s were indeed *Wunderjahre*.

Questioning the causes behind this unprecedented growth cycle in German economic history is not new. The conflict over economic policy, however, is not as important as an examination of the decisive macroeconomic factors. Giersch, Paqué, and Schmieding (1993: 5) have collected the most important figures, as can be seen in Table 9.2.

Clearly, the production capability within West German industry in the 1950s and 1960s was high. Levels of investment and productivity gains allowed the rapidly growing domestic and export demand to be trans-

Table 9.2 *The Growth of Output, Input, and Productivity, 1950–1989*

	1950–60 %	1960–73 %	1973–80 %	1980–89 %
(1) Real GDP[a]	8.2	4.4	2.2	1.9
(2) Active labour force[b]	3.3	0.3	0.0	0.3
(3) Labour volume[c]	0.9	−0.8	−1.0	−0.3
(4) Labour productivity[d]	7.3	5.2	3.2	2.2
(5) Capital stock[e]	4.8	6.1	3.8	2.8
(6) Capital productivity[f]	3.4	−1.6	−1.6	−0.9
(7) Joint factor productivity	6.9	3.0	1.6	1.2

Notes:
[a] Gross domestic product at constant prices.
[b] Number of employed persons.
[c] Number of hours worked by active labour force.
[d] Gross domestic product at constant prices divided by number of hours worked.
[e] Gross fixed capital at constant prices.
[f] Gross domestic product at constant prices divided by captal stock as defined in note to (5).
[g] Weighted productivity of labour and capital as defined in notes to (4) and (6), with weights being 0.7 for labour and 0.3 for capital.

Source: Giersch, Paqué, and Schmieding (1993).

formed into a growing supply of industrial goods, without the accompaniment of inflationary surges. Exports which grew from 10 per cent of industrial goods in 1951 to almost 25 per cent in 1970 benefited decisively from the undervalued DM of the Bretton Woods System; that this undervaluation did not also lead to inflation induced by export demand was due to the elasticity of supply. This was the result of specifically West German conditions after 1949, with a modern but underutilized capital stock on one hand, and a large, productive, and highly qualified labour force on the other. Hence, a flexible reaction was possible in response to the rapidly expanding international demand for West German industrial goods during the Korean Boom and the West European dollar gap (Abelshauser, 1975: 100 ff.; Buchheim, 1990: 81–98; Krengel, 1958). This favourable combination of circumstances at the start developed into a medium-term pattern of relatively inflation-free growth. Above all, this was the result of an economic policy aimed at upholding an elasticity of supply by promoting private capital accumulation and establishing a competitive environment in which market and price distortions were unlikely. To explore this further, Section 9.3 examines the concept and practice of Ludwig Erhard's *Soziale Marktwirtschaft*.

9.3. The Concept of the *Soziale Marktwirtschaft*

9.3.1. *The Emergence of Ordo-Liberalism before 1945*

In the past, the concept of a social market economy has been the topic of debate within economic history (Nichols, 1994: 203–40; Tribe, 1995; Motteli, 1961; Grosser *et al.*, 1990; Haselbach, 1991; Blum, 1969). The first discussions identified as part of the theoretical design of the social market economy arose in the context of the Great Depression. The classical liberal approach to economic theory was clearly strained by the extent and complexity of the 'crisis of capitalism'. In the opinion of young political economists such as Walter Eucken, Wilhelm Röpke, Alexander Rüstow, and Alfred Müller-Armack, a new orientation in terms of economic theory and policy was necessary.[10] In Germany this new orientation coincided with the political crisis of the Weimar Republic, with economic and political considerations becoming indistinguishable in any discussion of the nature and causes of the crisis (Borchardt and Schötz, 1991; Grotkopp, 1954). Yet no conceptual and pragmatic solution to the crisis could be found and the discussion of such matters was interrupted by the rise of National Socialism before a productive conclusion could be reached.[11]

Within the debate on the causes of the Great Depression, two basic theoretical and implicitly political positions can be identified, aside from Marxist crisis scenarios (Kuczynski, 1994: 357 ff.). First, before and during the 'Keynesian revolution', the extent and development of the crisis was seen as due to the failure of the market's balancing function on economic grounds for which state intervention should have compensated. Second, within the tradition of liberal thought, this 'failure of the market' was ascribed to concentration, centralization, and lobbyism on the one side, and to uncontrolled, unsystematic, and arbitrary state intervention in the economic process on the other. This form of regulating and controlling the market was seen as a handicap for the development of a dynamic form of entrepreneurship (Schumpeter, 1987: 99 ff.). It is here that Eucken, Rüstow, Müller-Armack, and Röpke—to name some of the most prominent figures involved in the German economic debate—showed themselves to be true students of Schumpeter (Haselbach, 1991).

The theory was this: the crisis was caused by the dynamic inherent to capitalism, leading to regulation, control, and the tendency to use the state for particular interests (given the pluralistic form of parliamentarism), in conjunction with the deterioration of the moral foundation of Western civilization. Walter Eucken in particular upheld this proposition in an elaborated form and with unambiguous clarity (Eucken, 1932: 297–321). This interpretation, which was thoroughly compatible with Carl Schmitt's critique of the republic (Schmitt, 1991), did not necessarily lead to homogeneous advice about how to remedy the crisis of capitalism. Alfred Müller-Armack especially did not argue in favour of a retreat of the state from the economy but—seemingly taken by Italian fascism—in favour of a strong interventionist state able to override particular interests and to break a cartel's control of the economy (Müller-Armack, 1932 and 1933). Eucken, Röpke, and Rüstow, however, argued in favour of a strong state—neutral *vis-à-vis* particular interests—which was supposed to limit itself to the creation of a functioning market regime by means of an energetic regulatory policy. The state was to maintain distance from daily economic affairs unless an unavoidable crisis situation demanded short-term intervention (Haselbach, 1991).

These 'ordo-liberal' economists were not clear on how to achieve this; they basically hoped for greater insight on the part of politicians and so placed great hopes in Papen's cabinet. Once Papen had also failed, the hope remained that greater insight, reason, and the 'good heart' of man would make a turn possible, especially since National Socialism initially presented itself as a strong state, with the power to reform the economy. Böhm's *Ordnung der Wirtschaft* (1937), the manifesto of ordo-liberalism and later of the social market economy, carried the implicit hope that National Socialism would re-establish a functioning market regime. This was despite the fact that it was already becoming clear that the Nazi dictatorship was aiming at the exact opposite of a liberal entrepreneurial economy, one with a fundamental reform of proprietary rights and powers of disposition for the war economy.[12]

Thus, the ordo-liberal economic debate increasingly ran into conflict with Nazi economic and regulatory practice.[13] While the Great Depression provided the first impetus to modify economic theory, a second arose through development of the economic system under a dictatorship. Although the dictatorial state had the power to override particular interests, it was clear this was only possible with the right advisers.[14] It was soon apparent that the 'strong state' alone was by no means a guarantee of a sensible economic system *(Ordnung der Wirtschaft)*; indeed, despite vague ordo-liberal hopes to the contrary, National Socialism increasingly tended towards a centralist economic dictatorship, which would handicap the entrepreneurial dynamic even more.[15]

The short-term hopes placed in National Socialism were swiftly shattered,[16] especially once it came to light that National Socialism had little to offer the national economy in ideological terms (Kruse, 1988: 48–70). The decisive discussions on political economy increasingly lost any constructive reference to the possible role of a strong state under the leadership of the NSDAP to the National Socialist system—despite their institutional proximity alongside Klasse IV of the Akademie für Deustches Recht (Brackmann, 1993; Haselbach, 1991; Herbst, 1982). On the contrary, political-economic debate moved towards open support of a liberal market model and attempted to substantiate this decision in theoretical terms. This task was carried out by Walter Eucken in particular (Eucken, 1941) who, at the same time, made it clear that political economy should be practical, thus claiming its political authority (Eucken, 1938). Here, the liberal concept was not primarily a concept of resistance in the political sense, even if in retrospect it has often been interpreted as such.[17] Above all, it was a clear rejection of direct state intervention in economic development, and support for re-establishing the market's capacity to function and the role of the creative entrepreneur. During the latter half of the war this concept found increasing support among entrepreneurs desiring the end of the command economy (Herbst, 1982: 350 ff.; W. Plumpe, 1992: 11–37). This approach was not National Socialist, at least in so far as National Socialism created and, during the war further perfected,[18] a state-enforced economic dictatorship. However, a clear political line of opposition against the regime was definitely not an element of ordo- and neo-liberal debate; the practical postwar planning of Ludwig Erhard (from as early as 1943) clearly emanated from neo-liberal thought and was to some extent developed in close co-ordination with high-level National Socialists. Within National Socialism the question of the economic constitution appears to have been open, at least in an academic sense (Hentschel, 1996; Herbst, 1977: 305 ff.).

Thus, the political and military defeat of National Socialism in 1945 did not also signify the collapse of the dominant political economic doctrine; on the contrary, the neo- and ordo-liberal stance retained a role both institutionally and theoretically. In cultural and theoretical terms it had experienced a turning-point at the end of the Weimar Republic which became more pronounced during the National Socialist era under forced inner emigration. After 1945 this development enabled it to couch a description of its own economic approach in 'anti-fascist' terms. The diagnosis of the crisis at the end of the Weimar Republic was based on the collapse of mass democracy and the resulting weak and corruptible interventionist state. In exile, Wilhelm Röpke and Alexander Rüstow further developed these anti-modernist observations; Alfred Müller-Armack did so from within Germany. Thus, after 1945 National Socialism was no longer interpreted as a possibly significant antidote to the flawed development of modernity for which hopes had been raised in 1933. As Alfred Müller-Armack explicitly stated, it was now interpreted as the result of unchecked modernity; as the consequence of a mass society without God.

9.3.2. *The Concept of the Social Market Economy*

The German ordo-liberals' ideas on regulation and their critique of culture merged with the concept of the 'social market economy' as formulated by Müller-Armack in 1947 (Müller-Armack, 1981). In April of that year ideas on economic and social reorganization first found political articulation.[19] They met with some resistance, not least within German industry, given that the majority of employers' organizations fundamentally rejected the existing form of a planned economy (W. Plumpe, 1987: 235 ff.). While direct influence can only be identified in a limited sense, these considerations were the basis for economic reform in 1948, largely because ordo-liberal concepts appealed to Ludwig Erhard. Erhard had often spoken in favour of rapid liberalization of the West German economy (Brackmann, 1993: 231 ff.). At the end of the war Erhard became the Minister of Economic Affairs in Bavaria and from 1947 he was head of the Special Bureau for Monetary and Currency Matters *(Sondersstelle Geld und Kredit)*. During the war Erhard had argued in favour of a liberal solution to financial and monetary problems and he maintained this position in the years that followed. In March 1948 he became head of economic administration in the Bizone in Frankfurt, and was thus the most important figure within the West German economy. His appointment was also a public signal of favour for a liberal solution to the German postwar economic crisis, which was the American choice as well (Nicholls, 1994).

In addition, the liberal economic position swiftly gained the upper hand within the newly created academic advisory council of the Economics Administration (Wissenschaftlicher Beirat der Verwaltung für Wirtschaft, later Bundesministerium für Wirtschaft), and this remained the case until well into the 1960s. Within the advisory council, ordo-liberal ideas of the 1930s were implemented—at least in part. The ordo-liberals had always felt themselves to be the decisive advisers in national economic affairs and had demanded policies to be devised in line with academic debate.[20] At the end of May 1948, shortly before currency reform, Müller-Armack wrote a 'Denkschrift der Volkswirtschaftlichen Gesellschaft zur Verwirklichung der Sozialen Markwirtschaft',[21] in which the concept of a social market economy was clearly defined. At least until the mid-1960s, this concept was the guiding principle of West German economic policy. In a sixteen-point plan Müller-Armack presented a clear conception of the future liberal economic order and outlined the preconditions necessary for its realization. Leaving aside problems resulting from war, Müller-Armack argued in favour of a liberal West German market economy, integrated into the world market, where the state would reduce itself to guaranteeing the general setting for free enterprise.

The dismantlement of price and wage controls and the reintegration of the German economy under non-discriminatory conditions into the world market seemed to Müller-Armack to be the most effective way of accelerating reconstruction. He not only denied that any notable social problems would arise with the liberalization of the economy, but he argued that only this path would stimulate enough production to create a significant rise in the supply of goods. In the event of a large rise in prices, intervention in favour of the needy would be possible, in the form of goods, coupons, etc. However, Müller-Armack rejected the possibility of direct state intervention in the price mechanism both in theoretical and practical terms.

This concept was not new. Furthermore, its social components were quite concealed, in so far as it was a functioning market mechanism designed to lead to a larger supply of goods at low prices, improving the market for the general population. The decisive element in Müller-Armack's concept was not the notion of a free-market economy—it was the new role of the state. This new state was to be reserved in its daily economic affairs but strong and incorruptible in its role as guarantor of the economic system. Hence, its main function was to guarantee the market regime, and especially to maintain free competition. The creative powers of entrepreneurship, in particular, would be able to develop fully within a non-monopolistic, non-cartelized market.

A liberal market regime was therefore the centre-piece of the social market economy which, in the German case, was first to be created and then protected by the state. Accordingly, the legislation accompanying the currency reform of 1948 was close to neo-liberal ideas, while the result was patchwork, as the legal repression of cartels and monopolies did not follow. The neo-liberal analysis of the crisis at the end of the 1920s said that capitalist economies tend to destroy their own base under the impulse towards market regulation and the instrumentalization of politics. As a consequence, the social market economy seemed to be secure only if the state would simultaneously prevent private enterprise from developing either cartel or monopoly power.

Previously, a conceptual agreement existed between neo-liberal theorists, the group around Ludwig Erhard, and those representing German industry. On this point, however, agreement soon evaporated. While industry had welcomed the legislation accompanying currency reform and strongly supported the development of the appropriate tax policy,[22] its support of a move towards monopoly control was limited. Here industry argued in favour of limited state intervention, so as not to reduce its own actions (Berghahn, 1985: 152 ff.).

Next to the disputed question of monopoly control was the issue of a workable economic and social policy as a cornerstone of the social market economy. Contrary to the widespread critique of the neo-liberal concept, its theorists were in favour of state measures in economic and social affairs, but they wanted these to be limited:

The neoliberals accepted a certain level of state support for social purposes, but they wanted this to be selflimiting as far as possible. Therefore they thought in terms of remedial help rather than continous or, as they may have put it chronic, aid to less successful areas of the economy or society. An ailing industry should not be propped up by subsidies, but money should be provided to retain its labor force in more economic activities. So far as personal welfare was concerned, the theory of the social market demanded that as much should be done by individuals as possible, which meant that pensions and health services should be funded on an insurance basis and should not just be a charge on public expenditure. If people were poor, state help could be provided, but it should take the form of targeted support for individuals or families over such matters as rent supplements, rather than blanket projects which might not discriminate between those who could pay and those who could not. (Nicholls, 1994)

Consequently, the concept of the social market economy rested on the state guaranteeing free competition as well as on the principle of subsidiarity. Practical measures arising from the state economic and social policy were not entirely ruled out, but were limited. The role the state would actually play in the economic and social development of the young Bonn Republic and its industry was to be decided on a day-to-day basis. After the 'victory' of the social market economy in 1948–9, it was clear on paper at least that a return to the interventionist tradition of the 1920s would be difficult. The break with the economic theory (Kruse, 1988) and practice (Herbst, 1982) of National Socialism could not have been more radical, in so far as the actual direction of the economy via production targets and steering of investments (*Investitonslenkung*) was ruled out.

9.4. The Practice of the Social Market Economy

This section provides a brief insight into the main features of West German economic policy and the handling of its economic system during the 1950s and 1960s. First, essential aspects of economic development and economic policy will be discussed. An outline of competitive policy and foreign trade will follow. The problem of regulating postwar industrial relations and the organization of the West German labour market cannot be dealt with here (W. Plumpe, 1996*b*: 389–419). Nevertheless, in contrast to input and output markets, the labour market remained regulated to a large extent, as legislation conceded great autonomy to the bargaining parties and guaranteed their liability. At the same time, various rules on co-determination extended this predefined organization of the labour market into plants and companies. Liberal labour relations were an impossibility in the Federal Republic. The West German labour market was almost entirely cartelized: an aspect long viewed as a pillar of the economic miracle. Indeed, cartelization of the labour market was an advantage as long as trade unions were prepared to base their pay policy on productivity. However, by the 1960s this exception to the social market economy had become a decisive handicap to adapting the labour market to a changing (world) economic setting. According to leading liberal economists, high unemployment since 1975 is the economic price paid for labour-market cartels.

Prior to the currency reform of 1948, basic principles of West German economic policy were highly controversial. In brief, two opposing camps existed with ideas on economic policy that clashed within the Sonderstelle Geld und Kredit, which was supposed to prepare the currency reform and economic policy which followed. While one camp upheld a traditional position of retaining the controlling mechanisms of a planned economy and believed the greatest boost for growth to be the resolute promotion of raw materials and producer goods industries, the liberal free-market economists led by Ludwig Erhard had a fundamentally different view. In their opinion, the success of thorough currency reform depended not least on whether the introduction of a new currency would be bound to a noticeable increase in the supply of consumer goods. Due to his own origins, Ludwig Erhard favoured the promotion of the consumer goods industry. Finally, the liberal concept was also adopted because, in this case, the support of the American occupying forces could be counted upon (Ambrosius, 1977).

Erhard's concept was characterized by three main elements: (1) the dismantlement of price-fixing and goods allocation; (2) the promotion of the consumer-goods industry; and (3) waiting for the effects of Marshall Plan Aid (Adamsen, 1981: 40 ff.). However, Erhard did not envisage an independent role for the state within the economic process. He was concerned with the re-establishment of a free-market economy and a state guarantee of market operations. Hence, the fight for monopoly control was central within state economic and regulatory policy in the 1950s (Hentschel, 1996; Laitenberger, 1986).

The neo-liberal concept of reconstruction was consolidated during the currency reform of 1948 and in the subsequent law on the guiding principles of economic policy, then linked to Ludwig Erhard (Buchheim, 1988: 189–231). On 21 June 1948, state price-fixing and goods allocation was stopped, with the exception of basic foodstuffs and certain other basic products (coal, steel, energy). In these areas goods allocation and price-fixing were transferred to newly created specialist bureaux, in which the relevant employers' associations effectively continued what remained of an economic direction (*Bewirtschaftungssystem*) (W. Plumpe, 1987: 297–305).

The consequences of currency reform can hardly be exaggerated. At first, the ability of the market to operate was restored via decontrol of prices. However, next to basic foodstuffs, certain industrial products like coal and steel were excluded, leading to a rapid increase in labour productivity because wages had not been decontrolled and prices had increased significantly. This also stimulated the production of non-durable and consumer goods (Ritschl, 1985: 136–65), but the boom in demand had already collapsed at the end of 1948. Domestic demand was too weak to lead to a long-term recovery and an expansion in exports had not yet begun. The figures shown in Fig. 9.1 reflect the significance of currency reform at the break in reconstruction in 1949. Thus, as 1949 turned into 1950, the neo-liberal economic policy followed by the Economics Ministry came under massive pressure. There was pressure from trade unions because of high unemployment and from occupying Allied forces who feared reconstruction and then demanded an active economic policy from the federal government. Erhard saw this as a 'Generalangriff auf die deutsche Marktwirtschaft', an unjustified fear as Abelshauser points out, since the Allied occupying forces did not favour an alternative to the liberal market economy but merely wanted to prevent a destabilization of the economy and society in the Federal Republic (Abelshauser, 1983: 66 ff.).

The economic programmes[23] devised under this pressure had not become law when in June 1950 the Korean War broke out. This radically changed the international economic setting to the advantage of the West

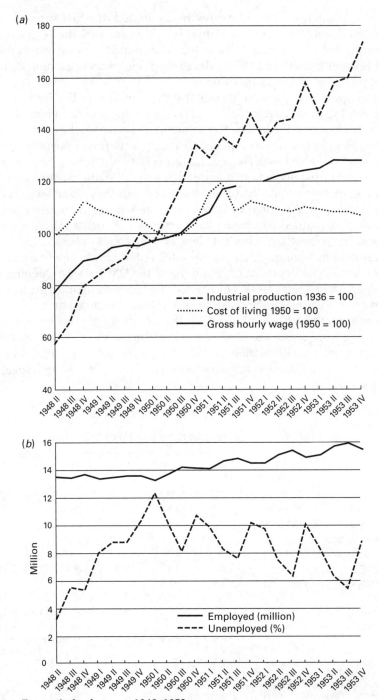

Fig 9.1 *Economic development, 1948–1953*

German economy. Economic growth accelerated due to a surge of international demand for German industrial goods. By 1952 the West German economy was in the midst of a boom. The immediate postwar problems had been overcome and the model of the social market economy was, at least publicly, no longer questioned.

How great was the significance of state economic policy for industrial recovery? Currency reform and its accompanying legislation had led to a massive change in the investment structures essential to the economic miracle. The structure of investment financing was fundamentally altered. This was connected with changes in the tax structure which the occupying forces had implemented on their own. In particular, the rate of income tax and corporate profit tax had been set at a prohibitively high level in 1946. The German side wanted to halve these rates through currency reform; however, the Allied occupying forces prevented such a far-reaching tax reform for fear of large budget deficits. In order to promote necessary investment financing within industry, the federal government decided to ease commercial depreciation. In addition, the DM-Balance Opening Law (*DM-Bilanz-Eröffnungsgesetz*) of August 1949 gave companies greater freedom in evaluating existing assets. After 1948, in the context of rapidly expanding production and turnover, the structures of prewar investment financing were reformed. Next to market liberalization, the promotion of private capital accumulation can be seen as the decisive contribution of politics to West German reconstruction. The figures in Table 9.3 speak for themselves.

Table 9.3   *Sources of Capital Accumulation, 1948–1953*

	1948/II	1949	1950	1951	1952	1953
Gross savings[a] (in absolute terms in milliard DM)	8.8	17.1	22.1	29.2	34.3	35.4
Gross savings (in hundred DM)						
Private savings	22.7	14.0	9.0	7.9	12.6	15.3
Company savings[b]	53.4	61.4	65.2	65.1	61.7	52.8
State[c]	23.9	24.6	25.8	27.0	25.7	31.9
State including tax measures[d]	—	35.7	36.2	33.6	34.7	42.4

Notes:
[a] Inventory accumulation inclusive.
[b] Savings through tax depreciation inclusive.
[c] Including social insurance.
[d] Possible tax depreciation and resulting budget losses.

Source: Roskamp (1965).

Although exact figures are not available for the interwar years, the level and structure of capital accumulation after currency reform does represent a clear break with the pre-1939 period. The volume of investment was 21 per cent above the 1936 rate on average between 1949 and 1951, and 63 per cent higher on average between 1952 and 1954. At the same time the order in its financing had altered: 'The earlier order of capital market, state and self-finance had been turned upside down. This was a reflection of the development of a massive state subsidy for business capital formation' (Adamsen, 1981: 46 f.).

The internal accumulation of capital within enterprise took on new proportions despite the collapse of the capital market. Barely functioning after the breakup of major banks, it effectively dropped out of the statistics on investment financing. State tax concessions were the main reason for this rise. Undoubtedly, the state itself played a big part as an investor in the areas of infrastructure and house building; it also used ERP counterpart funds to promote economic areas with a deficit, or those characterized by shortages and bottlenecks. The promotion of reconstruction as such, however, occurred indirectly through private-capital accumulation.

Next to the structure of investment financing, the clearest illustration of this policy was the tax loss suffered by the state on the basis of special write-off facilities. During the early years of the Republic this probably amounted to almost 10 per cent of tax revenue. At the end of the 1950s it represented about 7 per cent of total tax revenue, nationally and of the *Länder* (Jakli, 1990: 312). This indirect but very effective subsidy of capital accumulation did not favour any economic branch in particular. Nevertheless, industry in particular profited, in that investments were made and production was successful. Although exact figures are only available for the late 1950s and early 1960s, Table 9.4 still gives an impression of the structural setting of the 1950s.

Table 9.4 *Tax Subsidies on Central and Regional Levels, 1959–1967 (in million DM)*

Year	Total	Agriculture	Industry	Transport	Housing
1959	3,910	680	2,135	560	535
1960	4,300	725	2,500	470	605
1961	5,410	810	3,480	475	645
1962	5,925	805	4,000	475	645
1963	7,255	850	5,155	565	685
1964	7,720	900	5,500	595	725
1965	8,635	1,195	5,950	595	725
1966	9,185	1,280	6,245	845	815
1967	9,475	1,290	6,490	860	835

Source: Jakli (1990: 308).

Werner Plumpe

Thus in the postwar era the real 'policy of promoting industry' (*Industrieforderungspolitik*) pursued by the federal government consisted of tax concessions which were consciously taken into account and even promoted. Moreover, these did not follow a planned structural change; companies which were successful anyway were additionally rewarded. The resulting improvement in the elasticity of supply within West German industry thus contributed—albeit unplanned and indirectly—to the increased ability of West German industry to compete on an international level. National economic policy under Ludwig Erhard with regard to direct economic intervention in favour of individual companies remained extremely reserved. Erhard was also successful with this, as the summary of the development of direct national subsidies in Table 9.5 shows.

Table 9.5 *National Financial Aid (Direct Subsidies), 1951–1968 (in million DM)*

Year	Total	Agriculture	Mining/Energy	Financial aid
1951	179.8	149.3	—	159.5
1952	318.7	276.9	—	292.1
1953	255.8	209.2	—	224.7
1954	374.0	332.6	—	340.9
1955	515.5	446.3	1.5	463.9
1956	1,442.2	1,021.0	207.5	1,374.7
1957	2,164.2	1,674.7	249.5	2,059.1
1958	2,078.4	1,739.8	1.5	1,954.6
1959	2,089.3	1,861.4	1.5	1,947.9
1960	1,994.3	1,655.3	36.8	1,796.8
1961	2,842.3	2,311.6	103.7	2,448.4
1962	3,272.1	2,732.4	91.7	2,858.3
1963	3,695.4	2,890.9	261.0	3,213.4
1964	3,959.8	2,890.5	439.5	3,398.4
1965	4,726.8	3,417.6	527.4	4,167.0
1966	4,597.9	3,170.4	478.1	3,881.1
1967	5,247.3	3,501.3	564.4	4,337.3
1968	6,881.4	4,800.7	772.7	6,074.7

Note:
[a] Payments to the following are not included: Deutsche Bundesbahn. Deutsche Lufthansa, airport companies, housing.
Source: Jakli (1990: 307).

During the 1950s and early 1960s there can be no question of the federal government having promoted particular branches of industry. The proportion of the federal budget reserved for direct financial aid was on average 1.4 per cent during the first half of the 1950s, 5.7 per cent between 1955 and 1960, and 5.9 per cent during the first half of the 1960s (Jakli, 1990:

308). Up until the mid-1960s, over 90 per cent of direct subsidies—usually in the form of financial aid—were allocated to agriculture, a sector which had to survive on social grounds. At the end of the 1950s the coal industry was subsidized too. Coal was a sector with difficulties due to similar weaknesses in competitive ability, although its subsidization was fought for strongly at first. Here Erhard's anti-subsidy stance failed for the same reasons as it did in the area of agriculture: the pressures of social policy and certain groups seemed to make a large reduction in the German coal industry impossible (Abelshauser, 1984: 87 ff.).

The federal government's policy on subsidies—which was in effect its industrial policy—changed to some extent after the mid-1960s. However, the first significant changes ocurred after the mid-1970s, when the government reacted to changing international competition, the accompanying fall in growth rates, and growing unemployment, with industrial subsidies and programmes to fight the downward economic trend. Between 1966 and 1976 the volume of direct state financial aid doubled from 6 to 12 million DM. Industry profited significantly, but so did house building, and private households increasingly came to benefit from state subsidies. In volume, tax subsidies increased even more rapidly, reaching the 25-million-DM mark for the first time in 1976. During the first half of the 1970s tax subsidies were on average as follows: 13.6 per cent for agriculture, 37.7 per cent for industry, 4.6 per cent for transport, 12.7 per cent for housing, and 18.2 per cent for the promotion of private savings (Jakli, 1990: 316). Adding all subsidies and tax concessions together in order to assess their structural significance, Jakli presents the following picture:

In 1980 each individual in gainful employment in industry was subsidized (financial aid and tax concessions) to the tune of 1.044 DM by central governemt. Single branches, however, received much more: each person employed in the coal industry cost central government 11.009 DM, while in 1970 the rate had been 1.710 DM. In agriculture subsidies—including EC market expenditure—ran at 6.903 DM per employed person. Those employed in the aerospace industry received barely less (6.764 DM) but those in the shipbuilding industry received only 4.379 DM while in 1970 the rate had been 368 DM. The average subsidy per employed person in the steel industry was fairly small, at 255 DM in 1980. (Jakli, 1990: 47)

In summary, it is clear that both the economic miracle and high growth rates during the reconstruction period were sustained by private capital accumulation. The federal government aggressively promoted the latter, at first rarely resorting to direct economic intervention and then only after the mid-1950s on grounds of social welfare. Although the manner and volume of aid in both taxes and direct form changed after the mid-1970s, subsidies in the areas of coal, agriculture, and shipbuilding, aiming at conservation, dominate until today. Jakli speaks of a functional, rather than a primarily socially defensive, subsidy policy after this period. Most important, the expansion of subsidies in West Germany was a reaction, not a plan. Expansion was not a prerequisite to the economic miracle, but a result of its discontinuation in the 1960s. Admittedly, one precondition for the success of this liberal model was the ample supply of qualified and cheap labour, and large and modern capital stock, particularly in the capital goods industry. Both factors were present in West Germany at the end of the 1940s, because capital assets had been expanded and modernized during the war. The influx of refugees after the war more than compensated for the losses in labour supply (Abelshauser, 1983: 20 ff.).

Promotion of private capital formation involved mainly the supply side of economic development. The demand side was thought about fairly little, given the great need for goods of all types both in West Germany and the rest of Europe. Here the priority was to put the national and international exchange of goods back in order and keep possible inflation in check. Consequently, the second central element of Erhard's economic policy was composed of the Marshall Plan, European economic co-operation, and, in this context, the liberalization of foreign trade. Initially the policy of liberalizing exports and imports seemed to be a risk, since, until a recovery in mid-1950, the trade balance was briefly negative. However, the resulting criticism of Erhard's economic policy soon disappeared. In 1951 and 1952, after the crisis in foreign exchange, exports were successful (Hentschel, 1989: 715–58). Above all, during the Korean Boom and boost in exports, West Germany's specific advantages as a producer of high-quality capital goods (which did not have to be paid for in dollars) (Buchheim, 1990: 81–98) proved to be decisive. In addition, West Germany was the only large industrial country within Western Europe not immediately obliged to use its capacities for armaments after 1950.

The success of Erhard's foreign trade policy was also due to free and competitive industrial capacity which could be utilized profitably. One simply had to exploit existing strengths decisively and this was exactly what the federal government did. It pursued a return to the world commodity market, accompanied by the promotion of private-capital formation, preventing foreign demand from importing inflation through additional investments. According to Giersch, Paqué, and Schmieding these successes can be attributed to the federal government and its liberal trade policy, even if one element of this liberalization was, in fact, the result of the forced renunciation of autarky under occupation:

However, it was for endogenous reasons that West Germany gradually turned into a pacemaker for liberalization. With less inflation than almost everywhere else in Europe and benefiting from its traditional strength in high-quality goods, which were in high demand in Europe and beyond, West Germany started to accumulate huge balance-of-trade surpluses. With a relatively far-reaching and rapid liberalization of imports and a faster growth of productivity than in most other EPU countries, West Germany outpaced its OEEC partners in terms of export and import growth and gained market shares overseas while other European countries became slightly more dependent on intra-European exchanges. Most importantly, West Germany increased its share of the North American market more rapidly than the rest of the OEEC. (Giersch, Paqué, and Schmieding, 1993: 115 f.)

West Germany also profited from the undervalued DM and from the relatively low labour piece rates which were around 10–15 per cent under the OECD levels. In investment and the capital market, however, it was again the federal government's liberal economic policy which created an environment in which German industry could fully exploit its specific advantages. Here the American approach to Europe in trade and economic terms was very much welcomed on the German side (Berger and Ritschl, 1995: 473–519; Bührer, 1990: 139–62). Whatever the cause, foreign trade was a strong and lasting pillar of the German economy and when necessary it was able to more than compensate for losses in demand in the home market.

The real test of the concept of a social market economy, however, lay neither in capital accumulation nor in a boost of exports, but in cartel legislation. After 1945 the Allies had implemented a thorough decartelization and deconcentration of German industry despite business opposition. Nevertheless, it remained entirely open whether these regulations would be adopted in German law, and if so what form this should take (Berghahn, 1985: 152 ff.). As already outlined, the alliance between government, neo-liberal theory, and industry soon collapsed on this point. The latter was not set on returning to the cartel practices of the prewar years, which had not been as successful as the occupying powers claimed after 1945 (Hentschel, 1979: 119–41); but German businessmen had no interest whatsoever in either suffering restrictions under narrow antitrust legislation and merger controls or conceding an unlimited supervisory right to the state.[24] This was the decisive issue for advocates of the social market economy: 'Above all, however, there was the concept of state-protected competition. This was an indispensable component of the social market system' (Nicholls, 1994: 324). After preliminary work in 1947, a first draft was on the table in Erhard's house in the summer of 1949. It proposed a prohibition of cartels and harsh measures to fight market domination by individual companies. The timing of this proposal was unfortunate, because at the same time the occupying powers' deconcentration measures were also being discussed, giving the impression that German support existed for them. It also met with strong criticism from industry, not necessarily because of the cartel ban itself, but because the 'antitrust elements' surpassed even the American tradition (Berghahn, 1985: 153 ff.). Although the first proposal was unsuccessful, Erhard maintained his position.

In December 1949 a German delegation under the leadership of neo-liberal Franz Böhm travelled to the US in order to study American antitrust legislation. On their return, they produced a memorandum which strengthened Erhard's position, and he made it clear that he rejected any restrictions on competition, whether state directed or exercised by entrepreneurs. But Erhard was not a 'hardliner',[25] for he did not plan to carry through with these measures to the detriment of German industrial productivity. Accordingly, he rejected the economically absurd measures of heavy industry deconcentration as proposed by the Allies because, in his opinion, the primary aim was to weaken German industry (Berghahn, 1985: 155).

Hence simple solutions were not possible. Erhard was convinced that only well-functioning, large-scale companies could survive within a liberalized global market. But productivity considerations were not the only cause of Erhard's or other neo-liberals' reservations regarding working out a practical policy concerning the concentration of cartels. From the perspective of small- and medium-sized industries, cartels were ambivalent in character: they pushed up prices but they also provided a certain protection against the unscrupulous business practices of large-scale companies. Thus, any cartel ban had to be accompanied by effective monopoly control (Nicholls, 1994: 330 ff.). Along with these reservations, opposition from businessmen, single ministers, and politicians developed against German anti-cartel legislation. Even within Erhard's own department, the anti-cartel issue was controversial (Berghahn, 1985: 169 ff.).

Nevertheless, in the summer of 1952 Erhard introduced a bill into the *Bundestag* which banned cartels but made certain exceptions. Industrial and political opposition prevented this law from even being debated during the parliamentary session. After Erhard reintroduced the bill in 1954, a political fight broke out during which Adenauer also put pressure on the Federal Chancellor to reach a compromise with industry, particularly with the BDI. However, Erhard did not give up on the central question. In July 1957 the *Bundestag* passed the bill which provided for a cartel ban with some exceptions. In this sense the cartel law was a compromise. It was not a true magna carta of the social market economy but a vindication of those opposing cartels and those advocating competition. 'In the end, Erhard did succeed in getting this key act of social-market legislation in the statute book. It was by no means an ideal measure for believers in perfect competition' (Nicholls, 1994: 336 ff.).

The significance of this act is controversial. Historically, it represents a turn away from the stronger protectionist cartel practices of industry towards a strategy of adaptation, with liberal and world-market orientation. But originally, this breakthrough was not connected to the anti-cartel legislation; that legislation did not handicap the concentration waves of the 1960s and 1970s either. The change in attitude on the part of large-scale German companies corresponded far more to the possibilities and challenges presented by the dynamic global market of the 1950s and 1960s and the resulting structural change within industry, which made relative the strong influence of cartel-prone heavy industry. The liberalization of foreign trade and its consequences were far more decisive for the Americanization of West German industry than cartel policy and control. These symbolized a breakthrough in the clearest way, as an American observer commented in May 1954: if the anti-cartel bill be rejected 'West Germany may well slip back into the economic authoritarianism of the old days'. But if accepted 'even in modified form, this would mean a major victory, perhaps the greatest victory ever won in Europe, for the principles of dynamic American-style capitalism' (Berghahn, 1985: 173; Nicholls, 1994: 337).

The concept of a liberal market economy favoured by Erhard, with strong private-capital accumulation, more intensive international contacts, and an effective regulatory policy, functioned surprisingly smoothly between 1950 and the mid-1960s. Hence Erhard's self-confidence over the success of his social market economy was strong in the early 1960s (Erhard, 1962). Yet the liberal economic miracle had its costs and negative side, apart from the structural changes to industry it provoked and the downfall of traditional industries after the 1950s. The social market economy got off to a bad start in those areas which had been disadvantaged by legislation following currency reform. This was especially true of the iron and steel industry which was twice the victim: of deconcentration and dismantlement.[26] In addition, its products were not cleared in 1948 but were subject, just as coal and energy were, to rationing and price-fixing. Capital accumulation thus had a paralytic effect, particularly in the area of basic and producer goods. As in the coal industry, this industrial segment did not take part in the self-financed investment boom of the early years of the Federal Republic.

After the outbreak of the Korean War and the beginning of the Korean Boom this area turned into a decisive bottleneck within the economic miracle. Heavy industry reached its capacity limit at the end of 1950. The absence of wide-reaching rationalization and new construction, particularly within the coal industry, now became noticeable, as did the dismantlement of significant capacity within the iron and steel industry. Shortly after the end of state economic direction *(Bewirtschaftung)*, the steering mechanism *(Wirtschaftslenkung)* returned to the iron and steel industry. This development has been subject to historical debate. While it is interpreted as an exception and therefore in conformity with the free-market model, others interpret specific measures introduced to overcome the crisis in heavy industry as the end of the liberal model of reconstruction.

9.5. The Investment Aid Act—An Exception?

Let us take a closer look at this area which, in the early 1950s, demanded a break from the neo-liberal model of reconstruction and, according to Werner Abelshauser, pointed the way back to traditional German corporatism. The background to this development was the growth bottleneck within heavy industry which began at the end of 1950 and seemed to jeopardize the success of the West German recovery. From early 1950 on, coal production growth rates fell; haulage productivity stagnated. Between November 1950 and November 1952 coal haulage was persistently set at a daily production of 400,000 tons and the abolition of coal rationing in April 1950 soon proved to be an extremely dangerous decision in the face of the growing coal shortage (Abelshauser, 1983: 76 f.). Although steel production markedly increased between 1949 and 1950, its prewar high was only reached in 1955 while industrial production otherwise reached its 1938 level in 1951 (Wiel, 1970: 236). In contrast, the capital and consumer goods industries boomed. Production was 46 per cent and 42 per cent respectively above the 1936 level in November 1951, while the mining industry was only 10 per cent up on the prewar level, which neither steel nor iron production had reached (see Fig. 9.2).

What were the origins of this bottleneck? First, there were legal difficulties created by production quotas and dismantlement during the occupation which stopped in the autumn of 1949, affecting important plants within the iron and steel industry of Rhineland-Westphalia. But, aside from these, the main reason for the bottleneck in basic industry was currency reform. In contrast to the capital-goods and consumer-goods industries, price-fixing and state direction were abandoned in 1950. As a consequence heavy industry could take part to a very limited extent in the capital accumulation boom. Initially the head of the Economics Ministry was deaf to demands for control of capital beneficial to areas on the verge of a bottleneck, especially since under American control the biggest portion of ERP counterpart funds had been used to boost bottleneck industries. Table 9.6 illustrates the significance of ERP counterpart funds for investments within heavy industry.

Roughly 10–15 per cent of investment in heavy industry between 1949 and 1952 was covered by Marshall Aid; in the coal industry it was more than 40 per cent. Between 1948 and 1959, the iron and steel industry received more than 460 million DM or 6.8 per cent of total counterpart funds. This was surpassed only in the areas of electricity supply, mining, the national railways, and house building (Bankmann, 1965: 1083 ff.). Furthermore, this 'mini planned economy' was not unwelcome to leading elements of the Economics Ministry because the necessary intervention in

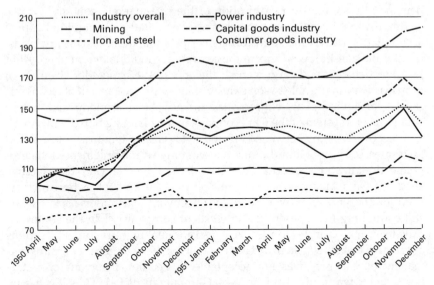

Fig 9.2 *Index of industrial production, 1950–1951*

investment flow and the free economy could be presented as a consequence of American policy (Abelshauser, 1983: 59 f.).

However, this 'steering of capital' *(Kapitallenkung)* to the benefit of heavy industry was not able to settle the deficit in investment. In 1951 the threat of bottlenecks was so great that the Allied High Commission directly intervened. In March 1951 the American High Commissioner, John McCloy,

Table **9.6**   *The Stake of ERP Funds in Gross Investment in Fixed Assets (in hundred DM)*

	1949	1950	1951	1952
Overall[a]	6.4	8.6	4.5	2.3
Industry	7.1	13.0	4.5	2.3
Within industry: mining	47.0	40.0	13.0	4.9
Within industry: basic and producer goods industries	0.8	14.0	6.1	1.8
Within industry: iron and steel	—	18.0	14.0	2.0
Power supply	14.0	24.0	21.0	5.5
Telecommunications and transport	20.0	7.1	3.3	2.2
Housing	0.7	4.6	2.9	2.3
Agriculture	2.0	13.0	2.7	3.7
Other industry	—	0.4	0.5	0.3

Note:
[a] Gross investment in fixed assets within public administration are not included.

Source: Baumgart (1961: 122–5).

demanded a significant modification of the free-market economy. On the German side it became clear too that non-regulated and unguided capital accumulation had to find some form of correction in the area of heavy industry. But the question which form the correction should take remained. After lengthy debates and arguments, the Bundesverband der Deutschen Industrie was finally able to solve the problem with the concept of 'economic self-responsibility'. This concept had already been implemented within Albert Speer's system of the war economy, in the planning bureaucracy used to direct the economy between 1945 and 1948. This system functioned as follows: measures to steer and direct the economy were implemented via economic organizations because the state lacked the relevant bureaucratic apparatus and business had no interest in creating such a bureaucracy. Economic organizations were therefore effectively instruments of state while still continuing to represent the interests of companies.[27] In the context of private property and decentralized decision-making structures, a serious alternative to such a system did not exist, given that a large and perhaps permanent bureaucracy was not acceptable. A decision in favour of a state bureaucracy was unthinkable in West Germany in 1950–1. Thus it is hardly surprising that the BDI succeeded in implementing its proposals on steering investment *(Investitionslenkung)* and controlling bottleneck goods via newly created bodies of 'economic self-responsibility'.

The first of the areas discussed above involved investment steering (Adamsen, 1981). The *Investitionshilfegesetz* of January 1952 planned a transfer of capital amounting to 1 million DM for urgent investment projects in coal and iron, power, water, and the railways—a proposal which had its origins in a BDI plan of April 1951. The investment-aid legislation did not entail direct state intervention in the investment process; rather, various member-associations within the BDI committed themselves to collecting relevant amounts from their member companies and channelled them into heavy industry. For companies benefiting from investment aid, the process involved neither intervention in proprietary rights and company powers of disposition, nor in the regulation of production and sales. The allocation of investment aid in the form of reduced-interest loans was carried out in principle by industry, or rather by a board of trustees dominated by industry, which allocated loans according to certain criteria. Companies were not subject to intervention; moreover the state had only an indirect influence on the iron and steel industry through a corporate governing body. In essence this measure involved a transfer of capital from previously favoured to not-yet-favoured industries carried out by industry's own organizations (Adamsen, 1981: 199 ff.).

The success of investment aid was remarkable. While it is true that numerous other factors were also involved, investment structures within German industry changed markedly during the allocation of investment aid (1952–5).

Table 9.7 *Investment Development and Investment Structure of Economic Branches Covered by Investment Aid Legislation*

Branches of industry	Index of investment development[a]			Single branch's share in gross investment in fixed assets[b]		
	1951	1953	1955	1951 %	1953 %	1955 %
Areas favoured by Investment Aid						
Coal	100	217	222	5.4	9.5	6.6
Iron	100	225	393	3.6	6.6	7.8
Power industry	100	131	168	14.6	15.5	13.5
Compulsory contributors						
Basic and producer goods industries[c]	100	138	231	18.4	20.5	23.3
Capital goods industry	100	118	192	14.2	13.6	15.0
Consumer goods industry	100	96	131	9.2	7.2	6.7
Food and luxury goods	100	104	125	6.1	5.1	4.2
Small industrial businesses[d]	100	92	167	5.4	4.0	5.0
Building trade	100	136	267	3.5	3.9	5.2
Commerce	100	107	167	12.2	10.6	11.2
Banking and insurance	100	124	155	3.0	3.0	2.5
Other services	100	108	161	5.6	4.9	5.0
Average in total	100	124	182	—	—	—

Notes:
[a] On the basis of gross investments in fixed assets.
[b] Of the listed industries, that is without the state, agriculture and forestry, transport and housing in relevant prices.
[c] Including the iron-manufacturing industry.
[d] Including craft businesses and other producing industries.

Source: Adamson (1981: 272).

Overall, investment aid was distributed as follows: 25 per cent went to both the mining and electricity industries, 10 per cent to gas, and 30 per cent to the iron and steel industry—the major beneficiary of capital transfer, which received almost 300 million DM (Adamsen, 1981: 264). Of all the remarkable increases in investment, rapid growth in this industry was due largely to the impetus from investment aid. The exploitation of an unusually favourable economic situation also played a part. Indeed, within the iron and steel industry the share of investment aid as a part of overall investment was not very significant. Reconstruction aid was moderate in comparison to the funds which were invested after the mid-1950s as a consequence of strong demand, leading to great returns when capacities were fully utilized. While 2.2 million DM were invested between 1949 and 1952 (gross investment of fixed assets in the iron-manufacturing industry), almost 2.1 million DM were invested in 1955 alone, and between 1953 and 1955 a total of over 4.7 million DM was invested (G. Plumpe, 1981: 180–90). Overall, between 1952 and 1955 less than 5 per cent of investments in the iron and steel industry were financed by investment aid; together with Marshall Aid the iron and steel industry received a total of 760 million DM in reduced-interest investment loans. This corresponds to about 11 per cent of total investment between 1949 and 1955.

The success of investment aid vindicated the programme because it helped to clear short-term bottlenecks and to improve the performance of the West German coal industry. It would not have been able to do so on the basis of its own strength. Neither politically nor practically was this a programme of planning and regulation because it was explicitly limited to the elimination of bottlenecks. Neither were planned aims set for the economy nor instruments developed which would have made planned economic steering possible. The organization of investment aid by the BDI was a clear argument against any state claim to planning and regulation. The state not only kept itself out of direct investment financing but, via the BDI, also guaranteed that investment aid would not become a pawn for the institutionalization of a state planning bureaucracy.

The same interpretation applies to the reintroduction of rationing for strategic goods in short supply (particularly coal) in 1952. In a similar process to that of investment aid allocation, bodies of industrial self-managers took on all the practical work involved in allocating coal and thereby made an independent state agency irrelevant, an agency which was abolished in 1950 anyway. The takeover of 'steering functions' (*Lenkungsfunktionen*) by private associations was criticized by academic neo-liberals who attacked a 'supremacy of associations' as much as a state planned economy (Abelshauser, 1983: 76–84). But the significance of such private planning bodies should not be exaggerated. They stopped work the moment they were no longer necessary. Within the young, West German market economy, they were an unlikely vehicle for reform of political structures given that the industry which carried them had no interest in such a change. And the longer the economic miracle lasted, the more large-scale, West German companies oriented themselves towards European and global market-setting, limiting the reach of national regulations, whether of a corporate or cartel nature. Investment aid and the rationing of coal were therefore only exceptions of short-term significance and did not alter structures. It seems tenuous then to interpret them as a turning-point of postwar economic policy. These measures were rather the exception than the rule.

9.6. Liberal Economic Policy and the Development of Enterprise

The West German economic miracle that took place from 1948 to 1967 was the result of a number of concurring factors. The elasticity of supply in West German industry was high well into the 1960s and in this way Germany profited from the investment boom of the war economy and the influx of labour after 1945. In addition, favourable conditions within the global market aided exploitation of this situation. Finally, for a long time the focus of West German economic policy was directed towards preservation of this combination of circumstances—which the policy itself partly created through the promotion of private capital accumulation, the reconstruction of the capital market, the liberalization of foreign trade, and through a social consensus safeguarded by the state.

The role of the state (federal government) remained restricted to guaranteeing a positive environment and to favouring capital accumulation. Direct economic intervention was accepted only to clear bottlenecks or to minimize social effects, with the notable exception of agriculture. Once economic conditions changed after the mid-1960s, a process of political rethinking began. With this in mind, Erhard's neo-liberalism must be seen as ambivalent. He did not create the conditions for the economic miracle, but he made their rigorous exploitation possible. In this sense his success was inextricably linked to specific preconditions. Once the conditions for growth changed in the mid-1960s, neo-liberal economic policy was pushed on to the defensive and was abandoned in favour of a moderate Keynesian approach.

Aside from these points, Erhard's economic policy signified a break with the National Socialist past and also with pre-1933 economic policy (James, 1986). The role of the state in economic development in quantitative terms diminished during the 1950s and early 1960s, contrary to the general trend. While public expenditure (without social insurance) represented 16 per cent of the gross national product in 1913, 24 per cent in the 1920s, and 37 per cent in 1938, it still represented 29.8 per cent in 1950, dropping to 28.8 per cent in the ten years leading up to 1962. At 29.9 per cent in 1973 it was exactly as high as it was in 1950 (Abelshauser, 1983: 88). This low share of public expenditure in the GNP was not always advantageous, as in the lack of public expenditure on education at the end of the 1950s, which ignored the requirements of an advanced industrial state (Abelshauser, 1983: 97). At the end of the 1960s one was certain that with the renaissance of Keynesian models, a more active state would lead to improvement in the economic conditions for growth (Hagemann, 1984; Scherf, 1987). However, what is notable about the economic miracle is the parallel occurrence of high economic growth and a low share of public expenditure in the GNP. This is a clear illustration of contemporary neo-liberal economic policy; one that recognized a link between relatively low rates of state investment and high net investment rates.[28]

The second major break with the economic policy of the interwar and National Socialist periods involved the abandonment of the direct intervention in industrial development which had been used to achieve arms policy objectives. The shift in the structure of German industry in favour of the metalworking industries had been the result of state investment projects, particularly during wartime. On the basis of massive state investments, a new industrial structure had been created which could only have resulted from arms production. It was particularly favourable for capital-intensive and very specialized plants (Geyer, 1984: 166). In short, the National Socialist wartime economy had caused a thorough modernization and increase in German capital assets.[29] It was this significant development which eased the break with industrial and political traditions after 1949.

At the same time, the global orientation of industry, pursued by Erhard with American help, was not new in Germany. German foreign-trade links had been extremely strong before 1914 and had only diminished during the collapse of international economic relations after 1918. In 1928 exports represented 17 per cent of national income, much below the pre-war (1913) figure of 20.2 per cent, while imports reached 19.3 per cent, almost the level attained in 1913 (21.5 per cent). Germany's share in European domestic trade had fallen from 25.3 per cent in 1913 to 21.5 per cent in 1928. Other European states had suffered losses too, though the US did not.

During the Great Depression, international economic relations in Germany collapsed (Ziebura, 1984: 157 ff.); exports and imports represented only 11 per cent and 13 per cent of national income respectively, falling further during the National Socialist arms boom.[30] Industry's move away from the world market was dictated by Versailles, the Great Depression, and National Socialist preparations for war. The decision was not freely made by German industry nor was it a result of industry's inclination towards autarky. Under the pre-1914 liberal conditions of the global economy, German industry had forcefully sought for and realized its opportunities in the world market. Similarly, after 1923, and even during National Socialism, a majority of large-scale German companies tried to maintain their share in the world market and their international contacts. This was the situation in 1949 when they had relatively open access to the dynamic global market. Thus Erhard restored a 'normal situation' which had been interrupted by the 'thirty years war' between 1914 and 1948.

With the withdrawal of the state from the economy and from the task of steering industrial policy, a third change involved cartel and monopoly policy, the centre-piece of the 'social market economy'. The efforts of Erhard and his neo-liberal, academic advisers to break with the German cartel tradition were successful, though not to the extent that many radical ordo-liberals would have hoped. At the same time this breakthrough had a symbolic significance and, at least immediately after 1949, it signalled Erhard's anti-cartel stance to the industrial branches hoping for recartelization. It indicated that political support would not be forthcoming, indeed that massive political opposition would be provoked. Neither Erhard nor anti-cartel legislation prevented the wave of mergers in the 1960s and 1970s, which to some extent corrected the consequences of postwar dismantlement. Indeed, Erhard made it clear he believed productive, large-scale companies to be desirable and for this reason criticized Allied dismantlement policy (Berghahn, 1985: 152 ff.). The consequences, especially of American dismantlement measures, were corrected or at least modified by reconstruction efforts in the iron and steel industries, and in the banking sector. Thus, these found the federal government openly supportive (Horstmann, 1991).

What was the significance of changes in the national and global economy for West German enterprise? Present research allows only very hypothetical answers. It is relatively easy to answer the question of how industrial associations reacted to Erhard's neo-liberal economic policy. German industry basically shared Erhard's economic orientation towards supply and the world market. From 1948, the promotion of private-capital accumulation in particular met with repeated industry demands. Indeed, the tax and monetary policy pursued by Adenauer's government fufilled the hopes of enterprise (W. Plumpe, 1987: 235 ff.). Industry viewed the role of the state with some scepticism when it went beyond creating favourable conditions or restricting industry's scope of activity. Industry's readiness to run down what was left of state direction after 1948 was based precisely on the conviction that the active role of the state should be as small as possible. Similarly, the BDI found validation for its support of investment aid legislation: if such intervention was unavoidable, the creation of a state bureaucracy was to be prevented. Opposition to the concept of monopoly control in competition law sprang from similar motives (Berghahn, 1985). Overall one can assume that both the federal government and organized industry trusted the concept of the social market economy. Of course each had its own fitting interpretation. Businessmen in particular assessed the benefits of the social market economy in a pragmatic manner.

It is not surprising that many companies were interested in closely co-operating with state agencies. However, this developed into a kind of market-regulating cartel under exceptional conditions in the areas of agriculture, mining, and the power industry, where political motives were dominant. The preservation of agriculture and mining was politically motivated, as was the expansion of nuclear power (Radkau, 1983). Other sectors of the economy were highly regulated, such as energy, telecommunications, and transport. Here a number of companies were publicly owned (Soltwedel *et al.*, 1986). Within this regulated section of the market, state authorities and individual companies kept in close contact, as in the case of Siemens and the federal postal system. And, finally, the direct role of industry in state control was not small. In the case of Volkswagen, Simon Reich recently attempted to illustrate that the entire postwar, neo-liberal success story was, in fact, a fairy tale. Indeed, according to Reich, the case of Volkswagen shows how the forms of close co-operation between state and industry, created and used by the Nazis, continued to be effective after 1945 (Reich, 1990). These were selectively beneficial to single companies, Volkswagen being only one example:

Like the German state in the Third Reich, although perhaps less consciously, the Bonn Republic was drawn to a discriminatory web. On a less general scale I have sought to identify the configuration of political relationship between state and individual firms in the interwar auto industry. Although this analysis is confined to one industry, it too suggests that the fascist state policy acted as a modernizing force whose influence on the postwar period cannot be understated or ignored. (Reich, 1990: 315)

While Reich's interpretation on a number of points can be accepted, his overall concept is misleading as it questions the break in economic policy during 1948 and 1949. The National Socialist prewar and wartime economy, and the investment boom of 1944 in particular, modernized the structure of German industry and was therefore beneficial to reconstruction; but this insight is not new. Reich's assertion about the continuity of state economic policy does not apply at either the macroeconomic or the microeconomic level. At both levels, interruptions are clearly dominant. Accepting that his conclusions are correct, it is at least open to question whether the car industry was really representative of West German industry, the heart of the German economic miracle. It is also questionable whether Volkswagen, a company with a majority state holding, was a good example of the relationship between state and private sectors. Reich's interpretation is also not convincing given that research done on other companies paints a different picture (Stokes, 1994b).[31]

Scholarly work on individual companies is not uniform. The proposition of the 'Americanization of West German industry'—upheld by Volker Berghahn (1986)—must be treated cautiously. After 1950, American management methods were eagerly adopted. But German businessmen—at least many leading representatives (Hartmann, 1959)—soon regained their former pride in industry, as German industry's competitive ability was seen in the global market. Furthermore, assessing the attitude of German industrialists towards America is difficult because the America of the 1920s was often used as an excuse for their own plans and strategies

(Kleinschmidt and Welskopp, 1994: 73–103). Additionally, in the case of organization structures and strategic company policy, the adaption of American methods occurred comparatively late. During the diversification and divisionalization of companies in the 1970s, certain developments suggested American methods were being adopted.[32] Similarly, a general orientation towards America cannot be found among the industrial élite. Individual cases undoubtedly existed and Berghahn's examples are impressive (Berghahn, 1986).

This new generation had taken over during the 1930s and 1940s. There is much to be said for the assertion that the economic miracle was directed by those technocratic managers who had grown up within the National Socialist prewar and wartime economy (Erker, 1993: 26 ff., 75 ff.). This is just as true for the case of the successor companies of IG Farben as for the iron and steel industry of the Ruhr area (Stokes, 1988). Kurt Pritzkoleit, a West German economic journalist with intimate knowledge of German industry in the 1950s, was able to illustrate convincingly how the majority of large-scale German companies remained true to their own corporate traditions and strategies after 1949–50 (Pritzkoleit, 1953). A reorientation developed through continuous adaptation to changing market demands, not as an abrupt change of key concepts within corporate policy. This interpretation was presented in *Capital*, a business magazine, in April 1968.[33] According to the article, the ability to persevere and adapt during the Third Reich was the basis for the success of this generation of German managers after 1945.

Finally, it is possible to identify clear connections between the business policies of the majority of large-scale German companies and their prewar strategies. After 1933 many companies had unwillingly given up their global market orientation; in the majority of cases attempts were made to preserve business contacts and early preparations were made to rebuild foreign trade links. The restoration of foreign trade relations took priority in German companies' plans for the postwar period (W. Plumpe, 1992: 11–37). After the liberalization of German foreign trade relations in 1949–50, this aim was realized. In doing so German industry not only followed American standards or wishes but by 1951 restoration of trade with the East was being pursued (Mai, 1992: 203–26; Neebe, 1992: 163–202). These strategies were not only true of foreign trade. At home, the business policies of the majority of companies followed traditional lines of development; major changes first occurred at the end of the 1950s and at the beginning of the 1960s, once a surge of technological development made old patterns of behaviour obsolete (Stokes, 1994b). The abandonment of cartel practices within German industry was not so much the result of a 'change in convictions' after 1950 but based on the fact it had became irrelevant in a liberal, non-discriminatory world economic system with high-growth rates.[34] In the early 1950s the number of cartels thus increased,

after a drop following disentanglement, without much economic significance. The tradition of 'cooperative capitalism' (Windolf and Beyer, 1996)
was also not impinged upon by the disentanglement measure and later
cartel legislation. Thus, it can be assumed that the immediate influence of
cartel policy on business strategies was small, especially since corporate
concentration accelerated in the 1960s.

The decisive element in the development of West German enterprise is
that after 1949–50 changing national and international economic settings
and growing national and international competition demanded adaptation. On the basis of their technological and economic strengths, and with
management flexibility, they were able to meet these challenges. In this
manner old cartel and protectionist traditions were dropped during the
1950s and 1960s, not necessarily on principle but pragmatically. Within a
dynamic global market, cartel strategies—especially national ones—were
obsolete. Company survival depended far more on size, technical
strength, flexibility, and successful marketing strategies, while the protectionist securing of markets was profitable only in a handful of cases.
Hence, under market pressures and despite the lack of a break after the
war, company structures and strategies continually changed.

Thus the economic miracle was the result of a variety of factors. It profited from National Socialist industrial policy just as it did from the liberal
American concept of world trade: a thoroughly modernized industrial
structure and an almost unlimited national and international demand for
goods. Erhard's economic policy allowed German industry to exploit
these possibilities by pursuing liberalization of the national economy and
of foreign trade, despite massive opposition from Social Democrats, trade
unions, and the occupying forces. Furthermore, Erhard's tax and monetary policy prevented the strong pull on demand from causing inflation.
As well, direct economic intervention was limited to a minimum. This
reserved approach was possible because the competitive ability of
German industry was unchallenged in an international context. In this
sense the neo-liberalism of the 1950s remained untested. Once the international economic setting changed in the 1960s, the desire to return to
direct economic intervention soon came back to West Germany.

Indeed, the state was not only given responsibility for the market
regime, but also for practical results (demand management). Admittedly,
this does not alter the fact that after 1949 West Germany was a model of
neo-liberalism for two decades. Economic corporatism and the active
steering of the economy (*Wirtschaftssteuerung*) returned once growth rates
fell after the mid-1960s. Measures designed to steer investments in the
early 1950s do not alter this picture; these were interventionist exceptions
to the liberal rule.

NOTES

1. Translated by Kirsten Petrak.
2. Over the last few years there has been a change of paradigm within the presentation of the postwar economic history of Europe. In this context the role of politics in the process of reconstruction has been requestioned, but up until now, no new concept has been defined due to the lack of empirical research (Toniolo, 1998: 252–67).
3. Typical of this are Ludwig Erhard's writings on policy, which were swiftly translated into English. See especially Erhard (1957 and 1962).
4. For a recent summary of the discussion to date see Berger and Ritschl (1995: 473–519).
5. On National Socialist economic policy see Buchheim (1994: 97–122).
6. Buchheim (1990). The post-1933 development demands special attention. In the case of IG Farben, management did not follow a domestic market strategy but tried to retain their strong international position—albeit under the politically unfavourable conditions of the 1930s and 1940s. Furthermore, the successor companies did not take a new course after 1949, even if technologically speaking there was a different emphasis. See Gottfried Plumpe (1990: 560).
7. The energy sector and nuclear technology are probably the most important exceptions. See Radkau (1983).
8. See Nicholls (1994) 9. In the 1960s, research critical of liberalism, for example, Shonfield (1968), denied the 'liberal legend of the economic miracle' but did not, in the German case, as opposed to France, observe a decisive state industrial policy. However, Kidron (1970) followed a stronger argument of 'industrial policy' in connection with the arms industry. But Germany does not fit in with this pattern in the 1950s because a state arms policy was insignificant until the end of the decade.
9. The regulation of economic activities cannot be dealt with comprehensively here, given that the focus of regulation did not and does not rest on manufacturing industry but on the service sector and the infrastructure; see Soltwedel *et al.*, (1986). Soltwedel deals in particular with the regulation of the self-employed, of retail trade, financial markets, communications, of supply, and of transport markets.
10. The link between economic development and economic theory is largely ignored in the relevant literature which is consequently weak in interpretation. See, amongst others, Brandt (1993) and Stavenhagen (1964).
11. A reflection of this open situation can be found in economic history, particularly in the Borchardt debate on the possibilities for action during the great crisis; see Krüdener (1990).
12. In economic history the character of Nazi economic policy has remained controversial until today. See Temin (1989). Temin speaks of a 'socialist' economic system. For a critique of Temin see Barkai (1988) and Buchheim (1994: 97–122).
13. The issue of political resistance remains. In time, all leading ordo-liberals had trouble with the Nazi regime and emigrated or withdrew from 'public life'.

Nevertheless they remained as academics in the context of contemporary debate. While their conservative critique of National Socialism does not meet with today's concepts of democracy, this does not disqualify them in any sense. See Nicholls (1994), particularly 90 ff.

14. In the preface, titled 'Unsere Aufgabe', to the series 'Ordnung der Wirtschaft', Walter Eucken, Franz Böhm, and Hans Großmann-Doerth openly declared that the quality of economic policy depended on the quality of academic debate and in four maxims claimed for themselves the advisory role. These maxims related to the restoration and implementation of academic reason (expressed in political economy and law) when designing an economic constitution (p. xviii), to the necessity of focusing on the economic constitution (p. xviii), to an orientation to 'konkretes Ordnungsdenken' and practice (p. XIX) and finally and fourthly to understanding the system of law as the economic constitution (pp. xix f.). Here Schmoller's historicism was rejected because of its theoretical relativism, which denied any security in questions of political advice and of the economic system. These seemed to be the necessary precondition of clear academic debate and effective regulatory action.

15. The characteristics of Nazi economic policy remain controversial. This debate relates primarily to questions of the evaluation of the relationship between state and private sector, as to the social character of the economic system. However, it is clear that National Socialism favoured anything but a liberal market economy both during the prewar period and during the war itself. On Nazi economic policy see Petzina (1977: 108 ff.) and Mollin (1988).

16. On Müller-Armack see Haselbach (1991: 118 ff.). The biography of Johannes Popitz, onetime Prussian Chancellor of the Exchequer and later member of the opposition, is typical of this group of theorists and practical men; see Bentin (1972).

17. In this context Günter Schmölders's memoirs are of interest as chairman of Klasse IV of the Akademie für Deutsches Recht and later professor in Cologne (Schmölders, 1988).

18. For a comprehensive if problematic discussion see Eichholtz (1984, 1985, 1996).

19. The relevant essays are printed in Müller-Armack (1981).

20. For the various positions in the academic advisory council see Wissenschaftlicher Beirat (1973). Also Eucken (1938).

21. Printed in Müller-Armack (1981).

22. Arbeitsgemeinschaft der Industrie- und Handelskammern des Vereinigten Wirtschaftsgebietes, Leitsätze zur Finanz- und Steuerreform, 19.12.1948, Bundestag-Parlamentsarchiv 2/713.

23. Both programmes were each supposed to provide 1 milliard DM for job-creation purposes. One-half of the second programme was to be financed through bank of issue loans, the other through bills of exchange for job creation. If implemented it would have been close to an omission of the failure of the social market economy, according to Volker Hentschel, but it was made irrelevant by the consequences of the Korean War; see Hentschel (1989: 716).

24. See Arbeitskreis Kartellgesetz des BDI, Zehn Jahre Kartellgesetz—Eine Würdigung aus der Sicht der deutschen Industrie, 1968.

25. Berghahn correctly points out that Erhard's neo-liberalism was by no means academic and radical in form but extremely pragmatic. Erhard can therefore

not simply be identified as belonging to the group of ordo-liberal theorists. See Berghahn (1985: 156).

26. The significance of deconcentration and dismantlement for heavy industry in Rhineland-Wesphalia had not yet been analysed. Contemporaries believed the consequences of Allied intervention to be significant and that they caused at least part of the problems of the early 1950s. Although contemporary analysis is plausible, more research is necessary. See Werner Plumpe (1996: 290–303).

27. For a comprehensive analysis of this system of 'economic self-responsibility' see Werner Plumpe (1987).

28. Net investment rates (10.5 per cent in the 1920s and on average 12.9 per cent between 1935 and 1938) continuously increased after 1950, from 14.6 per cent in 1950/4, to 16.1 per cent in 1955/9, and finally to 17.9 per cent in 1965/9 before then falling. For the figures see Petzina (1977: 177).

29. According to the calculations of the Deutsche Institut für Wirtschafts-forschung gross fixed assets in West Germany were in 1945 20.6 per cent larger than in 1936. Even in 1948 after dismantlemant and restorations they still exceeded the 1936 level by 11 per cent (DIW, 1958: 98 ff.).

30. In 1936 imports and exports represented 6–7 per cent of the national product (Petzina, 1977: 187).

31. Tolliday (1995) shows VW's success was not based on state support. Volkswagen is thus not an example of successful West German industrial policy or a simple continuation of Nazi traditions.

32. Dyas and Thanheiser (1976) and Poensgen (1973). In the area of iron and steel, dismantlement was responsible for 'American company structures' only being adopted after reconcentration, so that dismantlement was a handicap to Americanization.

33. 'Deutsche Top Manager. Von Hitler erzogen', in *Capital*, 4 (1968).

34. The practice of market agreements and international cartels in the 1920s was also not a consequence of a dominant pro-cartel mentality but an expression of the politically caused collapse of the world economy and international economic relations (Gottfried Plumpe, 1990: 182 ff.).

REFERENCES

Abelshauser, W. (1975) *Wirtschaft in Westdeutschland 1945–1948. Rekonstruktion und Wachstumsbedingungen in der amerikanischen und britischen Zone* (Stuttgart: Deutsche Verlagsanstalt).

—— (1983), *Wirtschaftsgeschichte der Bundesrepublik Deutschland 1945–1980* (Frankfurt-on-Main: Suhrkamp).

—— (1984), 'The First Post-Liberal Nation: Stages in the Development of Modern Corporatism in Germany', *European History Quarterly*, 14. 285–318.

—— (1987a), *Der Ruhrbergbau seit 1945* (Munich: Beck).

Abelshauser, W. (1987*b*), *Die Langen Fünfziger Jahre. Wirtschaft und Gesellschaft der Bundesrepublik Deutschland 1949–1966*, (Düsseldorf: Schwann).

Adamsen, H. R. (1981), *Investitionshilfe für die Ruhr. Wiederaufbau, Verbände und soziale Marktwirtschaft 1948–1952* (Wuppertal: Hammer).

Ambrosius, G. (1977), *Die Durchsetzung der Sozialen Marktwirtschaft in Westdeutschland 1945–1949* (Stuttgart: Deutsche Verlagsanstalt).

Bankmann, J. (1965), 'Die Entwicklung der Finanzierungsprobleme der Eisen- und Stahlindustrie von 1948 bis heute', *Stahl und Eisen*, 85. 1083 ff.

Barkai, A. (1988), *Das Wirtschaftssystem des Nationalsozialismus. Ideologie, Theorie, Politik 1933–1945* (Frankfurt-on-Main: Fischer, 2nd edn.).

Baumgart, E. R. (1961), 'Investitionen und ERP-Finanzierung', *DIW-Sonderhefte*, NS 56 (Berlin), 122–5.

Bentin, L. A. (1972), *Johannes Popitz, und Carl Schmitt. Zur wirtschaftlichen Theorie des totalen Staates in Deutschland* (Munich: Beck).

Berger, H., and Ritschl, A. (1995), 'Die Rekonstruktion der Arbeitsteilung in Europa. Eine neue Sicht des Marshallplans in Deutschland 1947–1951', *VfZ*, 43. 473–519.

Berghahn, V. (1985), *Unternehmer und Politik in der Bundesrepublik* (Frankfurt-on-Main: Suhrkamp).

—— (1986), *The Americanization of West German Industry 1945–1973* (Leamington Spa: Berg).

Blum, R. (1969), *Soziale Marktwirtschaft. Wirtschaftspolitik zwischen Neoliberalismus und Ordoliberalismus* (Tübingen: Mohr).

Böhm, F. (1937), *Die Ordnung der Wirtschaft als geschichtliche Aufgabe und rechtsschöpferische Leistung*, Schriftenreihe, 'Ordnung der Wirtschaft', 1 (Berlin: Kohlhammer).

Borchardt, K. (1976), 'Wachstum und Wechsellagen 1914–1970', in H. Aubin and W. Zorn (eds.), *Handbuch der deutschen Wirtschafts und Sozialgeschichte* (Stuttgart: Union-Verl.), ii. 724.

—— and Schötz, O. (1991) (eds.), *Wirtschaftspolitik in der Krise. Die (Geheim) Konferenz der Friedrich List-Gesellschaft im September 1931 über Möglichkeiten und Folgen einer Kreditausweitung* (Baden-Baden: Nomos-Verlagsgesellschaft).

Brackmann, M. (1993), *Vom totalen Krieg zum Wirtschaftswunder. Die Vorgeschichte der westdeutschen Währungsreform* (Essen: Klartext-Verlag).

Brandt, K. (1993), *Geschichte der deutschen Volkswirtschaftslehre*, ii.*Vom Historismus zur Neoklassik* (Freiburg: Haufe).

Buchheim, Ch. (1988), 'Die Währungsreform 1948 in Westdeutschland', in *VfZ* 36. 189–231.

—— (1990*a*), 'Die Bundesrepublik und die Überwindung der Dollar-Lücke', in L. Herbst, W. Bührer and H. Sowade, (eds.), *Vom Marshall-Plan zur EWG. Die Eingliederung der Bundesrepublik Deutschland in die westliche Welt* (Munich: Oldenbourg), 81–98.

—— (1990*b*), *Die Wiedereingliederung Westdeutschlands in die Weltwirtschaft 1945–1958* (Munich: Oldenbourg).

—— (1994), 'Zur Natur des Wirtschaftsaufschwungs in der NS-Zeit', in Ch. Buchheim, M. Hutter, and H. James (eds.), *Zerrissene Zwischenkriegszeit. Wirtschaftshistorische Beiträge. Knut Borchardt zum 65, Geburtstag* (Baden-Baden: Nomos-Verlagsgesellschaft), 97–122.

Bührer, W. (1992), 'Erzwungene oder freiwillige Liberalisierung? Die USA, die OEEC und die westdeutsche Außenhandelspolitik 1949–1952', in L. Herbst *et al* (eds), *Vom Marshallplan zur EWG* (Munich: Oldenbourg), 139–62.

Eichholtz, D. (1984, 1985, 1996), *Geschichte der deutschen Kriegswirtschaft*, 3 vols. (Berlin: Akademie-Verlag).

Erhard, L. (1957), *Wohlstand für Alle* (Düsseldorf: Econ).

—— (1962), *Deutsche Wirtschaftspolitik. Der Weg der Sozialen Marktwirtschaft. Reden und Aufsätze* (Düsseldorf: Econ).

Erker, P. (1993), *Industrieeliten in der NS-Zeit. Anpassungsbereitschaft und Eigeninteresse von Unternehmern in der Rüstungs und Kriegswirtschaft 1936–1945*, (Passau: Wissenschaflicher Verlag Rothe).

Eucken, W. (1932), 'Staatliche Strukturwandlungen und die Krise des Kapitalismus', *Weltwirtschaftliches Archiv*, 36. 297–321.

—— (1938), *Nationalökonomie—wozu?* (Leipzig: Meiner; 2nd edn., Godesberg, 1947).

—— (1941), *Die Grundlagen der Nationalökonomie* (Jena: Fischer, 2nd edn.).

Dyas, G. P., and Thanheiser, H. T. (1976), *The Emerging European Enterprise: Strategy and Structure in French and German Industry* (Basingstoke: Macmillan).

Geyer, M. (1984), *Deutsche Rüstungspolitik 1860–1980* (Frankfurt-on-Main: Suhrkamp).

Giersch, H., Paqué, K. H., and Schmieding, H. (1993), *The Fading Miracle: Four Decades of Market Economy in Germany* (Cambridge: Cambridge University Press).

Glastetter, W., Högemann, G., and Marquardt, R. (1991), *Die Wirtschaftliche Entwicklung in der Bundesrepublik Deutschland 1950–1989* (Frankfurt-on-Main: Campus Verlag).

Grosser, D., *et al.* (1990), *Soziale Marktwirtschaft. Geschichte, Konzept, Leistung* (Stuttgart: Kohlhammer).

Grotkopp, W. (1954), *Die Große Krise. Lehren Aus der Überwindung der Weltwirtschaftskrise 1929–1932* (Düsseldorf: Econ).

Hagemann, W. (1984), *Von der Ordnungs zur Konjunkturpolitik. Zur Funktionsentwicklung staatlicher Wirtschaftspolitik in Westdeutschland von 1948 bis 1967* (Essen: RWE Essen).

Hartmann, H. (1959), *Der Deutsche Unternehmer. Autorität und Organization* (Frankfurt-on-Main: Europäische Verlags-Anstalt).

Haselbach, D. (1991), *Autoritärer Liberalismus und Soziale Marktwirtschaft. Gesellschaft und Politik im Ordoliberalismus* (Baden-Baden: Nomos Verlagsgesellschaft).

Hentschel, V. (1979), 'Schwerindustrielle Syndikatsbildung und Kartellpolitik im Ruhrgebiet von der wilhelminischen Zeit bis zur Gegenwart', in K. Rohe (ed.), *Politik und Gesellschaft im Ruhrgebiet* (Königstein-on-Taunus: Hain), 119–41.

—— (1989), 'Die Europäische Zahlungsunion und die Deutschen Devisenkrisen 1950–51', *VfZ*, 37.

—— (1996), *Ludwig Erhard. Ein Politikerleben* (Munich: Olzog).

Herbst, L. (1977), 'Krisenüberwindung und Wirtschaftsneuordnung. Ludwig Erhards Beteiligung an den Nachkriegsplanungen am Ende des Zweiten Weltkrieges', *VfZ*, 25. 305 ff.

—— (1982), *Der Totale Krieg und die Ordnung der Wirtschaft. Die Kriegswirtschaft im Spannungsfeld von Politik. Ideologie und Propaganda 1939–1945* (Stuttgart).

Horstmann, Theo (1991), *Die Alliierten und die deutsche Grossbanken, Bankenpolitik nach dem Zweiten Weltkrieg in Westdeutschland* (Bonn).

Huggschmid, J. (1970), *Die Politik des Kapitals, Konzentration und Wirtschaftspolitik in der Bundesrepublik* (Frankfurt-on-Main).

Jakli, Z. (1990), *Vom Marshallplan zum Kohlepfennig. Grundrisse der Subventionspolitik in der Bundesrepublik Deutschland* (Opladen: Westdeutscher Verlag).

James, H. (1986), *The Great Slump* (Oxford: Oxford University Press).

Kidron, M. (1970), *Rüstung und Wirtschaftliches Wachstum. Ein Essay über den Westlichen Kapitalismus Nach 1845* (Frankfurt-on-Main: Suhrkamp; 1st edn. London, 1968).

Kleinschmidt, C., and Welskopp, T. (1994), 'Amerika aus Deutscher Perspektive. Reiseeindrücke Deutscher Ingenieure über die Eisen und Stahlindustrie der USA 1900–1930', *Zeitschrift für Unternehmensgeschichte*, 39. 73–103.

Kramer, A. (1991), *The West German Economy, 1945–1955* (New York and Oxford: Berg).

Krengel, R. (1958), *Anlagevermögen, Produktion, und Beschäftigung der Industrie im Gebiet der Bundesrepublik von 1924 bis 1956* (Berlin: Duncker and Humblot).

Krüdener. J. von (1990) (ed.), *Economic Crisis and Political Collapse. The Weimar Republic 1924–1933* (New York and Oxford: Berg).

Kruse, C. (1988), *Die Volkswirtschaftslehre im Nationalsozialismus* (Freiburg: Haufe).

Kuczynski, J. (1994), 'Die Zwischenkriegszeit—ein neuer Kapitalismus nimmt Gestalt an', in Ch. Buchheim *et al.* (eds.), *Zerrissene Zwischenkriegszeit. Wirtschaftshistorische Beiträge. Knut Borchardt zum 65. Geburtstag* (Baden-Baden: Nomos-Verlagsgesellschaft), 357–65.

Laitenberger, V. (1986), *Ludwig Erhard. Der Nationalökonom und Politiker* (Göttingen: Musters-Schmidt).

Mai, G. (1992), 'Osthandel und Westintegration 1947–1957. Europa, die USA und die Entstehung einer hegemonialen Partnerschaft', in L. Herbst *et al.*, *Vom Marshallplan zur EWG* (Munich: Oldenbourg), 203–26.

Mollin, G. T. (1988), *Montankonzerne und Drittes Reich. Der Gegensatz zwischen Monopolindustrie und Befehlswirtschaft in der deutschen Rüstung und Expansion 1936–1944* (Göttingen: Vanderhoeck and Ruprecht).

Motteli, C. (1961), *Licht und Schaten der sozialen Marktwirtschaft: Leitbild und Wirklichkeit der Bundesrepublik Deutschland* (Zurich: Rentsch).

Müller-Armack, A. (1932), *Entwicklungsgesetze des Kapitalismus. Ökonomische, geschichtstheoretische und soziologische Studien zur modernen Wirtschaftsverfassung* (Berlin: Junker and Dünnhaupt).

—— (1933), *Ders., Staatsidee und Wirtschaftsordnung im neuen Reich* (Berlin: Junker and Dünnhaupt).

—— (1981), *Genealogie der Sozialen Marktwirtschaft* (Berne and Stuttgart: Haupt).

Neebe, R. (1992), 'Optionen Westdeutscher Außenwirtschaftspolitik 1949–1953', in W. Bührer *et al.* (eds.), *Vom Marshallplan zur EWG* (Munich: Oldenbourg), 163–202.

Nicholls, A. J. (1994), *Freedom with Responsibility: The Social Market Economy in Germany 1918–1963* (Oxford: Oxford University Press).

Petzina, D. (1977), *Die Deutsche Wirtschaft in der Zwischenkriegszeit* (Wiesbaden: Steiner).

Plumpe, G. (1981), 'Ökonomische Entwicklung und technologische Veränderungen in der westdeutschen Eisen und Stahlindustrie seit dem Zweiten Weltkrieg', in D. Petzina and G. van Roon (eds.), *Konjunktur, Krise, Gesellschaft. Wirtschaftliche Wechsellagen und soziale Entwicklung im 19. und 20. Jahrhundert* (Stuttgart: Klett-Cotta), 180–90.

—— (1990), *Die I.G. Farbenindustrie AG. Wirtschaft, Technik, Politik 1904–1945* (Berlin: Duncker and Humblot).

Plumpe, W. (1987), *Vom Plan zum Markt. Wirtschaftsverwaltung und Unternehmerverbände in der britischen Zone* (Düsseldorf: Schwann).

—— (1992), 'Politische Zäsur und Funktionale Kontinuität: Industrielle Nachkriegsplanungen und der Übergang zur Friedenswirtschaft 1944–1946', *1999. Zeitschrift für Sozialgeschichte des 20. und 21. Jahrhunderts*, 4. 11–37.

—— (1996*a*), 'Desintegration und Reintegration: Anpassungszwänge und Handlungsstrategien der Schwerindustrie des Ruhrgebietes in der Nachkriegszeit', in E. Schremmer (ed.), *Wirtschaftliche und soziale Integration in historischer Sicht. Arbeitstagung der Gesellschaft für Sozial und Wirtschaftsgeschichte in Marburg 1995, Beihefte der VSWG 128* (Stuttgart: Deutsche Verlagsgesellschaft), 290–303.

—— (1996*b*), 'Industrielle Beziehungen', in G. Ambrosius, D. Petzina, and W. Plumpe (eds.), *Moderne Wirtschaftsgeschichte. Eine Einführung für Historiker und Ökonomen* (Stuttgart: Oldenbourg), 389–419.

Poensgen, O. H. (1973), *Geschäftsbereichsorganisation* (Opladen: Westdeutscher Verlag).

Priebe, H. (1985), *Die subventionierte Unvernunft* (Berlin: Siedler).

Pritzkoleit, K. (1953), *Männer, Mächte, Monopole. Hinter den Türen der westdeutschen Wirtschaft* (Düsseldorf: Rauch).

Radkau, J. (1983), *Aufstieg und Krise der deutschen Atomwirtschaft 1945–1975. Verdrängte Alternativen in der Kerntechnik und der Ursprung der nuklearen Kontroverse* (Reinbek: Rowohlt).

Reich, S. (1990), *The Fruits of Fascism: Postwar Prosperity in Historical Perspective* (Ithaca, NY: Cornell University Press).

Ritschl, A. (1985), 'Die Währungsreform von 1948 und der Wiederaufstieg der westdeutschen Industrie', *VfZ*, 33. 136–65.

—— (1991), 'Die NS-Wirtschaftsideologie—Modernisierungsprogramm oder reaktionäre Utopie', in M. Prinz and R. Zitelmann (eds.), *Nationalsozialismus und Modernisierung* (Darmstadt: Wissenschaftliche Buchgesellschaft), 48–70.

Roskamp, K. W. (1965), *Capital Formation in West Germany* (Detroit: Wayne State University Press).

Scherf, H. (1987), *Die Wirtschaftspolitik der sozialliberalen Koalition* (Göttingen: Vanderhoeck and Ruprecht).

Schmitt, C. (1991), *Die geistesgeschichtliche Lage des heutigen Parlamentarismus* (Berlin: Duncker and Humblot, 7th edn., 1st edn., 1923).

Schmölders, G. (1988), 'Gut durchgekommen?', *Lebenserinnerungen* (Berlin: Duncker and Humblot).

Schumpeter, J. A. (1987), *Theorie der wirtschaftlichen Entwicklung. Eine Untersuchung über Unternehmergewinn, Kapital, Kredit, Zins und den Konjunkturzyklus* (Berlin: Duncker and Humblot, 7th edn.; 1st edn. 1911).

Shonfield, A. (1968), *Geplanter Kapitalismus. Wirtschaftspolitik in Westeuropa und US* (Cologne: Kiepenhauer and Witsch; 1st edn., London, 1965).

290 *Werner Plumpe*

Soltwedel, R., *et al.* (1986), *Deregulierungspotentiale in der Bundesrepublik*, Kieler Studien, 202 (Tübingen: Mohr).

Stavenhagen, G. (1964), *Geschichte der Wirtschaftstheorie* (Göttingen: Vanderhoeck and Ruprecht, 3rd edn.).

Stokes, R. (1988), *Divide and Prosper: The Heirs of I.G. Farben Under Allied Authority 1945–1951* (Berkeley: University of California Press).

—— (1994a), *Opting for Oil* (Cambridge: Cambridge University Press).

—— (1994b), *The Political Economy of Technological Change in West Germany* (Cambridge: Cambridge University Press).

Temin, P. (1989), *Lessons from the Great Depression* (Cambridge, Mass.: MIT Press).

Tolliday, S. (1995), 'Enterprise and State in the West German *Wirtschaftwunder*: Volkswagen and the Automobile Industry, 1939–1962', *Business History Review*, 69. 273–350.

Toniolo, G. (1998), 'Europe's Golden Age, 1950–1973: Speculations from a Long-Run Perspective', *Economic History Review*, 51. 252–67.

Tribe, K. (1995), 'The Genealogy of the Social Market Economy: 1937–1948', in *Strategies of Economic Order: German Economic Discourse 1750–1950* (Cambridge: Cambridge University Press), 203–40.

Windolf, P., and Beyer, J. (1996), 'Cooperative Capitalism: Corporate Networks in Germany and Britain', in *British Journal of Sociology*, 47. 205–31.

Wissenschaftlicher Beirat beim BMWi (1973), Sammelband der Gutachten 1948–1972. ed. BMWi (Göttingen).

Ziebura, G. (1984), *Weltwirtschaft und Weltpolitik 1922/24-1931* (Frankfurt-on-Main: Suhrkamp).

10

Coherence and Limitations of French Industrial Policy during the Boom Period
It Was Not So Bad After All

PHILIPPE MIOCHE

10.1. Introduction

Defined as a part of state economic policy, industrial policy is based on targets which are proposed or imposed on private or nationalized enterprises. This chapter proposes a chronology of the industrial policies conducted in France from 1945 to 1978, during the boom period which followed the Second World War. In particular I will try to evaluate their degree of continuity and coherence, and to characterize their nature. Are they mainly part of the planned economy, with targets chosen by the government and imposed on companies? Or are they part of a liberal policy, giving advice and indications to companies and helping to establish their strategies?

I will conclude with an evaluation of the efficiency of these policies in terms of company competitiveness. Unfortunately, it is not possible to explore here all the means which can be used by the state to plan its industrial policy. There are a great number of them: legislative, fiscal, monetary, etc. This chapter gives only an analysis of a few of the leading policy tools, in particular those using macroeconomic and sector planning.

Access to archives made possible only a few examples from the 1970s, but it is generally agreed that 1984 marked a historic turning-point. Policy changes with respect to the biggest bankruptcy in the country's history—the bankruptcy of the Creusot-Loire firm—turned a strategy of attack into a withdrawal policy, which resulted in various forms of deregulation (Cohen, 1989).

It is not my intention to conduct a detailed study of all industrial sectors and, therefore, the examples in this chapter will deal mainly with the steel industry. This industry has occupied a central place in French industrial policy. Industrial output represented nearly 5 per cent of world production in 1946, 10 per cent of exports in the 1960s, and about 6 per cent in the 1970s. Furthermore, the industry's image placed it at the heart of political debates. It symbolized national power, economic power, and independence. Steel policies were generally perceived as exemplary until the mid-1970s. At that time, during the financial collapse which led Prime Minister Raymond Barre to take control of the sector in 1978, the steel industry was the subject of a long dispute. Having once been the symbol of France's revival, steel was now the embodiment of inefficiency, revealing the risks of certain types of industry. It is perhaps time to wonder whether the radical condemnation of the 1980s should not be qualified.

10.2. Modernization of French Industry by virtue of the Monnet Plan and the Dollars of the Marshall Plan (1945–1952)

On the whole, French industry achieved real growth between 1945 and 1952 as production levels reached and exceeded those of the prewar years. The production level of the 1937–9 steel industry was reached again between 1948 and 1949. The 1929 level—around 10 million tons—was exceeded in 1951. This was the result of the industrial policy of the Monnet Plan, American aid provided by the Marshall Plan, and, finally, the recovered dynamism of French society, from the working class to employers.

Industrial policy was inspired by a variety of experiences. First there were the debates and attempts at an industrial policy during the crisis of the 1930s, including inconclusive policy experiments in the active period of the Vichy government (1940–1). For example, the first macroeconomic plans were drawn up under the German occupation. There were many common elements between the prewar and postwar period—often major ones—which concerned men, ideologies, and practices.

But, after 1945, Keynesianism began to dominate economic theory filling the gap between the liberal discourses of the prewar period and the practice of interventionism (Sirinelli, 1994). There was also a fairly far-reaching renewal of the political community taking place with the emergence in government of former members of the Resistance. These men followed left-wing policies until 1947 and were concerned with 'controlling the means of production' more than anything else. Nationalizations were carried out on a large scale: the coal industry, electricity, the deposit banks, the car company Renault, etc. Decisions regarding which industries should be nationalized were shaped by political considerations more than economic concerns.

That the steel industry was not nationalized initially was due to political hesitancy and the efficiency of corporate action in the profession (Mioche, 1992). Employers in the steel industry managed to re-establish their legitimacy fairly rapidly after accusations of Nazi collaboration, because it was accepted that their confiscation by occupying forces was perpetrated against their will. In 1945 the Employers' Federation of the French steel industry—a professional organization stemming directly from the prewar Ironworks Comity, *Comité des forges*—was officially reinstated (Mioche, 1992). It managed to put off nationalization until 1949.

Management of the new public sector differed greatly from one company to another. For example, the communist minister Marcel Paul directed ex-directors of private companies to run the public group of electric utilities while the communist Secretary of State, Auguste Lecoeur, placed trade unionists at the head of the public coal industry. The Communist Party was wracked with indecision (Bloch-Lainé and Bouvier, 1986: 116). Generally speaking, state economic policy was ill defined and showed deep political contradictions. In 1945 and 1946, industrial policy was trying to find its way. It was the planning of Jean Monnet which gave it the coherence that it lacked before.

Paradoxically, the first general adviser for the Plan (Commissaire Général du Plan) knew none of the experiments of the prewar or war period, unlike the civil servants with whom he was to work. He had no sympathy at all with communism and did not refer explicitly to Keynesian theory, though he met J. M. Keynes many times. J. Monnet acted as a consultant to American decision-makers and benefited from the expertise of American advisers such as Robert Nathan, one of the fathers of the Victory Programme (Duchêne, 1994). The general adviser for the Plan took up his post at the beginning of 1946.

The Plan was based on the setting up of commissions of modernization in those sectors (sixteen commissions were created in 1946) which were to define the necessary resources in raw materials, machinery, and labour, before reaching—in four years—the 1929 level plus 25 per cent. This prospective work was also to include an evaluation of financial requirements and indications about changes in industrial structures (cooperation, mergers, etc.).

The commissions brought together managers, union workers, and civil servants who represented the ministers concerned. Most of them worked towards expansion and growth, since the various groups wanted to modernize national industry. Their motives were different. Managers wanted to make up for the technological backwardness caused by the war and demonstrate their desire for modernization, despite accusations of Malthusianism made against them. Civil servants were converted to the Keynesian economic policy. The trade unionists wanted the country's recovery to escape from American rule. This political and social context was the key to the success of the Plan. This is why some commission proposals led to an acceleration of projects. The best example is that of electricity.

The commission responsible for the modernization of electricity was appointed on 12 February 1946. It included twenty-two members: six trade unionists, four ministry representatives, six managers, and six experts (Mioche, 1987). It was chaired by a manager, Roger Bouteville. The structure of the industry was totally transformed when the nationalization law took effect, soon after the work of the commission began. The whole industry in this sector was brought together under one state-owned body: Electricité de France. The programmes for electrical equipment were increased. An increase in production capacity of nearly 10 thousand million kWh was forecast for the period 1947–51, which would put the country's overall hydraulic production at more than 25 thousand million in 1951 with total production at 40 thousand million kWh.[1] The amount of hydraulic equipment necessary increased threefold; investment was 220 thousand million current francs.

The achievements of the commission responsible for modernizing the steel industry were more modest. Large investments were approved, in particular two: a rolling mill in Denain in the north and another at Seremange in the east. Their equipment alone represented more than half the total investment in the steel industry. That equipment made it possible for the country to catch up in the thin sheet rolling industry and thus ensure supplies to car factories at the beginning of the mass-consumption period.

The Monnet Plan was revised when the results of the French–American financial negotiations in May 1946 (the Blum–Byrnes Agreement) proved to be disappointing to the French. Generally the Plan was kept intact, but its aims were limited to six key sectors: coal, electricity, steel, cement, railways, and tractors as shown in Table 10.1.

One must stress the pragmatism of the Plan implemented by Monnet. Funds were provided by the Marshall Plan beginning in 1948 and by the Modernization and Equipment Fund (FME) at the Ministry of Finances. Funds were used largely to give loans to firms that made productive investments. If an investment application had first been accepted by the Plan, long-term credits were granted at a much lower rate than that of the money market. Otherwise firms had to organize their own financing at higher costs with banks, since the stock exchange was still very weak.

Such financing methods explained the 'guiding' feature of French planning, as opposed, for instance, to the authoritarian system applied in the

Table 10.1 *Programme for Key Sectors for 1947 with a Forecast for 1950 (in absolute terms)*

	1938	1946	1947	1950
Coal (thousand of tons)	47	50	55.5	65
Electricity (billion of kWh)	20.7	23.5	26	37
Crude steel (thousand of tuns)	6.2	4.2	7	11
Cement (thousand of tons)	3.8	3	6	13.5
Railways (thousand of tons consigned)	133	130	160	240
Tractors (thousand units)	2.7	1.7	12.3	—

Source: Mioche (1987: 165).

USSR. Private enterprise did not have to follow the Plan, but if they did they were granted very attractive credits. However, this relative freedom did not apply to nationalized enterprises which received the bulk of the loans. Those enterprises had to follow the Plan's directives. But as they were, to a great extent, associated with the preparation of the Plan, they were obligated to follow its guidelines. This was made very clear, for instance, in the case of the National Electricity Board (EDF) and the Railways (SNCF).

The steel industry was the main private beneficiary of Marshall Plan aid. The volume of investment went from 0.5 thousand million in constant francs (1990) in 1946 to 4.5 thousand million in 1950—that is, more than 20 per cent of turnover. Almost the whole of that sum (94 per cent) came from Marshall Plan aid (Margairaz, 1991: 1250 ff.). In this way the public debt of the steel industry became an essential financial resource. Again, in 1950, self-financing was reduced to less than 20 per cent (see Fig. 10.1). In the long term, public financing peaked at two points: 1949–54 and 1966–8. The first period coincided with a loan offer generated by the Marshall Plan; the second coincided with the sector plan of 1966. Easy access to public credit thus eliminated self-financing and capital increases from such financing.

Managers were very active in the steel commission. They supported the production targets and investment programme but refused to support restructuring that would have meant closing some outdated plants. Results were therefore very limited. One noticed a small number of mergers with the creation of Usinor in 1946, the rolling co-operative Sollac in 1948, and Sidelor in 1950. From 100 companies three or four groups emerged, owning roughly 150 establishments. Industrial policy in that first period was very active. It brought together nationalization, planning, public financing of investments, price control of raw material, and basic products. This last point was important. As early as before the war governments instituted price controls in order to slow down inflation.

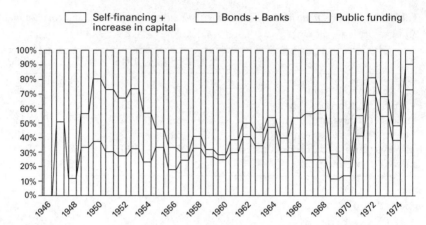

Fig 10.1 *Financing of the steel industry, 1945–1978, as a percentage of total long-term financing*

Between 1938 and 1947, for instance, overall increase in wholesale prices was twice that of electricity (Woronoff, 1994: 511).

Price control weighed heavily on basic industries but benefited manufacturing. What basic industries lost in receipts, they got back in the public funds used for investment in industry as part of the Marshall Plan.

The industrial policy of that period was clever—it allowed an increase in competition among private manufacturers as a result of transfers from basic sectors. Such transfers were compensated for with public funds from the Marshall Plan in 1948–52, and then from public savings and budget resources.

10.3. The Uncertainties of Industrial Policy, 1952–1962

The end of the Fourth Republic was characterized by government instability and colonial wars. For example, Pierre Mendès France, *Président du Conseil* in 1954, focused on peace in Indochina and did not have time to carry out his economic programme (Margairaz, 1988). For four or five years, France had no economic policy. Politicians, especially Edgar Faure, got caught up in the growth taking place at the time even though they had done nothing to promote it.

The role of planning diminished during the Second (1952–7) and Third Plans (1958–61). The Plan helped industrial decision-making by proposing development scenarios, but it was no longer decisive in formulating economic policy. His weakness mirrored that of political power and institutions. Implementation and the public perception of the Second Plan was damaged by its difference from the more dynamic First Plan. Jean Monnet, the father of planning, would have liked to have integrated French planning into European construction and to have made some progress towards a 'communautarian plan'. But the difficulties of ECSC caused that scheme to fail. The Economic Advisory Committee (Commissariat du Plan) was put under the authority of the Ministry of Finance in 1956 and was no longer under the supervision of the executive. This new administrative position weakened the authority of the Plan and subjected it to budgetary arbitration.

The targets decided upon by planning were 'basic actions' aimed at improving the general environment of the enterprises. The Plan was meant first to guide manufacturing industries and then to take public equipment into account. Planning could use the tools of national accounts, but these were not really operational until the Fourth Plan (B. Cazes in Lévy-Leboyer and Casanova, 1991). Overall, the Second Plan lost credibility with the public and contractors. Its priorities and strategies differed from the First Plan. The continuing public effort to support basic industries was halted. Certain needs were particularly strong, as in housing, whose modernization had been delayed up until that point. A reorientation was necessary both socially and politically, and it was an important change in the priorities of industrial policy.

The weaknesses of planning were even more obvious in the Third Plan: its drafting and implementation coincided with the setting up of the new regime (1958), which was to define a new economic policy. Also, the Plan was under a political obligation to include 'French Algeria' in its forecast, which made the Plan practically null and void (Fourquet, 1982).

In the absence of a coherent and clear industrial policy after 1953–4, however, growth and investment were particularly strong. France contributed to the world increase in investment and, in spite of a relative lag, managed to overtake the United States in this field as is shown Table 10.2.

Table 10.2 *Investment Rate as a percentage of Gross Domestic Product (GDP)*

	1950	1955	1960
France	17.5	19.1	20.1
West Germany	19.5	23.4	24.3
United States	19	18.5	17.9
Japan	20.5	19.8	30.1

Source: OCDE.

After the Korean Boom in 1950 and the big reduction in investments in 1951, growth became steadier. The annual average rate of industrial production growth came to 5.3 per cent for the period 1949–69 (Carré, Dubois, and Malinvaud, 1984). These performances were not the consequence of industrial policy as defined at the beginning of this chapter. The state economic policy had not disappeared but it came out with indirect incentives. Some examples are the 1951 tax policy that induced accelerated pay-off, reform of indirect taxation, and the creation of the Value-Added Tax in 1954, all of which helped productive investment. Export subsidies compensated for monetary depreciation in 1957. A policy of regional decentralization encouraged redeployment and the modernization of industry in general. The Economic and Social Development Fund (FDES) replaced the Modernization and Equipment Fund (FME) in 1955, and allocation of public funds to investment continued within this new body. Financing was no longer drawn from Marshall Plan aid but from budget resources. However, the share of public spending devoted to industry and commerce would never again reach the levels attained in postwar years (see Fig. 10.2).

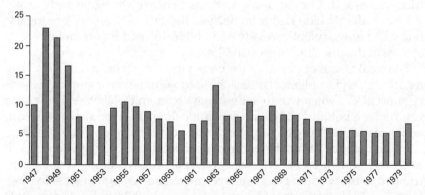

Fig 10.2 *The percentage of public spending on industry and commerce in overall public spending from 1947 to 1980*

By this point the reconstruction phase was complete and the market had regained its independent capacity. Countries—France included—had gone from an economy of producers to an economy of traders (Caron, 1995). On the finance side, the stock exchange regained great vitality and the market index doubled between 1947 and 1952, covering an increasing portion of enterprises' financial needs. Consumption was boosted by income supplements from the social benefits provided by the welfare state (Social Security Act in 1945). These benefits progressively reached one-third of available income. France, in its turn, had entered the mass-consumption society. Industrial growth was not as dependent on public action as it once was.

In this context the first stages of European reconstruction began. Following Robert Schuman's declaration on May 1950, the Treaty of Paris established the European Coal and Steel Community (ECSC) in 1951. The Community was to take over national industrial policy as far as coal and steel were concerned. For a brief period, those industries were placed in a situation which set them apart from other industries.

The aims of the founder members of the ECSC were complex and diverse, as much in international relations as in economic interests. The members wanted to settle the German issue while guaranteeing peace; they also wanted to guarantee industrial development by ensuring the supply of coke in the Ruhr (Milward, 1984). Finally they wanted to improve the competitiveness of manufacturing industries by lowering steel prices (Kipping, 1994: 73–93).

The Treaty of Paris included ambitious targets for industrial controls: investments as well as disinvestments were submitted for authorization. The Community executive—the High Authority—could establish guiding programmes, modernization targets, etc. (Article 46). Tacit combines (cartels) were prohibited. On the other hand, selling prices from industrialists in official schemes knew total freedom. The Treaty was partly inspired by antitrust laws in the United States. Jean Monnet asserted, in June 1950, that 'the main idea was the condemning of all cartels' (Barjot, 1994: 124). Afraid that their private cartels should disappear, some steel producers started a vigorous battle to prevent implementation of the Schuman Plan. But it failed because some managers preferred compromise to confrontation. This strategy prevailed and in 1951 the profession obtained subsidization from public funds of all the bond issues it had contracted before (Schwabe, 1988: 305–18).

Claiming that their competitiveness was markedly inferior to that of German steel producers in particular, the French obtained financing from their government which allowed for equipment modernization that began with the Monnet Plan and continued into the 1950s. This created a precedent which was picked up during various stages: modernizing with the help of public funds to be better prepared when markets opened. In practical terms, this new contribution made it possible to finance the first true coastal plant, that at Dunkirk, akin to the seaside steel industry in Japan.

In fact the practices of the ECSC were as different from the initial project as its founders and its texts were contradictory (Spirenburg and Poideuin, 1993). Some partners favoured a supranational planned economy; others—particularly the Germans—leaned towards the liberal management of markets. All of them maintained their desire to give priority to their national markets. Steel producers were very satisfied to find that they could maintain their cartel in the national market. Simultaneously they

combined with their European counterparts to become the 'steel producers' club' reviving the steel agreements of prewar years.

The ECSC did not implement an industrial policy, as I have defined it.
Its role was confined to helping to restructure some coal mines, mainly in
Belgium. The opening up of frontiers resulted in important modifications
of the markets, especially in the medium term. They were only half-unex-
pected. Although German competition remained bearable, the French
market was subjected to strong penetration from Belgium and Luxem-
bourg, while in Italy the dynamism of the steel industry was taking shape.
After the final failure of the European Defence Community in 1954, the
ECSC was weakened and therefore prevented from implementing its initial projects. The boost of Messina (1955) and the Treaty of Rome (1957) did
not lead to a renewal of European industrial policy.

The creation of the European Economic Community (EEC) was marked
by a liberal-minded desire to confine its action to customs disarmament.
The Treaty included its intentions in its Articles 3 and 6: 'The action of the
Community includes the institution of a common policy regarding trans-
ports, the establishment of a regime ensuring that competition is not distorted by the common market, the implementing of procedures allowing
the co-ordination of the economics policies of the member states and the
prevention of destabilization in the balance of payments.' But this was just
the framework of a treaty whose enforcement was still to be worked out.
Thus, until the beginning of the 1980s (Davignon Plan), nothing was produced that resembled a common industrial policy.

There were two reasons why this was so: on the one hand the founders,
especially the German liberals, were greatly hostile to the idea of an industrial policy. On the other hand, European reconstruction was going through
a long period of difficulties, due to the position of General de Gaulle. In the
end the Community's efforts had two results during the years 1960–70: the
setting up of a costly agricultural policy and a successful customs disarmament. The Europeans participated fully in the Kennedy round of GATT
negotiations in 1960, and therefore the common exterior tariff planned by
the Treaty of Rome did not play its protectionist role.

This period was characterized by a distinct weakening of industrial
postwar voluntarism. Of course, this was only a relative weakening.
Compared with other European countries—West Germany and Belgium
for instance—French governments had important means of intervention
at their disposal with the state sector fully maintained, planning already
under way, public aid to productive investment, taxation, and the price
control of basic products. But these means were used less intensively and
less coherently than before. The ECSC and the EEC, for different reasons,
did not make up for the absence of national intervention.

Altogether, the end of the Fourth Republic was a time of slack industrial
policy. However, these same years showed a very strong growth. This

growth was not explained by a weakening of industrial policy but rather it was a consequence of the voluntarist policy followed earlier.

It was during the 1950s that France felt the effects of the structural reforms of the Liberation. The failings of economic policy during the 1950s were partly responsible for the rebirth of an industrial policy during the Fifth Republic.

10.4. The Renewal and Decline of the Industrial Policy of the Fifth Republic, 1962–1978

The first years of the Fifth Republic, 1958–62, were dominated by the settling of the colonial war in Algeria. As soon as December 1958, however, General de Gaulle adopted a series of economic measures—the Rueff–Armand Plan—which took effect at the end of the year. It included spending reductions and credit and price cuts. The franc was greatly devalued.

For the most part the plan was confirmation of the French commitment to European reconstruction. In a rather unexpected way, General de Gaulle accepted the Treaty of Rome and his subsequent policy encouraged the abolition of tariffs between member countries on 1 July 1968. The French government also asked for and obtained a reform of community institutions and the implementation of a common agricultural policy particularly favourable for France.

It was with the Fourth Plan (1962–5) that planning found its new direction. It was a 'burning obligation' for the President of the Republic. He meant it to become a priority once again for government. Social dialogue was the main tool used and planning became a prime example for some of the unions and the political left wing. For the liberal Jacques Rueff, the Plan did not contribute to growth, but simply recorded it. It was obvious that growth could not come about by planning alone. Other European countries had known strong growth without the kind of official planning used in France. However, the influence of planning must not be underrated. Research has proved the correspondence between the achievements of the national economy and the targets fixed by planning, in particular those of the Fourth Plan (Estrin and Holmes, 1983). The Economic Advisory Committee was one of the few places for social dialogue in a society marked by numerous social conflicts. According to the widely quoted quantitative survey of French growth, planning was a real, but not quantifiable, cause of growth (Carré, Dubois, and Malinvaud, 1984).

The apparent success of French planning brought it international notoriety, particularly in the United Kingdom. This was why, in 1961, the National Economic Development Council and the National Plan were created, partially following the French example. As for French planners, they thought the national method was a model to be followed: 'So rationality should lead to something which would be in accordance with the spirit of the Plan. If French methods are not immediately applicable in different contexts, they retain a general value, by their analysis of the nature of problems in a modern economy, and by creation of a framework of thought open to adaptations. The French Plan could therefore one day bring its contribution to the organization of development in the group of industrialized nations' (Introduction by P. Massé in Schonfield, 1967). British economic theory paid close attention to the French experiment (Meade, 1970). In fact, observers probably gave too much credit to the coherence and efficiency of planning in France (Holmes, in *Divers auteurs*, 1990).

At the end of the 1960s, those in favour of the Plan met its first detractors. It had been weakened in 1964 by the failure of income policy and it was broken by the political and social events of May–June 1968 and again by the oil crisis of 1973.

The weakening of macroeconomic planning in the mid-1960s was compensated for by totally new forms of sector interventions. Industrial policy came to rely on some 'national champions', following the policies of Georges Pompidou, who became prime minister in 1962. Sectors and enterprises were to serve as examples and to receive public aid in the form of long-term financing which was a much more attractive option. This policy expressed the will to prepare France for the widening of European and international market openings. It was in line with the politics of national greatness of Gaullism and was a way of making up for the loss of the colonial empire by industrial power. Finally, it was meant to be an answer to American economic penetration from 1960 to 1967, since half the foreign capital invested in France at that time was of American origin. However, this only represented 3.3 per cent of French investment, compared with 5.9 per cent in the Federal Republic of Germany, which was considerably more 'penetrated'. The American presence in France was strongly resented, as shown by the success of Jean Jacques Servan-Schreiber's book, *The American Challenge*, published in 1967 (Lévy-Leboyer and Casanova, 1991).

It is fairly difficult to claim that the choice of the sectors that would become 'national champions' was made after an analysis of 'comparative advantages'. Some sectors were founded on high technology where the country showed real capacity, like aeronautics; others were not, like the shipbuilding industry. The strategy of the industrial policy aimed to compensate for the market's failure, as in the computer industry, but the desire for national independence took complete precedence over economic analysis. Pompidou's policy resulted in a series of big sector programmes. After the buyout of the Machines Bull Company by General Electric, the government created the CII in 1966 and implemented its 'Calculation Plan' from 1967 to 1971. It aimed to create a national French computer industry, particularly for the manufacturing of nuclear armament. Manufacturing's aircraft plan conceptualized the French–British Concorde in 1962 and resulted in the making of the European Airbus in 1969. Plans for space research were part of the aircraft industry project. In every case, public financing had to be granted in order to modernize the sectors concerned. Their concentration then gave them the necessary scale for world expansion while insuring the country's technological and industrial independence. The project was ambitious and coherent and its results were debatable and debated (Stoffaes, 1978; Stoléru, 1969). In the long term, the aerospace industry came through the crisis with great panache, but the shipbuilding industry met with failure.

One of the first sector plans was for the steel industry and took place from 1966 to 1970. General de Gaulle's governments had set their own priorities in 1951: reinforcing and modernizing the sector first, then allowing confrontation with European competition. This scheme was reinforced in 1961 at the start of the world crisis in the steel industry. From that year on international competition, especially Japanese competition on 'distant markets', and the relative drop in productivity gains in Europe, caused grave upheaval. Prices were going down and, on the initiative of Belgian competitors, cartels were abandoned.

During the next four years, from 1962 to 1966, steel producers and authorities had face-to-face negotiations in an attempt to tackle a double problem. How were they to reinforce competitiveness in the steel industry in view of the market's disorder and how were they to deal with the 1968 deadline for opening up European markets?

The government wanted to concentrate sectors into one or two enterprises. In that way three steel groups emerged: two for ordinary steel—Usinor and Sacilor, and one for special steel—Creusot-Loire. The negotiation was threefold: the structures of the sector, the financing of a new investment programme, and a social policy including an attempt at planned redundancy concerning 15,000 jobs. Concentrating sectors was not desired by all industrialists; it was required by the government in exchange for a new programme of public financing (Mioche and Roux, 1988). The whole industrial policy was set up as a model of neocorporatism. Implementation of this plan was carried out until 1970. In the context of the economic recovery of 1968–9, authorities added to the investment programme the construction of a big coastal plant at Fos-sur-mer. This was how the third investment cycle, 1966–73, reached unequalled highs.

The 1960s and the beginning of the 1970s witnessed a remarkable opening to the world and particularly to Europe of French industry. De Gaulle's uncompromising attitude on certain big issues (the veto of the United Kingdom's entry into the EEC in 1963 and 1967; France leaving NATO in 1966; etc.) must not hide the dynamic of industrial internationalization. Furthermore, the new President in 1969, Georges Pompidou, extended this policy of opening up by encouraging international co-operation, particularly with European partners. In the long term, one sees that the most successful programmes were based on co-operation (Woronoff, 1994: 563).

We can characterize the industrial policy of that time in terms of Saint-Simonism, opening up, and European co-operation. The results were spectacular. The share of foreign trade as part of GDP went from 22.7 per cent in 1950 to 34.1 per cent in 1973. The opening up was also accompanied by a redeployment of trade—trade with the 'overseas territories' since they became independent had considerably diminished in favour of that with Europe (Marseille, 1984). Half France's trade was now with the six member countries of the EEC and West Germany became France's first client supplier. From one year to the next, France maintained its influence in rapidly growing world trade, attaining between 7 and 8 per cent of world trade. It also maintained its rank among the great industrial powers (see Table 10.3).

Table 10.3 *Countries Ranked in Accordance to Exports of Manufactured Products*

1952	1965	1971
United States	United States	West Germany
United Kingdom	West Germany	United States
West Germany	United Kingdom	Japan
France	Japan	France
Benelux	France	United Kingdom

Source: Lévy-Leboyer and Casanova (1991).

The French steel industry believed it would reap the fruits of this policy in 1974, when, from all points of view, results were excellent. But, as early as 1975, prices, sales, and production collapsed. The industrial policy at the end of the 1960s had not stopped the course of industrial depression. The steel industry was confronted with a contra-cyclic financing of its investments, and the withdrawal of the policy of sale price controls in 1971 did not benefit the sector since the market embarked on a downward trend. The financial costs and level of debt in the enterprises became politically unbearable considering the advantages granted by the authorities.

In 1978, Prime Minister Barre undertook the conversion of public loans into shares, which amounted to bringing the three steel groups under state control. This salvage measure should not be considered as a renewal of interventionism. It was a technical decision which was part of a totally different political project: 'Internal and international competition must from now on be the fundamental law of our industrial activity' (R. Barre, Apr. 1978, in Caron, 1995: 394). This state control was preceded by four years of nationalization, the main consequence of which was the saving of big industrial companies by bringing them more capital. In this sense, what happened in the steel industry was a 'general rehearsal' for overall relations between the state and industry when facing depression.

10.5. Concluding Remarks

All the means at the state's disposal to conduct an industrial policy in France during the boom period—planning, public financing, sale price controls, etc.—were impressive. We have seen that, paradoxically, industrial policy was less planned during the Fourth Republic, when the governmental or parliamentary left wing was influential, than during the Gaullism-inspired Fifth Republic. The industrial policy of Charles de Gaulle's governments, when growth was at its fastest, was not liberal but drawn from a tradition of Saint-Simonism.

Observed from abroad, French industrial policy may have seemed particularly state planned to the Western world. This opinion is sometimes taken up by national historians who study the public archives of the Ministry of Finance or Ministry of Industry.

However, is it not a kind of illusion that the high civil servants and the politicians have their own power of intervention ? If one reads about the events of that period in the light of questions asked by the historian Jean Bouvier (Fridenson and Strauss, 1987), one draws the conclusion that the France of the 'thirty glorious years' was more liberal than state controlled or one has to qualify what one means by the state control of French industrial policy.

Similar reasoning is valid regarding the evaluation of industrial policies during that period. It leads to two conclusions. French industrial policy, on the whole, has not been constant—consensus and unity around the Monnet Plan from 1946 to 1952, hesitancy and dispersion during the second part of the Fourth Republic (1953–8). The third period, from 1958 to the end of the 1960s (with some extension into the 1970s), characterized by a more intensive industrial policy; one based on sectors rather than macro-economic targets.

We will start with the hypothesis that the efficiency of an industrial policy depends more on its long-term constancy than its short-term modalities. From this point of view it appears that policy towards the steel industry knew considerable fluctuations, particularly as a result of the ECSC episode, to the extent that it came close to resembling a 'stop and go' British-type policy. The extent of those fluctuations sheds light on the specific difficulties of the industrial sector during the 1970s and 1980s: early signs of depression and financial bankruptcy.

As for the general efficiency of industrial policies in France, one tends to stay clear of short-term, impassioned judgement. Literature has not stopped praising the 'national specificity' combining water and fire, as it were, in a competitive and open market with an efficient industrial policy. The fame of French policy at the time aroused international interest. When industrial depression reached its maximum intensity, during 1970–80, state intervention—exaggerated to serve the purpose of the time—stood accused.

But what can one say today, twenty-five years later? Year in, year out, France has maintained its rank in world trade and its ability to innovate (Lévy-Leboyer and Casanova, 1991). The steel industry which yesterday was bankrupt was privatized in 1995 and now shows a healthy financial position. Indeed the changes in the industrial system, marked in particular by a considerable rise in unemployment, are not yet at an end but one can already claim that the industry has not disappeared in the storm, both in France and Europe. How can one avoid the question: Isn't the recovery now taking place partly the result of the industrial policies that were followed during the 'thirty glorious years'?

Couldn't it be said that those policies, while not overestimating their rigidity or their national originality, were not so harmful after all?

NOTE

1. AN 80 AJ 10 (French National Archives), 'Premier rapport de la commission de modernisation de l'électricité, Novembre 1946'.

REFERENCES

Barjot, Dominique (1994) (ed.), *Vues nouvelles sur les cartels internationaux* (Caen: Edition-Diffusion du Lys).

Bloch-Lainé, François, and Bouvier, Jean (1986), *La France restaurée, 1944–1954: dialogue sur les choix d'un modernisation* (Paris: Fayard).

Caron, François (1995), Histoire économique de la France, XIXe–XXe siècles (Paris: Armand Colin, 2nd edn.).

Carré, J. J., Dubois, P., and Malinvaud, E. (1984), *Abrégé de la croissance française* (Paris: Seuil).

Cohen, Elie (1989), *L'État brancardier* (Paris: Calmann-Lévy).

Delorme, Robert, and André, Christine (1983), *L'État et l'économie, un essai d'explication de l'évolution des dépenses publiques en France (1870–1980)* (Paris: Seuil).

Divers auteurs (1990), *De Gaulle en son siècle* (Paris: Unesco).

Duchêne, François (1994), *Jean Monnet: The First Statesman of Interdependence* (New York and London: W. W. Norton and Co.).

Estrin, Saul, and Holmes, Peter (1983), *French Planning in Theory and Practice* (London: George Allen and Unwin).

Fourquet, François (1982), *Les Comptes de la puissance: histoire de la comptabilité nationale et du plan* (Paris: Encres).

Fridenson, P., and Strauss, A. (eds.) (1987), *Le Capitalisme français au 19ème-20ème siècles, blocages et dynamismes d'une croissance* (Paris: Fayard).

Kipping, Mathias (1994), 'La Construction européenne: une solution aux problèmes français de compétitivité', *Entreprises et Histoire*, 5.

Lévy-Leboyer, Maurice , and Casanova, Jean Claude (1991) (eds.), *Entre l'état et le marché: l'économie française des années 1880 à nos jours* (Paris: Gallimard).

Margairaz, Michel (1988) (ed.), *Pierre Mendes France et l'économie* (Paris: Odile Jacob).

—— (1991), *L'État, les finances et l'économie: histoire d'une conversion, 1932–1952*, 2 vols. (Paris: Ministère des Finances, 'Historie économique et financière').

Marseille, Jacques (1984), *Empire colonial et capitalisme français: Histoire d'un divorce* (Paris: Albin Michel).

Meade, James (1970), *The Theory of Indicative Planning* (Manchester: Manchester University Press).

Milward, Alan S. (1984), *The Reconstruction of Western Europe, 1945–1951* (London: Methuen).

Mioche, Philippe (1987), *Le Plan Monnet, genèse et élaboration 1941–1947* (Paris: Publications de la Sorbonne).

—— (1992), 'La Sidérugie et l'état en France des années 1940 aux années 1960', Ph.D. diss., University of Paris IV.

—— and Roux, Jacques (1988), *Henri Malcor, un héritier des maîtres des forges* (Lyons: Éditions du CNRS).

Schonfield, Andrew (1967), *Le Capitalisme aujourd'hui: l'état et l'entreprise* (Paris: Gallimard).

Schwabe, Klaus (1988), *The Beginnings of the Schuman Plan* (Baden Baden and Paris: Nomos and LGDJ).

Sirinelli, Jean François (1994) (ed.), *Dictionnaire historique de la vie politique française au XXe siècle* (Paris: PUF).

Spirenburg, Dirk, and Poidevin, Raymond (1993), *Histoire de la Haute Autorité de la Communauté Européenne du Charbon et de l'Acier: une expérience supranationale* (Brussels: Bruylant).

Stoffaes, Christian (1978), *La Grande Menace industrielle* (Paris: Callmann-Lévy).

Stoléru, Lionel (1969), *L'Impératif industriel* (Paris: Seuil).

Woronoff, Denis (1994), *Histoire de l'industrie en France du XVIe siècle à nos jours* (Paris: Seuil).

11

Harmful or Irrelevant?
Italian Industrial Policy, 1945–1973

GIOVANNI FEDERICO

11.1. Introduction

The performance of the Italian economy during the 'golden years' of the postwar period was exceedingly good. From 1950 to 1973 the industrial value added grew at an impressive 6.8 per cent yearly (Rossi, Sorgato, and Toniolo, 1993: table 1.A) and the GDP per capita at 4.8 per cent, the second best performance (along with Germany) among the seven major industrialized countries after Japan (Maddison, 1991: table 1). The Italian *miracolo economico* was even more impressive than the German *Wirschaftswunder*. In fact in 1951 Italy, unlike Germany, was not a fully fledged member of the club of advanced countries. Agriculture still accounted for a quarter of GDP (ISTAT, 1985: table 8.18) and employed 9 million people out of an active population of about 20 million (Zamagni, 1986: table A.1). Twenty years later, Italy was undoubtedly an advanced industrial country, even if it was still lagging behind others in Europe.

How much did state intervention contribute to this success? Most scholars would say very little or nothing at all. Italian industrial policy enjoys a very bad reputation. At best, it is credited with having helped some industries to grow; at worst it is regarded as a squandering of the taxpayers' money for political purposes. Bollino blames the 'complexity, inconsistency and ineffectiveness of many policies accumulated over time by numerous short-lived governments'; the 'ex post approach'; the 'ad hoc attitude, merely responding to a sequence of external market shocks'; the 'attitude on the part of public authorities to transform a winner into a loser in order to pursue social and political objectives'; and the 'intrinsic myopia of the government coupled with an inconsistency in the assignment of instruments to targets from an economic viewpoint' (Bollino, 1983: 263, 265, 268).

This reputation was largely built in the 1970s, when government(s) reacted to the oil shocks by massively subsidizing industries and by defending existing jobs at all cost. Perhaps the case of the 1950s–1960s was different. Perhaps state intervention then did help growth. Clearly, a good performance is not in itself sufficient to endorse an optimistic view. In fact, it does not rule out the possibility that a different policy would have yielded a faster (or more balanced, or more socially equitable) growth. The question can be dealt with only by analysing the characteristics, aims, and tools of the actual policies.

This chapter begins with an overview of the situation in 1945 and of the main problems government had to tackle, notably widespread unemployment and the North–South income gap. It then deals with the solutions, considering first macroeconomic policies regarding trade and planning and then microeconomic support to firms. The next two sections discuss how these policies affected industry—first presenting case-studies within the three main industries and then outlining the peculiar relationships between the state and the industrial companies. The seventh and final section draws some conclusions. As yet, they do not lend much support to a revisionist stance. However, it is necessary to stress that any conclusions regarding the issue are still provisional. In fact, they are based on incomplete evidence, as first-hand research is still scarce. Historians have only recently begun to study the period, and as yet have dealt mainly with the 1940s and early 1950s. Company archives are only now being (slowly) opened and much of the 'sensitive' information on relationships with the state and politicians are unlikely to have been kept there.

11.2. Italy 1945: What To Do?

In 1945 the Italian economy was in decidedly poor condition. Actually, the physical damage was not as serious as one would have expected after five years of war. According to the most recent estimates, capital stock and equipment were only 4.3 per cent and 8.2 per cent respectively less than their 1942 peak (Rossi, Sorgato, and Toniolo, 1993: table 5). However, markets were disorganized, communications were interrupted, and the supply of raw materials was very scarce, as those materials had to be imported and foreign currency was chronically lacking. As a result output was barely a fourth of its 1940 peak (Rossi, Sorgato, and Toniolo, 1993: table 1.B).

The recovery (*ricostruzione*) took four years: in 1949, the total manufacturing VA and capital stocks were back to their prewar maximum. This was remarkable—if not exceptional in Europe. Industrial policy contributed little to it and was not intended to do so. The government (a centre-right coalition organized around the Christian Democrats) adopted a hands-off policy (*linea Einaudi*), partially to mark the discontinuity with the interventionist behaviour of the Fascist regime. Firms were given free access to credit, until the money crunch of mid-1947, and as much freedom as was possible in the circumstances (e.g. for a while they were not allowed to fire workers or to use the proceeds of exports at will).

Historians have analysed the political economy of this strategy, in much greater detail than its economic consequences (Bottiglieri, 1984; Daneo, 1975; Harper, 1986; Salvati, 1982; Zamagni, 1986). Many seem to endorse the opinion of American experts, who, in a well-known document (the country study of the ECA in June 1949), harshly criticized the Italian government for its overcautious approach. It is impossible to assess whether a bolder policy was politically and administratively feasible, and *a fortiori* whether it could have sped up the return to normalcy and/or improved the welfare of the population. The counterfactual is too complex and vague to be tested.

By its nature the *ricostruzione* could not and did not solve the traditional problems of the Italian economy. In the short run the most serious one was unemployment, both open and disguised (many industrial workers were paid to do very little or nothing at all because firms could not fire them for social reasons). According to some estimates, there were more than 2 million jobless workers at the time (Mori, 1994). In the long run the increase in industrial employment had to be much larger, to absorb the millions of people still working in the fields. Most of them lived in the south, which was almost an industrial desert. Piedmont, Liguria, and Lombardy accounted for 54 per cent of the total workforce, the other regions of the centre and the north for another 40 per cent, and the south for only 7 per cent (Svimez, 1961: table 210). As a consequence, the per capita income in the south was a mere 40 per cent of that in the Northwest (Svimez, 1961: table 386). Industrialization of the southern regions could solve both problems—even if few people in the 1950s believed it possible.

Other issues, such as the level of competition, seemed much less important. The Americans had not imposed an antitrust policy as they had done in Japan or in Germany, partly for political reasons (Italy had been officially an ally since 1943) and partly because they did not find anything comparable—in economic and political terms—to the Japanese *zaibatsu* or to the German *Konzerns*. Actually, Italian industry was not highly concentrated (Giannetti, Federico, and Toninelli, 1994: table 1), in spite of the policy of the Fascist regime. There were some exceptions in heavy industries, but most of the companies belonged to the state via the IRI (Istituto per la

Ricostruzione industriale). The IRI controlled the production of all weapons, 90 per cent of shipbuilding, 80 per cent of the production of rolling stock, 40 per cent of the steel industry, etc. (Toniolo, 1980: 250).[1] In the 1950s some opposition parties waged a strong campaign against the 'monopolies', but they targeted two specific industries, fertilizer production and the generation and distribution of electric power. As we will see, both problems were 'solved', and the need for comprehensive antitrust legislation was to become a real issue of political contention only in the 1980s. As late as 1965, Law 170 granted tax deductions to mergers, provided they did not contradict the (non-existing) antitrust law.

The consensus on the priorities did not entail an agreement on how to tackle them—even within the government (Barca, 1997). The Liberal Party and right-wing factions of the Christian Democratic Party wanted to go on with the relatively liberal policy of the Recovery period; the left wing of the same Christian Democratic Party suggested more intervention. The opposition parties (the Socialists and Communists) favoured a more active role for the state, but they proposed a different set of priorities. As we will see later, the extension of the ruling coalition to the Socialist Party in 1962 (Centro-sinistra) was to cause a deep change in the aims and tools of the industrial policy.

11.3. The Macroeconomic Framework: Trade Liberalization, Planning, Industrial Relations

The main event of the 1950s was trade liberalization. It entailed a great break with a legacy of protectionism that dated back to the 1880s. Tariffs on manufactures had not on average been very high, but in the 1930s they had been supplemented by a wide array of restrictions ('autarchic policy'). Many of these restrictions lasted until the late 1940s, to distribute the available (scarce) foreign currency. The majority of industrialists criticized the system as illiberal, but regarded protection as indispensable in withstanding international competition. Their requests were embodied in the new tariff of 1950, which was accepted by other European countries in the international conferences of Annecy and Torquay. It was rather protective, getting an average duty on manufactured goods close to 20 per cent—with peaks of up to 41 per cent for cars (Pierucci and Ulizzi, 1973: table 2). Behind such a shield, Italy could afford to abolish the administrative restriction to trade as early as 1951, earlier than most European countries.

In the same year, Italy took a decisive step towards liberalization by joining the European Community for Steel and Coal (Ranieri, 1985). The decision to join coincided with the appointment of a staunch free-trader, Ugo La Malfa, as Minister of Trade, but it would be excessive to attribute him with all the merit. The United States, whose opinion had to be taken very seriously, strongly favoured this move, and Italy was economically and politically too weak to remain alone in Europe. In spite of the gloomy predictions of many industrialists and experts, the Italian steel industry was not swept away by foreign competition. Actually, the whole of Italian industry proved to be very competitive in the world market in the 1950s. Exports of manufactures grew at 10.4 per cent p.a. from 1950 to 1958, and Italy's share of total world exports rose from 3.65 per cent in 1950 to 4.1 per cent in 1959 (Maizels, 1963). In the years following, Italy was quite active in the foundation of the Common Market (Willis, 1971), with little or no opposition from the industrialists (De Cleva, 1992). The liberalization of imports was gradual, and duties were totally abolished in 1968. In the new environment, Italian industry thrived. Its share in the world market for manufactures reached a peak of 5.5 per cent in 1970 (Guerrieri and Milana, 1990: table 23). Indeed, some scholars have argued that the whole *miracolo economico* was an example of export-led growth. The issue is still controversial, but the wisdom of liberalization cannot be denied. It has been called 'the most important decision of industrial policy in the last forty years' (CER-IRS, 1986: 141).

The industrial boom of the 1950s greatly reduced unemployment; full employment was attained in 1962. However, it did not solve the North–South gap and heightened perception of other shortcomings in Italian economy and society. Planning appeared to be the right solution. After long discussions and an aborted attempt in 1955—the *Piano Vanoni*—(Barucci, 1978) the principle was officially accepted only by the new centre-left government in a famous *nota aggiuntiva* (added memorandum) to the 1962 budget. The first outline of a five-year plan (the 'Saraceno Report') was drafted in January 1964. The law was submitted to parliament in January 1965 and approved in July 1967 (D'Antonio, 1968).

Italy was surely not alone in Europe in adopting macroeconomic planning. It was only in Italy, however, that it acquired the role of panacea for all shortcomings and distortions. It should have guaranteed a high and stable growth of GDP, reduced the North–South gap and the dualism in the labour market (i.e. the gap between agricultural and industrial wages), eliminated market failures, improved the efficiency of the civil service, and even 'created the conditions so that the cultural values could develop for their own sake and not as a by-product of the economic activity' (Lombardini, 1967: 110). Thus the plan not only set out detailed targets for the macroeconomic variables, but also dealt with practically every aspect of economic and social life, with an endless list of reforms (a 'dream-book' according to its foes). It was never implemented (Barca, 1997; Podbielsky, 1974: table 17). Only one of the proposed reforms was actually approved, while 'it is not possible to find any relation or consistency between the guidelines of the plans published by the centre-left governments in the 1960s and the content of the laws on industrial policy which began to be approved in those years' (Momigliano and Pent Fornengo, 1986: 8).

To some extent, failure was inevitable for such an ambitious undertaking, but that it was a total fiasco needs some additional explanation. The believers in planning were a minority even in the government, while most were indifferent or opposed the reforms. As Ruffolo, secretary of planning, put it, the plan failed because of the 'pre-industrial residuals of backwardness and parasitism' (Ruffolo, 1973: p. xvii). In a recent article, Magnani (1994) put the blame mainly on the Communist Party, which induced trade unions not to follow the guidelines of the plan for wage increases.

As anticipated, there was an exception to the generalized failure of reforms. Law 300, 1970 (known as *Statuto dei Lavoratori*) created a new framework for industrial relations (Pontarollo, 1979). It protected individual workers against unjustified firing and other abuses (quite frequent in those years) and gave the trade unions a legal right to discuss with entrepreneurs any issue concerning the workers' well-being (safety standards, intensity of work, hierarchies, etc.), including wages. The entrepreneurs loudly complained that the *Statuto dei Lavoratori* thwarted their freedom and thereby reduced Italy's competitiveness. This complaint was not totally unfounded. In the 1970s trade unions often adopted a very aggressive attitude towards the firms and were uncritically supported by labour judges. Moreover, the *Statuto* applied only to medium and large companies, while the workers of small enterprises were not protected at all. This difference increased the competitiveness of small industries and the diffusion of a 'black' labour market. Thus, the Statuto caused a serious market failure, beyond the good intention of its authors.

11.4. The Microeconomic Policy: Subsidies and Bailouts

11.4.1. An Overview

The postwar period marked a discontinuity not only in macroeconomic policy but also in microeconomic (supply-side) policy. Since the 1880s, support had focused mainly on the military-industrial complex—iron and steel, heavy engineering, shipbuilding, etc.—which was deemed indispensable if Italy was to be a great power. These industries were the only ones to get high duties, public procurements accounted for a substantial amount of the total output (possibly a third in 1938), and, if necessary, firms were sure to be bailed out. Of course, these motivations were no longer acceptable after the war. But the strategy was not replaced by another one. Planning was now in vogue and the first specific industrial plans (*piani di settore*) were drafted in the early 1970s.

There was no coherent policy to favour 'national champions' even where it was possible, as in the case of the pharmaceutical industry, where the state was almost a monopsonist. Discrimination by industry was replaced by discrimination based on size and geographical location, entailing major changes in the tools of industrial policy. Trade was liberalized, as noted earlier. Public procurements lost importance, accounting for 1.5–2 per cent of the total output of manufactures (Loraschi, 1979). Bailouts were extended to all companies of a certain size in order to prevent those firms from going bankrupt and consequently dismissing their workers. Bankruptcy applied only to craftsmen and to small industrial firms. But the main innovation was the use of state money to subsidize companies.

11.4.2. The Bailouts

The practice of bailing out companies in trouble was resumed in the late 1940s. Some engineering firms benefited from this policy because they were unable to withstand the reconversion from wartime weapons production to a peacetime economy (Bottiglieri, 1984; Doria, 1987). The government set up a FIM (*Fondo per le industrie meccaniche*), which first financed companies and then became their owner. In 1962, the government decided to transform it into a permanent holding, called EFIM. The boom of the 1950s and early 1960s made bailouts largely unnecessary, but, when the need arose, the government did not hesitate. For instance, ENI (the state holding for energy) bailed out Pignone, a Florentine engineering firm, at the request of the city's mayor, who happened to belong to the same faction of the Christian Democratic Party as the president of ENI.

Bailouts resumed in the late 1960s, when economic growth slowed and the situation of many large companies was made worse by wage increases and the growing power of trade unions. Large conglomerates, such as FIAT and Montedison, seized the opportunity to get rid of their loss-making subsidiaries. The mining activities of the latter were transferred to a new holding, EGAM (*Ente Gestione Aziende Minerarie*), established in 1971. In the same year, the needs of small and medium enterprises were addressed by setting up a fifth holding, GEPI. In theory, this was set up to adopt the innovative formula of a joint venture between the state (which provided the funds) and a private partner (to manage the firm and become its owner after some time). However, the system worked only in a few cases—and most companies became permanent state property.

The massive waves of bailouts swelled the size of state-owned industry and very few firms were privatized until the 1990s. The state-owned industries employed (in manufacturing only) 185,000 workers in 1953, 236,600 in 1968; and 451,500 in 1974 (Grassini, 1979: table 1). This boom was not guided by any industrial strategy—simply by chance (the quality of management, etc.) and by the vagaries of the economic cycle. The state ended up owning firms which produced everything—from cakes to warships. For example, EFIM diversified from engineering into aluminium, rubber, paper, food processing, and cattle raising [sic] (Alzona, 1975). And there were few or no attempts at all to rationalize companies after their acquisition, as such measures would have required a reduction in the workforce. It is not surprising, then, that all holdings of PPSS lost vast sums in the 1970s and 1980s. It is difficult to justify this policy. With some goodwill, it is possible to regard the prewar policy of targeted bailing-out as an effort to save precious technical capabilities (Zamagni, 1994), but the generalized postwar bailout was a massive waste of resources, inspired by purely political interests.

11.4.3. The Subsidies

The heading of subsidy covers a broad array of measures, divided here into two categories—financing for investment, with contributions (*contributi a fondo perduto*) or soft loans (*credito agevolato*) and other subsidies.

Financing for investment began in the 1940s, to help with the reconstruction of plants. The Italian state contributed about 140 billion lire, mainly distributed by the previously quoted FIM, while the United States supplied 230 billion dollars from the European Recovery Program and the Eximbank (Bottiglieri, 1984; Daneo, 1975). Most of the funds were given to the engineering industry. These sums were substantial, as in those years the GDP in engineering barely exceeded 500 billion lire (ISTAT, 1956: table 13). But the American money was particularly important. First it accrued mainly to large companies (98 per cent of the ERP funds and 80 per cent of the Eximbank ones); second, it made it possible to import American machinery, which greatly helped overcome the traditional backwardness of Italian industry worsened by the isolation of the 1930s and the war.

After the Reconstruction, the flow of money dried up to a trickle. However, there was an important institutional innovation: the setting-up of a network of banks (*istituti di credito speciale*) that specialized in long-term credit which joined the IMI (established in 1931)—the *sezioni di credito speciale* of the Banca Nazionale del Lavoro, Banco di Napoli and Banco di Sicilia, the Mediocredito Centrale (with a branch in every region), the ISVEIMER, IRFIS, etc. These were necessary because high-street banks were officially forbidden to finance long-term investments since the enactment of the banking law of 1936—approved in the aftermath of the Great Crisis of the 1930s. The *sezioni di credito speciale* handles nearly all financing for investment until the present day.

The sums became substantial again only in the late 1950s, with the passing of Laws 634 (1957) for the industrialization of the south and 623 (1959) for the support of small and medium enterprises. The late 1960s and 1970s marked the heyday of *credito agevolato*. A list of all laws with their extensions, refinancing, etc., would be unnecessarily tedious (Marzano, 1979; Serrani, 1971; Pontarollo, 1980), but it is important to stress two points. First, financial investment conditions were very favourable. For instance Law 717 (1965) for investments in the south granted a contribution equivalent to 20 per cent of the capital free, and credit on the remaining 70 per cent at the rate of 4 per cent. With a small budget adjustment, a firm could build a factory without putting up a single lira. Second, there was a far-reaching change in the underlying strategy for industrialization in the south. Law 634 favoured local small enterprises—by setting an upper limit to the size of claimants. This clause was abolished in the early 1960s to make a southern location appealing to investments from large northern companies. Laws still favoured small companies, but large companies soon discovered how to claim these advantages, by simply dividing new plants into companies of the required size.

Other types of subsidies were comparatively negligible until the late 1960s. The change was heralded by the passing of Laws 1089 and 1115 in 1968 (Pontarollo, 1979). The former offered southern firms a partial exemption from welfare payments (*fiscalizzazione degli oneri sociali*) to newly hired workers.[2] The latter increased the amount and the scope of the existing subsidies for the temporary laying-off of redundant workers (or *cassa integrazione guadagni*). Neither provision seemed revolutionary at first, but became so in the next decade because their scope was progressively extended. In 1972 Law 464 extended the right to the *cassa integrazione* to all company crises (including those caused by internal mismanagement) and abolished the limit of duration (nine months) subject to an official authorization. In the 1970s, the *fiscalizzazione* was granted to more and more workers, and eventually to all industrial employees in 1977, and the share of exempted payments was raised.

11.4.4. The Role of Subsidies in Industrial Development

Any assessment of the role of subsidies in Italian industrial development has to begin with a quantitative analysis. The available data (in constant 1970 billion lire) are collected in Tables 11.1 and 11.2. Table 11.1 refers to the amount of resources made available for investment—either as soft loans or contributions. They were very substantial, accounting for about a quarter of total investment in manufacturing (with peaks of up to a third in some years), and for more than two-thirds of long-term credit for investment. This latter figure is surely overestimated, as an (unknown) amount of investments was financed with short-term loans.[3] In other words, state money contributed massively to the surge of investment which marked the second half of the 1960s until the oil crisis.

Table 11.2 reports the basic data on transfers to companies by category—subsidies to investment, credit to exports, exemption to welfare payments, and subsidies to temporary lay-offs.[4] The total grew sixfold from 1964 to 1975, or from 1.2 per cent to 4.6 per cent of national income.

Table 11.1   *Total Resources for Investment 1964–1979*
(billions of 1970 lire)

	(1)	(2)	(3)	(4)	(5)	(6)	(7)
1964	593.0	31.7	1941.7	477.7	63.3	18.4.	19.0
1965	589.6	22.7	2248.5	417.6	66.3	21.8	21.2
1966	627.9	32.0	2521.4	444.9	67.1	23.1	20.4
1967	1039.4	33.9	3163.6	801.7	69.1	56.3	32.4
1968	1130.9	35.7	3743.9	801.9	71.4	50.0	28.2
1969	1093.2	38.9	4144.8	758.3	72.5	66.2	24.2
1970	1141.6	31.8	4409.5	830.5	74.5	79.4	23.1
1971	1726.6	24.1	5379.8	1371.5	74.9	28.7	34.1
1972	1743.6	27.7	6258.4	1404.4	76.0	62.6	35.8
1973	1300.5	35.0	6024.0	1011.5	68.1	66.1	23.4
1974	925.8	26.5	4193.8	748.1	63.1	47.4	17.6
1975	1040.2	28.2	4704.3	862.4	61.4	91.6	24.3
1976	1056.3	36.8	4493.0	864.8	63.1	81.8	24.8
1977	1004.9	31.2	4329.0	690.5	60.8	72.4	20.13
1978	778.5	10.9	4197.9	439.6	57.2	75.5	13.8
1979	713.1	4.1	3813.4	451.3	54.9	94.3	13.4

Notes: (1) Total soft loans (*credito agevolato*) by year; (2) percentage of (1) to the small and medium-sized industries; (3) total outstanding soft loans; (4) total soft loans for investment (col. (1) less credit to exports and to commerce); (5) outstanding soft loans as a percentage of total credit to manufacturing; (6) subsidies to *investment* (*contributi in conto capitale*) in the south; (7) soft loans and subsidies (cols. (4) and (6) as a percentage of total investments in manufacturing.

Source: Silvestri (1983: tables 3.1, 3.2, 3.10); investment in manufacturing ISTAT (1985: table 8.29); implicit price index for investment goods from ISTAT (1985: tables 8.29 and 8.30).

Table 11. 2   *Total Transfers to Manufacturing*

	(1)	(2)	(3)	(4)	(5)	(6)
1964	128.3	7.8	—	—	136.1	1.24
1965	141.9	9.5	—	—	151.4	1.34
1966	133.1	10.1	—	—	143.2	1.17
1967	259.0	14.0	—	—	272.9	2.03
1968	254.0	23.4	4.1	4.8	286.3	1.97
1969	283.7	24.1	72.4	1.4	381.6	2.49
1970	353.5	21.5	113.1	1.8	489.9	2.95
1971	377.2	33.2	148.2	32.1	590.7	3.58
1972	456.8	24.9	185.8	39.6	707.1	4.07
1973	306.2	12.4	196.8	9.6	525.0	2.77
1974	220.8	7.2	250.0	22.9	500.9	2.71
1975	387.2	15.7	333.2	77.6	813.7	4.61
1976	388.1	28.3	300.1	60.3	776.8	4.06
1977	371.1	59.0	356.8	27.3	814.2	4.20
1978	301.1	59.2	386.1	77.9	824.3	4.03
1979	327.6	43.1	428.5	32.7	831.9	3.77

Notes: (1) Resources for investments (direct subsidies and subsidization on soft loans); (2) credit to exports; (3) exemptions on welfare payments (*fiscalizzazione degli oneri sociali*); (4) net subsidies to temporary lay-offs (*cassa integrazione guadagni*); (5) total transfers; (6) percentage on manufacturing value added.

Sources: (1) and (2) 1964–9 estimates of the author from Table 11.1; (3) and (4) 1968–9 Brosio (1983); other, Brosio and Silvestri (1983: table 2.1); implicit price index for investment goods ISTAT (1985: tables 8.29 and 8.30), value added ISTAT (1985: tables 8.18 and 8.19) (adjusting for the change in definition according to the new series).

It was to reach an all-time peak of 8.9 per cent in 1984 (Ranci, 1987). This growth is impressive, but even more impressive is the change within the aggregate. Subsidies for investment increased greatly in the 1960s but remained constant in the 1970s, with wide fluctuations from one year to another. Other types of subsidies soared from a few billion lire in the early 1960s to more than 500 in the late 1970s, jumping from 5 per cent to over 60 per cent of the total (and to 90 per cent in the 1980s). This entailed a switch from support for investment to more short-term goals, such as preventing social unrest or easing a firm's financial situation.

11.4.5. Was This Money Well Spent?

An exhaustive reply is impossible, as it implies an unworkable counterfactual hypothesis. It is nevertheless likely that the effect differed with each recipient and type of subsidy.

Probably the most successful subsidy was as support for small- and medium-sized enterprises. It is well known that they are the most dynamic component of Italy's industry, even if Vera Zamagni (1994) regards this as a serious shortcoming of Italian industrialization. How much did state support contribute to their success? Opinion on this point diverges. Prodi and De Giovanni are rather sanguine, attributing to it 'the initial development of thousands of enterprises' (Prodi and De Giovanni, 1993: 37; Scognamiglio, 1979). Others pinpoint the unnecessary amount of red tape involved and the lack of a proper technical assessment of the applications with instead a purely bureaucratic check of adherence to the procedures (Bianchi, 1993). The small- and medium-sized enterprises only got about one-third of the *credito agevolato* (table 1, col. 2). There are no data on the allocation of the other categories of subsidies by the size of the claimants. It is likely that small companies got less than their 'fair' share, according to their share of the value added. In fact they were located almost exclusively in the north, while most subsidies (contributions for investment, the *fiscalizzazione*) were reserved for southern firms.

The usefulness of support for investment in the south is uncertain. It would be unfair to say that it has had no effect whatsoever (Sicca, 1979). From 1951 to 1981, the per capita GDP in the south rose at 2.5 per cent yearly—that is nearly as much as the national one. The number of industrial workers increased by 2.5 times, or from 13 per cent to 20.5 per cent of the Italian total. Most of these additional jobs were created in factories financed by the state. In 1973 state-owned companies and the two largest private firms, FIAT and Montedison, accounted for about two-thirds of the southern industrial output and employed more than 70 per cent of the workers (Dal Monte and Giannola, 1979: table 8.11). They were almost exclusively capital-intensive activities, which were clearly unsuited to the southern factor endowment. Besides that, they did not stimulate the development of local companies—so plants were commonly nicknamed 'cathedrals in the desert'. In fact, these activities were severely hit during the crisis of heavy industry in the 1980s. The policy for the south was therefore effective at least in the short run, but could hardly be considered an efficient use of taxpayers' money. It is not, however, easy to suggest an alternative and to prove that it would have been more successful.

The 'other' subsidies seem decidedly unhelpful—with the possible exception of credit to export. In fact neither the *fiscalizzazione* nor the CIG were the result of a coherent industrial strategy. Both were conceived as short-term relief for certain types of activities and then transformed into a permanent and universal subsidy. They were also likely to cause additional market failures as they were reserved for certain classes of industries.

On the whole, therefore, microeconomic policy was not a great success (to put it mildly). In the 1970s it caused a serious misallocation of resources and kept a lot of inefficient enterprises alive. In the 1960s it may not have been so damaging, as the sums were rather small, but the measures of the late 1960s created the framework for the subsequent rush to subsidization.

11.5. The Unintentional Supply-Side Policy: Steel and Chemicals and Energy

The lack of an explicit policy to foster some industries did not imply that state intervention was equitable among industries. Quite the contrary. It did favour heavy industries in the allocation of resources. They were the traditional core business of state-owned manufacturing companies and received the lion's share of financing for investment. As Table 11.3 shows, metalworking, chemicals, and engineering got on average between one-half and three-quarters of total resources. The real beneficiary, though, was the chemical industry, whose transfer/value added ratio constantly exceeded the aggregate one. The ratio for metalworking was also usually

Table 11.3 *Distribution by Industry of Resources for Investment*

	% of industries on total resources			% of resources on value added			
	Steel	Chemical	Engineering	Steel	Chemical	Engineering	Total
1964	18.4	18.6	15.8	3.9	1.9	0.6	1.2
1965	7.3	25.7	19.8	1.6	2.6	0.8	1.3
1966	9.5	15.4	21.3	1.7	1.2	0.8	1.1
1967	7.2	29.5	14.6	2.1	4.0	0.8	1.9
1968	6.1	24.4	23.4	1.8	3.2	1.2	1.7
1969	6.9	27.0	24.2	1.9	3.4	1.3	1.8
1970	17.5	26.5	24.3	4.0	4.2	1.3	2.1
1971	18.4	26.6	28.7	6.4	5.6	2.0	2.3
1972	35.0	20.2	20.8	13.1	4.7	1.5	2.7
1973	5.6	26.9	23.4	1.0	3.3	1.0	1.7
1974	14.3	23.6	21.0	1.7	2.1	0.6	1.2
1975	18.5	20.9	25.2	4.8	3.8	1.3	2.3
1976	9.2	22.9	30.0	2.3	3.9	1.5	2.1
1977	7.2	20.0	38.0	1.9	3.8	1.8	2.0
1978	15.5	6.2	44.6	3.0	0.9	1.6	1.6
1979	9.3	5.3	43.2	1.6	0.7	1.5	1.6

Source: Silvestri (1983: tables 3.11 and 3.14*a*) (adjusted to the new series of value added).

quite high, while engineering always got less than if total transfers had been distributed according to size.

It could be argued that some additional support for the development of heavy industries, and especially to steel and chemicals, was justified. Those industries are considered indispensable for any large industrial country yet their history did not support an optimistic assessment of their prospects in, say, 1950. Heavy industries had always been quite backward in Italy. The steel industry was substantial but it had a long and inglorious history of protection and bailouts, and an entrenched reputation for being inefficient. The chemical industry had developed somewhat in the 1920s–30s, but the bulk of its output still consisted of traditional goods, above all fertilizers (Zamagni, 1990). Thirty years later, apparently, the situation had changed. Both industries had been growing quite fast— more than the growth rate of industrial total output (9.7 per cent p.a. chemical, 8.4 per cent metalworking) and Italy could boast a production of steel and chemical products as large as other advanced European countries. Would the same results have been achieved without state support? Let us briefly consider the effects of industrial policy on both these industries and also on the energy supply—another strategic field where the state intervened on a massive scale.

11.5.1. *The Supply of Energy*

Lack of energy has always haunted Italian industrialization. Italy has abundant water power (in the north) but neither coal nor oil, and thus has had to import a large share of its energy needs. This task has been performed by private traders or foreign large oil companies. In 1926, in its avowed quest for national autonomy, the Fascist regime established a company (AGIP) to search for and sell oil in Italy and in its colonies, but with little success (large oil fields in Libya were discovered just before the beginning of the war). Therefore, in 1945 the government decided to close it. It escaped its fate only because the appointed liquidator, Mattei, realized the importance of natural gas deposits, discovered during the war in the Po valley. In the confusion of the postwar years, Mattei succeeded in delaying the liquidation of AGIP until the deposits began to produce. Mattei was then able to boast the value of a 'national' source of energy.[5] Gas was cheaper than imported coal or oil, and in a few years AGIP had built a network of pipelines to distribute it. The undertaking was highly profitable, and AGIP used its resources to diversify into the chemical industry. In 1952, AGIP was subsumed in a new public holding, ENI (Ente Nazionale Idrocarburi), with the task of providing low-cost energy. And

ENI fulfilled its task in a very aggressive way, searching for new deposits of oil all over the world, in tough competition with the Seven Sisters (Barca and Trento, 1997).

No one would doubt, therefore, that AGIP/ENI had been a success story—at least as a national supplier of energy. However, its success owed a lot to its monopolistic position. In the 1950s many foreign companies asked for the right to search for gas in the Po valley, but their requests were turned down by the government after intense lobbying by AGIP. The question was hotly debated at that time for its political implications. However, the ownership of the extraction rights would really have mattered for Italian development only if AGIP and foreign companies had behaved differently—that is, if the former had charged lower prices or built a more extensive distribution network than the latter (as it boasted it was doing when trying to convince the government of its merits). In other words, AGIP would have had to renounce the exploitation of its monopoly power. No one can say for sure, but this does seem somewhat implausible.

Unlike gas, the production and distribution of electrical power had a long tradition, beginning in the 1890s. In the 1950s the industry was a thriving and profitable business. It was much criticized, however (AAVV, 1994; Barca, 1997). The electric companies were accused of being technically backward, of charging urban consumers too much, and of under-supplying rural and backward areas, thus hindering their development. It was alleged that only nationalization could solve these structural short-comings (Rossi, 1962; Scalfari, 1963). These arguments were not new, as nationalization had been proposed for the first time in the 1910s. They suddenly became convincing when the Socialist Party made nationalization a *conditio sine qua non* to enter the new centre-left coalition. Consequently, in 1962 the government nationalized the commercial production of electrical power, creating a new agency, the Ente Nazionale Energia Elettrica (ENEL). These measures covered private companies (which produced about 45 per cent of total energy) and state-owned ones (which produced another 30 per cent), but not the electrical plants of industrial firms (about 10 per cent) and those owned by local authorities (the remaining 15 per cent). Officially, the nationalization had three aims. First and foremost it had to benefit consumers by providing power to all Italian households at the same (and possibly reduced) price. It was designed to make planning easier, giving government control of a strategic resource. Finally, it was intended to force the nationalized companies to diversify into new activities, using the (huge) compensation payments they received. But nationalization was also inspired by less noble political considerations. In fact, the electric companies had been the main financial backers of the right wing of the Christian Democratic Party, the political adversaries of the PSI within the coalition.

Most of the aims of nationalization were fulfilled. ENEL expanded the network to all rural areas, connected the different regional networks into a unified national one, and therefore rationalized the production and distribution of energy, exploiting economies of scale. ENEL also lowered prices—a little too much. The nominal rates for domestic households increased by 15 per cent from 1962 to 1972 (i.e. fell by 15 per cent in real terms) and then remained stable or decreased until 1980—falling in real terms by 85 per cent (ISTAT, 1985: table 16.8). This decrease far outpaced the increase of productivity, and the ensuing losses were shouldered by the state, causing a massive hidden subsidization of electrical power consumption.

11.5.2. The Steel Industry

The steel industry is the best-known success story of state-owned enterprises. Yet in 1945 its prospects were not appealing. Factories which before the war had produced about half of the Italian output of steel, were seriously damaged. Many questioned the wisdom of rebuilding them, suggesting the demand for steel could be met by private producers or by imports. But the president of Finsider (the steel subholding of IRI), Sinigaglia, instead put forward a plan to increase their productive capacity (Balconi, 1991; Barca and Trento, 1997; Posner and Woolf, 1967; Ranieri, 1993). It returned to a plan (the *piano autarchico per l'acciaio*) which had been conceived by the same Sinigaglia and partially implemented before the war. The *pièce de resistance* was the reconstruction of the Cornigliano factory (near Genoa) with American technology. The new mill specialized in the production of coils and plates for car-making and engineering, leaving 'private' companies the market for bars and rods for building. Sinigaglia argued that the scale economies were large enough to overcome the extra cost of imported coal and iron ore, making protection unnecessary. He even quoted explicitly the possibility of exporting, something which had previously been unthinkable.

Private producers were very sceptical. They did not believe in the growth of demand and therefore regarded a modest increase in the productive capacity of their plants more than sufficient for the foreseeable future. None the less, Sinigaglia succeeded in having his plan approved (January 1948) and funded by the ERP plan, in spite of American mistrust of state-owned enterprise. He proved to be right. The demand for steel increased beyond expectation, the production of cars growing from 43,000 units in 1948 to 878,000 in 1962. Growth in demand actually exceeded Sinigaglia's expectations and in the 1950s the Italian productive capacity was fully exploited. In spite of the prudent advice of a commission of experts, Finsider (Sinigaglia had died in 1953) decided to bet on the future. In 1960, it decided to build a fourth large, integrated plant in the southern town of Taranto (Apulia), with a production capacity of 3.5 million tons per year, using compensation payments from the nationalization of electric companies. Again, the gamble succeeded, when in the 1960s the demand grew beyond the most optimistic forecasts. The Italian output of steel soared from about 2 million tons per year (the prewar level, reached again in 1948) to 17.2 in 1970, and Finsider's share from 44 per cent in 1952 to 59 per cent in 1965 (Balconi, 1991).

For the first time Italy had a large, modern, and competitive steel industry (it was even a net exporter for some time in the 1950s). This was largely due to the aggressive strategy pursued by Finsider, which acquired an undisputed price leadership and forced private firms to modernize. In other words, Sinigaglia's strategy was a resounding success.

At this point, in the late 1960s, Finsider, emboldened by its previous successes and trusting projections suggesting further growth in consumption, decided to increase its production capacity. This time, the alternative was between expanding the Piombino plant (near Leghorn) or Taranto. The president of Finsider chose the latter, following the government's suggestions but against the advice of most top managers (Osti, 1993). This choice proved to be a serious mistake. The hoped-for scale economies never materialized, as the Taranto plant was too large (a production capacity of 10 million tons per year) to be manageable. Balconi blames Finsider for worshipping gigantism because it misunderstood the peculiar social situation that made the Japanese strategy viable. Moreover, in the 1970s demand grew much less than expected. The market difficulties highlighted some structural shortcomings of Finsider, such as defective marketing, imperfect division of labour among the plants (e.g. in the production of pipes), neglect of some potentially promising market niches, and excessive resort to bank credit for financing, which had been concealed by the demand boom. In the late 1970s and in the 1980s Finsider lost a huge amount of money, while the smaller and more flexible private companies (mini-mills) made profits and increased their market shares. One of them bought back big state companies when they were eventually privatized in the early 1990s.

11.5.3. *The Chemical Industry*

The Italian chemical industry in the early 1950s was not only backward, it was also highly concentrated. By far the largest company was the Montecatini, which supplied about three-quarters of Italian fertilizers. It charged high prices, and therefore the market was ripe for new entries.

Both Edison, the largest electrical company, and ANIC, AGIP's chemical firm, built new plants. These companies were searching for alternatives to their core businesses, which were threatened by the campaign for nationalization. This move triggered a price war, which substantially lowered the price of fertilizers. However in 1959 the government brokered an agreement between the two competitors—further evidence of its lukewarm (to say the least) commitment to an antitrust policy.

In the meantime, all over the world the chemical industry was changing from coal-based to oil-based products. This change was perceived in Italy as a great opportunity to overcome traditional backwardness with a fresh start. The petrochemical industry was regarded as the new frontier of Italian industrialization—as steel production had been ten years before. Unlike in the steel industry, however, there were at least three main players: Montecatini, ANIC, and another aggressive private firm (SIR). In 1966 Montecatini, in parlous financial condition, merged with Edison into a new company (Montedison). These three companies formulated the same strategy: to create an integrated production cycle from oil to plastics and fibres. This strategy needed considerable investment, as the production of ethylene (the first intermediate product) was subject to very large-scale economies. The money was provided by the state, as detailed in the previous section. Unfortunately, the Italian market was not large enough to absorb the whole production of three optimally sized factories. Time and again, experts and the government suggested that the companies specialize in different final products. All these suggestions were dropped because of the fierce competition between the three firms (it was known as the 'chemical war'). Each company went on with its plans. The result was an inordinate rush to build new factories. According to one estimate, the cumulated total of approved investments from 1966–76 was close to 10,000 billion lire; at the end of the period the Italian productive capacity for ethylene was about 85 per cent of France's and 115 per cent of Britain's (Filippi, 1979; Marchi and Marchionatti, 1992). In 1971 the government had tried to regulate growth by drafting a chemical plan. It was decidedly too sanguine, however, as it forecast a 10 per cent increase in output on the basis of a 7.5–8.5 per cent growth in GDP. Yet the actual increase of productive capacity was even greater, as each producer wanted to supply the whole increase. Some cases are almost unbelievable. For instance, SIR and Montedison built two *identical* plants for the production of synthetic fibres in the *same* Sardinian village; another company, Liquichimica, built a whole factory for the production of proteins from oil before having the necessary health authorization (which was never granted).

The results were not brilliant. Output did increase but the Italian industry was not really competitive, and, despite all the plans, Italy still ran a trade deficit. An expansion financed almost exclusively with borrowed money was a recipe for disaster. And disaster came as a consequence of the Oil Shock and the general economic crisis of the 1970s. As usual, the state had to come to the rescue of private companies, bailing out SIR and Liquichimica and taking over most of the Montedison plants. Not unreasonably, the state's support of the chemical industry has been called the 'biggest mistake of Italian industrial policy' (Grassini, 1979: 17).

11.6. The Microeconomics of Italian Industrial Policy: The Italian Government and the Firms

Traditionally, the Italian state supported industries without interfering with managerial decisions—a 'liberal protectionism' according to Amato (1972). This line of conduct was also followed during the 1930s when investments were officially tightly controlled and subject to authorization. In fact, the overseeing agencies were dominated by large companies which could have their decisions approved easily. Administrative controls were totally dismantled after the war, and, for companies, the 1950s were years of almost complete freedom. The largest ones (notably FIAT) wielded considerable power, because of the social and economic consequences of their business decisions. They buttressed their influence by financing the ruling parties through associations such as the Confindustria or the ANIDEL of electrical industries.

In theory, the situation of state-owned companies was different, as they were subject to the will of IRI and, hence, of the government. In practice managers enjoyed great freedom and behaved like private entrepreneurs. In a (slightly idealized) version, 'the first and foremost task of the *enti pubblici* (IRI and ENI) was to give some entrepreneurs, thanks to state ownership, a control on some industries and services, which those people would not have been able to control with their own financial means' (Barca and Trento, 1997: 195–6); more bluntly Ranieri (1993) calls the system a 'privatization of the state intervention'. Were official authorization or allocation of public resources necessary, people like Mattei or Sinigaglia could get them, thanks to their personal links with political parties or politicians. Mattei was particularly able in this game, where he used all the means at his disposal (including bribery). ENI was his own feud, and the law to establish it was approved with the acquiescence of the neo-fascist party and substantial help from the Communist and Socialist Parties, but against many in the Christian Democratic Party, to which Mattei belonged. A biographer of his—quite an apologetic one—writes that 'Mattei's energy and his skill to push forward the political discussion on real issues are at the origin of what was to be called 'the system of state-owned enterprises' (Colitti, 1979: 162).

The balance of power between firms and the state began to shift in the early 1960s. The change was preceded and made possible by two institutional innovations, the outcome of which bore little resemblance to the ideas of the law-makers.

The first innovation was to give the Ministero delle Partecipazioni Statali power to supervise both IRI and ENI in 1956 (Barca and Trento, 1997). The law was somewhat vague regarding its powers but it did present an important novelty. It quoted 'social purposes', including the already quoted increase of investments in the south, along with 'profitability' as the aims of state-owned enterprises, without making the meaning of these words explicit. This uncertainty enabled the Minister to justify almost any intervention.

The second innovation was planning. The first law did not enter into details, but subsequent laws increased the power of the state. For instance, from 1971 all investments exceeding a given size were subject to official permission. That permission had to be given by a ministerial committee, the 'Comitato per la Programmazione Economica' (or CIPE), with the technical support of the ISPE ('Segretariato alla programmazione'). The system never worked as designed. Agencies were understaffed and powerless, and CIPE was pletoric and ineffective, as none of its members was ready to renounce part of their authority (Ruffolo, 1973). But the system gave each member ample personal power; he could use his position to speed up or slow down an authorization for a new plant, an application for a contribution for investment, or for a subsidy by the Cassa Integrazione Guadagni, etc. In almost all cases, the politicians used this power to enhance their personal influence. Of course, they found it much easier to exert their power on state-owned enterprises than on private companies. It is thus necessary to deal with these two cases separately.

Unfortunately, discussion of business–government relations cannot be exhaustive in either case. The issue has not yet been researched, as the archives are still closed to historians. What follows is therefore a first outline, which will hopefully be superseded by further research (Balconi, Orsenigo, and Toninelli, 1995). It is unlikely that a full account will ever be possible. Some of these transactions were not entirely lawful, and therefore records are not likely to be kept in the archives.

The government intervened for the first time in an operative decision of a state-owned enterprise in the late 1950s, when it strongly favoured the choice of Taranto as a location for Finsider's next big steel plant (Balconi, 1991). From an economic point of view it was a mistake, as this location imposed additional costs in transporting products to northern consumers. But it was a noble mistake. It was hoped that the plant could boost the economy of a poor area and create large spillovers of opportunity for the entire south (which never materialized). In fact, the choice was supported by all the southern members of parliament, by trade unions, and by left-wing opposition parties.

Real trouble began in the 1960s, when politicians realized how useful state-owned enterprises could be for gaining votes. Ministers, influential leaders, and members of parliament (or local authorities) began to meddle in day-to-day management. They asked the managers to locate factories in their constituencies, to avoid dismissal of workers, to bail out private firms in trouble, or to hire the politicians' protégés.

In 1975 the government literally promised to build a fifth steel plant in Calabria just to placate those involved in a popular uprising (the decision was scrapped in 1978). Managers were appointed according to their political affiliation and not their skills. In the 1970s and 1980s it was an undisputed matter of fact that IRI 'belonged' to the Christian Democrats (i.e. that the party had the 'right' to designate top managers of the holding company and of most of its subsidiaries); the ENI to PSI; the EFIM to PSDI. The very decision to set up this latter holding (instead of transferring the companies to IRI) was inspired largely by the desire to create more positions. These managers strictly followed the suggestions of their party or, quite often, of their faction within the party. They allegedly used the companies' funds to finance their political patrons—but this claim has yet to be proven.

One might discuss at length whether this degeneration was inherent to state ownership or a consequence of the peculiar Italian political situation, evidenced by the stability of the ruling coalition. It is more fruitful to stress that the autonomy of management also depended on its financial independence. Mattei's ENI could finance its investments with the very substantial rent from the sale of natural gas. IRI was not so lucky, as profits were not large enough to finance all its investments. During the 1960s it resorted to compensation for the nationalization of its electrical companies and issued bonds, which investors welcomed because of the state guarantee. The economic crisis of the early 1970s drastically reduced the amount of these 'autonomous' resources. For the whole state-owned enterprise, they fell from 55 per cent of the total resources in 1966–9 to 31 per cent in 1970–3 (Ravazzi, 1983). Therefore the holdings had to rely increasingly on the *fondi di dotazione* (i.e. direct transfers from the state) and on the *credito agevolato*—both dependent on the government's goodwill. This started a vicious circle. The increase of the share of these 'politically controlled' resources increased politicians' clout; the uneconomical decisions they imposed augmented losses and, hence, the need for 'political' funds. This vicious circle caused the Participazioni Statali (state-owned enterprises) to lose money from 1970 on and was only partially broken in the late 1980s.

The situation for private companies was obviously different. Small and medium-sized companies had relatively little contact with politicians. Their credit applications were assessed by the *istituti di credito speciale*. The management of these banks was appointed by the government and because of this, a political acquaintance might help to get a larger sum, to get it in a short time, or to avoid a too-detailed examination of a shaky application. But political patronage was not really vital. Personal networks were as important as the political ones, and a good firm with a sound plan could get the money anyway. The 'political' use of funds became more widespread in the 1980s, especially in the south. In principle, bailing out was a different matter, as it implied a discretionary act by the (politically controlled) EFIM or GEPI. However, there was widespread support for these operations from local authorities, trade unions, and the public at large—including the opposition parties. The acquisition was almost automatic.

From the point of view of politicians seeking to widen their power, large enterprises were much more appealing than small- and medium-sized ones. They needed more and could give more. Each big chemical plant required contributions of hundreds of billion lire to investments and soft loans; the acquisition of one of their subsidiaries could cost the Partecipazioni Statali billions of lire and burden the budget with losses for many years to come. These operations were appealing from the politicians' point of view; by engineering it they enhanced their reputation as a provider of jobs. At least some companies financed political parties directly (instead of contributing to institutional financing through associations as they did in the 1950s). Unfortunately, it is practically impossible to measure these contributions, as they flowed in many ways, some of which were illegal. Two points, however, seem well established. First, most of the funds accrued to the ruling parties (Christian Democrat and Socialist); second, chemical companies were particularly liberal (Scalfari and Turani, 1975). Each of them forged strict links with one political patron—ENI with the Socialist Party, and the two private companies with two different factions within the Christian Democrat Party. The chemical war, therefore, was a political war as well, and this may explain why the government was unable to stop it or to rationalize the use of its own funds.

It is likely that the exchange was as convenient for the companies as it was for the politicians. Unfortunately it is extremely difficult to assess to what extent. In principle, it is possible to estimate the amount of 'politically controlled resources' each company received by summing up contributions and soft loans for investment, 'other' subsidies, and the savings on the subsidiaries they transferred to the Partecipazioni Statali. Of course, such an estimate would require much work with budgets and a dose of creativity, especially for the last item on the list. But it is not possible to assess to what extent the support of the politicians was necessary to obtain these benefits. It is, however, very unlikely that the exchange was fruitful for Italian development. It implied a massive distortion in the allocation of resources and a large, directly unproductive rent-seeking.

11.7. Conclusion

A definitive reply to the initial question of how much state intervention contributed to development is almost impossible. The information about some issues is scarce, and the implicit counterfactual questions ('What would have happened had a real planning been implemented?') are too complex. It is nevertheless possible to put forward a tentative answer: very little or perhaps not at all, with the exception of trade liberalization. This statement might seem somewhat unfair in regard to the policies of the late 1940s–early 1950s, especially with regard to the role of state-owned enterprises. It could be argued that private capital—Italian or foreign— would have been found anyway, as state-owned enterprises were profitable. The main point is that their achievements came about because of the initiative of a few enterprising managers, with little or no input from the government. Amato (1972: 72) bluntly states that 'the PPSS acted without any hint of a recognizable economic policy'. And it would be hard to defend the policies of the 1960s–1970s. The support to private enterprises was not very efficient. The best one can say is that it benefited innovative companies. Planning was a total failure, and the only real decision implemented was the nationalization of electrical production.

In the 1960s, industrial policy was hardly relevant but neither was it really harmful, as sums were comparatively small. The decisions of those years created the institutional framework for the mismanagement of the 1970s. The situation was somewhat improved by attempts to change strategy in the 1980s. Policies were better devised, but were very poorly implemented.

The failure may not be casual. Industrial policy failed because the state was inefficient, the government afraid to implement any policy which could have hurt organized interests (industrialists, trade unions, etc.), and politicians were more interested in their own personal affairs than in the general well-being. Some of these problems were deeply rooted in Italian history and still exist today, beneath the surface of sweeping changes. This fact may have ominous implications for Italy's economic future.

Currently, the traditional tools of industrial policy (subsidies, planning, direct state ownership) are widely discredited. On the contrary, there is some consensus about implementing a 'liberal' industrial policy aimed at enhancing the country's competitiveness. It would need to use quite sophisticated tools (support to R. & D. and to education, regulation of competitive markets, etc.), of a kind which the Italian state has never proved able to manage. If these policies are necessary for a modern industrial economy (the issue is rather controversial), Italy's future is likely to be deeply troubled.

NOTES

1. IRI owned also three of the most important Italian banks and most utilities (tele-phones, water, 30 per cent of electrical companies, etc.). On the whole the state-owned companies accounted for about two-fifths of the total capital of joint-stock companies (Toniolo, 1980: 250) and produced about a sixth of the GDP (Mori, 1994: 148).
2. It also financed private R. & D. for the first time, but the sums were very small. They would become substantial in the 1980s.
3. This practice was in principle forbidden by the bank law, but was none the less quite widespread.
4. The table omits direct payments to state-owned enterprises, which may be assimilated (with some goodwill) to shareholders' subscription of an increase in capital.
5. The exploitation of this 'nationalistic' attitude was ruthless: AGIP publicized its fuel as 'Supercortemaggiore, the powerful Italian fuel' but only a small amount of it was extracted in Cortemaggiore, the rest being purchased abroad.

REFERENCES

AAVV (1994), *Storia dell'industria elettrica in Italia* [*A History of the Electrical Industry in Italy*], iv and v (Bari).

Alzona, G. (1975), *L'EFIM* (Milan).

Amato, G. (1972), *Il governo dell'industria in Italia* [*The Governance of Industry in Italy*] (Bologna).

—— Orsenigo, L., and Toninelli, P. L. (1995), 'Tra gerarchie politiche e mercati' ['Between Markets and Political Hierarchies'], in M. Magatti (ed.), *Potere gerarchie e mercati* [*Power Markets and Hierarchies*] (Bologna), 299–338.

Balconi, M. (1991), *La siderurgia italiana 1945–1990* [*The Italian Steel Industry*] (Bologna).

Baldassarri, M. (1993) (ed.), *Industrial Policy in Italy 1945–1990* (Basingstoke and London).

Barca, F. (1997), 'Compromesso senza riforme nel capitalismo italiano' ['Compromise without Reforms in Italian Capitalism'] in F. Barca (ed.), *Storia del capitalismo italiano* [*A History of Italian Capitalism*] (Rome), 3–115.

—— and Trento, S. (1997), 'La parabola delle partecipazioni statali: una missione tradita' ['The Evolution of State-Owned Enterprises: A betrayed destiny'], in F. Barca (ed.), *Storia del capitalismo italiano* (Rome), 185–236.

Barucci, P. (1978), *Ricostruzione, pianificazione, Mezzogiorno* [*Recovery, Planning and the South*] (Bologna).

Bianchi, P. (1993), 'Industrial Policies for Small and Medium Frms and the New Direction of European Commodity Policies', in Baldassarri (1993: 161–188).

Bollino, A. (1983), 'Industrial Policy in Italy: A Survey', in F. G. Adams and L. R. Klein (eds.) *Industrial Policy for Growth and Competitiveness* (Lexington, Mass.), 283–305.

Bottiglieri, B. (1984), *La politica economica dell'Italia centrista* (Milan).

Brosio, G. (1983), 'Le sovvenzioni sul costo del lavoro' ['The Subsidy to Labour'], in Ranci (1983: 149–75).

—— and Silvestri, P. (1983), 'Uno sguardo d'assieme' ['A General Overview'], in Ranci (1983: 17–34).

CER-IRS (1986), *Quale strategia per l'industria?* [*Which Strategy for Industry?*] (Bologna).

Ciocca, P. L. (1994) (ed.), *Il progresso economico dell'Italia* [*Italy's Economic Progress*] (Bologna).

Colitti, M. (1979), *Energia e sviluppo in Italia. La vicenda di Enrico Mattei* [*Energy and Growth in Italy. Mattei's Life*] (Bari).

Dal Monte, A., and Giannola, A. (1978), *Il mezzogiorno nell'economia italiana* [*The South in the Italian Economy*] (Bologna).

Daneo, C. (1975), *La politica economica della ricostruzione* [*The Economic Policy during the Recovery Period*] (Turin).

D'Antonio, M. (1968), *Commento al programma economico nazionale* [*The National Economic Planning: A Comment*] (Bologna).

De Cleva, E. (1992), 'Integrazione europea e iniziativa privata. Gli ambienti milanesi e la nascita del MEC (1955–1957)' ['European Integration and Private Enterprise. Milanese businessmen and the Creation of the Common Market (1955–1957)'] in E. Di Nolfo, R. Rainero, and B. Vigezzi (eds.) *L'Italia e la politica di potenza in Europa* (Milan), 439–81.

Di Maio, A., and Fausto, D. (1987), 'Il ruolo delle imprese pubbliche nello sviluppo del Mezzogiorno' ['The Role of Public Enterprise in the Development of the South'], in *Piccola e grande impresa: un problema storico* [*Small and Large Enterprise in Historical Perspective*] (Milan), 202–61.

Doria, M. (1987), 'Note sull'industria meccanica italiana nella ricostruzione' ['Notes on Engineering during the Recovery'], *Rivista di storia economica*, 4. 35–75.

Filippi, E. (1979), 'I problemi dei piani di settore' ['The Problems of the Plans by Industry'], in A. Cassone (ed.), *Politica industriale e piani di settore* [*Industrial Policy and the Plans by Industry*] (Milan), 63–78.

Giannetti, R., Federico, G., and Toninelli, P. A. (1994), 'Size and Strategy of Italian Industrial Enterprises (1907–1940): Empirical Evidence and Some Conjectures', *Industrial and Corporate Change*, 3. 491–512.

Grassini, F. A. (1979), 'Le imprese pubbliche' ['Public enterprises'], in Grassini and Scognamiglio (1979: 79–114).

—— and Scognamiglio, C. (1979) (eds.), *Stato ed industria in Europa: l'Italia* [*State and Industry in Europe: Italy*] (Bologna), 155–192.

Guerrieri, P., and Milana, C. (1990), *L'Italia ed il commercio mondiale* [*Italy and World Trade*] (Bologna).

Harper, J. L. (1986), *America and the Reconstruction of Italy* (Cambridge).

ISTAT (1957), 'Indagine statistica sullo sviluppo del redito nazionale dell'Italia dal

1861 al 1956' ['A Statistical Enquiry on the Development of Italian National Income, 1861–1956'], in *Annali di statistica*, 8: 9 (Rome).

—— (1985), *Sommario di statistiche storiche* [*Italian Historical Statistics*] (Rome).

Lombardini, S. (1967), *La programmazione. Idee, esperienze, problemi* [*Planning. Ideas, Experiences, Problems*] (Turin).

Loraschi, G. C. (1979), 'Gli acquisti del settore pubblico allargato' ['Public Procurements'], in Grassini and Scognamiglio (1979: 361–86).

Maddison, A. (1991), *Dynamic Forces in Capitalistic Development* (Oxford).

Magnani, M. (1994), 'L'appuntamento mancato degli anni '60' ['The Failed Opportunity of the 1960s'], in Ciocca (1994: 161–76).

Maizels, A. (1963), *Industrial Growth and World Trade* (London).

Marchi, A., and Marchionatti, R. (1992), *Montedison (1966–1989)* (Milan).

Marzano, F. (1979), *Incentivi e sviluppo del Mezzogiorno* [*Incentives and Development of the South*] (Milan).

Momigliano, F., and Pent Fornengo, G., (1986), 'Quadro Generale' ['General overview'], in F. Momigliano (ed.), *Le leggi della politica industriale in Italia* [*The Laws of Industrial Policy in Italy*] (Bologna), 7–35.

Mori, G. (1994), 'L'economia italiana fra la fine della seconda guerra mondiale e il "secondo miracolo economico" ' ['The Italian Economy between the end of the Second World War and the "Economic Miracle" '], in *Storia dell'Italia repubblicana* [*History of Italy during the Republic*] (Turin), 129–230.

Osti, G. L. (1993), *L'industria di stato dall'ascesa al degrado* [*Public Enterprise from the Ascent to the Degradation*] (Bologna).

Pierucci, C. M., and Ulizzi, A. (1973), 'Evoluzione delle tariffe doganali italiane dei prodotti manufatti nel quadro della integrazione economica europea' ['Italian Tariffs on Manufactures in the Framework of European Integration'], *Contributi alla ricerca economica della Banca d'Italia*, 269–82.

Podbielsky, G. (1974), *Italy: Development and Crisis in the Postwar Economy* (Oxford).

Pontarollo, E. (1979), 'La politica del lavoro' [Policies for Work], in Grassini and Scognamiglio (1979: 217–49).

—— (1980), 'Le politiche di ristrutturazione industriale in Italia dal 1961 al 1977' ['Industrial Restructuring in Italy from 1961 to 1977'], *L'industria*,1. 369–94.

Posner, M. V. and Woolf, S. (1967), *Italian Public Enterprises* (London).

Prodi, R., and De Giovanni, D. (1993), 'Forty-five Years of Industrial Policy in Italy: Protagonists, Objectives and Instruments', in Baldassarri (1993: 31–54).

Ranci, P. (1983) (ed.), *I trasferimenti dello stato alle imprese industriali negli anni Settanta* [*The Transfers from the State to Industrial Companies in the 1970s*] (Bologna).

—— (1987), 'Italy: The Weak state', in F. Duchene and G. Shepherd (eds.), *Managing Industrial Change in Western Europe* (London and New York), 110–43.

Ranieri, R. (1985), 'La siderurgia italiana e gli inizi dell'integrazione europea' ['Italian Steel Industry and the Beginnings of European Integration'], *Passato e Presente*, 4. 65–85.

—— (1993), 'La grande siderurgia in Italia' ['The Large Steel Frms in Italy'], in Osti (1993: 9–98).

Ravazzi, P. (1983), 'I conferimenti ai fondi di dotazione delle partecipazioni statali' ['The Tranfers to State-Owned Enterprises'] in Ranci (1983: 83–148).

Rossi, E. (1962), *Elettricità senza baroni* [*Electricity without Godfathers*] (Bari).

Rossi, N., Sorgato, A., and Toniolo, G. (1993), 'I conti economici italiani: una ricostruzione statistica, 1890–1990' ['Italian National Accounts: A Statistical Reconstruction'], *Rivista di storia economica*, 10. 1–47.

Ruffolo, G. (1973), *Rapporto sulla programmazione* [*A Report on Planning*] (Bari).

Salvati, M. (1982), *Stato ed industria nella ricostruzione* [*State and Industry during the Recovery*] (Milan).

Scalfari, E. (1963), *Storia segreta dell'industria elettrica* [*Secret History of the Electrical Industry*] (Bari).

—— and Turani, G. (1975), *Razza padrona* [*The Bosses*] (Milan).

Scognamiglio, C. (1979), 'Strategia industriale e programmazione' ['Industrial Strategy and Planning'], in Grassini and Scognamiglio (1979: 29–78).

Serrani, D. (1971), *Lo Stato finanziatore* [*The State as a Provider of Funds*] (Milan).

Sicca, L. (1979), 'Gli strumenti di politica industriale per il Mezzogiorno d'Italia ed i risultati dell'intervento' ['The Industrial Policy for the South and the Outcomes of the Intervention'], in Grassini and Scognamiglio (1979: 155–92).

Silvestri, P. (1983), 'Agevolazioni sul credito e contributi in conto capitale (1964–1979)' ['Soft Loans and Contributions to Investments'], in Ranci (1983: 35–82).

SVIMEZ (1961), *Un secolo di statistiche italiane* [*A Century of Italian Statistics*] (Rome).

Toniolo, G. (1980), *L'economia dell'Italia fascista* [*The Economy of Fascist Italy*] (Bari).

Willis, R. (1971), *Italy Chooses Europe* (Oxford).

Zamagni, V. (1986), 'Betting on the Future. The Reconstruction of Italian Industry', in J. Becker and F. Knipping (eds.), *Power in Europe* (Berlin and New York), 283–301.

—— (1987), 'A Century of Change: Trends in the Composition of the Italian Labor Force 1881–1981', *Historical Social Research*, 44. 36–97.

—— (1990), 'L'industria chimica in Italia dalle origini agli anni Cinquanta' ['The Chemical Industry in Italy from the Beginning to the 1950s'], in F. Amatori and B. Bezza (eds.), *Montecatini 1886–1966* (Bologna), 46–148.

—— (1994), 'Alcune tesi sull'intervento dello stato in una prospettiva di lungo periodo' ['Some Theses on State Intervention in the Long Run'], in Ciocca (1994: 151–60).

INDEX